"十四五"职业教育国家规划教材

民航运输类专业系列教材

民航空乘英语实用口语教程

第三版

李屹然　主编

Practical Spoken English Courses for Civil Aviation Service

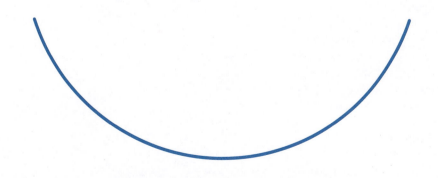

Civil Aviation

化学工业出版社

·北京·

内容简介

本书以高等职业教育人才培养目标为依据，结合教育部高等职业人才培养要求及国家相关行业职业规范的知识技能要求，以行业企业典型案例为载体，突出训练学生的综合岗位职业能力。

本书内容包括航前准备、登机服务、起飞前地面服务、安全检查、细微服务、餐饮服务、国际航班、特殊情况、紧急情况、着陆前后等共10个项目28个工作任务，基本涵盖了民航空乘一线工作的全部内容。同时，每个工作任务由课前问题、行业情景会话、高频词汇、实用句式、客舱广播词与服务技巧、知识拓展与巩固练习等内容构成，涉及民航英语、客舱设备操作、航空播音、客舱服务与服务礼仪、客舱安全与管理等多方面行业知识。为方便教学，本书提供与教学内容配套的教学音频、教学视频、多媒体课件等颗粒化教学资源。其中教学音频、教学视频以二维码形式植入教材，直接扫描书中二维码便可获取。

本书可作为高等职业院校、中等职业院校等相关院校空中乘务专业的教学用书、成人高等教育同类专业教材，也可以作为民航空乘人员的参考书及航空公司培训用书。

图书在版编目（CIP）数据

民航空乘英语实用口语教程 / 李屹然主编 . -- 3 版 .
北京 : 化学工业出版社，2025. 3. --（"十四五"职业教育国家规划教材）. -- ISBN 978-7-122-48059-0

Ⅰ. F560.9

中国国家版本馆 CIP 数据核字第 2025X90S11 号

责任编辑：王　可　旷英姿
责任校对：李露洁
装帧设计：王晓宇

出版发行：化学工业出版社
　　　　　（北京市东城区青年湖南街13号　邮政编码100011）
印　　装：三河市君旺印务有限公司
787mm×1092mm　1/16　印张17¼　字数487千字
2025年8月北京第3版第1次印刷

购书咨询：010-64518888
售后服务：010-64518899
网　　址：http://www.cip.com.cn
凡购买本书，如有缺损质量问题，本社销售中心负责调换。

定　　价：55.00元

 前言

　　《民航空乘英语实用口语教程》于2019年首次出版，全书融入全新的高职课改理念，坚持项目引领、任务驱动、校企合作等先进教改模式。自发行以来，深受全国同类高职院校及航空公司同行的厚爱。2020年被遴选为"十三五"职业教育国家规划教材。2023年入选"十四五"职业教育国家规划教材。

　　教材第三版继续秉承前几版的精髓，以高等职业教育人才培养目标为依据，结合教育部高等职业人才培养要求、国家相关行业职业规范的知识技能要求，融理论教学、实践操作、企业案例于一体，注重教材的新颖性、专业性、系统性、实践性与实用性。

　　修订后的教材突出以下特点：

　　（1）融入"增强文化自信，围绕举旗帜、聚民心、育新人、兴文化、展形象建设社会主义文化强国"等党的二十大精神，有助于培养学生的家国情怀，提高道德修养。

　　（2）以项目为引领、工作过程为导向、典型工作任务为驱动，深化产教融合，选取行业企业一线案例为教学载体。

　　（3）突出课岗融通，强化立德树人，加强职业技能和培养综合技能，要求教学中教师在"教中做"、学生在"练中学"，并与职业技能鉴定相结合。

　　（4）教材编写侧重营造实际工作场景，且在教材编写的每一个阶段都充分考虑到了空乘专业学习者自身语言学习需求及未来的工作需要。

　　（5）为方便教学，本教材提供与教学内容配套的教学音频、教学视频及多媒体课件等颗粒化教学资源，其中教学音频、教学视频以二维码形式植入教材，直接扫描书中二维码便可获取。

　　本教材参考学时为144学时，建议采用理实一体教学模式安排学时：理论72学时，实训72学时。

　　本书主编李屹然是南京旅游职业学院专任教师，中国航协航空乘务教员，TESOL国际英语教师，具备教育部全国高职高专空乘专业"双师"资质，曾任中国国际航空股份有限公司飞行乘务员，长期从事民航空乘及专业英语教学等工作。本书由南京蓝天教育集团有限公司朱正华参编，南京交通职业技术学院胡海青主审。

　　本教材在编写过程中参考和借鉴了同行的相关资料、文献，在此一并表示诚挚感谢！限于编者水平，难免存在疏漏，敬请读者不吝赐教，以便修正，日臻完善。

编　者

2025年7月

目录

Civil Aviation

Preparations before Flights
航前准备

Task 1 Briefing 航前准备会

I. Warm-up Questions

1. What's the content of "briefing"?

2. What does a flight attendant need to do before the briefing?

3. Why is it necessary for airlines to hire flight attendants from foreign countries?

4. What's the routine of cooperating with foreign flight attendants before getting on board?

II. Dialogues

Dialogue 1: Briefing I

Situation: Flight attendants are necessary crew members assigned by airlines to be on duty in cabin in consideration of passengers' safety, and their main duties and responsibilities are to ensure cabin safety. Cabin safety is the most important part during a regular flight. Normally, a briefing is conducted before crew members getting on board.

Principle: Flight attendants should arrive on time and do necessary preparations previously. And at present, cabin crew still need to follow personal protection measures.

Example (CF: Chief Purser, PS: Regional Purser, FA: Flight Attendant)

CF: Hello, everyone! Attendant No. 2, our announcer, would you please introduce the flight route information?

FA2: Hello, Chief Purser, nice to meet you! The distance between Beijing and Frankfurt is about 8,260 km. The estimated flight time is 10 hours. The time difference between Beijing and Frankfurt is 6 hours. We will be flying over the countries as China, Mongolia, Russia, Belarus, Poland, Czech Republic, Germany, and the seas as the Baltic Sea and the North Sea.

CF: Cabin safety is the most important task for a flight. Flight attendants must check all the in-flight emergency equipment and report to regional pursers. And regional pursers report to me. Now I'd like to invite attendant No. 5 to review how to use the Halon Extinguisher.

FA5: Right hand grasps the handle; left hand rolls and pulls out the safety pin. Hold the bottle vertically 2 to 3 meters from fire source, aim at the bottom, press the trigger, and move horizontally to fight fire.

音频扫一扫

CF: Okay. Thank you for your attention!

FAs: Got it!

情景会话1：航前准备会1

主任乘务长：大家好！我们的广播员，也就是2号乘务员，可以请你来介绍一下这次航线信息吗？

2号乘务员：您好，主任乘务长，很高兴见到您。北京到法兰克福的飞行距离是8260公里，预计飞行时间是10小时，北京与法兰克福的时差是6个小时。在这条航线上，我们将飞越的国家有中国、蒙古、俄罗斯、白俄罗斯、波兰、捷克、德国，飞越的海洋有波罗的海和北海。

主任乘务长：安全是航班中的头等大事。各位置乘务员要检查本区域的应急设备，报告给区域乘务长，区域乘务长再报告给我。现在请5号乘务员带领大家复习一下海伦灭火瓶的使用方法。

5号乘务员：右手握住手柄；左手转动并拔出安全销。垂直握住瓶体，距离火源2至3米，对准火源底部，按下触发器，平行移动灭火。

主任乘务长：好的，谢谢大家！

乘务员们：明白！

音频扫一扫

Dialogue 2: Briefing Ⅱ

Situation: The preparation of international flights usually requires certain English knowledge. Normally, we should use English to do self-introduction, assign working positions and simulate emergency evacuation procedures. In some internationally renowned airlines, flight preparation is an important part in terms of international cooperation. In order to create a relaxed and pleasant atmosphere, we should introduce foreign colleagues or green hands to the whole group during the briefing.

Principle: Be prepared before the briefing; enter the briefing room at least five minutes in advance.

Example (CF: Chief Purser)

CF: Good afternoon, everyone! Nice to meet you here to join the flight from Beijing to Seattle. My name is William. I'm the chief purser of the flight. I have been flying for 8 years. And this is our regional purser, Evelyn.

PS: Nice to see you!

CF: Today we have a foreign colleague working with us, that is Amy, and she is new to the business class. Hope we'll have a nice cooperation today!

Amy: Hello, everyone. I'll try my best on this flight.

CF: Amy, if you have any questions, you may ask your colleague, Katherine. She can help you.

Amy: That's great!

CF: Shall we begin the briefing now?

FAs: Yes, we are ready!

CF: First, I'd like to assign working positions by seniority and qualifications. John, you have the longest seniority in the business class, so you work as SS3. Jessica, you are SS8. And in the middle class, SS4 is Linda, and SS5 is Sara. Amy, how about SS9 for you in the business class?

Amy: No problem.

CF: Then in the economy class. Kathy, is SS11 OK for you?

Kathy: Sure, but it is my first time to work on the galley job, I'm afraid...

CF: Don't worry, our regional purser and I will help you out with it. But do remember to follow the standards.

Kathy: OK.

CF: Then SS6 is Alex while SS7 is Frank. Is there any questions about your working positions?

FAs: No, we are good.

CF: Then let's move on. For the requirement, SS6 is responsible for the VIP service in the economy class, and SS8 in the business class. SS3, SS4 and SS11, you must make sure that you make a clear check of the in-flight supplies and meals, especially for the VIP meals. And the WCHR passenger will be sitting in the R-aisle side, SS7, please take good care of him. Do remember to introduce him the facilities on board around him, and remind him to disembark till the ground staff come to pick him up.

FAs: Got it.

CF: Now let's have a review of the evacuation procedures. Today we fly with Airbus 330-300 plane, and totally we have 11 cabin crews. John, could you please tell me your responsibilities in land evacuation?

John: OK, I'm No.3 cabin crew today. I'm responsible for the front galley and stand in Row 11 of R-aisle for safety demo. I'm in charge of the clearance and security check from Row 11 to Row 20 of R-aisle. And I'm responsible for R1 door and evacuate from R1. The emergency item I should carry is flashlight.

CF: Perfect, thank you.

情景会话2：航前准备会2

主任乘务长：各位同事，大家下午好！很高兴跟大家一起执飞北京到西雅图的航班。我叫威廉，是本次航班的主任乘务长。我已经飞行8年了。这是我们的区域乘务长，艾芙琳。

区域乘务长：大家好！

主任乘务长：今天有位外籍同事跟我们一起飞行，她叫艾米，刚开始飞公务舱。希望我们今天合作愉快！

艾米：大家好，我将尽力飞好这次航班。

主任乘务长：艾米，如果你有问题，可以问同事，凯瑟琳。她会帮你的。

艾米：好的。

主任乘务长：现在我们可以开始开准备会了吗？

乘务员们：是，我们准备好了！

主任乘务长：首先，我将依据飞行年限和资质来进行号位分工。约翰，你是执飞公务舱资历最久的，那你在3号位。杰西卡，你担任8号位。中舱的话，琳达4号位，萨拉5号位。艾米，你担任公务舱的9号位怎么样？

艾米：没问题。

主任乘务长：接下来看看经济舱。凯西，你担任11号位，可以吗？

凯西：可以的，只不过这是我第一次干厨房工作，我恐怕……

主任乘务长：别担心，我和区域乘务长会帮你的。但你一定要记住按标准执行程序。

凯西：好的。

主任乘务长：接下来，艾历克斯6号位，弗兰克7号位。你们对号位分工有什么问题吗？

乘务员们：没有问题。

主任乘务长：那我们继续。职责上要求，6号位乘务员负责经济舱的贵宾服务，8号位负责公务舱的服务。3号、4号和11号位乘务员，请你们确保仔细检查机供品和餐食，尤其是贵宾的餐食。本次航班有一位轮椅旅客，他会坐在右通道那一侧，7号位乘务员，请你照顾好他。一定记得给他介绍周围的设施设备，并且记得提醒他：落地后不要着急下飞机，坐在座位上不要走，要等到地面工作人员来接他。

乘务员们：明白。

主任乘务长：现在我们来复习一下应急撤离程序。今天我们执飞的机型是空客330-300型飞机，共配备了11名机组成员。约翰，你能告诉我你在陆地撤离时的职责是什么吗？

约翰：好的，我今天承担的是3号位。我负责前厨房的工作，站在右通道的第11排进行客舱安全演示。我负责右通道第11至20排的清舱和安全检查，负责右一门，并且从右一门撤离。陆地撤离时，我要携带的应急设备是手电筒。

主任乘务长：很好，谢谢你。

音频扫一扫

Dialogue 3: Briefing Ⅲ

Situation: Besides the briefing among cabin attendants, flight crew should conduct "triple-side cooperation" among the entire crew before passengers getting on board.

Principle: Being well-prepared.

Example (CAP: Captain, SF: Aviation Safety Officer, PS: Purser)

PS: Excuse me, Captain. I'm the purser of this flight. May I have a look at the Pre-flight Report?

CAP: OK. Here you are.

SF: Captain, how do we contact each other during the flight?

CAP: Just as we settled before.

PS: How's the weather today on route? What's the intensity and duration time of turbulence?

CAP: We may encounter severe turbulence after two hours taking off, above Wuhan. It will take about half an hour.

PS: Do you have any special requirements on safety and service of today's flight? How long shall we taxi?

CAP: Just as we discussed before.

FA: OK. Do you have any requirements for your meal? When would you like to have the meal?

CAP: After the passengers, after your meal and beverage service.

FA: No problem.

情景会话 3：航前准备会 3

乘务长：打扰一下，机长，我是本次航班的乘务长，我可以检查一下任务书吗？

机长：好的，给您。

航空安全员：机长，在飞行中我们怎样互相联络呢？

机长：就跟之前制定的一样。

乘务长：请问今天的航路天气怎么样？有几级颠簸，预计持续多久？

机长：我们大概起飞后两小时，飞到武汉上空的时候，会遇有重度颠簸，持续大约半小时。

乘务长：对于今天航班的安全和服务您还有什么特殊要求吗？我们将滑行多久？

机长：就跟协同准备时候说的一样。

乘务员：好的。您对您的餐食有什么要求吗？您打算什么时候用餐？

机长：你们餐饮服务结束，旅客用完餐了再给我开餐吧。

乘务员：没问题。

Dialogue 4: Communication and Teamwork

音频扫一扫

Situation: With the development of the airlines, the influx of foreign talents, the international routes have been gradually increased. We may often encounter foreign captains during flights. In addition to discussing about flight time, turbulence, hijacking and other information, as flight attendants, we also need to conduct "cockpit communication". Therefore, we need some basic communication skills.

Principle: Flight attendants should stay open-minded.

Example

FA: How's going, Captain? Pleased to meet you again, do you still remember me? I'm Jane.

CAP: It's you, Jane! Nice to see you again. Just call me Jin. Today we will fly to Guangzhou together. The flight time is 2 hours and 50 minutes. This is the first officer, Dong.

PS: I'm the purser, please call me Lily. And this is flight attendant No. 3, Li and No. 8, Tang. Li will take care of the cockpit service today. And our security guard, Wang.

CAP: If the emergency occurs, everyone stands by, waiting for my command; if I failed, listen to the first officer, then the purser, regional purser, or the sequence of your working position.

PS: OK. Got it. When would you like to make the passenger announcement?

CAP: Maybe before they finish boarding and the airplane descending.

PS: How long will we taxi before take-off?

CAP: We're at W207, so the taxiing time will be around 10 minutes. Please let me know you are ready and sit tight before take-off and descending.

PS: Sure, I'll give you a "cabin ready" signal.

CAP: It's quite windy today, so might be a little bumpy 20 minutes after we take off. If it's severe, I'll give you two chimes and make an announcement. Everyone takes a seat and stops working.

PS: So one chime is for the mild one?

CAP: Yes, you're right. For turbulence, I'll give you one time ring; if it is bad, I'll give you twice.

FAs: OK!

FA3: When would you like to have your meal? Before take-off or after that?

CAP: Maybe after take-off.

FA3: Do you have any requirements for the meal?

CAP: Nope. We prefer the crew meal. Thank you!

FA3: My pleasure.

情景会话4：机组、乘务组之间沟通交流

乘务员：你好，机长。很高兴再次跟你一起飞航班，还记得我吗？我是简。

机长：简，是你啊，很高兴再次见到你！可以叫我金机长。今天我们一起执飞北京——广州航线，飞行时间2小时50分钟。这是副驾小董。

乘务长：我是本次航班的乘务长，叫我丽丽就好了，这是3号乘务员小李和8号乘务员小唐。小李负责今日的驾驶舱服务。这是安全员小王。

机长：如遇紧急情况，所有人听从我的指挥。如果我失能，指挥权交由副驾驶，接着转交乘务长、区域乘务长，或者是依照你们工作号位顺序交接。

乘务长：好的，明白。请问您何时做客舱广播？

机长：大约在客人结束登机之前和飞机下降之前。

乘务长：起飞前我们滑行多久？

机长：飞机在W207，滑行时间大约10分钟。起飞、下降前坐好后，请告知我。

乘务长：好的，我会给您回铃"客舱就绪"的。

机长：今天风很大，所以起飞后20分钟内可能会有些颠簸。如果颠得严重，我将打两声铃，与此同时，我会做客舱广播，所有人停止服务并就座。

乘务长：轻度颠簸打一声铃？

机长：是的。轻度颠簸打一声铃，颠簸严重打两声铃。

乘务员们：好的！

乘务员3：请问你们何时用餐？起飞前还是起飞后？

机长：起飞后吧。

乘务员3：那你们对餐食有要求吗？

机长：没有，机组配的餐就行。谢谢你！

乘务员3：不客气。

Dialogue 5: Work with foreign colleagues

音频扫一扫

Situation: With the rapid development of airlines, more and more foreign flight attendants will work with us on our daily flights. What should a flight attendant say when flying with foreign flight attendants during a flight?

Principle: Flight attendants should keep polite and friendly.

Example

(1) Greetings between colleagues

FA1: Hi, there! Are you doing the Seattle flight? I'm Qin, nice to see you.

FA2: Hi, Qin! I'm Zhang. Do you remember me? We flew together before. How is everything going?

FA1: Not bad.

FA2: You look great today!

(2) Chatting when taking the crew shuttle bus

FA1: Do you have any plan in Seattle? Shopping or going to the downtown for sightseeing？
/ Is this your first time doing this flight? We can go out together.

FA2: That's great! I'd love to.

*(3) Assistance from colleagues on board

FA1: Let's distribute the blankets now.

FA2: Just a moment…

FA1: Are you looking for something? Do you need my help?

FA2: I'm looking for the pencil and writing paper because I could not understand what that passenger said.

FA1: It's okay. I will talk to the passenger. Erm... Another passenger just pressed the call button.
/ Could you help me to check with the passenger sitting at 42A, what did he say? I didn't get him.

FA2: I will go and answer the call button.

FA1: OK.

*(4) Communication during the meal and beverage service

(Before the meal and beverage service)

FA1: Shall we go and take order now? And do you know where is the tissue pack?

FA2: Sure, here you are. After that, we will do one round of drink first.

FA1: Could you prepare a cup of coffee for me, please? The passenger at 32D just asked.

(During the meal and beverage service)

FA2: Qin, could you pass me the ice bucket？ And please give me one more bread tongs.

FA1: Here you go.

FA1: Do you have any more beef with rice?

FA2: Yes, I have three extra. Here you are.

FA3: I've done the forward cabin. Please give me a few rows, I will serve the passengers here.

情景会话5：和外籍乘务员一起飞航班

（1）首先从熟悉彼此开始：问候与回复

乘务员1：你好，你是飞西雅图吗？我是小琴，很高兴见到你。

乘务员2：你好，小琴！我是小章，你还记得我吗？我们之前一起飞过。你最近怎么样？

乘务员1：还不错。

乘务员2：你今天看起来真不错！

（2）在机组车上聊天

乘务员1：你在西雅图有什么计划吗？是要去购物还是去市区观光？

/ 这是你第一次飞这趟航班吗？我们可以一起出去。

乘务员2：太好了，我也想出去走走。

*（3）飞机上，工作过程中互相帮助

乘务员1：我们去发毛毯吧。

乘务员2：稍等一下。

乘务员1：你在找什么东西吗？需要我帮忙吗？

乘务员2：我听不懂那位旅客在说什么，正在找铅笔和书写纸，想让他写下来。

乘务员1：没事的，我去跟那位旅客说。呃，又有一位旅客按呼唤铃。

/ 可以帮我问一下42A的旅客在说什么吗？我没听懂。

乘务员2：我去答复那个呼唤铃吧！

乘务员1：好的。

*（4）发餐过程中的交谈

（餐饮服务前的准备）

乘务员1：现在我们去点餐吧！还有，你知道餐巾纸包在哪儿吗？

乘务员2：当然，给你。点餐结束，我们先发一遍饮料。

乘务员1：可以帮我准备一杯咖啡吗？32排D座的旅客刚刚跟我要的。

（餐饮服务时）

乘务员2：小琴，可以把冰桶递给我吗？请再给我一个面包夹。

乘务员1：好的，给你。

乘务员1：你那儿还有牛肉米饭吗？

乘务员2：有的，我这辆餐车还富余三份。这份给你。

乘务员3：前舱我发完了，请给我留几排，我来给这些旅客发。

Ⅲ. Popular Words and Phrases

| passenger | ['pæsɪndʒə(r)] | n. 旅客，乘客 |

cabin crew		客舱机组，机组成员
crew member		机组成员
captain	[ˈkæptɪn]	n. 机长
pilot	[ˈpaɪlət]	n. 飞行员
purser	[ˈpɜrsə]	n. 乘务长
flight attendant		空乘，飞行乘务员
cabin attendant		空乘
steward/ stewardess	[ˈstjuːəd] / [ˌstjuːədes]	n. 空乘
air hostess		（旧，客机上的）女乘务员
aviation safety officer / security guard		n.（航空）安全员
air marshal		n. 空警
assign	[əˈsaɪn]	v. 分配
seniority	[ˌsiːniˈɒrəti]	n. 资历
qualification	[ˌkwɒlɪfɪˈkeɪʃn]	n. 资质
assign the working positions by seniority and qualification		根据飞行时长和资质来进行号位分工
have been flying for...year(s)		已经飞行……年了
flight number		航班号
in-flight supplies		机供品
standard	[sˈtændəd]	n. 标准
be responsible for		对……负责
be in charge of		负责……
bumpy	[ˈbʌmpi]	adj. 颠簸的
chime	[tʃaɪm]	n. 铃声
key point		关键点
purser's log		乘务日志
advisory	[ədˈvaɪzəri]	n. 业务通告

IV. Practical Expressions

1. There are totally 8 cabin crew members on today's flight. One purser, two business class flight attendants, four economy class flight attendants and one security guard.

今天的航班中共有八位机组成员。一名乘务长，两名公务舱乘务员，四名经济舱乘务员和一名安全员。

2. Good morning! I am the first class flight attendant. So glad to fly with you!

早上好，我是头等舱乘务员，很高兴一起飞行！

3. How many portions of meal for this flight? Any special meal?

请问这次有多少份餐食，有特殊餐吗？

4. Captain, do you have any requirements for your meal? When would you like to have the meal?

机长，您对餐食有什么要求吗？您想什么时候用餐？

5. Excuse me, Captain. Do you have any requirements on safety and service of today's flight?

打扰一下，机长，对于今天航班的安全和服务您有什么要求吗？

6. Excuse me, Captain. How long will we taxi?

打扰一下，机长，我们的滑行时间大概是多久？

7. How's the weather today on route? What's the intensity and duration time of turbulence?

今天的航路天气怎么样？有几级颠簸，预计持续多久？

8. Is there any special passenger on this flight?

本次航班有特殊旅客吗？

V. Tips

Communications among crew members 机组成员间的沟通交流

Good morning/ afternoon/ evening! I'm...

Nice/ Glad/ Pleased to meet you! I'm...

How are you?/ How's going recently?/ How are you doing?/ How's going?

Nice to see you. I'm the purser of today's flight. It's our honor to have this flight with you.

Excuse me, Captain, if you want to have the meal, please don't hesitate to call our attendants.

Excuse me, Captain, all the passengers are on board now and all the necessary flight documents have been confirmed, shall I close the cabin door now?

VI. Supplementary Reading

1. Captain 机长

Captain is the commander of an airplane. The Pilot in Command (PIC) of an aircraft is the person aboard who is ultimately responsible for its operation and safety during the flight. The PIC is the person legally in charge of the aircraft and its flight safety and operation, and would normally be the primary person liable for an infraction of any flight rule. The Pilot in Command must hold the rank of Captain, and typically sits in the left seat. The second in command can be the first officer or another captain, and will take the right seat.

During the entire flight operation, the PIC is responsible for directing the airplane and aircrew, on-board passengers and cargo. The PIC has the authority of controlling and managing the airplane. The PIC has the right to make the final decision. In order to guarantee the safety of on-board personnel and keep a good order in cabin, PIC will order within his power limit. Crew members must listen to PIC's order and be subject to PIC. When the airplane is in emergency, PIC will command crew members and others on board to adopt all necessary rescuing measures. In evacuation, the captain will get off airplane at last.

2. Purser 乘务长

The cabin manager (chief flight attendant) is often called the purser. The purser oversees flight attendants by making sure airline passengers are safe and comfortable. A flight purser completes detailed reports and verifies all safety procedures followed.

Purser mainly fulfills the responsibilities of cabin management, which include but not limit to these: abide by the laws, regulations and company policies, carry out the work according to the company manual and procedures, and assure occupants safety; manage cabin work, organize, supervise and coordinate cabin crew members to implement procedures and standards in the flight mission according to the manual requirements, and properly assign the mission; obey the instructions of PIC, report to PIC, and maintain communication with flight crew and cabin crew members; coordinate and communicate with ground support department, complete handover and record; collect the passenger feedback information, information of flight mission, and cabin equipment information, and make records and feedback; evaluate and record cabin crew performance; organize and handle irregularities in cabin.

3. Flight Attendants 空乘（客舱乘务员）

The main responsibilities of flight attendants are to ensure cabin safety, which includes but not limits to these: abide by the laws, regulations and company policies, carry out the work according to the company manual and procedures, and assure occupants safety; obey the management of PIC and chief purser, report to PIC and chief purser, and maintain communication with PIC, chief purser and other cabin crew members; ask passengers to abide by the laws, regulations, company policy manual and crew instructions, maintain the order in cabin, and assist PIC and security officer in security work; provided safety is met and assured, provide proper service for passengers; collect passenger feedback information, information in flight operation and cabin equipment information, and report to chief purser; handle irregularities in cabin; complete necessary training, and ensure personal qualification meets the requirements of flight operation; ensure physical and mental health meets flight requirements.

4. Aviation Safety Officer 航空安全员

Aviation safety officer or security guard refers to one qualified as an aviation safety officer who performs security tasks on a civil aircraft in order to ensure the safety of the aircraft and its personnel. Their main responsibilities are to prevent and stop hijacking and bombing; prevent and stop illegal interference and disturbance; maintain on-board order, protect passengers and their properties, and therefore maintain national security. PIC is responsible for the security work in flight. Supervised by PIC, the safety officer shall undertake the specific work of in-flight security. Other crew members shall assist PIC and safety officer to ensure cabin safety.

The crew members shall perform the following duties in accordance with relevant regulations: carry out security inspection on aircraft cockpit and cabin according to working areas; check identifications of the on-board ground staff, except the original passengers and crew members; prevent unauthorized persons or articles from entering the cockpit or cabin; take necessary control measures or require them to leave the aircraft before takeoff and after landing for those who disturb the order in the aircraft or hinder the crew members from performing their duties and do not listen to dissuasion; take necessary measures against acts seriously endangering flight safety; implement safety measures for carrying out tasks such as carrying weapons, escorting suspects and repatriation personnel; other duties prescribed by laws, administrative regulations and rules.

VII. Exercises

1. Answer the following questions according to the dialogues.

(1) What's the main duty and responsibility of a cabin attendant?

Answer:

(2) What's the time difference between Beijing and Munich?

Answer:

(3) How to operate the Halon fire extinguisher?

Answer:

2. Fill the blanks in following dialogues.

> briefing, distance, standards, weather, turbulence, time difference, cabin safety,
> safety and service, assign the working positions, it is my first time to...

(1) PS: Please let attendant No. 2 to introduce the flight route information.

FA: Hello, Purser, nice to meet you! The _____ between Beijing and Frankfurt is about 8,260km. The estimated flight time is 10 hours. The _____ between Beijing and Frankfurt is 6 hours.

PS: _____ is the most important task for the flight. Flight attendants must check all the in-flight emergency equipment and report to pursers.

(2) PS: Shall we begin the _____ now?

FAs: Yes, we are ready!

PS: First, I'd like to _____ by seniority and qualifications. John, you have the longest seniority in the business class, so you work as SS3. Jessica, you are SS8. And in the middle class, SS4 is Linda, and SS5 is Sara. Amy, how about SS9 for you in the business class?

Amy: No problem.

PS: Then in the economy class, Kathy, is SS11 OK for you?

Kathy: Sure, but _____ work on the galley job, I'm afraid...

PS: Don't worry, our regional purser and I will help you out with it. But do remember to follow the _____.

Kathy: OK.

(3) PS: Excuse me, Captain. How's the _____ today on route? What's the intensity and duration time of turbulence?

CAP: We may encounter severe _____ after two hours taking off, above Wuhan. It will take about half an hour.

PS: Do you have any special requirements on _____ of today's flight? How long will we taxi?

CAP: Just as we discussed before.

3. Translate the following terms into Chinese or English.

assign	be in charge of
seniority	旅客/乘客
qualification	机长
assign the working positions	乘务长
have been flying for...year(s)	空乘/飞行乘务员
flight number	航空安全员
in-flight supplies	客舱机组
standards	机组成员
be responsible for	

4. Translate the following sentences into Chinese or English.

(1) 早上好，我是今天的头等舱乘务员，很高兴一起飞行！

(2) 请问今天有多少份餐食，有特殊餐吗？

(3) How long will we taxi?

(4) Is there any special passenger on this flight?

(5) There are totally eight cabin crew members on today's flight. One purser, two business class flight attendants, four economy class flight attendants and one security guard.

5. Group work: choose one topic to start a conversation. (TIME LIMIT: 10 minutes)

(1) Briefing: route information

(2) Briefing: in-flight emergency equipment

(3) Briefing: an international flight

Task 2　Special Inspection before Boarding 航班特殊检查

Ⅰ.Warm-up Questions

1. How to communicate with foreign colleagues effectively on board?

2. What should flight attendants do before boarding and after landing?

3. What is "TSA" ?

4. What is "SAFA" ?

Ⅱ.Dialogues

音频扫一扫

Dialogue 1: SAFA (Safety Assessment of Foreign Aircraft) Ramp Inspection

Situation: After all ground service staff have left the cabin, before the passengers start boarding, flight attendants should cooperate with the security guard to complete cabin clearance. Open and check all carts and containers in the galley. The cabin attendant who is in charge of crew restroom safety should report to the purser before boarding. Sometimes, "Safety Assessment of Foreign Aircraft" ramp inspection will be conducted before international flights.

Principle: The cabin crew should be well prepared and be professional.

Example (IO: Inspection Officer, CC: Cabin Crew)

IO: Can I see your certificates/ licenses?

CC: Yes. Here your are.

IO: How do you confirm and introduce emergency exits?

FA1: Before the last cabin door is closed, cabin crew should confirm the passengers sitting on emergency exit seats, introduce door opening procedures, escape routes and their responsibilities in emergency situations.

IO: How do you operate a Water Extinguisher?

FA2: Hold the Water Extinguisher upright with the left hand. Turn the handle fully clockwise with the right hand. Make the nozzle aim at the base of fire and discharge. Stand 6 to 10 feet away from fire on initial discharge and move closer. The spurt time is about 40 seconds.

IO: How do you operate a Portable Oxygen Bottle

FA3: Ensure the dispensing tube and oxygen mask are connected to the selected flow outlet of the oxygen bottle. Turn the control knob anticlockwise on fully. Check the flow indicator on the dispensing tube to ensure a flow of oxygen. Put on and adjust the oxygen mask on the passenger's face. Monitor the passenger's condition.

IO: What is the pre-flight check of a flashlight?

FA4: Secure and the green indicator light is flashing.

IO: Please make the introduction of an emergency exit.

FA5: Standard phrase: The seat you're taking today is an emergency exit seat, please do not touch the door handle in normal situations and assist us if there is an emergency. Here is the *Exit Seat Instruction Card*, please read it. If there is any question, please let us know. Thank you.

IO: Would you please introduce the operation procedures with passengers on board during fuelling?

FA6: Make sure the "No Smoking" sign is on. The chief purser should make the announcement. At least one cabin crew stationed at each evacuation gate throughout the fuelling operation. The door area is clear of obstruction. Boarding aisles are free from obstruction. If the evacuation cannot be implemented due to uncontrolled cabin order, cabin crew should inform cockpit immediately. The chief purser should require one cabin crew responsible for transmitting information when the communication between cockpit and the outside cannot be made.

情景会话 1：外国航空器安全评估停机坪检查

检查员：请出示客舱乘务员证照。

机组成员：好的，给您。

检查员：如何做应急出口确认？

乘务员 1：乘务员在机门关闭前，必须确认坐在应急出口座位的旅客，介绍出口的使用方法、撤离路线及紧急情况下他们的任务。

检查员：请说明水灭火瓶的使用方法。

乘务员 2：左手垂直握住瓶体，右手顺时针转动手柄到底。距离火源 6 至 10 英尺，对准火源底部，按下触发器，平行移动灭火。喷射时间大约 40 秒钟。

检查员：请说明氧气瓶的使用方法。

乘务员 3：选择流量出口，确认接好氧气面罩；逆时针打开阀门到底，确认氧气流出。为病人戴好氧气面罩，观察其状况。

检查员：如何检查手电筒？

乘务员 4：手电筒固定好，观察电源指示灯是否闪亮。

检查员：请介绍应急出口。

乘务员 5：标准用语是：您今天坐的是应急出口的座位，正常情况下请勿触动舱门手柄，在紧急情况下请协助我们。这是"出口座位须知卡"，请您阅读。如有疑问，请及时和我们联系，谢谢。

检查员：请介绍飞机加油期间旅客登机的操作程序。

乘务员 6：确认"禁止吸烟"信号灯亮；主任乘务长广播通知旅客飞机正在加油；飞机加油时，每个应急出口至少要有一名乘务员；门区不能有障碍物；客舱通道保持畅通；当客舱秩序失控无法执行应急撤离，乘务组要立即报告驾驶舱；当驾驶舱与机组联络出现障碍时，主任乘务长应指定一名乘务员负责信息传递。

Dialogue 2: TSA (U.S. Transportation Security Administration) Inspection

Situation: Whenever an inspection shows the existence of a potential safety threat, or shows that an aircraft does not comply with international safety standards, the aircraft is prohibited from taking off until appropriate corrective measures are taken.

音频扫一扫

Principle: During TSA inspection, crew members should strictly follow standard procedures in terms of safety.

Example

IO: Can I see your certificates/ licenses?

CC: Yes. Here your are.

CAP: As we've discussed during the briefing, everyone, please take your responsibilities. And do report me the situation after the inspection.

CF: Just follow standard inspection procedures and our captain's instructions. We should cooperate with the security guard to complete cabin clearance before passengers' boarding. Open and check all carts and containers in the galley. Please report to me that everything is okay. That's all for cabin clearance before boarding. The cabin clearance after passengers' disembarkation is also important. We are a family, although we work in different areas.

CC: OK!

(After the chief purser's announcement, the inspection begins)

CF: Ground staff, please leave the aircraft. Thank you! Cabin security inspection/ clearance starts now!

(After cooperation and inspection...)

FA4: Purser, the cabin is okay.

FA10: Purser, the galleys are okay.

SF: Purser, the lavatories are okay.

CF: Got it!

(10 minutes before passengers' boarding, the second inspection)

情景会话2：美国运输安全管理局检查

检查员：请出示客舱乘务员证照。

机组成员：好的，给您。

机长：依照准备会上说过的，每位机组成员请肩负起自己的职责。清舱结束后向我汇报情况。

主任乘务长：请大家严格执行标准的检查程序和机长的要求。我们应在上客前配合安全员做好清舱工作。厨房里的所有餐车和格子都要打开仔细检查，完成检查后，旅客登机前完成所有清舱工作，向我汇报。旅客下机后的清舱工作同样重要。请大家注意配合，分工不分家。

机组成员：好的！

（主任乘务长发布口令后，清舱工作正式开始）

主任乘务长：请地面人员离机，客舱安保检查工作开始。

（经过配合检查……）

乘务员4：报告乘务长，客舱清舱完毕。

乘务员10：报告乘务长，厨房清舱完毕。

航空安全员：报告乘务长，洗手间清舱完毕。

主任乘务长：好的，收到！

（旅客登机前10分钟，进行二次检查）

Ⅲ. Popular Words and Phrases

clearance	['klɪərəns]	n. 清舱；放行（许可）
departure	[dɪ'pɑːtʃə]	n. 离开；出发
depart	[dɪ'pɑːt]	v. 离开；出发
gesture	['dʒestʃə]	n. 手势，姿态
precaution	[prɪ'kɔːʃn]	n. 预防
parking apron	['pɑːkɪŋ 'eiprən]	n. 停机坪
alcohol test		酒精测试
Medical Certificate		体检合格证
Training Certificate		训练合格证
flight document		随机文件，飞行文件
cloakroom	['kləʊkruːm; −rʊm]	n. 衣帽间
cockpit	['kɒkpɪt]	n. 驾驶舱

equipment	[ɪˈkwɪpmənt]	n. 设备，设施
facility	[fəˈsɪlətɪ]	n. 设施
emergency	[ɪˈmɜːdʒənsɪ]	n. 紧急
Emergency Locator Transmitter		应急定位发射机
Protective Breathing Equipment		防护式呼吸装置
Portable Oxygen Bottle		手提式氧气瓶
extinguisher	[ɪkˈstɪŋwɪʃə]	n. 灭火器，灭火瓶
flashlight	[ˈflæʃlaɪt]	n. 手电筒
scheduled flight	[ˈʃedjuːld flaɪt]	定期航班
outbound flight	[ˈaʊtbaʊnd flaɪt]	出港航班
inbound flight	[ˈɪnbaʊnd flaɪt]	进港航班
domestic flight	[dəˈmestɪk flaɪt]	国内航班
international flight	[ɪntəˈnæʃ(ə)n(ə)l flaɪt]	国际航班
extra section flight	[ˈekstrə ˈsekʃ(ə)n flaɪt]	加班飞行
charter flight	[ˈtʃɑːtə flaɪt]	包机，包机航空
business flight	[ˈbɪznɪs flaɪt]	公务飞行

IV. Practical Expressions

1. Before the last cabin door is closed, we should confirm the passengers sitting on emergency exit seats, introduce door opening procedures, escape routes and their responsibilities in emergency situations.

在机门关闭前，必须确认坐在应急出口座位的旅客、介绍出口的使用方法、撤离路线及紧急情况下他们的任务。

2. Hold the extinguisher upright. Turn the handle fully clockwise . Make the nozzle aim at the base of fire and discharge. Stand 6 to 10 feet away from fire on initial discharge and move closer.

垂直握灭火器，顺时针转动手柄到底。距离火源6至10英尺，对准火源底部，按下触发器，平行移动灭火。

3. Ensure the dispensing tube and oxygen mask are connected to the selected flow outlet of the oxygen bottle. Turn the control knob anticlockwise on fully. Check the flow indicator on the dispensing tube to ensure a flow of oxygen.

选择流量出口，确认接好氧气面罩；逆时针打开阀门到底，确认氧气流出。

4. Put on and adjust the oxygen mask on the passenger's face. Monitor the passenger's condition.
为病人戴好氧气面罩，观察其状况。

5. At least one cabin crew stationed at each evacuation gate throughout the fuelling period.
飞机加油时，每个应急出口至少要有一名乘务员。

6. We should cooperate with the security guard to complete cabin clearance before passengers' boarding.
我们应在上客前配合安全员做好清舱工作。

7. Open and check all carts and containers in the galley.
厨房里的所有餐车和格子都要打开仔细检查。

8. The cabin clearance after passengers' disembarkation is also important.
旅客下机后的清舱工作同样重要。

V. Tips

Individual Necessary Items and Certificates 乘务员个人必备物品及现行有效证件
(1) Announcement handbook (purser, announcer)

(2) Flight attendant training certificate

(3) Physical examination certificate

(4) Flight attendants personal boarding badges

(5) Accurately worked wrist watches

VI. Supplementary Reading

1. SAFA (Safety Assessment of Foreign Aircraft) 外国航空器安全评估计划

The EU Ramp Inspection Programme is a European programme regarding the performance of ramp inspections on aircraft used by the third country operators (SAFA) or used by operators under the regulatory oversight of another EU Member State (SACA).

Authorised inspectors are using a checklist with inspection items during Safety Assessment of Foreign Aircraft (SAFA) ramp checks. The checks may include pilots licenses, procedures and manuals carried in the cockpit, compliance with these procedures by flight and cabin crew, safety equipment in cockpit and cabin, cargo carried in the aircraft and the technical condition of the aircraft. Some oversight authorities of the Participating States engaged in the EU Ramp Inspections Programme carry out random inspections while others try to target aircraft or airlines that they suspect may not comply with the applicable standards.

If the findings indicate that the safety of the aircraft and its occupants is impaired, corrective actions will be required. Normally the aircraft captain will be asked to address the serious deficiencies which are brought to his attention. In rare cases, where inspectors have reason to believe that the aircraft captain does not intend to take the necessary measures on the deficiencies reported to him, they will formally ground the aircraft. The formal act of grounding by the State of Inspection means that the aircraft is prohibited from resuming its flights until appropriate corrective measures are taken.

2. TSA (U.S.Transportation Security Admin-istration) 美国运输安全管理局

Transportation Security Administration (TSA) aims at protecting the nation's transportation systems to ensure freedom of movement for people and commerce. On the morning of September 11, 2001, nearly 3,000 people were killed in a series of coordinated terrorist attacks in New York, Pennsylvania and Virginia. The attacks resulted in the creation of Transportation Security Administration, designed to prevent similar attacks in the future. Driven by a desire to help the nation, tens of thousands of people joined TSA and committed themselves to strengthening the transportation systems while ensuring the freedom of movement for people and commerce.

The Aviation and Transportation Security Act, passed by the 107th Congress and signed on November 19, 2001, established TSA, with core values: Integrity, Respect and Commitment.

VII. Exercises

1. Answer the following questions according to the dialogues.

(1) How do you confirm and introduce emergency exits?

Answer:

民航空乘英语实用口语教程　第三版

(2) Please make the emergency exit introduction.

Answer:

(3) Would you please introduce the operation procedures during fuelling with passengers on board?

Answer:

2. Translate the following words and phrases into Chinese or English.

clearance	extinguisher
departure	国内航班
precaution	国际航班
parking apron	驾驶舱
flight document	设备
Protective Breathing Equipment	应急定位发射机
Portable Oxygen Bottle	酒精测试

3. Translate the following sentences into English or Chinese.

(1) 在机门关闭前，必须确认坐在应急出口座位的旅客、介绍出口的使用方法、撤离路线及紧急情况下的任务。

(2) 飞机加油时，每个应急出口至少要有一名乘务员。

(3) We should cooperate with the security guard to complete cabin clearance before passengers' boarding.

(4) Open and check all carts and containers in the galley.

4. Group work: choose one topic to start a conversation. (TIME LIMIT: 10 minutes)

(1) Please confirm and introduce emergency exits.

(2) Please introduce the operation procedures during fuelling with passengers on board.

(3) How do you operate a water extinguisher?

Project 2

Civil Aviation

Boarding Service
登机服务

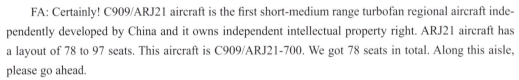

Task 3　Greeting Passengers 问候旅客

Ⅰ. Warm-up Questions

1. How to leave a passenger a good impression during boarding?

2. Talk about different ways of greeting.

3. What should a flight attendant bear in mind when standing in the cabin?

Ⅱ. Dialogues

Dialogue 1: Greeting a passenger Ⅰ

Situation: When boarding, the purser should stand at the front cabin door and other flight attendants should stand at the assigned area to welcome passengers.

Principle: Flight attendants should be warm and elegant.

Example (FA: Flight attendant, PAX: Passenger)

FA: Good morning, welcome aboard! May I have a look at your boarding pass?

PAX: Good morning! Here you are. Is this the C909/ARJ21 aircraft?

FA: Certainly! C909/ARJ21 aircraft is the first short-medium range turbofan regional aircraft independently developed by China and it owns independent intellectual property right. ARJ21 aircraft has a layout of 78 to 97 seats. This aircraft is C909/ARJ21-700. We got 78 seats in total. Along this aisle, please go ahead.

PAX: OK. Thanks. One more thing, when shall we take off? And the time to land?

FA: We shall take off at 9 a.m. and land at 10 a.m.

情景会话1：问候旅客1

（FA：乘务员，PAX：旅客）

乘务员：早上好，欢迎登机！我能看一下您的登机牌吗？

旅客：早上好！给你。这是C909/ARJ21型飞机吗？

乘务员：是呀！C909/ARJ21是中国首次自行研制、具有自主知识产权的中短程涡扇支线飞机，基本型布局为78～97座，这架飞机是C909/ARJ21-700，共有78个座位。请您沿着过道往前走。

旅客：好的，谢谢。再问下，我们什么时候起飞？什么时候落地？

乘务员：我们大约上午9点起飞，10点落地。

音频扫一扫

视频扫一扫

Dialogue 2: Greeting a passenger Ⅱ

音频扫一扫

Situation: When boarding, flight attendants should stand at the assigned area to welcome passengers.

Principle: Flight attendants should be informative and professional.

Example (FA: Flight attendant, PAX: Passenger)

FA: Good afternoon, welcome aboard!

PAX: Good afternoon! It's my first time to travel alone. I don't know my seat number.

FA: Don't worry! May I take a look at your boarding pass?

PAX: Here you are. The ground staff told me that this is the C919 aircraft.

FA: Yes, that true! C919 aircraft is a large civil jet aircraft independently developed by China and owns independent intellectual property right. C919 aircraft has a layout of 156 to 168 seats. Today we got 156 seats in total. Please walk along the aisle till row 13. It's the third row in the economy class. And your seat is by the aisle, 13C.

PAX: OK. Thank you!

FA: My pleasure.

情景会话2：问候旅客2

（FA：乘务员，PAX：旅客）

乘务员：下午好，欢迎登机！

旅客：下午好！这是我第一次独自旅行。我不清楚我的座位号。

乘务员：别担心，我能看一下您的登机牌吗？

旅客：给你。地服人员告诉我这是C919型飞机。

乘务员：是呀！中国商飞C919型飞机是中国自主研发的具有自主知识产权的大型民用喷气式客机，基本型布局为156～168座，今天这架飞机共有156个座位。请沿着这条过道往前走到13排。您的座位在经济舱13排C座，靠过道的座位。

旅客：好的，谢谢。

乘务员：不客气。

Dialogue 3: Describe the aircraft

音频扫一扫

Situation: When boarding, more and more passengers are paying attention to the basic information of the chosen aircraft.

Principle: As a flight attendant, you should answer questions professionally.

Example

PAX: What's the type of this airplane?

FA: Well, it is Boeing 737-800/ Airbus 330-300.

PAX: Erm... How many seats on this plane altogether?

FA: (Boeing 737-800) 159 in total with 147 seats in economy class/ (Airbus 330-300) 301 in total with 271 seats in economy class.

PAX: Wow, that's interesting. What about the height and length of this aircraft?

FA: (Boeing 737-800) It is 12.5 metres in height and 39.5 metres in length. / (Airbus 330-300) It is 16.85 metres in height and 63.6 metres in length.

PAX: Thanks a lot.

FA: My pleasure.

情景会话 3：描述飞机

旅客：这是什么机型的飞机？

乘务员：这是波音737-800/ 空客330-300机型。

旅客：嗯……机上一共有多少个座位？

乘务员：这架（波音737-800）飞机一共有159个座位，经济舱一共147个座位/ 这架（空客330-300）飞机一共有301个座位，经济舱一共271个座位。

旅客：哇，挺有意思的。那机高和机长是多少呀？

乘务员：（波音737-800）高12.5米，长39.5米。/（空客330-300）高16.85米，长63.6米。

Dialogue 4: Introduce the aircraft — This is an A320 aircraft

Situation: When boarding, more and more passengers are paying attention to the basic information of the chosen aircraft.

Principle: As a flight attendant, you should answer questions professionally. Briefly introduce the cabin layout of A320 aircraft.

Example

PAX: Excuse me, you know this is my first time to board a plane. May I ask what type of plane this is?

FA: Of course. This is an Airbus 320 aircraft.

PAX: I am curious about this aircraft. Could you please introduce it?

FA: Sure. Let's start from the galley. There are two galleys on this aircraft. As you can see, this is the place where we prepare drinks and meals for passengers. Now we go through into the cabin area. There are three lavatories. There is no first class. This is the business class compartment. There are only 8 seats in this part, so it is very comfortable. Then we come to the economy class. This is the biggest part and most of passengers are seated here. There are 144 seats in economy class, among which you will find 24 premium economy class seats.

PAX: OK.

FA: There are eight emergency exits. In case of emergency, we can evacuate from these exits.

PAX: I got it, and that is very nice of you.

情景会话 4：机型介绍——空客 320 机型

旅客：打扰一下，我是第一次乘机。我能问下这是什么机型吗？

乘务员：当然可以，这是空客320机型。

旅客：我对这个机型挺好奇的，能给我介绍一下吗？

乘务员：好的，我们从厨房讲起，飞机上共有两个厨房，正如您所看到的，这里是我们为旅客准备餐饮的地方。现在我们穿过客舱，本架飞机共有3个卫生间，没有头等舱，这是商务舱。商务舱只有8个座位，所以还是很舒适的。接下来是经济舱，这是客舱最大的部分，大多数旅客都坐在这个舱位，这个舱位共有144个座位，其中包含超级经济舱的24个座位。

旅客：嗯。

乘务员：本架飞机有8个紧急出口。一旦发生紧急情况，我们从这些出口撤离。

旅客：好的，我知道了，谢谢你。

Dialogue 5: Introduce the aircraft— This is a B787 aircraft

Situation: When boarding, more and more passengers are paying attention to the basic information of the chosen aircraft.

Principle: As a flight attendant, you should answer questions professionally. Be warm and elegant.

Example

PAX: Excuse me, Miss. May I ask what type of plane this is?

FA: Sure. This is an aircraft of Boeing 787.

PAX: How many seats are there on this plane?

FA: Actually there are more than 200 seats.

PAX: It's a new type, right? The cabin looks pretty and smells good.

FA: Yes. Boeing 787 Dreamliner is faster and lighter. It's the newest type of Boeing series. Our company often use this type of aircraft to fly to America, and use A330 to fly to Europe.

PAX: That's interesting. Thank you.

FA: It's my pleasure. If there is anything I can do for you, please feel comfortable to let me know.

情景会话5：机型介绍——波音787机型

旅客：打扰一下，女士。我能问问这是什么机型吗？

乘务员：当然。这是波音787型飞机。

旅客：这架飞机上能载多少客人呢？

乘务员：实际上有超过200个座位。

旅客：这是新机型，对吗？客舱里看上去不错，气味也还好。

乘务员：是的。波音787梦想系列机型更快更轻。它是波音系列的最新机型。我们公司通常使用波音787执飞美国航线，使用空客330执飞欧洲航线。

旅客：听上去挺有意思。谢谢你了。

乘务员：乐意效劳。如果您有什么需要，请随时找我。

Ⅲ. Popular Words and Phrases

greet	[griːt]	v. 问候
greeting	[ˈgriːtɪŋ]	n. 招呼，问候；v. 问候（greet 的现在分词）
board	[bɔːd]	v. 登机
boarding	[ˈbɔːdɪŋ]	n. 上飞机；v. 登机（board 的现在分词）
boarding pass		登机牌
passport	[ˈpæspɔːt]	n. 护照
visa	[ˈviːzə]	n. （护照等的）签证，背签
ID, Identification Card		身份证
embark	[ɪmˈbɑːk]	v. 上机；上船
disembark	[ˌdɪsɪmˈbɑːk]	v. 下机；下船
Frequent Flyer Program		常旅客奖励计划，常旅客计划
membership	[ˈmembəʃɪp]	n. 会员
mileage	[ˈmaɪlɪdʒ]	n. 英里，里程
flight plan		飞行计划
seating capacity		载客量
aircraft	[ˈeəkrɑːft]	n. 飞机，航空器
first class		头等舱
business class		商务舱，公务舱
premium economy class		高端经济舱，超级经济舱
economy class		经济舱，普通舱

configuration/ layout	[kən,fɪɡə'reɪʃ(ə)n]/ ['leɪaʊt]	n. 布局
row	[rəʊ]	n. 排
aisle	[aɪl]	n. 过道，通道
window	['wɪndəʊ]	n. 窗户
galley	['ɡælɪ]	n. 机上厨房
lavatory	['lævət(ə)rɪ]	n. 盥洗室，卫生间

Ⅳ. Practical Expressions

1. Hello/ Good morning/ Good afternoon/ Good evening, welcome aboard China ×× flight!

您好/早上好/下午好/晚上好，欢迎乘坐中国××公司航班！

2. Good morning! May I see your boarding pass? / May I have a look at your boarding pass?

早上好，可以看一下您的登机牌吗？

3. Hello! Nice/ Pleased to meet you!

您好！见到您很高兴！

4. How do you do?/ How are you?

你好！（表达"你好"/"你好吗"，初次见面时的问候语，一般用于正式场合。如果回答，可用"Good/ Very well/ …"）。

5. — How's it going?/ How are you doing?/ What's up?/ What's new?

— Not bad./ Pretty good.

——近来如何？（寒暄语，常用的打招呼方式，"最近怎样？"，含有"你好"的意思）

——还行。/挺好的。

6. C909/ARJ21 aircraft is the first short-medium range turbofan regional aircraft independently developed by China and it owns independent intellectual property right. ARJ21 aircraft has a layout of 78 to 97 seats.

C909/ARJ21是中国首次自行研制、具有自主知识产权的中短程涡扇支线飞机，基本型布局为78至97座。

7. C919 aircraft is a large civil jet aircraft independently developed by China and owns independent intellectual property right. C919 aircraft has a layout of 158 to 168 seats.

中国商飞C919型飞机是中国自主研发的具有自主知识产权的大型民用喷气式客机，基本型布局为158至168座。

8. There are two galleys on this aircraft. As you can see, this is the place where we prepare drinks and meals for passengers.

这架飞机上共有两个厨房，正如您所看到的，这里是我们为旅客准备餐饮的地方。

9. Now we go through into the cabin area. There are three lavatories.

现在我们穿过客舱，本架飞机共有3个卫生间。

10. There is no first class. This is the business class. There are only 8 seats in this part, so it is very comfortable.

这里没有头等舱，这是商务舱。商务舱只有8个座位，所以还是很舒适的。

11. Then we come to the economy class. This is the biggest part and most of passengers are seated here. There are 144 seats in economy class, among which you will find 24 premium economy class seats.

接下来是经济舱，这是客舱最大的部分，大多数旅客都坐在这个舱位，这个舱位共有144个座位，其中包含超级经济舱的24个座位。

12. Our company often use this type of aircraft to fly to America, and use A330 to fly to Europe.

我们公司通常使用这一机型执飞美国航线，使用空客330执飞欧洲航线。

Ⅴ. Tips

The Boarding Pass 登机牌

A boarding pass is a document provided by an airline during check-in, giving a passenger permission to enter the restricted area of an airport and to board the airplane for a particular flight. At a minimum, it identifies the passenger, the flight number, and the date and scheduled time for departure. In some cases, passengers can check in online and print their boarding passes themselves. A boarding pass may be required for a passenger to enter a secure area of an airport.

Generally, a passenger with an electronic ticket will only need a boarding pass. If a passenger has a paper airline ticket, that ticket (or flight coupon) may be required to be attached to the boarding pass for him or her to board the aircraft. The paper boarding pass (and ticket, if any), or portions thereof, are sometimes collected and counted for cross-check of passenger counts by gate agents, but more frequently are scanned (via barcode or magnetic strip). The standards for bar codes and magnetic stripes on boarding passes are published by IATA. Most airports and airlines have automatic readers that will verify the validity of the boarding pass at the jetway door or boarding gate. This also automatically updates the airline's database that shows the passenger has boarded and the seat is used, and that the checked baggage for that passenger may stay aboard. This speeds up the paperwork process at the gate, but requires passengers with paper tickets to check in, surrender the ticket, and receive the digitized boarding pass.

Ⅵ. Supplementary Reading

1. COMAC 中国商飞 (established: May 11, 2008)

COMAC (Commercial Aircraft Corporation of China Limited), is a centrally managed core enterprise in civil aircraft industry of China and a central backbone enterprise, which is formed with the approval of the State Council, jointly invested by State-Owned Assets Supervision and Administration Commission (SASAC) of the State Council, Shanghai Guo Sheng (Group) Co., Limited, Aviation Industry Corporation of China (AVIC), Aluminum Corporation of China Limited (CHALCO), China Baowu Steel Group Corporation Limited, and Sinochem Corporation. The headquarter of COMAC is in Pudong, Shanghai.

COMAC functions as the main vehicle in implementing large passenger aircraft programs in China. It is also mandated with the overall planning of developing trunk liner and regional jet programs and realizing the industrialization of civil aircraft in China. COMAC adheres to the principle of "development with Chinese characteristics" and attaches great importance to technological progress and self-reliant advancement in the process of marketing, integration, industrialization and globalization. The company endeavors to manufacture large passenger aircraft that are safer, cost-effective, comfortable and environment-friendly.

Product: C909/ARJ21, C919, Commercial airliners

(1) C909/ARJ21 (old friend, new look) aircraft is the first short-medium range turbofan regional aircraft independently developed by China in accordance with international civil aviation regulations, it owns independent intellectual property right. C909/ARJ21 aircraft has a layout of 78 to 97 seats, and a range of 2,225 to 3,700 kilometers. C909/ARJ21-700 aircraft obtained the Type Certificate from Civil Aviation Administration of China (CAAC) on December 30th, 2014 and the Production Certificate (PC) from CAAC on July 9th, 2017.

(2) C919 aircraft is a large civil jet aircraft independently developed by China in accordance with international civil aviation regulations, and owns independent intellectual property right. C919 aircraft has a layout of 158 to 168 seats, and a range of 4,075 to 5,555 kilometers. The first aircraft rolled out on November 2nd, 2015. On May 5th 2017, C919 made the first test flight.

【背景阅读】

　　中国商用飞机有限责任公司（简称中国商飞，COMAC），于2008年5月11日在上海成立，是我国实施国家大型飞机重大专项中大型客机项目的主体，也是统筹干线飞机和支线飞机发展、实现我国民用飞机产业化的主要载体。中国商飞公司注册资本501.01亿元，总部设在上海。

　　C909/ARJ21支线客机：C909/ARJ21是中国按照国际标准研制的具有自主知识产权的中短航程支线涡扇飞机，基本型布局为78~97座，标准航程为2225公里，最大航程为3700公里，以中国中西部和北部地区机场起降和复杂航路越障为目标的营运要求，具有良好的高温高原性能和抗侧风能力。ARJ21-700是C909/ARJ21翔凤客机系列的基本型。据中国新闻网，自2016年6月投入航线运营以来，国产客机C909/ARJ21已累计交付国航、东航、南航、成都航空、天骄航空和江西航空等客户38余架。C909/ARJ21飞机拥有支线客机中最宽敞的客舱，为乘客提供更多的行李空间和舒适的乘坐环境，与150座级干线飞机具有相近的飞行性能和相媲美的舒适性，同时可提高飞机调配使用的灵活性。2024年11月12日，中国商飞宣布ARJ21飞机增加新名称C909。

　　2025年7月1日，北京时间9时35分，由中国国航C909机型执飞的CA757航班，从呼和浩特白塔国际机场平稳飞抵乌兰巴托国际机场，开启了国航C909运营国际商业航班的新篇章。国航C909执飞呼和浩特—乌兰巴托国际航线，是在推动国产民机国际化运营道路上的重要突破，也是积极响应"一带一路"倡议、拓展"一带一路"航线网络的重要举措，在促进我国睦邻友好的同时，让"中国航空制造"服务更多国际旅客，展示中国制造的实力和能力。增进周边国家参与构建人类命运共同体的信心和决心，积极参与分享中国经济高质量发展和文明进步的红利。

　　C919是中国商用飞机有限责任公司COMAC自主研发的大型民航客机，是国产中短程干线客机，基本型布局为158~168座，标准航程为4075公里，最大航程为5555公里，经济寿命达9万飞行小时，与空客A320、波音737属同级别飞机。C是China的首字母，也是中国商用飞机有限责任公司英文缩写COMAC的首字母，同时寓意跻身国际大型客机市场，要与Airbus（空中客车公司）和Boeing（波音）一道在国际大型客机制造业中形成ABC并立的格局。第一个"9"的寓意是天长地久，"19"代表的是中国首型大型客机最大载客量为190座。C919于2017年5月5日成功进行首飞，于2022年9月29日获中国民用航空局颁发的型号合格证。2025年，中国东航、国航、南航C919已成功完成"春运"航班任务，各航司该机型均已执飞多条航线。C919以中国国内为切入点，同时兼顾国外市场，提供多等级、多种航程的产品，希望之后为民用航空市场提供安全、舒适、节能、环保、具有竞争力的中短程单通道商用运输机。

2. Boeing 波音 (established: July 15, 1916)

The Boeing Company is an American multinational corporation that designs, manufactures, and sells airplanes, rotorcraft, rockets, and satellites worldwide. The Boeing Company's corporate headquarters are located in Chicago. Boeing is organized into three business units: Boeing Commercial Airplanes (BCA); Boeing Defense, Space & Security (BDS); and Boeing Global Services, which began operations on July 1, 2017. Supporting these units is Boeing Capital Corporation, a global provider of financing solutions. Boeing is among the largest global aircraft manufacturers. As America's biggest manufacturing exporter, the company supports airlines and U.S. and allied government customers in more than 150 countries.

Product: B737, B747, B767, B777, B787 family

As America's biggest manufacturing exporter, the Boeing company supports airlines and U.S. and allied government customers in more than 150 countries. The Next-Generation 737, including B737-800, provides airline customers with superior reliability, fuel efficiency and high-value returns operators require in today's competitive market. The B737-800 usually seats from 159 to 189 passengers and has a maximum capacity of 180 passengers.

【背景阅读】

波音公司是美国的一家航空航天公司，是美国最大的制造出口商，总部位于美国芝加哥（2001年前在西雅图）。波音的产品以及定制的服务包括：民用和军用飞机、卫星、发射系统和通信系统等。1972年中国民用航空总局订购了10架波音707客机。波音707是美国波音公司研制的四发远程喷气运输机。

波音737（即B737）系列飞机是美国波音公司研制生产的单通道双发中短程客机，至今发展出14个型号。B737-800是B737-700的机身延长型号。B737-800可以载客159~189名，在两级机舱配置下，可载159人；全为经济客位单级配置下，载客量可达189人。续航距离为5,665公里。B737-800是B737NG的其中一员。B737系列飞机包括B737-200、B737-300、B737-700、B737-800、B737-900和B737-800MAX等组成了单通道飞机系列，满足了航空公司可靠、简捷，且极具运营和维护成本经济性的需求。

3. Airbus 空客 (established: December, 1970)

The Airbus Company is a global leader in aeronautics, space and related services, built on its strong European heritage to become truly international – with roughly 180 locations and 12,000 direct suppliers globally. It is based in Toulouse, France, with production and manufacturing facilities mainly in France, Germany, Spain, China, United Kingdom and the United States. The company produces and markets the first commercially viable digital fly-by-wire airliner, the Airbus A320, and one of the world's largest passenger airliner, the A380. Passenger comfort is a major design consideration for Airbus, which is why the company's product line of modern jetliners has built a reputation for delivering the most enjoyable experiences aloft today.

Product: A300, A310, A318, A319, A320, A321, A330, A340, A350, A380

Since Airbus launched the A320 single-aisle jetliner family, it has become the world's most comfortable short-to-medium-haul aircraft. The A320 usually seats from 140 to 170 passengers and has a maximum capacity of 180 passengers. With the widest single-aisle cabin, passengers can enjoy more personal space, wider seats and generous overhead compartments to store their luggage. The A320 also has an extremely quiet cabin. It's easy to relax and enjoy the flight. Like all A320 Family members, the A320 shares the same fly-by-wire digital flight controls and cabin management systems and this consistency makes life easier for the crew members and passengers.

【背景阅读】

空中客车公司，又称空客公司，是欧洲一家飞机制造、研发公司，总部位于法国图卢兹，有三个装配厂分别位于法国的图卢兹、德国的汉堡及中国的天津。1985年中国民航总局华东管理局引进一架A310，这是在中国大陆运营的首架空中客车飞机。空中客车的生产线是从A300型号开始的，它是世界上第一个双通道、双引擎的飞机，比A300更短的变型被称为A310。

空客320系列飞机包括A318、A319、A320和A321型飞机，这一系列是欧洲空中客车公司研制生产的单通道双发中短程客机。空客320通常设置有140~170个座位，最大座位数可达180。空客320是第一款使用数字电传操纵飞行控制系统的商用飞机，也是第一款放宽静稳定度设计的民航客机，客舱适应性和舒适性较好，满足了航空公司低成本运营中短程航线和旅客舒适性的需求。

VII. Exercises

1. List at least three ways of greetings when passengers getting on board.

(1)

(2)

(3)

2. Translate the following words and phrases into Chinese or English.

常旅客计划	boarding pass
过道	passport
窗户	first class
galley	business class
lavatory	economy class

3. Translate the following sentences into English.

(1) 早上好，欢迎登机！

(2) 下午好，可以看一下您的登机牌吗？

(3) 这架空客330-200机型飞机一共有237个座位，经济舱有207个座位。

(4) 这架波音737-800机型飞机一共有167个座位，头等舱有8个座位。

4. Group work: choose one topic to start a conversation. (TIME LIMIT: 3 minutes)

(1) Describe an aircraft.

(2) The principles of greeting a passenger when boarding.

(3) The importance of greeting passengers warmly on board.

Task 4　Baggage Arrangement 安放行李

Ⅰ. Warm-up Questions

1. How to assist passengers to arrange their luggage appropriately?

2. Could you list several items that could not be stowed in the overhead compartment?

3. According to your understanding, passengers are not allowed to put their hand baggage on which part of the cabin?

Ⅱ. Dialogues

Dialogue 1: Give a hand to a passenger

Situation: When boarding, passengers usually take more than one piece of hand luggage and they need time to arrange them. Under this circumstance, the aisle always gets blocked.

Principle: Keep an eye on passengers' hand luggage and arrange bags with flexibility.

Example

FA: Excuse me, Madam. May I help you?

PAX: Um... Could you please give me a hand? It's too heavy for me...

FA: Sure. Could you please give way to the passengers behind by stepping aside a little bit? I will try my best to help you.

PAX: Alright.

FA: Thank you for your cooperation.

音频扫一扫

情景会话 1：给旅客搭下手

乘务员：您好，女士，请问需要帮忙吗？

旅客：呃……能帮忙搭把手（放行李箱）吗？箱子有点儿沉。

乘务员：好的。烦请您稍微侧一下身以便后面的旅客通过，谢谢。我尽力帮您（安放行李）。

旅客：好。

乘务员：感谢您的配合。

Dialogue 2: The handcart

Situation: During boarding session, not all passengers understand the rules of cabin baggage arrangement. And cabin crew need to pay attention to the onboard baggage at this time.

Principle: Keep an eye on passengers' hand baggage and arrange bags with flexibility.

Example

FA: Whose handcart is this?

PAX: It's mine. What's up?

FA: I'm afraid you can't leave it here. It might fall down in case of turbulence and hurt someone. Would you please put it somewhere else?

音频扫一扫

PAX: Could I leave it on the aisle?

FA: I'm afraid not. Would you mind if I take care of it? I'll put it in the cloakroom and bring it to you after landing. Is that okay?

PAX: All right. Thank you so much!

FA: My pleasure.

情景会话2：手推车

乘务员：请问这是谁的手推车？

旅客：是我的，怎么了？

乘务员：抱歉您不能把它放在这里。如果发生颠簸，手推车有可能倒下砸伤旅客。您介意将它放到其他地方吗？

旅客：那我放过道可以吗？

乘务员：不可以的。如果您不介意的话，我可以将它放置在衣帽间里，落地后我再给您送过来，这样您看可以吗？

旅客：好的，非常感谢你！

乘务员：不客气的。

音频扫一扫

Dialogue 3: Checked luggage on board

Situation: When boarding, passengers oftentimes bring oversize hand luggage due to very short flight time or long-distance international flight. In this case, passengers usually ask for help.

Principle: Keep professional and deliver notices about in-flight checked baggage to the passenger involved.

Example

PAX: Excuse me, lady. There's no space for my luggage.

FA: Don't worry! Let me see. (After looking around the overhead compartment and area nearby) I've checked the overhead compartment and the size of your luggage. I'm sorry to tell you that your luggage is too big to go into the overhead compartment.

PAX: Could you please help me?

FA: May I help you check it in? One of our ground staff is at the front door and it's totally free.

PAX: Well, then. But how can I get it back?

FA: That won't be a problem. When we arrive at our destination, you may claim your baggage at the baggage claim area. Just make sure that no lithium battery and portable power bank in your luggage. Please also take your passport and personal items including the valuables as well as breakable objects out of your luggage.

PAX: Alright.

FA: Thank you for your understanding.

情景会话3：机上的托运行李

旅客：你好，女士。我没有地方放行李了。

乘务员：别着急，我帮您看一下。（看下其座位上方的行李架及附近行李存放区域）我帮您看过了，由于您的行李尺寸过大，抱歉地跟您说，您的行李没有办法放进行李架。

旅客：那怎么办？能帮帮我吗？

乘务员：您需要办理机上托运手续。在前登机门处，有一名机场的地面工作人员为您办理，您放心，办理是完全免费的。

旅客：那好吧。不过我怎么取回我的行李呢？

乘务员：那不成问题。当我们到达目的地时，您正常到行李提取处去提取就可以了。请您确保这件需要托运的行李里没有锂电池及充电宝。同时，确认护照证件及贵重易碎物品已全部取出。

旅客：好的。

乘务员：谢谢您的理解。

Dialogue 4: Limited space for carry-on luggage (1)

音频扫一扫

Situation: When boarding, passengers oftentimes bring over one piece of hand luggage due to short flight. Under this circumstance, passengers usually ask for assistance. Flight attendants meet this case on the single-aisle aircraft frequently.

Principle: Be polite and patient during the process, with sincere apology. Try to communicate with the passenger actively and pay attention to your attitude and gestures.

Example

PAX: Excuse me, Miss?

FA: May I help you?

PAX: I don't think I can find room for my carry-on bags.

FA: Don't worry about it. I'll help you. One moment, please.

PAX: OK.

(After looking around the overhead compartment and the nearby area...)

FA: Thank you for your waiting! Sir, I do apologize for no space in the overhead locker above your seat. I understand you would like to keep your bags close to you. May I suggest you stow them on the overhead compartment? Just two rows ahead of you as you can see from here.

PAX: No problem.

FA: Please make sure that you take the valuable and breakable items out of the bags, just in case.

PAX: Alright.

FA: Thank you for your cooperation. Carry your bags and follow me, please.

PAX: Thank you actually.

FA: My pleasure.

情景会话4：行李存放空间有限（1）

旅客：你好？

乘务员：您好，请问需要帮忙吗？

旅客：我带的行李放不下了。

乘务员：别着急，我马上来帮您，请稍等一下。

旅客：好的。

（查看下其座位上方行李架及前后行李架）

乘务员：先生，让您久等了。很抱歉，您座位上方的行李架已满，我理解您想把行李放在身边。您介意把行李放在您前面的行李架上吗？您看，就在您前面两排的位置。

旅客：可以。

乘务员：为您着想，请您确认将行李里的贵重易碎物品取出。

旅客：好的。

乘务员：谢谢您的配合，请跟我来。

旅客：是我该谢谢你。

乘务员：这是我的荣幸。

Dialogue 5: Limited space for carry-on luggage (2)

Situation: During the boarding period, it is the responsibility of cabin crew to assist passengers to arrange their baggage due to limited time and space.

Principle: Be polite and patient during the process. Try to communicate with passengers instead of neglecting them.

Example

PAX1: Excuse me, Miss?

FA: Yes. What can I do for you?

PAX1: Just look at it. There's no room left.

FA: I do apologize that there is no space in the overhead locker above your seat. I understand you would like to keep your bag close to you. May I suggest you stow it under the seat in front of you?

PAX1: I tried but it doesn't fit.

FA: Got it. (Turning around...) Excuse me, whose baggage is it?

PAX2: It's mine. What's wrong?

FA: Sir, this lady wants to put her bag into the overhead compartment as well. But there is no enough room left. Could I lean your bag a bit to put her bag in?

PAX2: Sure.

FA: Thanks!

情景会话5：行李存放空间有限（2）

旅客1：打扰一下，乘务员？

乘务员：您好，请问有什么可以帮您的？

旅客1：你自己看吧，没地方放行李了。

乘务员：我很抱歉您座椅上方的行李架满了，我也明白您想把包放在自己身边。我建议您放在您前面座椅下方好吗？

旅客1：我试过了，但是放不下。

乘务员：好的。（转过身……）打扰一下，请问这是谁的行李？

旅客2：我的。怎么了？

乘务员：先生，是这样的，这位女士也想将她的包放在行李架上，但是空间有限，能否将您的包稍微倾斜一下，把她的包放到里面去？

旅客2：可以啊。

乘务员：谢谢您！

Ⅲ. Popular Words and Phrases

stow	[stəʊ]	v. 将某物装好收起
overhead bin		（头顶上方的）行李架
overhead compartment		（头顶上方的）行李架
luggage	[ˈlʌgɪdʒ]	n.（英）行李，（美）皮箱
baggage	[ˈbægɪdʒ]	n. 行李
baggage claim tag		行李牌
suitcase	[ˈsjuːtkeɪs]	n. 手提箱
briefcase	[ˈbriːfkeɪs]	n. 公文包
carry-on baggage/ carry-on luggage		随身行李

hand baggage/ hand luggage		手提行李
checked baggage/ registered baggage		托运行李
oversized baggage		超规行李
lost baggage		丢失的行李
delayed baggage		延误的行李
valuables	['væljʊəb̩z]	n. 贵重物品
laptop	['læptɒp]	n. 笔记本电脑
block	[blɒk]	v. 阻挡
occupied	['ɒkjʊpaɪd]	adj. 被占了，没空了
offload	[ˌɒf'ləʊd]	v. 卸下
oversize	['əʊvəsaɪz]	adj. 过大的
fragile	['frædʒaɪl]	adj. 易碎的
breakable	['breɪkəbl]	adj. 易碎的
belongings	[bɪ'lɒŋɪŋz]	n. 随身财物
item	['aɪtəm]	n. 物品
baby stroller	['beibi 'strəʊlə]	婴儿车
closet/ cloakroom	[klɒzɪt]/['kləʊkruːm]	n. 衣帽间

IV. Practical Expressions

1. May I help you with your bag?

请问需要帮忙放行李吗？

2. I am afraid your baggage is too big to go into the overhead compartment. May I help you check it in? One of our ground staff is at the front door and it's totally free.

恐怕您的行李太大，行李架里放不下。建议您托运吧？我们的一名地面人员就在前登机门，可以免费帮您办理托运手续。

3. May I advise you to take your passport and personal items including the valuables as well as breakable objects out of your luggage?

请取出您行李中的护照及随身要用的物品，包括贵重及易碎物品好吗？

/ Would you mind taking out your passport, the valuables and fragile items from your luggage?

请您取出行李中的护照、贵重和易碎物品好吗？

4. Could you please take out all valuable items and important documents from your pockets? Thank you.

请您把贵重物品和重要文件从口袋中取出好吗？谢谢。

5. Excuse me, is this your luggage? May I advise you to put it under the seat in front of you or into the overhead compartment?

您好，请问这是您的行李吗？请放在您前方座椅下，或放在行李架上。

6. I do apologize for no space in the overhead locker above your seat. I understand you would like to keep your bag close to you. May I suggest you stow it under the seat in front of you?

对不起，您座椅上方的行李架满了。我明白您想把包放在身边，我建议您放在前面座椅的下面好吗？

7. Excuse me, whose bag is it? This lady wants to put her bag into the overhead compartment as well. But there is not enough room left. Could I lean your bag a bit to put her bag in?

打扰一下，请问这是谁的包？这位女士也想将她的包放在行李架上，但是空间有限，能否将您的包稍微倾斜一下，把她的包放到里面去？

8. Sir/ Madam, may I help you hang up your coat in the closet?

先生/女士，我帮您把外套挂在衣帽间，好吗？

9. Please carry your bag and follow me.

请带上您的行李跟我走。

10. Excuse me, Madam. Is this your baggage? It's the emergency exit. For your safety, would you mind putting it into the overhead compartment?

女士，打扰一下。请问这是您的行李吗？这里是应急出口，出于安全考虑，请您将您的包放在行李架上好吗？

11. Please don't put your handcart/ baby stroller in the overhead compartment. It might fall down because of wheels. Thank you!

手推车/婴儿车的底部有轮子容易滑落，请不要放在行李架上，谢谢！

12. If there is some space left in other compartments, would you mind putting it there?

如果其他行李架有空位置，您介意把您的行李放到那儿吗？

13. Would you mind if I put your baggage in the overhead compartment in Row 35?

您介意我把您的行李放到35排的行李架吗？

14. After landing, you may get your baggage at the baggage claim area.

落地后，您到行李提取处就可以拿到您的行李了。

V. Tips

1. What are the key points on placing baggage on the overhead compartment? 在行李架上安放行李要注意什么？

Monitor passengers to place baggage on the overhead compartment, forbid baggage stacking except clothing; forbid overweight baggage, easily sliding bottles and other metal objects to be placed on the overhead compartment.

2. What kind of location is not suitable for accommodating baggage on board？ 机上哪些位置不宜安放行李？

Emergency exits, the space under the first row of seats, vacant trolley locations in the kitchen, the bathroom, the emergency equipment storage locations, crew rest seats and spaces without fixers, including the gap between the last row of seats (the back) and the plane wallboard of all models and cabins.

VI. Supplementary Reading

1. The International Air Transport Association (IATA) 国际航空运输协会	

IATA was founded in Havana, Cuba, on 19 April 1945. It is the prime vehicle for inter-airline cooperation in promoting safe, reliable, secure and economical air services, for the benefit of the world's consumers. IATA offers over 400 titles consisting of standards, manuals and guidelines that cover a variety of aviation topics, from Safety, Passenger, Cargo, to Security and more. Ensuring that the industry adapts and adheres to these global standards and recommended practices underpins a safe, secure, and integrated global air transport system. The international scheduled air transport industry is more than 100 times larger than it was in 1945. Few industries can match the dynamism of that growth, which would have been much less spectacular without the standards, practices and procedures developed within IATA.

2. The International Civil Aviation Organization (ICAO) 国际民用航空组织

The International Civil Aviation Organization (ICAO) is a specialized agency of the United Nations. It codifies the principles and techniques of international air navigation and fosters the planning and development of international air transport to ensure safe and orderly growth. Its headquarter is located in Montreal, Quebec, Canada. The ICAO Council adopts the standards and recommended practices concerning air navigation, its infrastructure, flight inspection, prevention of unlawful interference, and facilitation of border-crossing procedures for international civil aviation. ICAO defines the protocols for air accident investigation followed by transport safety authorities in countries signatory to the Chicago Convention on International Civil Aviation.

3. Baggage Allowance 行李额度

Baggage is considered as appropriate or necessary objects, items and other personal assets for passengers clothing, usage or comfort. For your own safety, please check if there are any dangerous items in your baggage. Please pack your own baggage or follow the packing procedures for your own safety. When packing your baggage, please check all sealed boxes, packages and wrappings. Additionally, do not accept any items to take from someone else if you don't know what the content is. Always carry jewelry, money, cell phones, laptops, documents and other valuable goods in your hand luggage.

On the commercial transportation, mostly with airlines, the baggage allowance is the amount of checked baggage or hand/ carry-on luggage the company allows per passenger. There may be the limit on the amount that is allowed free of charge, and hard limit on the amount that is allowed. The limit varies per airline and depends on the class, elite status, type of ticket, flight origin and destination. If a flight is booked together with another flight, it may be different (e.g. if another flight on the same ticket is a long-haul flight). The exact baggage conditions are mentioned in the ticket information online.

VII. Exercises

1. List several cases of baggage arrangement when passengers getting on board.

(1)

(2)

(3)

(4)

2. Translate the following words and phrases into Chinese or English.

stow	行李
valuables	行李牌
laptop	手提行李
block	托运行李
occupied	易碎的
行李架	

3. Translate the following sentences into English.

(1) 请问需要帮忙放行李吗？

(2) 您的行李太大，行李架里放不下。建议您办理机上托运，地面人员就在前登机门，可以免费帮您办理托运手续。

(3) 请取出您行李中的护照及随身要用的物品，包括贵重及易碎物品。

(4) 您好，请问这是您的行李吗？请放在您头顶上方的行李架上。

(5) 对不起，先生，您座椅上方的行李架没地方了。我明白您想把包放在身边，我建议您放在前面座椅的下面好吗？

(6) 婴儿车底部有轮子容易滑落，请不要放在行李架上，谢谢。

4. Group work: choose one topic to start a conversation. (TIME LIMIT: 10 minutes)

(1) No space for carry-on luggage.

(2) Oversize luggage on board.

(3) In-flight checked baggage.

Task 5   Seating Assistance 协助入座

Ⅰ. Warm-up Questions

1. How to recognize the seat number on a boarding pass?

2. Could you figure out several cases where passengers need to change their seats when boarding?

3. The principles of seating assistance.

Ⅱ. Dialogues

Dialogue 1: "Stay with my daughter"

Situation: When boarding, it is often the case that the family members are separated by seats and they would like to seat together. Aircraft is different from trains and cars, which requires weight balance. For the reason of safety, in order to ensure the balance of stowage and flight safety, passengers are not allowed to change their seats randomly during flight. However, when passengers request, we should try our best to solve the problem under the premise of ensuring safety.

Principle: Give priority to safety, be patient and arrange seats with flexibility.

Example

PAX1: Excuse me, Miss ?

FA: May I help you?/ What can I do for you?

PAX1: My daughter is only 4 years old. And our seats are separated somehow. Can I change the seat with the lady beside my daughter? She is too young to take care of herself. We would like to sit together. Could you please help me?

FA: Well, you could talk with that lady directly./ OK. I will try to help you./ I will try my best to arrange for you. May I see your boarding pass?

音频扫一扫

视频扫一扫

PAX1: Here you are.

FA: OK! Your seat number is 31A and your daughter's is 42F.

(Walking towards 42H...)

FA: Excuse me, Madam. This little girl sits here by herself, but her mother sits in the first row of the cabin. Her mother wants to change the seat with you to take care of her daughter. Her mother's seat is 31A. It is a window seat with more space. And you could get off the aircraft a little bit earlier after landing. It is more convenient and comfortable. Are you willing to sit there?

PAX2: Okay, I'd love to.

FA: Thank you so much!

(Going back to 31A...)

FA: Thank you for your waiting, Madam. The lady agrees to change her seat with you. You could change the seat now and please don't forget to take all your personal items.

PAX1: Thanks a lot.

FA: My pleasure.

情景会话 1："和我女儿坐在一起"

旅客 1：打扰一下，女士。

乘务员：您好，请问有什么可以帮您？

旅客 1：我的女儿只有四岁大。我们俩的座位不知怎么分开了。我能和我女儿旁边的女士换个座位吗？她还太小，不能照顾自己，我们希望能坐在一起。您能帮帮忙吗？

乘务员：这样，您可以直接和那位女士商量一下。/ 好的，我会尽量帮您的。/ 我尽量帮您安排，我能看看您的登机牌吗？

旅客 1：给您。

乘务员：好的，您的座位号是 31A，您女儿的座位号是 42F。

（乘务员走向 42 排 H 座……）

乘务员：打扰您了，女士。这位小姑娘自己一个人坐在这儿，而她妈妈在客舱的第一排。她妈妈想和您换一下座位以便照顾她的小孩。她妈妈的座位是 31A。那是一个靠窗的座位且空间较大，落地以后您可以早些下飞机，既方便又舒适。请问您愿意坐到那儿吗？

旅客 2：好的，我非常愿意。

乘务员：非常感谢您！

（乘务员走回 31 排 A 座……）

乘务员：让您久等了，女士。那位女士同意和您换座位。您可以现在就换过去，请带好您的全部个人物品。

旅客 1：非常感谢。

乘务员：您太客气了。

Dialogue 2: Language barrier

Situation: When boarding, it is often the case that a group of people, usually partners or friends, get separated seat numbers and they couldn't communicate well enough.

Principle: Safety always comes first; arrange seats with flexibility.

Example

PA1: Excuse me, Sir. I can't speak Chinese at all. I'd like to sit with my friends. Could you help me?

FA: Sure. That passenger is not on board. Later after boarding, I will ask if that passenger would like to change his or her seat with you. Please take the assigned seat now. I'll let you know when it's possible.

音频扫一扫

PAX1: OK! Thanks a lot.

(After a while...)

FA: Excuse me, Sir. A foreign passenger would like to sit with his friends and he is wondering whether he could change the seat with you. His seat number is 39D, an aisle seat. Would you like to change the seat with him?

PAX2: No worries.

FA: Thanks for your kindness. Would you like me to help you with your baggage? If there are some valuables in it, you may take them out and stow them in the seat pocket in front of you.

PAX2: Thanks for your reminding.

(Walking towards the foreign passenger...)

FA: Excuse me, Sir. The gentleman beside your friend is willing to change his seat with you. You could sit with your friends now. Please take all your personal belongings.

PAX1: Wow, thank you so much!

FA: It's my pleasure.

情景会话 2：语言障碍

旅客 1：先生，您好。我不会说中文，我想和我的朋友们坐一起，您能帮帮我吗？

乘务员：好的。现在那位旅客还没登机，稍后登机完毕我将询问下他/她是否愿意和您换座位。现在请您先坐在指定座位上。如果可以换座位，我会马上告诉您。

旅客 1：好的，谢谢您。

（过了一会儿……）

乘务员：抱歉先生，打扰您一下。有位外国旅客想和您换座位，以便和朋友坐在一起。他的座位号是 39D，靠过道的座位，您愿意跟他换吗？

旅客 2：没问题。

乘务员：太谢谢您了，需要我协助您安放行李吗？如果您行李中有贵重物品，请您拿出来，放到您座位前面的座椅口袋内。

旅客 2：谢谢你的提醒。

（乘务员走向那位外国旅客……）

乘务员：先生，打扰您了。坐在您朋友旁边的先生愿意和您换座位，现在您可以和您的朋友们坐在一起了，请您换座位时携带好全部个人物品。

旅客 1：啊！太谢谢你了。

乘务员：不客气。

Dialogue 3: Take the wrong seat

Situation: As is often the case, some passengers may take the wrong seats because of carelessness.

Principle: Flight attendants should recognize this kind of cases and help the passengers as soon as possible.

Example

PAX1: Excuse me, Miss?

FA: What can I do for you, Sir?

PAX1: My seat is 32J, but it is occupied by someone else. Could you help me with it?

FA: Sure. Could I take a look at your boarding pass, please?

PAX1: Here it is.

FA: I am afraid the lady might be in the wrong seat. Please stay here for a few seconds.

音频扫一扫

PAX1: OK.

(Walking towards 32J...)

FA: Excuse me, Madam. May I see your boarding pass, please?

PAX2: Here you are.

FA: Madam, your seat number is 42J and this is 32J.

PAX2: Oh, that's right. I am sorry. I'll move right now.

FA: Thank you for your cooperation. Would you like me to help you with your baggage?

PAX2: No, thank you. It's not that heavy.

FA: My pleasure.

FA: Thank you for your waiting, Sir. You may take 32J.

PAX1: Thanks a lot.

FA: You're welcome.

情景会话 3：旅客坐错座位（座位被占）

旅客 1：打扰一下您可以吗，女士？

乘务员：先生，我能为您做点儿什么呢？

旅客 1：我的座位是 32J，但是现在被别人占了。您能帮我一下吗？

乘务员：当然，我能看一下您的登机牌吗？

旅客 1：给您。

乘务员：恐怕那位女士坐错位子了。请您在这儿稍等一下。

旅客 1：好的。

（走向座位 32J⋯⋯）

乘务员：打扰您一下，女士。我能看一下您的登机牌吗？

旅客 2：给您。

乘务员：女士，您的座位号是 42J，而这个座位是 32J。

旅客 2：哦，是啊。对不起。我马上回我的座位去。

乘务员：感谢您的配合。需要我帮您拿行李吗？

旅客 2：不用了，谢谢。没多重。

乘务员：不客气的。

乘务员：久等了，先生。您可以坐到 32 排 J 座去了。

旅客 1：非常感谢。

乘务员：不客气。

Dialogue 4: The same seat number

Situation: During boarding, cabin crew may encounter the situation of passengers' boarding passes with the "same" seat number. This may be caused by the system mistake or the overbooked flight.

Principle: Cabin crew should be sincere and patient. First of all, a cabin attendant should apologize to the passengers, check the information on the boarding passes carefully and ask if one of them will need a transfer. Try to figure out the situation. If the "double-booked" situation is true, the ground staff should be contacted immediately to adjust seats for the passenger. During the waiting period, the crew should take good care of the passenger.

Example

PAX: Miss, come here, please!

FA: Yes, Sir. May I help you?

音频扫一扫

PAX: Why do we have the same seat?

FA: Could you please show me your boarding passes? I'm terribly sorry. I'm afraid there is something wrong with the system. I'll report to our purser immediately. Could you please wait a moment? The ground staff will rearrange your seat immediately.

FA: Sir, the ground staff has rearranged a seat for you. The seat number is 36A, in the front of the cabin. We apologize for this inconvenience.

PAX: Well, it's okay.

情景会话 4：座位重号（重座）或超售

旅客：女士，请过来一下！

乘务员：好的，先生。我能帮助您吗？

旅客：为什么我们是同一个座位？

乘务员：能让我看一下你们的登机牌吗？非常抱歉，恐怕是系统出错了。我马上报告乘务长。您稍等一下好吗？地面工作人员将马上重新安排您的座位。

乘务员：先生，地面人员重新给您安排了座位。座位号是36A，就在客舱前部。我们很抱歉为您带来了不便。

旅客：没事的。

音频扫一扫

Dialogue 5: On-board upgrading

Situation: In some certain flights, economy class is allowed to be upgraded to business class, and business class to first class, so some can be upgraded directly with extra money.

Principle: Flight attendants should be aware of the latest upgrading information previously.

Example

FA: Excuse me, Sir. May I see your boarding pass? Well, your seat number is 41B and here is 18C. Could you please go back to your seat?

PAX: It's very uncomfortable if I sit in the rear of the cabin. Can I just take this one, please? After all, it's unoccupied.

FA: Sir, if you want to sit here, you can upgrade your seat.

PAX: Oh, can I upgrade now?

FA: Sir, please wait for a moment. I will check if there is a vacant seat in business class.

FA: Excuse me, Sir. You are so lucky. There are some vacant seats in business class. But you need to pay extra money for upgrading, would you like me to upgrade for you?

PAX: Yes. How much should I pay?

FA: (Domestic flights) You need to pay half of the full ticket fare of economy class.

/ (International flights) You are in economy class, so you need to pay RMB 3500.

PAX: No problem. How can I pay for it?

FA: You can pay by cash and credit card.

PAX: I prefer credit card. Thank you. You are so nice.

FA: It's my pleasure.

情景会话 5：机上升舱

乘务员：打扰一下，先生，请给我看一下您的登机牌好吗？是这样，您的座位在41排B座，这是18排C座。请您回到您原来的座位上吧？

旅客：坐在后面真的太不舒服了。我能就坐在这儿吗？再说，这儿又没人。

乘务员：先生，如果您想坐在这儿的话，可以办理升舱。

旅客：哦，那我能现在升舱吗？

乘务员：先生，请先稍等一会儿，我去查看一下商务舱是否有空座。

乘务员：先生，您很幸运，商务舱还有空座。但是您需要支付额外的费用，需要我为您办理升舱吗？

旅客：是的，那我需要额外支付多少钱呢？

乘务员：（国内航班）您需要额外支付经济舱全票价的一半。

/（国际航班）您所在的是经济舱舱位，所以您需要额外支付人民币3500元。

旅客：没有问题，请问怎么支付呢？

乘务员：您可以使用现金或信用卡进行支付。

旅客：好的，我用信用卡吧。你真好，谢谢你。

乘务员：很乐意为您服务。

Dialogue 6: Crew seats

Situation: When boarding, a passenger would like to be more comfortable during the flight and changed his seat to the crew seat area.

Principle: Crew seats should be managed by an assigned cabin attendant. Flight attendants should pay attention to the potential needs of the passengers. When the passenger sits in the crew seat area, the flight attendant should be polite and let the passenger know. If possible, adjust the seat appropriately for the passenger. But be careful not to adjust to the area of upgrade seats in case of causing dissatisfaction from other passengers.

Example

FA: Excuse me, Sir. May I see your boarding pass?

PAX: Sure.

FA: Okay, your seat number is 54D, an aisle seat.

PAX: I know. But, may I sit here? Nobody's here.

FA: I'm afraid you couldn't. This is a crew seat, as you can see the "Crew Only" pattern. May I kindly ask you to return to your original seat?

PAX: Fine.

FA: Thank you for your cooperation.

情景会话 6：机组座位

乘务员：打扰一下，先生，可以看一下您的登机牌吗？

旅客：可以啊。

乘务员：嗯，您的座位号是54排D座，一个靠过道的座位。

旅客：我知道。但是，这里没人，我能坐在这里吗？

乘务员：抱歉不可以哦，这是机组座位，您看座位上有"机组座位"的字样，请您回到您原来的座位好吗？

旅客：好吧。

乘务员：感谢您的合作。

Dialogue 7: "I'm afraid you can't change seats at will"

Situation: When boarding, a passenger would like to change his seat and be more comfortable during the flight. Passengers can't change their seats at will.

音频扫一扫

音频扫一扫

Principle: Flight attendants should be polite and let the passenger understand the situation.

Example

PS: (Announcement) Ladies and gentlemen, please take your assigned seat and do not change seats at will.

PAX: May I take this seat? Nobody's here.

FA: Hi, Sir. I'm afraid you can't change seats on the plane at will.

PAX: There are so many vacant seats. Why?

FA: According to the requirements , each passenger's assigned seat on the aircraft needs to be matched with the corresponding passenger's personal information. In addition, changing seats at will will also affect the weight balance of the aircraft and cause potential safety problems.

PAX: Fine.

FA: Thank you for your understanding and support.

情景会话 7："您不可以随意换座"

乘务长：（广播）女士们先生们，请您按照登机牌上的座位号就座，不要随意更换座位。

旅客：这里没人，我能坐在这里吗？

乘务员：先生您好，飞机上是不可以随意更换座位的。

旅客：那么多的空余座位，为什么不让我坐？

乘务员：飞机上的每个座位都需要与旅客个人信息相匹配。另外，随意换座位也会影响飞机的配载平衡，造成安全隐患。

旅客：好吧。

乘务员：非常感谢您的理解和支持。

Ⅲ. Popular Words and Phrases

cabin	['kæbɪn]	n. 客舱
in-flight upgrade		机上升舱
assigned seat		指定座位
original seat		原来的座位
seat number		座位号
convenience	[kən'viːnjəns]	n. 方便
lead	[liːd]	v. 带领，领导
assist	[ə'sɪst]	v. 协助，帮助
follow	['fɑləʊ]	v. 跟随
rear	[rɪə(r)]	n. 后部，背面；adj. 后面的；adv. 向后地
window seat		靠窗座位
middle seat		中间座位
aisle seat		靠过道座位
vacant seat		空的座位

in the front (of the cabin)		在（客舱的）前部
in the middle (of the cabin)		在（客舱的）中部
in the back/rear (of the cabin)		在（客舱的）后部
on the right		在右边
on the left		在左边
crew seat		机组座位
available	[ə'veɪləbl]	*adj.* 空的，可用的
vacant	['veɪkənt]	*adj.* 空的，可用的

Ⅳ. Practical Expressions

1. Good morning. This aisle/ way, please.

早上好，请从这边通道往前走。

2. Your seat number is indicated under the overhead compartment.

您的座位号在行李架下方。

/ The seat number is on the edge of the overhead locker. 座位号在行李架的边缘。

/ The seat number is on the edge of the rack. 座位号在行李架的边缘。

/ Seat numbers are indicated on overhead bins. 座位号位于舱顶行李箱上。

3. Your seat number is 32D. Follow me, please.

您的座位是32排D座，请跟我来。

4. Excuse me, Sir. Could you please give way to the passengers behind. Thank you.

先生，麻烦您侧身让后面的旅客过一下，谢谢。

/ Could you please step aside a little bit and let other passengers go through.

请您稍微移步一下，让其他旅客通过。

/ Would you mind to step aside and make room for others to go through. You can arrange your baggage later. Don't worry, let's find a place to put your baggage later.

请您稍微移步一下，让出地方给其他旅客通过。您可以稍后再放行李，别担心，稍后我会帮您一起找地方安放的。

5. Sure. I'll see if there is any vacant seat for you in the first row after boarding.

好的，旅客登机完毕后，我帮您看看第一排有没有空座位。

6. Seat 37J is available. You could go to sit there after take-off.

37排J座没有旅客，起飞后您可以去坐。

/ The seat 45L is available and you can change your seat after like 30 minutes take-off.

45排L座没有旅客，飞机平飞后您可以换到那儿坐，大约在起飞后三十分钟。

7. I'm really sorry about this, would you mind taking a seat first? I will check with the ground staff straight away.

（旅客重座）非常抱歉，请您先在座位上休息一下，我马上让地服人员查询一下。

/ I am sorry. Please stay here for a moment. I will check it with the ground staff and be back soon.

对不起，请您先在这儿休息片刻，我去问一下（我请地服人员查询一下），马上就回来。

8. This seat has been double booked. There could be something wrong with our system.

这个座位重号了，可能是我们的系统出问题了。

9. I'll report to our purser immediately.

我马上报告乘务长。

10. The ground staff will rearrange your seat immediately.

地面工作人员将立即重新为您安排座位。

11. Thank you for waiting. It's our fault. Your seat number is 56F. I'll show you the way.

让您久等了，是我们工作失误。您的座位号是56排F座，我带您过去。

/ Thank you for your waiting. It is our mistake. Your seat number is 33D. I will take you there.

让您久等了，是我们工作失误。您现在的座位号是33排D座，我带您过去。

12. Excuse me, Sir/ Madam, the lady next to you wants to sit together with her child. Would you mind changing your seat with her?

打扰一下，先生/女士，您旁边的女士想和她的孩子坐在一起，请问您愿意和她换座位吗？

13. The girl beside your friend is willing to change the seat with you.

坐在您朋友旁边的那位女孩愿意和您换一下座位。

14. I'm so sorry, I have talked with that passenger, but he still prefers the window seat.

实在抱歉，我已经沟通过了，但那位旅客还是愿意坐靠窗的座位。

15. According to the latest regulations, you can upgrade your class and pay the extra.

根据最新规定，您可以升舱，不过需要您付差价部分的钱 / 升舱费用。

16. I'm afraid we couldn't upgrade for you on board. May I suggest you arrange the procedure in advance at check-in counter next time?

对不起，机上无法办理升舱手续。建议您下次在地面提前办理。

17. Excuse me, Sir, today we have some vacant seats in business class and the price is just 800 RMB for upgrading. Would you like me to upgrade for you?

（经济舱旅客换座到商务舱）打扰一下，先生，今天公务舱有空座，只需800元人民币就可以办理升舱。请问您是否需要升舱呢？

18. Sorry, Sir, if you need a more comfortable place, we have extra-pay seats on board for you to choose. How about Row 36 A, B and C?

（旅客换座到付费座位）抱歉，先生，如果您需要个更舒适的座位，我们机上有额外付费的座位可供您选择。您看36排A座、B座和C座怎么样？

19. The upgrading procedure in an international flight can be done by credit card.

国际航班中的升舱可通过信用卡支付来完成。

20. Excuse me, Sir, since we haven't got so many vacant seats on board today, how about taking turns to have a rest? Thank you for your cooperation!

（旅客占多个座位的情况）先生，您好，由于今天机上没有较多空座位，您看几位轮流使用休息如何？谢谢您的配合！

21. Excuse me, Sir. This is a crew seat. May I ask you kindly to return to your original seat? Thank you for your cooperation.

抱歉，先生，这是机组座位，请您回到原位。谢谢您的配合！

22. In order to keep the aircraft in balance, please return to your original seats. Thank you.

为了使飞机保持配载平衡，请你们回到原来的座位，谢谢。

Ⅴ. Tips

1. How to deal with double-booked seats? 如何处理重座情况？

旅客登机过程中，遇有"旅客重座"情况，在旅客等待期间，乘务组应尽量安排旅客在空座位上休息等候。乘务员处理时，沟通话术如下：

(1) Could you please show me your boarding pass?

能让我看一下你们的登机牌吗？

(2) I'm terribly sorry. / I'm really sorry about this.

非常抱歉。

(3) Would you mind taking a seat first? Please don't worry. I will check with the ground staff straight away.

请您在座位上休息一下，请不要担心，我马上让地服人员查询一下。

(4) I'm afraid there must be something wrong with the system.

可能是我们系统出错了。

(5) I'll report to our purser immediately. Could you please wait a moment?

我马上报告乘务长。您稍等一下好吗？

(6) The ground staff will rearrange your seat immediately.

地面工作人员将马上重新安排您的座位。

(7) The ground staff has rearranged a seat for you.

地面人员重新给您安排了座位。

(8) We apologize for this inconvenience.

我们很抱歉为您带来了不便。

2. On-board upgrading 机上付费升舱

旅客登机后，有时可能想要升舱。如需升舱，乘务员"机上付费升舱"沟通话术如下：

(1) Excuse me, Sir/ Madam. May I see your boarding pass? Could you please go back to your seat? If you would like to seat here, you may upgrade you seat.

打扰一下，先生/女士，请给我看一下您的登机牌好吗？请您回到原来的座位上好吗？如果您想坐在这里，可以办理升舱哦。

(2) I will check if there is vacant seat in business class... There are some vacant seats in business class. But you need to pay extra money for upgrading, would you like me to upgrade for you?

我去查一下看商务舱是否有空座……商务舱还有空座。但是您需要支付额外的费用，需要我为您办理升舱吗？

(3) You are in economy class. You need to pay half of the full ticket fare of economy class. Therefore, you need to pay extra RMB 3500.

您所在的是经济舱舱位，您需要额外支付经济舱全票价的一半。所以，您需要额外支付人民币3500元。

(4) According to the latest regulations, you may upgrade your class and pay the extra. You can pay by cash and credit card.

根据最新规定，您可以升舱，不过需要您付差价部分的钱/升舱费用。您可以使用现金或信用卡进行支付。

(5) Sorry, I' afraid we couldn't upgrade for you on board. May I suggest you arrange the procedure in advance at check-in counter next time?

对不起，机上无法办理升舱手续。建议您下次在地面提前办理。

VI. Supplementary Reading

Aircraft Weight and Balance 飞机载重与平衡

Airplane Empty Weight and Center of Gravity (CG) change when adding, removing or relocating seats and re-calculating empty weight values is critical to ensure flight safety. In the airline industry, load balancing is used to evenly distribute the weight of passengers, cargo, and fuel throughout an aircraft, so as to keep the aircraft's center of gravity close to its center of pressure to avoid losing pitch control. As a captain, he or she is responsible for the safe loading of the airplane and must ensure that it is not overloaded. The performance of an airplane is influenced by its weight and overloading, it will cause serious problems. The take-off run necessary to become airborne will be longer. In some cases, the required take-off run may be greater than the available runway. The angle of climb and the rate of climb will be reduced. Maximum ceiling will be lowered and range shortened. Landing speed will be higher and the landing roll longer. In addition, the additional weight may cause structural stresses during manoeuvres and turbulence that could lead to damage.

The total gross weight authorized for any particular type of airplane must therefore never be exceeded. A captain must be capable of estimating the proper ratio of fuel, oil and payload permissible for a flight of any given duration. The weight limitations of some general aviation airplanes do not allow for all seats to be filled, for the baggage compartment to be filled to capacity and for a full load of fuel as well. It is necessary, in this case, to choose between passengers, baggage and full fuel tanks. The distribution of weight is also of vital importance since the position of the center of gravity affects the stability of the airplane.

VII. Exercises

1. List at least three cases in terms of changing seats when boarding.

(1)

(2)

(3)

2. Translate the following words and phrases into Chinese or English.

lead	靠窗座位
assist	中间座位
follow	靠过道座位
in-flight upgrade	空座位
assigned seat	在（客舱的）前部
convenience	在（客舱的）后部
in the middle of ...	在右边
客舱	在左边
座位号	

3. Translate the following sentences into English.

(1) 座位号在行李架下方。

(2) 您的座位是45排A座，请跟我来。

(3) 先生，麻烦您侧身以便让其他旅客通过，谢谢。

(4) 旅客登机完毕后，我帮您看看第一排有没有空座位。

(5) 36J座位没有旅客，飞机平飞后您可以去坐，在起飞后三十分钟左右。

(6) 打扰一下，您旁边的旅客想和她的孩子坐在一起，请问您方便跟她换座位吗？

(7) 根据最新规定，您可以升舱，只需要您付差价部分的钱即可。

(8) 抱歉，机上无法办理升舱手续。建议您下次在地面提前办理。

(9) 抱歉，女士，这是机组座位，请您回到原位。谢谢您的配合！

(10) 为了使飞机保持配载平衡，请您回到原来的座位，谢谢您的配合。

(11) 抱歉，让您久等了，是我们工作失误。您现在的座位号是56排F座，我带您过去。

(12) 您好，您坐的是应急出口的位置，这是"出口座位须知卡"，请您仔细阅读，红色手柄不要触碰，在紧急情况下，请您协助我们的工作。谢谢配合。

4. Group work: choose one topic to start a conversation. (TIME LIMIT: 10 minutes)

(1) Emergency exit instruction.

(2) Seat assistance for a couple (foreigner).

(3) Seat assistance for the pregnant.

(4) In-flight upgrade.

Project 3

Ground Service before Take-off
起飞前地面服务

Task 6　On-board Amusements 机上娱乐

Ⅰ. Warm-up Questions

1. How do you help a passenger when he/she has difficulty in reclining his/her seat?

2. What will you say if a passenger asks for a piece of newspaper?

3. Why is it so significant to let the elderly know where the "call button" area is?

4. What would you like to say if you see a passenger looking around and asking for airline membership information?

Ⅱ. Dialogues

Dialogue 1: Newspapers and Magazines (1)

Situation: Normally, it is a routine to provide passengers with several kinds of newspapers and magazines after boarding.

Principle: Flight attendants should introduce patiently.

Example

FA: Excuse me, Miss. Would you like to read some magazines or newspapers? The magazines are in the seat pocket in front of you. And for newspapers, we have *Global Times* and *China Daily* today. Which one would you like?

PAX: Well, I'd like a copy of *Global Times*, please.

FA: One moment, please. I will be back with your newspaper.

PAX: Thank you.

FA: Here is your *Global Times*, Madam. Enjoy your flight!

情景会话1：报纸杂志（1）

乘务员：女士，您好。请问您想看杂志和报纸吗？杂志在您前面的座椅口袋里。我们今天准备的报纸有《环球时报》和《中国日报》。请问您喜欢哪种呢？

旅客：不错，请给我一份《环球时报》。

乘务员：请稍等一下。我马上为您拿来。

旅客：谢谢。

音频扫一扫

乘务员：女士，这是您的《环球时报》。祝您旅程愉快！

Dialogue 2: Newspapers and Magazines (2)

音频扫一扫

Situation: Normally, it is a routine to provide passengers with several kinds of newspapers and magazines after boarding.

Principle: Flight attendants should introduce patiently.

Example

FA: Excuse me, Sir. Did you press the call button?

PAX: Yes, I did.

FA: What can I do for you?

PAX: Have you got something to read?

FA: Yes, we have in-flight magazines and some newspapers. Which one would you like?

PAX: That's terrific. What kind of newspaper do you have?

FA: We have some international newspapers such as *The New York Times*, *Washington Post* and *The Economist*, some national newspapers such as *People's Daily*, *China Daily* and *Economy Daily*, and some local newspapers. Which would you like?

PAX: A copy of *People's Daily*, please.

FA: OK. Here you are.

情景会话2：报纸杂志（2）

乘务员：您好，先生，请问您刚才按了呼唤铃吗？

旅客：嗯，是的。

乘务员：我能为您做些什么呢？

旅客：你们有什么读物吗？

乘务员：有的，我们航班中配备了杂志和一些报纸。您想看哪种呢？

旅客：很好，报纸都有哪些？

乘务员：国际性的报纸有《纽约时报》《华盛顿邮报》和《经济学人》，国内报纸有《人民日报》《中国日报》和《经济日报》，此外还有一些地方报纸。您想看哪种？

旅客：请给我来份《人民日报》吧。

乘务员：好的，给您。

Dialogue 3: PSU Introduction

音频扫一扫

Situation: After taking their seats, lots of passengers would like to know everything nearby, especially the entertainment system on board. And normally, they would love to seek assistance from flight attendants.

Principle: Flight attendants should explain the functions and operation of PSU (Passenger Service Unit) , observe and answer questions patiently.

Example

PAX: Excuse me. This is my first time to take a flight. I'm so nervous.

FA: Take it easy, Madam.

PAX: Could you show me how to use all these buttons above my head?

FA: Yes, of course. This device is called PSU, which is short for Passenger Service Unit. It includes the call button, reading light and airflow system.

PAX: Okay... How can I use it?

FA: As you can see, we have the call button and the cancel call button on it. If you need anything, just press the call button, or press the cancel call button to cancel it.

PAX: Well...

FA: The reading light button turns on your overhead light. This one is the airflow system. By adjusting the knob, fresh air will flow in or be cut off. We also have "no-smoking" sign.

PAX: Oh, I see.

FA: By the way, this one is the seat-reclining button. If you press it, your seatback will recline as you like, so you can relax and be comfortable. But you should keep it in upright position when we take off, descend and meet turbulence. Now you can have a try.

PAX: I've got it, thank you.

FA: My pleasure.

情景会话3：介绍旅客服务组件

旅客：你好，这是我第一次乘机，我好紧张啊。

乘务员：女士，您别紧张。

旅客：你能帮我看看头顶上方的那些按钮怎么用吗？

乘务员：当然可以。这个装置叫旅客服务组件，它包括呼唤铃、阅读灯和通风系统。

旅客：嗯……怎么用呢？

乘务员：正如您所见，这上面有呼唤铃和解除呼唤铃。如果您需要什么，只需要按呼唤铃就可以了，如果不需要就按解除呼唤铃。

旅客：这样啊……

乘务员：阅读灯按钮打开的是您头顶上方的灯。这个是通风系统，可以通过调这个旋钮让新鲜空气流入或切断。这上面还有"请勿吸烟"标志。

旅客：哦，我明白了。

乘务员：顺便跟您介绍一下，这是座椅调节按钮。按住它，可以调节座椅靠背，放松休息。但是在起飞、下降以及遇有颠簸时，需要调直座椅靠背哦。现在您可以尝试一下。

旅客：我知道啦，谢谢你。

乘务员：不客气。

音频扫一扫

Dialogue 4: In-flight Wi-Fi

Situation: After taking the seats, lots of passengers would like to know everything nearby, for example, the entertainment system on board. And in-flight Wi-Fi may also be a popular choice. As is often the case, they would love to know information involved from flight attendants.

Principle: Flight attendants should be willing to observe and answer questions patiently.

Example

PAX: When can we connect with the Wi-Fi?

FA: The Wi-Fi system will be automatically switched on when the plane reaches 10,000 feet.

PAX: Why can't I access internet, but the passenger beside me does?

FA: Maybe you can check again a few moments later.

PAX: Why can't I watch videos?

FA: I am sorry, Madam, because all those video resources are blocked.

PAX: Can we use Facebook here?

FA: Maybe not, because we are using Chinese satellites for internet.

情景会话4：机上无线网络

旅客：我们什么时候可以连无线网络？

乘务员：当飞机到达10,000英尺高度，机上无线网络系统会自动开启。

旅客：为什么我连不上无线网络，但我旁边的旅客可以？

乘务员：或许您可以一会儿再试试。

旅客：为什么我不能看视频呢？

乘务员：抱歉，女士，因为所有视频资源都被限制了。

旅客：我能使用脸书吗？

乘务员：可能不行，因为我们使用的是中国的卫星网络。

Dialogue 5: Membership and Frequent Flyer Program (1)

音频扫一扫

Situation: With Frequent Flyer Program, passengers can benefit a lot. If our flight attendants could be more prepared, passengers on board would be more satisfied.

Principle: Flight attendants should be considerate and answer questions professionally.

Example

FA: Excuse me, have you ever heard of our membership reward program or Frequent Flyer Program?

PAX: No, what's that?/ A little. I've heard of it.

FA: You can apply our airline membership for free. I can introduce the basic information for you if you like.

PAX: Sure, I would love to.

FA: Our Frequent Flyer Program is a global loyalty and reward program.

PAX: Well, what benefits can I get?

FA: You can easily earn points when you fly with our partner airlines, stay at hotels, shop using your credit cards, rent cars and many other ways to exchange tickets and other gifts, upgrade by using the points.

PAX: Sounds nice. So will I get a free ticket?

FA: Yes, you have the chance to get free tickets. The more you fly with us, the more miles you collect, the higher chance you could get free tickets.

PAX: Okay, why not? Could you please get me a form?

FA: Sure, here is the application form and pen. You need to fill in these parts of the form.

PAX: Got it.

FA: You may check your redeem information and other information on our official website. If you have any questions, please contact us at our hotline. We are glad to help you at any time.

PAX: Thank you.

FA: You are welcome. We warmly welcome you to fly with our airline and get more benefits.

情景会话5：会员与常旅客计划（1）

乘务员：您好，请问您听说过我们的会员奖励计划或是常旅客计划吗？

旅客：没有呢，是什么呢？／一点点，我听别人说过。

乘务员：您可以免费申请成为我们公司的会员。如果您需要的话，我可以给您介绍一下基本内容。

旅客：好啊，非常乐意。

乘务员：我们的常旅客计划是一项全球性常旅客奖励计划。

旅客：那我能享受到什么好处呢？

乘务员：您可以通过乘坐我们合作航空公司的飞机、入住酒店、刷卡购物、租赁汽车等轻松获取积分来兑换机票和其他礼品，或是使用积分升舱。

旅客：听起来不错，那我可以兑换免费机票吗？

乘务员：可以的，您将有机会获得免费机票。您飞行越多，积累的里程越多，得到免票的机会就越大。

旅客：好的，为什么不呢，您能给我一张表格吗？

乘务员：好的，这是申请表和笔。您需要填写这张表格的这些部分。

旅客：好的。

乘务员：您可以在我们的官方网站上查询您的积分兑换信息和其他信息。如果您有任何问题，请拨打我们的服务热线，我们很乐意随时帮您。

旅客：谢谢。

乘务员：您客气了。非常欢迎您乘坐我们的航班，享受更多的优惠。

Dialogue 6: Membership and Frequent Flyer Program (2)

音频扫一扫

Situation: It is often the case that passengers would like to know more about Frequent Flyer Program from flight attendants. With this membership program, they can benefit a lot.

Principle: Flight attendants should be prepared and answer questions professionally.

Example

PAX: Excuse me, Miss. I'm quite interested in your membership program. Could you introduce it for me?

FA: Sure. You can apply our membership for free. This membership program is a global frequent flyer program for several member airline companies, such as XX Airlines etc.

PAX: Well, what benefits can I get?

FA: If you join it, you can earn extra award points when you fly with our member airlines or partners, stay at hotels, shop by credit card, rent cars and so on. And you have the opportunity to get free tickets with the collected points.

PAX: It sounds great. So how can I join it?

FA: You can join us by calling the hotline, or registering on our official website, airline application, or our WeChat official account.

FA: You may check your redeem information and other information on our official website.

PAX: All right.

FA: We warmly welcome you to fly with us again. Enjoy your flight!

情景会话 6：会员与常旅客计划（2）

旅客：您好，女士。我对你们的会员计划非常感兴趣，您能给我介绍一下吗？

乘务员：当然，您可以免费申请加入我们的会员。该会员计划是XX航空等几个成员航空公司共享的一项全球性常旅客奖励计划。

旅客：嗯，我能享受到什么优惠呢？

乘务员：加入常旅客计划，您可以通过乘坐我们的会员航空公司或合作航空公司的航班、入住酒店、刷卡购物、租赁汽车等消费获取额外的奖励积分，您还有机会用积分换机票。

旅客：听起来不错。那我怎么加入呢？

乘务员：您可以通过致电服务热线、登录公司官网注册、下载我们航空公司的应用程序或关注我们公司官方微信公众号注册入会。

乘务员：您可以在公司官网上查询您的积分兑换信息和其他信息。

旅客：好的。

乘务员：非常欢迎您下次再乘坐我们的航班。祝您旅途愉快！

Ⅲ. Popular Words and Phrases

newspaper	['njuːzpeipə; 'nuzpepə]	n. 报纸
magazine	[mægə'ziːn; 'mægəzin]	n. 杂志
China Daily		《中国日报》
Global Times		《环球时报》
call button		呼唤铃
seat pocket		座椅背后口袋
seat back		座椅靠背
remove	[rɪ'muːv]	v. 移动
helpful	['helpful; －f(ə)l]	adj. 有帮助的
improve	[ɪm'pruːv]	v. 提高；改善
inconvenience	[ɪnkən'viːnɪəns]	n. 不方便
interrupt	[ɪntə'rʌpt]	v. 打扰；打断
introduce	[ɪntrə'djuːs]	v. 介绍
USB socket	['sɒkɪt]	USB 插座
plug	[plʌg]	n. 电源插头
frequent	['frikwənt]	adj. 频繁的，经常的
alliance	[ə'laɪəns]	n. 同盟，联盟，联合
airline partner		合作航空公司
earn points		累积积分
application form		申请表
redeem information		积分兑换信息
service hotline		服务热线
exchange points		兑换积分
network	['netwɜːk]	n. 网络
nationality	[ˌnæʃə'næləti]	n. 国籍
citizen	['sɪtɪzn]	n. 公民
given name		（与姓相对而言的）名
surname	['sɜːneɪm]	n. 姓
family name		姓
priority	[praɪ'ɔrəti]	n. 优先权
rewarding	[rɪ'wɔːdɪŋ']	adj.（作为）报答的
contact information		联系信息
address	[ə'dres]	n. 住址，地址
signature	['sɪgnətʃə]	n. 署名，签名
according to		根据

access to		有权使用
baggage handling		行李处理
benefit	['benɪfɪt]	n. 收益，福利
counter	['kauntə]	n. 柜台
customer service center		客户服务中心
dial	[dail]	v. 拨打电话
detailed information		详细信息
global network		全球网络
hotline	['hɔtlain]	n. 热线电话
log in	[lɒg ɪn]	登录
membership terms		会员条款
official website		官网
relaxing	[rɪ'læksɪŋ]	adj. 舒缓的
purchase	['pɜːtʃəs]	v. 购买
redeem mileage		兑换里程
submit	[səb'mɪt]	v. 提交；呈递
worldwide	[wɔːld'waɪd]	adj. 全球范围的
Temporary Card		临时会员卡
Silver Membership Card		银卡会员
Gold Membership Card		金卡会员
Platinum Membership Card		白金卡会员

IV. Practical Expressions

1. This one is the call button and please press it if you need assistance.

这是呼唤铃，如果需要我们帮忙，请按它。

2. If you need any help, please press this call button. If you want to read, you can turn on the reading light. If you'd like to have a rest, you can press this button on your armrest and lean back at the same time. Here is the air vent. You can turn the knob here in whichever direction you like, or you can turn it off by turning it tightly to the right.

如果您需要任何帮助，请按呼唤铃；如果您想阅读，请打开阅读灯；如果您需要休息，可以按住座椅扶手上的按钮，同时身体向后仰，放倒座椅靠背。这是通风孔，您可以把它向任意方向调节，或向右旋紧关掉。

3. Excuse me, Sir. We have Chinese and English newspaper. Which one would you prefer?

您好，先生，我们有中英文报纸，请问您喜欢哪种？

4. The magazines are in the seat pocket in front of you. And for newspapers, we have *Global Times* and *China Daily* today.

杂志在您前面的座椅口袋里。我们今天准备的报纸有《环球时报》和《中国日报》。

5. This is our inflight entertainment device. But it can only be used during the cruising period. For the control handle, please put it back after using.

这是我们机上娱乐设备。但只能在巡航阶段使用。遥控器请您用完后放回。

/ Madam, sorry to disturb you, this is the entertainment system guide. If you have any question, please feel free to ask me. I will be glad to help you at any time.

/ 打扰您了，女士，这是娱乐系统指南。如有疑问，请随时找我，我将非常高兴随时为您提供帮助。

6. Excuse me, Sir. Would you like an application form for Frequent Flyer Program membership? To apply, please fill in the form and give it together with your boarding pass to a cabin attendant.

您好，先生，请问您需要我们公司的常旅客计划会员入会申请表吗？填写完表格后和登机牌一起交给乘务员就可以办理申请了。

7. Excuse me, have you ever heard of our Frequent Flyer Reward Program?

您好，请问您听说过我们的常旅客奖励计划吗？

8. You can apply our Frequent Flyer Reward Program membership for free. I can introduce some information for you if you would like.

您可以免费申请加入我们公司的常旅客奖励计划。如果您需要的话，我可以给您介绍一下。

9. Please make sure your address and telephone number is accurate.

请确认您的地址和电话号码准确无误。

10. Please collect your miles at the check-in counter.

请您在办理登机牌的柜台登记积累您的里程。

11. You may easily earn points when you fly with our partner airlines, stay at hotels, shop using your credit cards, rent cars and many other ways.

您可以通过乘坐我们合作航空公司的航班、入住酒店、刷卡购物、租赁汽车等轻松获取积分。

You can earn extra award points if you fly with our member airlines, stay at hotels, shop by credit card or rent cars.

您可以通过乘坐我们会员航空公司的航班、入住酒店、刷卡购物或租赁汽车消费获取额外的奖励积分。

12. You can exchange tickets and gifts, upgrade by using the award points.

这些奖励积分可以用于兑换机票和礼品，或是免费升舱。

13. You have the chance to get free tickets. The more you fly with us, the more miles you collect, the higher chance you get free tickets.

您有机会得到免费机票。您飞行越多，累积的里程数越多，得到免费机票的机会就越大。

14. If you have any question, please contact us on our hotline. We are glad to help you at any time.

如果您有任何问题，欢迎拨打我们的服务热线，我们很乐意随时帮您。

Ⅴ. Tips

The regular Procedure of Using In-flight WiFi 使用机上无线网络的常规步骤

Wi-Fi（wireless fidelity）无线网络，无线上网，又称作"行动热点"，Wi-Fi 与蓝牙技术一样，同属于短距离无线技术，是一种网络传输标准。在日常生活中，它早已得到普遍应用，并给人们带来极大的方便。

Example (How to connect with the Wi-Fi in the dreamliner 787-9?)

Step 1: Switch on your WLAN, and connect with the Wi-Fi "XX Airlines".

Step 2: After Step 1, it will pop out a portal page, or you can open a browser and input the website address "wifi.XXairlines.com".

Step 3: Click "WiFi", and then input your seat number and the last four numbers of your ID number.

Now you can surf the internet, and chat with your families and friends above in the air.

VI. Supplementary Reading

1. The World's Three Largest Global Airline Alliances — Star Alliance, SkyTeam and Oneworld

全球三大国际航空联盟——星空联盟、天合联盟和寰宇一家

	StarAlliance （星空联盟）	SkyTeam （天合联盟）	OneWorld （寰宇一家）
Number of Members	28	19	13
Year Established	1997	2000	1999
Annual Passenger Number	756 Million	630 Million	528 Million
Fleet	5046	3054	3553
Flights Per Day	18800	14500	13100
Staff Number	443703	392155	493650
Destinations (Countries)	193	176	158

（1）**Star Alliance** 星空联盟

Launch date: May 14, 1997.

Headquarter: Frankfurt am Main, Germany.

Alliance slogan: The Way the Earth Connects. 地球联结的方式。

Star Alliance is one of the world's largest global airline alliances. Founded on 14 May, 1997, its current CEO is Jeffrey Goh and its headquarters is located in Frankfurt am Main, Germany. Its slogan is "The Way the Earth Connects". Today, Star Alliance has 28 member airlines, each with its own distinctive culture and style of service. Alliance members come together to offer smooth connections across a vast global network. The member airlines include many of the world's top aviation companies as well as smaller regional airlines. Together, they offer easy connections to almost any destination in the world. Each airline maintains its own individual style and cultural identity, bringing the richness of diversity and multiculturalism to the alliance. At the same time each airline shares a common dedication to the highest standards of safety and customer service.

（2）**SkyTeam** 天合联盟

Launch date: June 22, 2000.

Headquarter: Amsterdam Airport Schiphol Haarlemmermeer, Netherlands.

Alliance slogan: Caring more about you 我们更关注您

SkyTeam is an airline alliance. Founded in June 2000, SkyTeam was the last of the three major airline alliances to be formed, the first two being Star Alliance and Oneworld. As of March 2014,

SkyTeam consists of 19 carriers from five continents and operates with the slogan "Caring more about you". It also operates a cargo alliance named SkyTeam Cargo, which partners ten carriers, all of them SkyTeam members. Its centralized management team, SkyTeam Central, is based at the World Trade Center Schiphol Airport on the grounds of Amsterdam Airport Schiphol in Haarlemmermeer, Netherlands. In 2004, the alliance had its biggest expansion when Continental Airlines, Northwest Airlines and KLM simultaneously joined as full members. The SkyTeam network operates nearly 17,343 daily flights to 1,074 destinations in 177 countries. Whether for business or leisure, the network of the member airlines makes global travel seamless.

（3）**Oneworld** 寰宇一家

Launch date: February 1, 1999.

Headquarter: New York City, New York, U.S.

Alliance slogan: An alliance of the world's leading airlines working as one. 世界顶尖航空公司联盟"寰宇一家"。

Oneworld is an airline alliance founded on February 1, 1999. The alliance's stated objective is to be the first-choice airline alliance for the world's frequent international travelers. Its central alliance office is currently based in New York City in the United States. As of August 2016, Oneworld is the third largest global alliance in terms of passenger numbers with more than 557.4 million passengers carried, behind Star Alliance (689.98 M) and SkyTeam (665.4 M).

2. Frequent Flyer Program 常旅客计划

A frequent flyer program (FFP) is a loyalty program offered by an airline. Many airlines have frequent flyer programs designed to encourage airline customers enrolled in the program to accumulate points (also called miles, kilometers or segments) which may then be redeemed for air travel or other rewards. Points earned under FFPs may be based on the class of fare, distance flown on that airline or its partners, or the amount paid. There are other ways to earn points. For example, in recent years, more points have been earned by using co-branded credit and debit cards than by air travel. Another way to earn points is spending money at associated retail outlets, car hire companies, hotels or other associated businesses.

Points can be redeemed for air travel, other goods or services, or for increased benefits, such as travel class upgrades, airport lounge access, fast track access or priority bookings. Frequent flyer programs can be seen as a certain type of virtual currency, one with unidirectional flow of money to purchase points, but no exchange back into money. Most larger airlines around the world have frequent flyer programs each having a program name, policies and restrictions regarding joining, accumulating and redeeming points. The primary method of obtaining points in a frequent flyer program until recent years was to fly with the associated airline.

【背景阅读】

常旅客计划通常是指航空公司、酒店等行业向经常使用其产品的客户推出的以里程累积或积分累计奖励里程为主的促销手段，是吸引公务商务旅客、提高公司竞争力的一种市场手段，是一项客户忠诚计划。

早在20世纪80年代初，航空公司就开始引入常旅客计划。那时作为一种客户忠诚度计划，的确取得了一定的效果。随后世界上几乎所有的航空公司都有了自己的常旅客计划。航空公司的常旅客计划被认为是民航史上最成功的市场创新活动。1994年，中国国际航空公司在国内最早推出了常旅客计划和相应的知音卡。中国东方航空公司1998年7月正式推出了常旅客计划。随后，厦航、南航、北航等也相继推出了自己的常旅客计划。

（1）**Air China and PhoenixMiles** 国航凤凰知音

Founded: July 1, 1988.

Headquarter: Shunyi District, Beijing, China.

Air China Limited is China's only national flag carrier, a member carrier of the world's largest airline network "Star Alliance" and one of the major airlines of China. Air China's flight operations are based at Beijing Capital International Airport. It was also the airline partner of the Olympics Beijing 2008. It is a Chinese carrier with the highest brand value in China's airline industry. It is in a leading position in China in terms of passenger transportation, cargo transportation and related services. Air China is the only designated carrier that also offers special flights for Chinese leaders on their official visit to other countries and foreign leaders traveling within China, which is another piece of convincing evidence of the exclusive status as China's only national flag carrier. Air China has a number of offshoots in different regions of China and also has some regional operational bases.

PhoenixMiles（凤凰知音）is a frequent flyer program conceived by Air China family carriers including Air China, Shenzhen Airlines, Shandong Airlines, Air Macao, Dalian Airlines, Inner Mongolia Airlines, Tibet Airlines and Beijing Airlines. PhoenixMiles allows passengers to earn mileage from numerous partners that can be redeemed for award flights, award upgrades and products from their online store. Passengers can earn mileage by flying with Air China family carriers and any of their airline partners, or by purchasing services from their non-airline partners.

（2）China Eastern Airlines and Eastern Miles 东航东方万里行 Founded: June 25, 1988. Headquarter: Shanghai, China.	

China Eastern Airlines Corporation Limited is an airline headquartered in the China Eastern Airlines Building, on the grounds of Shanghai Hongqiao International Airport in Changning District, Shanghai, China. It is a major Chinese airline operating international, domestic and regional routes. Its main hubs are at Shanghai Pudong International Airport and Shanghai Hongqiao International Airport, with secondary hubs at Beijing Capital International Airport, Kunming Changshui International Airport and Xi'an Xianyang International Airport.

China Eastern Airlines is China's second-largest carrier by passenger numbers. China Eastern and its subsidiary Shanghai Airlines became the 14th member of SkyTeam on 21 June, 2011. The parent company of China Eastern Airlines Corporation Limited is the China Eastern Airlines Group, a state-owned enterprise that was supervised by State-owned Assets Supervision and Administration Commission of the State Council.

China Eastern Airlines's frequent flyer program is called Eastern Miles（东方万里行）. Shanghai Airlines and China United Airlines, China Eastern's subsidiary, are also parts of the program. Enrollment is free of charge. Eastern Miles members can earn miles on flights as well as through consumption with China Eastern's credit card. When enough miles are collected, members can be upgraded to Elite. Elite membership of Eastern Miles can be divided into three tiers: Platinum Card membership, Gold Card membership and Silver Card membership. Elite membership can enjoy extra privileged services.

（3）China Southern Airlines and Sky Pearl Club 南航明珠俱乐部 Founded: July 1, 1988. Headquarter: Baiyun District, Guangzhou, Guangdong Province, China.	

China Southern Airlines Company Limited is an airline headquartered in Baiyun District, Guangzhou, Guangdong Province, China. Established on 1 July, 1988 following the restructuring of the Civil Aviation Administration of China that acquired and merged a number of domestic airlines, the airline became one of China's "Big Three" airlines (alongside Air China and China Eastern Airlines). With its main hubs at Guangzhou Baiyun International Airport and Beijing Capital International

Airport, the airline operates more than 2,000 flights to 208 destinations daily . The logo of the airline consists of a kapok flower on a blue tail fin.

China Southern Airlines's frequent flyer program is called Sky Pearl Club（明珠俱乐部）. Membership of Sky Pearl Club is divided into three tiers: Sky Pearl Gold Card, Sky Pearl Silver Card and Sky Pearl Member Card. The unit of mileage accumulation is based on kilometers. There are three membership levels in the Sky Pearl Club: gold card, silver card and base card. One qualification year is 12-month duration from January 1 and December 31, which is used to determine Elite levels.

（4）Hainan Airlines and Fortune Wings Club
海航金鹏俱乐部
Founded: May 2, 1993.
Headquarter: Haikou, Hainan, China.

Hainan Airlines Co., Ltd. (HNA, hereafter referred to as "Hainan Airlines") was founded and began operations on May 2, 1993 in Hainan Province, the largest special economy zone in China. As one of the fastest developing airlines in China, Hainan Airlines is committed to providing passengers with holistic, seamless and high-quality service. It is the largest civilian-run air transport company in China. It operates scheduled domestic and international services on 500 routes from Hainan and nine locations on the mainland, as well as charter services. Its main base is Haikou Meilan International Airport, with a hub at Beijing Capital International Airport and several focus cities.

HNA Group is a conglomerate developed against the backdrop of China's Reform and Opening Up. Maiden flight on May 2, 1993 signified the beginning of its undertakings.

According to *China Daily* (December 9, 2021), China's fourth-largest carrier Hainan Airlines announced that it has transferred its core aviation business to Liaoning Fangda Group Industrial Co., Ltd, its strategic investor, as the carrier's parent company HNA Group is in the process of going through bankruptcy and restructuring proceedings. The airline said since a court's final ruling on Oct 31, its reorganization process has been going on smoothly, and substantial progress has been made in risk mitigation. A joint working group will perform the duties of guidance, coordination and supervision, and continue to implement the group's bankruptcy and restructuring plans and other related risk management work. Liaoning Fangda Group has been a Chinese conglomerate involved in business sectors such as carbon, steel and pharmaceuticals. Earlier, Liaoning Fangda won the bid to become a strategic investor of Hainan Airlines over Shanghai Juneyao Group Co., Ltd, parent of Juneyao Airlines, and Fosun International, a major Chinese industry player in the tourism sector.

Hainan Airlines's frequent-flyer program is called Fortune Wings Club（金鹏俱乐部）. The Fortune Wings Club is the global frequent flyer program for 9 member airline companies, such as Hainan Airlines, Grand China Air, Tianjin Airlines, Hong Kong Airlines, Lucky Air, Capital Airlines, Fuzhou Airlines, Suparna Airlines and Guangxi Beibu Gulf Airlines. Members can earn miles on flights as well as through consumption with Hainan Airlines' credit card. When enough miles are collected, members can be upgraded to Elite members which are divided into two tiers: Fortune Wings Gold membership and Silver Card membership. Elite membership get extra services.

Ⅶ. Exercises

1. Please list three styles of in-flight entertainment for passengers right after boarding.
(1)

(2)

(3)

2. Translate the following words and phrases into Chinese or English.

呼唤铃	frequent
报纸	alliance
杂志	service hotline
累积积分	contact information
热线电话	address
官网	access to
银卡会员	benefit
金卡会员	counter
白金卡会员	membership terms
客户服务中心	submit

3. Translate the following sentences into English.

(1) 您好，女士，我们有中文报纸和英文报纸，请问您喜欢哪种？

(2) 杂志在您前面的座椅口袋里。报纸我们今天准备的有《环球时报》和《中国日报》。

(3) 这是我们的机上娱乐设备。但只能在巡航阶段使用。请您用完后放回前排座椅口袋里。

(4) 您好，请问您听说过我们的常旅客奖励计划吗？

(5) 您可以免费申请加入我们公司的常旅客奖励计划。如果您愿意，我可以为您介绍一下。

4. Group work: choose one topic to start a conversation. (TIME LIMIT: 10 minutes)

(1) Provide newspapers and magazines on board.

(2) Introduce in-flight Wi-Fi.

(3) Introduce Frequent Flyer Program.

Task 7　CIP/ VIP/First-Class and Business-Class Service 重要商务旅客/要客/头等舱和商务舱服务

Ⅰ. Warm-up Questions

1. How to serve distinguished guests on board?

2. What are the principles of working as a flight attendant in the first and business class?

3. In which aspect do you need to pay special attention to when you're providing service for VIPs?

Ⅱ. Dialogues

Dialogue 1: Would you like to hang up your clothes?

Situation: After boarding, cabin attendants should pay attention to passengers' demands, especially commercially and politically important passengers as well as the first class and business class passengers. Those passengers should be provided individual service. It is the responsibility of the first and business class attendants to hang up clothes for the passengers. And throughout the process, such as "hanging up the coat", cabin attendants can leave the passengers a good impression.

Principle: Cabin attendants should be considerate and pay attention to observing.

Example

FA: Excuse me, Mr. Lee, may I hang up your coat in the closet?

PAX: Yes, please!

FA: Are there any valuables in your pocket? Please keep them with you all the time.

PAX: No, thanks.

FA: It's my pleasure. May I know when you would like me to return your coat, Sir? Before landing or after landing?

PAX: Before landing. Thank you!

FA: Glad I can help you!

情景会话1：需要我为您挂衣服吗？

乘务员：李先生，您好，我帮您把衣服挂到衣帽间，好吗？

旅客：好的。

乘务员：您的衣服口袋里有贵重物品吗？如果有的话，请您随身携带。

旅客：没有，谢谢！

乘务员：不客气。您想在飞机落地前取回您的外套，还是在落地后取回呢？

旅客：降落之前，谢谢！

乘务员：不客气，很高兴为您服务！

Dialogue 2: Special greeting and first-round communication

音频扫一扫

Situation: It's usually the case that the purser greets and communicates with the VIP or the like first right after boarding or even during boarding. At this time, the purser can figure out how to address the passenger appropriately. And the flight attendant who is in charge of this cabin may introduce in-flight entertainment devices and corresponding service to this passenger.

Principle: A self-introduction should be done naturally during the first-round communication. According to a passenger's social position, dressing, manner and conversation style, flight attendants can communicate with him / her effectively in the limited time, especially in the first and business class.

Example

PS: Excuse me, Mr. Jackson, I am the flight purser. As you are our honorable Platinum Card member, we appreciate your support and would like to serve you better. Our crew will take your drink and meal order soon. Please feel free to contact us if you need any assistance. And this is my colleague, Ms. Zhang.

/ Welcome aboard, Sir. I'm the cabin purser of this flight. I'm not quite sure about the pronunciation of your name. How may I address you during the flight?

PAX: Okay, how do you do? Just call me Jackson.

PS and FA: Nice to meet you, Mr. Jackson.

PAX: Hi, Zhang. May I have a moment?

FA: Sure. I'm the cabin crew of the first class. It's my honor to fly with you today. In order to provide you a comfortable journey, in-flight entertainment devices will be available after taking off.

PAX: Great!

FA: Today we've prepared a variety of meal selections. These are the menu and wine list for you. Please have a look and I will take order for you later.

PAX: Thank you.

FA: Wish you a pleasant journey!

情景会话2：特殊问候与首轮沟通

乘务长：杰克逊先生，您好！我是本次航班的乘务长，您是我们尊贵的白金卡旅客，感谢您的支持，很高兴为您提供更优质的服务。稍后我们的客舱乘务员会为您预订餐食及饮料，如果您有任何需要，请随时联系我们。这是我的同事，小张。

/ 先生，欢迎您乘坐本次航班旅行。我是本次航班的乘务长。我不太确定您的名字的发音，请问航程中我应该怎样称呼您呢？

旅客：好的，你们好！叫我杰克逊就可以了。

乘务长和乘务员：杰克逊先生，很高兴遇见您。

旅客：嗨，小张，我能耽搁你一下吗？

乘务员：没问题。我是头等舱的乘务员，很荣幸今天能为您服务。为了您能够有一段愉快的旅程，机上旅客娱乐设备在飞机平飞后就可以使用了。

旅客：不错！

乘务员：今天我们为您准备了多种餐食，供您选择。这是餐谱和酒水单，请您过目，稍后我会来为您点餐。

旅客：谢谢！

乘务员：祝您旅途愉快！

音频扫一扫

Dialogue 3: Welcome service (hand out towels, boarding drinks and snacks)

Situation: It is the routine that flight attendants provide hot towels, boarding drinks and nuts for first class passengers, business class passengers, as well as very important and commercially important passengers. Based on such kind of service, the passengers could be at ease.

Principle: The flight attendants relevant should provide the service with flexibility and kindly remind the passengers of something necessary.

Example

FA: Excuse me, Mr. Lin. We have prepared a cold towel and a hot towel for you. Which one would you prefer?

PAX: A hot towel, please.

FA: Mr. Lin, for boarding drinks, we have prepared Champagne, freshly squeezed orange juice, mineral water and other drinks. What would you like to drink?

/ Jasmine tea is specially offered in this season. Would you like to have a try?

PAX: I prefer Champagne.

FA: OK. Would you like some mixed nuts?

PAX: Yes, thanks.

FA: Is there any nut you are allergic to?

PAX: Oh, yes, I'm allergic to peanuts. Em... I'd better not eat them. Thanks anyway.

FA: You are welcome!

情景会话3：迎宾服务（发毛巾、登机饮品和小吃）

乘务员：您好，林先生，我们为您准备了冷毛巾和热毛巾，请问您想要哪一种？

旅客：请给我热毛巾吧！

乘务员：林先生，我们为您准备了香槟、鲜榨橙汁、矿泉水以及其他饮品，您想喝点什么？

/我们在本季特意为您准备了茉莉花茶，您想尝一尝吗？

旅客：我想要香槟。

乘务员：好的。您想来一些混合果仁吗？

旅客：好的，谢谢。

乘务员：您对果仁有什么忌口吗？

旅客：哦，是的，我对花生过敏。嗯……我还是不吃了吧。谢谢了。

乘务员：不客气。

Dialogue 4: Special-prepared on-board entertainment service

音频扫一扫

Situation: After welcome beverage, flight attendants in the first and business class had better introduce on-board entertainment system to passengers and let them know how to use headphones. If they have extra time, newspapers and magazines should be recommended as well. And the reading light can be turned on after the passengers' permission.

Principle: Flight attendants should provide this kind of service with flexibility and proficiency, not in a hurry.

Example

FA: Excuse me, Mr. Chen, this is the headphone we prepared for you.

PAX: Well...

FA: The best feature is its noise-canceling function. Simply by turning on the switch on the right side, you may enjoy quiet environment.

/ It is our latest product on board and it adopts the most advanced technology. The digital chip in it can give you beautiful sound quality. No matter watching movies or listening to music, it can always help put on the best performance.

PAX: Sounds great. I'll try. Thanks for introducing it.

FA: And would you like a piece of newspaper? We have prepared English newspapers for you, such as *Financial Times, U.S.A. Today* and *The New York Times*.

PAX: *Financial Times*, please.

FA: Sure. Any magazines? We have prepared several kinds of Chinese and English magazines today. Would you like some?

PAX: *National Geographic* and *Vogue*.

FA: Here you are. Shall I turn on the reading light for you?

PAX: Thank you!

FA: My pleasure, Sir. Enjoy your flight.

情景会话4：特别准备的机上休闲娱乐服务

乘务员：陈先生，您好，这是我们为您准备的耳机。

旅客：好的……

乘务员：这款耳机最棒的特点是它的降噪功能，只需打开耳机右侧的开关就可以开启降噪功能，享受宁静的环境。

/这款耳机是我们机上的最新产品。它采用最先进的技术。其中的数字芯片能带给您美妙的音质。无论是看电影还是听音乐，它都能表现完美。

旅客：听起来很不错，我会试试的。谢谢你的介绍。

乘务员：另外，请问您需要报纸吗？我们为您准备了英文报纸，如《金融时报》《今日美国》和《纽约时报》。

旅客：请给我《金融时报》吧。

乘务员：好的，我们还准备了多种中英文杂志，请问您需要吗？

旅客：《国家地理》和《时尚》杂志。

乘务员：这是您的报纸和杂志。我为您打开阅读灯吧？

旅客：谢谢！

乘务员：不客气，先生。祝您旅途愉快！

Dialogue 5: Slippers, pajamas and amenity packs

Situation: It is part of a first-class or business-class flight attendant's job to distribute slippers, pajamas and amenity packs.

Principle: The flight attendants should be considerate.

Example

FA: Excuse me, Sir. Here's your pair of slippers. Would you like me to open the pack for you?

PAX: It's all right.

FA: What's more, these are pajamas and amenity packs for you. For the pajamas, there are different sizes from Small to Extra Large. The design for all of the three colors is the same. The pajamas made of pure cotton now are thinner and more comfortable. The simple designing style combines oriental elements and international fashion perfectly. Which size fits you?

PAX: I think "Small" fits me.

FA: OK. Here you are.

PAX: Great!

FA: The amenity pack changes a tri-fold bag to a zipper-style one with the brand LOGO zip-fastener and a metal LOGO of our airline on the front.

PAX: OK. So any changes inside?

FA: Still the same. There is hand lotion, a lip balm, wet wipes, an eyeshade, earplugs, socks, a toothpaste and a toothbrush in the pack.

情景会话 5：拖鞋、睡衣和洗漱包

乘务员：先生，您好，这是为您准备的拖鞋，需要我现在为您打开包装吗？

旅客：不用了，我自己来就行。

乘务员：我们还为您准备了睡衣和洗漱包。睡衣的尺码从小号到超大号不等。睡衣有三种颜色且样式都是一样的。纯棉材质更加轻薄、舒适。简单的设计风格完美地结合了东方元素与国际风尚。哪个尺码适合您呢？

旅客：我认为小号适合我。

乘务员：好的。给您。

旅客：不错！

乘务员：这款洗漱包将三折叠式更改为拉链式，同时配以品牌标志性拉链扣，正面装饰我们航空公司的金属标志牌。

旅客：好的。那洗漱包里面的东西有什么变化吗？

乘务员：还是一样的。洗漱包内有护手霜、一支润唇膏、湿纸巾、一个眼罩、耳塞、袜套、一支牙膏和一支牙刷。

Dialogue 6: Provide flight information service ahead

Situation: With the rapid development of economy and technology, more and more people would like to travel by plane. It is often the case that during a flight, over 40 percent of passengers are Gold Card members. And it's hard to greet them one by one during the short-haul flight. Therefore, the pre-service is very important.

Principle: The purser and flight attendants should be considerate and handle the situation with flexibility.

Example

FA: Good morning, Ms. Wang! It's a great honor for me to serve you on this flight and thank you for choosing our airline again.

PAX: Glad to see you!

FA: As you know, the flight time today is around three hours. And we could encounter slight turbulence during the catering service time.

PAX: I see.

FA: We have redesigned services for our Gold Card members. As you heard from our previous announcement, we have more than 50 Gold Card members on this flight. We will try our best to help you if you need any assistance.

PAX: It's okay.

FA: Thank you for your understanding and kindness. Have a good time!

情景会话6：提前告知飞行信息

乘务员：早上好，王女士！感谢您再次乘坐我们的航班，很荣幸为您服务。

旅客：见到你很高兴！

乘务员：可能您已经知道航班信息了，今天的飞行时间约为三小时。航程中餐饮服务过程中可能会有轻度的颠簸。

旅客：我知道了。

乘务员：我们公司针对金卡旅客，重新设计了服务项目。正如您先前听到的欢迎广播所说，本次航班上有超过五十名金卡常旅客。旅途中如果您有任何需要，我们将竭诚为您服务。

旅客：好的。

乘务员：您真好，感谢您的理解！祝您旅途愉快！

Ⅲ. Popular Words and Phrases

high-valued passenger		高价值旅客，高端旅客
platinum	['plætɪnəm]	n. 白金
upgrade	[ˌʌp'gred]	n. & v. 升舱，提高（……的待遇）
check-in counter		值机柜台
distinguished	[dɪ'stɪŋgwɪʃt]	adj. 尊贵的，受人尊敬的
distinguished guest		贵宾，尊贵的客人；嘉宾
honored guest		尊贵的客人
considerate	[kən'sɪdərɪt]	adj. 体贴的，体谅的；考虑周到的
towel	['taʊəl]	n. 毛巾
pajama	[pə'dʒɑːmə]	n. 休闲服，睡衣
slipper	['slɪpə]	n. 拖鞋
amenity kit	[ə'miːnətikɪt]	牙具包
toothbrush	['tuːθbrʌʃ]	n. 牙刷（复数 toothbrushes）

toothpaste	[ˈtuːθpeɪst]	*n.* 牙膏（复数 toothpastes）
quilt	[kwɪlt]	*n.* 小被子
eye shade		眼罩
ear plug		耳塞
lotion	[ˈləʊʃ(ə)n]	*n.* 乳液
comb	[kəʊm]	*n.* 梳子
lip balm	[lɪp bɑːm]	*n.* 润唇膏
be dedicated to		致力于
pleasure	[ˈpleʒə(r)]	*n.* 乐趣
prior to		优于
estimated flight time		预计飞行时间
flight route		飞行路线
departure time		出发时间
arrival time		抵达时间
cruising altitude		巡航高度
estimated time of arrival		预计到达时间
arrange	[əˈrendʒ]	*v.* 安排
at your service		愿为您服务
congratulation	[kənˌɡrætjuˈleiʃən]	*n.* 祝贺，恭喜
diplomatic	[ˌdɪpləˈmætɪk]	*adj.* 外交上的，外交人员的
distance	[ˈdɪstəns]	*n.* 距离
enjoyable	[ɪnˈdʒɔɪəbl]	*adj.* 愉快的
extend	[ɪkˈstɛnd]	*v.* 延伸，扩大
hesitate	[ˈhezɪteɪt]	*v.* 犹豫
honor	[ˈɒnə(r)]	*n.* 尊敬、荣誉
honorable	[ˈɒnərəbl]	*adj.* 可敬的，荣誉的
on behalf of		代表……
premier	[prɪˈmɪr]	*n.* 总理；首相
president	[ˈprezɪdənt]	*n.* 总统；董事长
shortly	[ˈʃɔrtli]	*adv.* 立刻；简短地
support	[səˈpɔrt]	*n. & v.* 支持，帮助
be filled with		充满
comfort	[ˈkʌmfət]	*n.* 舒适
healthy	[ˈhɛlθi]	*adj.* 健康的
journey	[ˈdʒɜːni]	*n.* 旅途
local time		当地时间
representative	[ˈreprɪˈzentətɪv]	*n.* 代表
respect	[rɪˈspɛkt]	*n.* 敬意
personnel	[ˌpɜsəˈnɛl]	*n.* 人员
special	[ˈspeʃəl]	*adj.* 特别的
securely	[sɪˈkjʊrli]	*adv.* 安全地；牢固地
assigned	[əˈsaɪnd]	*adj.* 指定的，指派的
entire	[ɛnˈtaɪr]	*adj.* 全部的；整个的

| Intercontinental | [ˌɪntəˌkɒntɪˈnentl] | *adj.* 跨洲的，洲际的 |
| continuing | [kənˈtɪnjʊɪŋ] | *adj.* 继续的，连续的，持续的 |

IV. Practical Expressions

1. How should I address you during the flight?

请问航程中我怎样称呼您呢？

2. Welcome aboard, Sir. I'm the cabin crew of the business class. My name is Lin. I'm not quite sure about the pronunciation of your name. How may I address you during the flight?

先生，您好！欢迎您乘坐本次班机旅行。我是今天商务舱的乘务员，我叫小林。我不太确定您名字的发音，请问我可以以怎样称呼您呢？

3. Excuse me, Madam, I'm your flight attendant of business class today. I'm Lee.

女士，您好，我是小李，是今天为您服务的公务舱乘务员。

/ Excuse me, Sir, my name is Kate. I'm working in this part of the cabin. Please let me know if there is anything I can do for you.

先生，您好，我叫凯特。本次航班我在这个区域服务。如您有任何需要，请随时联系我。

4. It's my honor to fly with you today. / It's my pleasure to be at your service.

我很荣幸 / 高兴今天能够为您服务。

5. I've been flying as an international flight attendant for almost two years.

我已经作为国际乘务员飞行快两年了。

6. The aircraft you are taking today is AirBus 330-200.

您今天乘坐的机型是空客330-200型飞机。

7. Excuse me, Sir, I am the flight purser. As you are our honorable Platinum Card member, we appreciate your support and would like to serve you better. Our crew will take your drink and meal order soon. Please feel free to contact us if you need any assistance.

先生，您好！我是本次航班的乘务长，您是我们尊贵的白金卡旅客，感谢您一直以来的支持，很高兴为您提供更优质的服务。稍后我们的客舱乘务员会为您预订餐食及饮料，如果您有任何需要，请随时联系我们。

8. I am really sorry that free upgrade service is no longer available on board. But the Platinum Card member can apply for the free upgrade at the check-in counter or online as usual.

非常遗憾，机上不再进行旅客免费升舱操作。但是，作为白金卡旅客，您仍然可以在地面值机柜台或者线上申请免费升舱。

9. Don't worry, wherever you are seated, we will provide considerate service to our distinguished Platinum Card member.

请您放心，无论您坐在哪个舱位，我们都将为尊贵的白金卡旅客提供周到贴心的服务。

10. We have prepared a cold towel and a hot towel for you.

我们为您准备了冷毛巾和热毛巾。

11. For boarding drinks, we have prepared champagne, freshly squeezed orange juice, mineral water and other hot drinks.

我们为您准备的登机饮品有香槟、鲜榨橙汁、矿泉水和一些热饮。

12. Excuse me, Sir. We have prepared orange juice, mineral water and champagne for you. Which one would you like?

您好，先生，我们为您准备了橙汁、矿泉水和香槟酒，请问您想要哪一种？

13. Excuse me, Madam. Would you like to put on the slippers? It will make you feel more comfortable.

您好，女士，请问您需要换一下拖鞋吗？这样会舒服些。

14. Excuse me, Sir. May I help you hang up your coat in the closet?

您好，先生，我帮您把大衣挂在衣帽间，好吗？

15. May I hang up your coat, Sir? I'll keep it in the cloakroom.

先生，需要我为您把外套挂起来吗？我将把它放在衣帽间里。

16. Would you mind taking out your passport, the valuables and the fragile items from your coat?

请您取出外套中的护照、贵重及易碎物品好吗？

17. Are there any valuables in your pocket? Please keep them with you all the time.

请问您口袋里有贵重物品吗？请您随时随身携带。

18. We've prepared a blanket and a pillow for you.

我们为您准备了毛毯和枕头。

19. We have prepared pajamas and amenity packs for you. We'll offer turn-down service after take-off.

我们为您准备了睡衣和洗漱包，起飞后我们还提供铺床服务。

20. We have prepared an amenity pack for you. There are some washing supplies, an eyeshade and earplugs in it.

我们为您准备了洗漱包。里面有一些洗漱用品、眼罩和耳塞。

21. We have prepared several kinds of mandarin and English magazines today.

今天我们准备了多种中英文杂志。

22. These are the menu and wine list for you. Please take a look. I will take your order later.

这是餐谱和酒水单，请您过目。稍后我来为您订餐。

23. These are the menu and wine list for you. Please have a look. If you would like to have dinner, I will take order for you after take-off.

这是本次航班的餐谱和酒水单，请您过目，如果需要用餐，起飞后我会来为您点餐。

24. Here is the menu. The flight takes about 2 hours, and we will be serving lunch after take-off. There are three options for the main course on this page. You can have a look at the menu first, and I will take your order soon.

这是今天的餐谱，今天的航班大约飞行2个小时，起飞后我们将为您提供午餐。主菜有三种选择，在这一页，您可以先看一下，稍后我帮您订餐。

25. The fragrance removes smell and keeps air clear effectively, creating a comfortable atmosphere for our passengers.

此款香氛有良好去除异味以及长时间持香的效果，能为旅客创造一个舒适惬意的环境。

26. We will take off at 1 p.m. and arrive in New York at 1:40 a.m. Beijing time on the next day.

我们下午1点起飞，到达纽约是北京时间第二天的凌晨1:40。

27. The flight time from Beijing to Milan is about 10 hours.

从北京到米兰的飞行时间大约是10个小时。

28. According to winter time, Beijing is 13 hours earlier than New York.

冬季时，北京比纽约早13个小时。

29. Now may I introduce our dining service? Our dinner starts with A, followed by B then C. We have also prepared D and E.

我现在可以为您介绍一下我们的餐食服务吗？我们首先为您准备了A，然后是B和C，我们还准备了D和E。（A、B、C、D、E为餐食名）

30. These are the pajamas in different sizes from Small to Triple Extra Large. Which one would you like?

这是为您准备的睡衣，型号从S号到XXXL号。您想要哪个尺码？

31. Would you like our wake-up service before catering service?

供餐前您需要叫醒服务吗？

32. I am really sorry that the shuttle bus is not available for the Platinum Card member in economy class.

非常抱歉，目前不提供经济舱白金卡旅客下机乘坐摆渡车服务。

V. Tips

How to communicate with CIPs effectively? 如何与商务旅客进行有效沟通？

(1) Greetings

Good morning/ afternoon/ evening!

Nice/ Pleased/ Glad to meet/ see you.

How are you?

(2) Self-introduction

Are you Mr./ Mrs. ××? / How may I address you?

I would like to spend a minute to introduce myself./ Please allow me to introduce myself to you. / I'd like to introduce myself to you. My name is ××, you can also call me ××.

I'll serve you for the whole flight, please feel free to contact me if you need anything or any help./ If you need anything, please let me know.

(3) Flight information and products

Our flight time is ×× hours and ×× minutes./ Our estimated time of the arrival is ××.

Today we've prepared two meals. For the first meal, it's a dinner, including ××, ×× and ××; for the second one, it's a breakfast for tomorrow morning, just three hours before landing, including ××, ×× and ××. We've also prepared cold and hot drinks and here's the menu for you.

(4) Ending

And we wish you a pleasant journey, if you need anything, please let me know/ feel free to tell us.

Enjoy your flight/ Have a good flight!

VI. Supplementary Reading

The business card 名片

(1) Basic information

company name 公司名称

person's name 本人姓名

position, title 职位、职称、头衔

telephone number 电话号码

fax number 传真号码

E-mail address 电子邮箱地址

company address 公司地址

(2) Proper business card etiquette in terms of receiving business cards

① Give with both hands and receive with both hands.

② When you receive it, pause a moment and look at it before you put it away. As you receive it and put it away, do gently.

③ Do not put the card in your wallet. It should go properly in your business card holder or business organizer. Do not chuck it on the table, or into a visible pile on your desk, or your back pocket or your handbag.

④ Do not write anything on the business card. Have respect for other people's business cards.

⑤ In more formal cultures, business cards are not only handed with both hands, they are handed with a slight nod or bow. If you are in that situation, try to do the same. When in Rome, do as the Romans do.

VII. Exercises

1. Answer the following questions according to the dialogues.

(1) What are the criteria of serving distinguished guests?

(2) How to address passengers on board?

(3) How to help passengers hang up their coats?

2. Translate the following words and phrases into Chinese or English.

on behalf of	休闲服，睡衣
upgrade	拖鞋
check-in counter	洗漱包
toothbrush	眼罩
toothpaste	耳塞

3. Translate the following sentences into Chinese or English.

(1) I'm the cabin crew of business class. How may I address you during the flight?

(2) It's my pleasure to be at your service.

(3) May I help you hang up your coat in the closet?

(4) I am really sorry that free upgrade service is no longer available on board. But the Platinum Card member can apply for the free upgrade at the check-in counter or online as usual.

(5) Don't worry, wherever you are seated, we will provide considerate service to our distinguished Platinum Card member.

(6) Would you like to put on the slippers? It will make you feel more comfortable.

(7) We have prepared an amenity pack for you.

4. Group work: each group chooses one topic to start a conversation. (TIME LIMIT: 5 minutes)

(1) Special greeting and first-round communication.

(2) Help passengers hang up their coats.

(3) Provide newspapers and magazines.

Task 8　Special Passengers 特殊旅客

I. Warm-up Questions

1. How would you explain the use of in-flight facilities to unaccompanied passengers?

2. What is the age limit for services to unaccompanied children?

3. What documents need to be provided if a child is flying by himself or herself?

4. What is the procedure for requesting an infant cradle?

5. Is there a limit on the number of infant passengers allowed on the flight?

6. How to look after the pregnant or infants during international long-distance flights?

7. How to provide services for the deaf on board?

8. How can we assist disabled passengers well?

II. Dialogues

Dialogue 1: The Baby Bassinet

音频扫一扫

Situation: In terms of long-distance flights, some parents may book a baby bassinet for their baby when buying tickets. And the parents would confirm it after getting on board.

Principle: Normally, the baby's weight cannot exceed the weight limitation. The baby bassinet provided by the company is applicable to the baby with the weight less than 25 pounds / 11kg and height less than 75cm.

Example

PAX: Excuse me, Miss, I need a baby bassinet. Can you help me?

FA: Yes, with pleasure, I will set up a baby bassinet for you after the airplane reaches the cruising altitude.

By the way, what's the baby's weight and height? Let me check whether a baby bassinet suitable for your baby or not?

(After checking...)

FA: Sorry, Miss, your baby's weight and height exceed the maximum of a bassinet, so it is not safe to let your baby in it.

PAX: Okay, then.

FA: Thank you for your understanding.

情景会话1：婴儿摇篮

旅客：打扰一下，乘务员，我需要一个婴儿摇篮，你能帮助我吗？

乘务员：当然，我很乐意为您服务。飞机到达平飞高度后，我将为您安装婴儿摇篮。

乘务员：顺便问一下，您的宝宝有多重多高呀？让我检查确认下摇篮大小是否适合您的宝宝。

（检查后……）

乘务员：对不起，女士，您宝宝的体重和身高超过了婴儿摇篮的最大限度，因此孩子在里面不安全。

旅客：那好吧。

乘务员：感谢您的理解。

Dialogue 2: Infant Passengers/ Passengers with Infants

音频扫一扫

Situation: In order to let the infant be more comfortable during the flight, the parents usually take multiple related items with them.

Principle: At this time, flight attendants should assist the passengers with their bags. After they have taken the seats, flight attendants should provide relevant services in time considerately.

Example

FA: Do you need a bassinet/ lactating towel/ napkin ?

PAX: Oh, you are so kind.

FA: I will set it up for you after 30 minutes taking off, but we have to stow it during take-off and descent. And please carry your baby carefully and fasten the seat belt if there is turbulence.

PAX: OK.

FA: Excuse me, Sir. This is a seatbelt for your baby. She will feel more comfortable with it and it will be safer during an emergency. Let me connect it with your seatbelt and you may adjust it as necessary.

PAX: Wow, you're so nice. By the way, could you please make a bottle of baby milk for my baby?

FA: Sure. How much warm water should I prepare?

PAX: 200ml will be fine.

(After a while...)

FA: Here is the baby milk, Sir. And have you ever reserved the baby food?

PAX: Yes.

FA: When do you need it?

PAX: Maybe later. I will let you know if I need it.

FA: Sure. By the way, the nappy changing tables are located in the rear lavatories of the left side with the sign. And if you need to change diapers for the baby, you can go there.

PAX: That's very sweet of you, and I really appreciate it.

FA: My pleasure.

情景会话2：婴儿旅客/带婴儿的旅客

乘务员：请问您需要婴儿摇篮/授乳巾/湿巾吗？

旅客：哦！你真体贴。

乘务员：飞机起飞后30分钟我会为您支好婴儿摇篮，但是，在起飞和落地时，我们得收起它。遇到颠簸时请抱好您的宝宝并系好安全带。

旅客：好的。

乘务员：打扰了，先生。这是给您宝宝的一条婴儿安全带。系上这条安全带，孩子会舒服一些。如果有紧急情况发生的话，也更安全些。让我为您把它连接到您的安全带上。必要时，您可以调节它的长度。

旅客：哇，你可真好。顺便问一下，你能帮我冲一瓶奶吗？

乘务员：当然。需要加多少热水？

旅客：200毫升就可以了。

（过了一会儿……）

乘务员：这是宝贝的牛奶，给您，先生。另外问一下，您预订婴儿餐了吗？

旅客：是的。

乘务员：您什么时候需要？

旅客：一会儿吧。如果我需要，我会告诉你的。

乘务员：好的。顺便和您说一下，给婴儿换尿布的置物板安置在客舱后部左侧带有标识的洗手间里。如果您需要给孩子换尿布的话，可以去那儿换。

旅客：你真好，非常感谢。

乘务员：不客气。

Dialogue 3: Infant Belts

Situation: When a passenger getting on board with an infant, flight attendants should provide an infant belt for the passenger.

Principle: For their safety, flight attendants ought to be considerate to provide the infant belt and

音频扫一扫

explain in time.

Example

FA: Excuse me, Madam, I'm afraid you can't fasten your seat belt with your baby. In case of an emergency, the seat belt may easily hurt your baby. Your baby needs to be seated on your lap during take-off and landing, fastened to your seat belt with a special baby belt. I'll go and get one for you.

PAX: Thanks!

(The flight attendant helps the passenger fasten the baby belt.)

FA: That's okay!

PAX: Thank you very much! And could you please heat the bottle of milk for my baby?

FA: I'm sorry we're busy now. Could you wait a moment until we've finished the service?

PAX: I'm afraid I have to feed my baby now. She's been crying for a long time.

FA: Leave it with me and I'll do it as soon as possible.

PAX: Can you find my bag from the overhead locker and take out the baby's bottle?

FA: Sure.

情景会话3：婴儿安全带

乘务员：您好，女士，恐怕您不能用您的安全带把您和孩子系在一起，万一发生紧急情况，这条安全带很容易伤着孩子。在飞机起飞或降落时您的孩子需要坐在您的腿上，用一条特殊的婴儿安全带系在您的安全带上。我马上就给您拿一条来。

旅客：谢谢！

（乘务员帮助这名旅客系好了婴儿安全带。）

乘务员：好了！

旅客：太谢谢了！可以请您帮我给宝宝热一下奶吗？

乘务员：抱歉我们眼下正忙。可以稍等一下，待我们忙完吗？

旅客：恐怕我现在得给孩子喂奶。她已经哭了很长时间了。

乘务员：把奶瓶给我，我马上就去为您加热。

旅客：您能在行李架上找到我的包拿出婴儿奶瓶吗？

乘务员：没问题。

Dialogue 4: The Pregnant

Situation: A pregnant passenger may find it a little difficult to travel alone, especially during the flight.

Principle: Flight attendants should be considerate.

Example

PAX: Excuse me, could you tell me where my seat is?

FA: Sure, it's 43A. Let me help you with your baggage and I'll lead you to your seat.

PAX: Thank you so much.

FA: Do you need to take something out? If not, may I put your baggage in the overhead bin?

PAX: Sure. Thanks a lot.

FA: Excuse me, Madam. I have prepared a blanket for you. You can put it on your belly and fasten your seatbelt around the root of your thighs. It will make you feel more comfortable.

PAX: I was thinking of asking for a blanket. It's so considerate of you.

FA: It's my pleasure. And we may experience turbulence during the flight. You can use the airsickness bag in the seat pocket in front of you if you feel uncomfortable, or you can call me at any

音频扫一扫

time. I am glad to be at your service.

PAX: I'm really lucky to have you here. Thank you so much!

情景会话4：孕妇旅客

旅客：您好，您能帮我看看我的座位在哪儿吗？

乘务员：当然，您的座位在43排A座，我来帮您拿行李，带您去座位上。

旅客：太谢谢您了！

乘务员：您有些东西要拿出来吗？如果不需要我就直接帮您把行李放到行李架上了。

旅客：好的，多谢。

乘务员：女士，我为您准备了一条毛毯，您可以把它盖在腹部上，把安全带系在大腿根的位置，这样会更舒服一些。

旅客：我正想找您要一条毛毯呢，您真贴心。

乘务员：这是我应该做的。在飞行中我们可能会遇到颠簸，如果您感到不适，可以使用您前方座椅口袋里的呕吐袋，或者随时叫我，我很乐意为您服务！

旅客：遇到您真是太幸运了，非常感谢！

音频扫一扫

Dialogue 5: UM (Unaccompanied Minor) Passengers

Situation: Due to diverse reasons, some children would travel by themselves.

Principle: Flight attendants should be considerate and pay attention to the unaccompanied minor during the whole flight.

Example

FA: Hello, Sweetie. Please stay in your seat and we will accompany you to look for your family after landing.

PAX1 UM: Sure.

FA: Please feel free to call me if you need any help in the flight, OK?

PAX1 UM: Okay, thank you!

FA: Excuse me, Lady, the child beside you is traveling on her own. If it's possible, could you please help contact us in case anything happened to her? Thanks.

PAX2: Sure.

FA: Enjoy your flight!

情景会话5：无人陪伴儿童

乘务员：你好呀，小可爱，落地后要在座位上等着哦，我们会陪你一起去找你的家人。

旅客1无成人陪伴儿童：好的。

乘务员：如果在航班上需要任何帮助，记得叫我哟，好不好？

旅客1无成人陪伴儿童：好的，谢谢！

乘务员：打扰了，女士，您旁边的这位小朋友是一个人出行的。您可以协助我们照顾一下她吗？如果她有什么需求，请帮助她联系我们。谢谢您。

旅客2：好的。

乘务员：祝你们旅途愉快呀！

音频扫一扫

Dialogue 6: The Elderly

Situation: Due to diverse reasons, some elderly passengers would travel by themselves.

Principle: Flight attendants should be considerate and pay attention to the elderly during the whole

 民航空乘英语实用口语教程　第三版

flight.

Example

FA: Sir, it's a long flight. During the flight we recommend you to do some simple in-seat-exercise several minutes per hour. Do drink more water. They are good for your health.

PAX: Thanks.

FA: You may feel a little uncomfortable in your ears during descent. But don't worry, it can be relieved by swallowing. And if you need anything, just press this call button.

PAX: Okay.

情景会话6：老人（无人陪伴老人）

乘务员：先生，本次航班航程时间较长，飞行中，我们建议您每小时在座位上做几分钟简单的运动。一定要多喝点儿水。这样对您的健康有好处。

旅客：谢谢。

乘务员：下降期间您可能会感到轻微耳痛。不过不要担心，您可以通过做吞咽动作缓解一下。如需任何帮助，可以按这个呼唤铃。

旅客：好的。

Dialogue 7: Wheelchair Passengers

Situation: Wheelchair passengers can be found in almost every flight, especially in international flights. Most of them are the elderly, disabled or injured passengers.

Principle: Flight attendants need to pay attention to wheelchair passengers and remind them of details during the flight.

音频扫一扫

Example

(Boarding...)

FA: Good morning, Sir. Please follow me, I will show you your seat.

PAX1: Well, thanks.

FA: Sir, this is your seat. Take your seat, please. I will introduce the service facilities to you so that you can get my help in time when you need.

PAX1: All right.

FA: There is a reading light button and a call button on your armrest. The button next to you can adjust the seat backwards. And the toilets are located in the rear of the cabin. If you need any help, just press the call button and the cabin crew will come to help you.

PAX1: Okay, thank you very much!

FA: Sir, there is one more matter for you to pay attention to. When disembarking, please don't follow others to disembark but wait for me to lead you to the cabin door. OK?

PAX1: All right!

FA: I will confirm it with you again before landing. I wish you a pleasant flight.

(Before landing...)

PAX2: Excuse me, Miss. I am wondering how to get off the plane.

FA: Don't worry, Madam. When the plane has come to a complete stop, the ground staff will bring a wheelchair and wait for you. Would you please stay in your seat and wait for me? When other passengers get off the plane, I'll be here to assist you.

PAX2: OK.

FA: After landing, our ground staff will go with you to the baggage claim area. Then you can claim your own wheelchair. By the way, if you need any assistance, please feel free to let us know by pressing the call button.

PAX2: I get it, thank you.

FA: It's my pleasure.

情景会话7：轮椅旅客

（登机过程中……）

乘务员：早上好，先生，请跟我来，我带您入座。

旅客1：好的，谢谢。

乘务员：先生，这是您的座位。请就座，我来给您介绍一下这些服务设施，以便在您需要时我能及时来帮助您。

旅客1：好的。

乘务员：在您座椅扶手上有阅读灯及呼唤铃按钮，您旁边的按钮可以调整座椅靠背，卫生间在客舱的后部。如果有什么需要帮忙的，就按呼唤铃，乘务员会过来帮您。

旅客1：好的，非常感谢！

乘务员：先生，还有一点需要您注意，在飞机落地旅客下机时，请不要跟着大家一起下机，等我带您去机舱门口，可以吗？

旅客1：好的。

乘务员：在飞机落地前我还会再过来和您确认一次，祝您旅途愉快！

（飞机落地前……）

旅客2：请问一下，我要怎么下飞机呢？

乘务员：别担心，女士。飞机完全停稳以后，地面工作人员会带着轮椅等候您的。您先在座位上等等好吗？等其他旅客下飞机后，我会来帮您的。

旅客2：好的。

乘务员：落地后，我们的地面工作人员会送您去行李提取处的，之后您就能取回自己的轮椅了。还有，如果您需要任何帮助，可以随时按呼唤铃联系我们。

旅客2：知道了，谢谢。

乘务员：很高兴为您服务。

Dialogue 8: Passengers with Visual Disability

音频扫一扫

Situation: Visual disability refers to the blind or very poor visual acuity. This kind of passengers can't move around easily on board.

Principle: Flight attendants need to pay attention to the passengers with visual disability and remind them of details during the flight. Avoid introducing the reading light to them.

Example

FA: Hello, Jim, I'm Lily, the cabin crew today. I will lead you to your seat. Here is my arm and elbow.

PAX: Okay.

FA: Jim, are you ready to go now?

PAX: Yes, please.

FA: Is this speed okay for you, Jim?

PAX: Erm... Hold on a moment...

FA: Sure. There is no one in the cabin right now... Your seat is 32C. We need to pass through the business class first, then reach the economy class. You seat is in the second row of the economy class, an aisle seat on our right side.

PAX: That's great!

FA: Jim, we have reached your seat 32C, and it is face to you. There are two more seats beside it. You may touch it and take your seat now.

PAX: Thank you so much!

FA: Don't mention it! If you need anything, just feel free to let us know.

情景会话8：视力障碍（视力残疾）旅客

乘务员：您好，吉姆，我是本次航班的乘务员莉莉，我将带您去您的座位，请握住我的手肘。

旅客：好的。

乘务员：吉姆，现在您准备好去座位上了吗？

旅客：好的，请吧。

乘务员：吉姆，这样的行走速度还可以吗？

旅客：呃……稍等一下。

乘务员：好的。现在客舱里没有人……您的座位在32排C座，我们需要穿过商务舱去到普通舱，您的座位在普通舱的第二排，是我们右侧靠过道的座位。

旅客：挺不错的！

乘务员：吉姆，到了，在您的正前方就是您的座位，32排C座。在您的座位旁边，还有两个座位。现在您可以感受一下，入座了。

旅客：非常感谢。

乘务员：不客气。有任何需要，随时联系我们。

Ⅲ. Popular Words and Phrases

baby bassinet		婴儿摇篮
baby stroller		婴儿车
diaper changing board		换尿布板
infant	['ɪnfənt]	n. 婴儿
pregnant	['pregnənt]	adj. 怀孕的
belly	['beli]	n. 腹部
root	[ruːt]	n. 根部
thigh	[θaɪ]	n. 大腿
lift cart		升降梯
wheelchair passenger		轮椅旅客
on-board wheelchair		机上轮椅
unaccompanied minor/ UM		无人陪伴儿童
adult	['ædʌlt]	n. 成人
elderly	['eldəli]	adj. 上年纪的
sick passenger		生病乘客
suspect	['sʌspekt]	n. 嫌疑犯
blind	[blaɪnd]	adj. 盲的
deaf	[def]	adj. 聋的
disabled	[dɪs'eɪbld]	adj. 残疾的
handicapped	['hændɪkæpt]	adj. 残疾的
insoluble	[in'sɔljubl]	adj. 不溶的，不溶解的

infant seatbelt		婴儿安全带
extension seatbelt		加长安全带
terminal	['tɜːmɪn(ə)l]	*n.* 候机楼
ground handling		地勤
conveyor	[kən'veɪə]	*n.* 输送带
airport passenger bus/ ferry		摆渡车
shuttle bus		摆渡车
ground power unit		地面电源车
air steps		机载客梯

IV. Practical Expressions

1. Would you like me to help you with your baggage/ baby stroller？

请问需要我帮您安放行李/ 婴儿车吗？

2. The nappy/ diaper changing tables are located in the rear lavatory of the left side. If you need to change diapers for your baby, you can go there.

后舱左侧卫生间里就有换尿布的安置板。如果您需要给孩子换尿布的话，可以去那儿。

/ You may go to the lavatory if you want to change diapers for the baby.

（对带婴儿旅客的温馨提示）您可以去卫生间给婴儿换尿布。

3. How much milk powder and water should I combine?/ How much warm water do you need?

需要加多少奶粉和水？ / 请问需要加多少热水？

4. May I bring you an infant seatbelt? Your baby will feel more comfortable with it and it will be safer during an emergency.

我可以为您拿一条婴儿安全带吗？系上婴儿安全带，您的宝宝会更舒服，紧急情况下也会更安全。

5. Let me connect it with your seat belt and you may adjust it as necessary.

让我来把它连在您的安全带上。必要时，您可以调节它的长度。

/ Here is the infant seatbelt specially for your baby. Please allow me to show you how to use it.

这是专为您宝宝准备的婴儿安全带，请让我为您展示如何使用它。

6. The armrest may crush your baby's finger. Please do be careful when you lift or put it down.

座椅扶手或许会夹伤您宝宝的手指。请您在抬放扶手时千万小心。

7. Here is a baby bassinet for you. And please fasten the seatbelt for your baby during the whole flight.

这是给您的婴儿摇篮。飞行全程中请为您的宝宝系好安全带。

8. Do you need a bassinet? I will set it up for you. But we have to stow it during take-off and descent.

您需要婴儿摇篮吗？我将给您安好。但是起飞和落地期间，我们得把它收起来。

9. I will set up a baby bassinet for you after the airplane reaches the cruising altitude.

飞机到达平飞高度后，我将为您安装婴儿摇篮。

10. By the way, what's the baby's weight and height? Let me check whether a baby bassinet suitable for your baby or not.

顺便问一下，您的宝宝有多重多高呀？让我检查下摇篮的大小是否适合您的宝宝。

11. Sorry, your baby's weight and height exceed the maximum of a bassinet, so it is not safe to let it in it.

对不起，您的宝宝的体重和身高超过了婴儿摇篮的最大限度，因此在里面不安全。

12. Excuse me, Miss, please allow me to stow the bassinet for you. Now, please fasten your seatbelt and hold your baby securely.

打扰下，女士，请允许我为您把婴儿摇篮收起来。现在请系好您的安全带，并把宝宝抱好。

13. If you would like to, you may reserve a baby/ child meal 24 hours before departure by dialing the hotline.

如果您有需要，可以在航班起飞前24小时拨打热线电话预订婴儿餐或儿童餐。

14. Excuse me, Madam. We have prepared biscuits instead of cheese peanuts for your baby just in case of being choked. Meanwhile, for the safety, we don't advise you to offer water-insoluble food for your baby during the flight.

打扰了，女士，我们为您的宝宝准备了饼干替代芝士花生以防孩子被噎住。同时，为了安全起见，我们也不建议您在飞行中喂宝宝非可溶性食物。

15. May I bring you a pillow? It will make you feel more comfortable.

（对怀孕旅客）我给您拿个枕头吧？这样会舒服一些。

16. One ground staff will take responsible for only one unaccompanied minor before boarding. Flight attendants will take good care of all unaccompanied minors during the whole journey.

每名无人陪伴儿童都会有一名地勤人员负责，直至登机。整个航程中，乘务员会认真照顾所有无人陪伴儿童。

17. I'll keep your traveling documents and the ticket. When you disembark, I'll give them to the ground staff.

（对无人陪伴旅客）我先帮您保管旅行证件和机票，当您下机时，我会将这些证件交接给地勤人员。

18. We will help you keep your crutch during the whole flight.

（对携带拐杖登机的旅客）我们将在整个航程中替您保管拐杖。

19. May I know your seat number? May I assist you with your hand luggage?

（登机时见到行动不便的旅客时）可以告诉我您的座位号吗？我帮您拿行李好吗？

20. Don't worry. How may I assist you?

别担心。请问我可以怎样协助您？

21. Our flight attendants can help you if you would like to go to the lavatory.

（对机上轮椅旅客）如果您想要去卫生间的话，我们的乘务员可以帮助您。

V. Tips

1. How to serve baby passengers? 如何为带婴儿旅客提供服务？

（1）乘务员应该主动协助旅客提拿安放行李。

Would you like me to help you with your baggage/ baby stroller?

（2）在引导婴儿旅客入座后，提示家长抬放扶手要小心。

The armrest may crush your baby's finger. Please do be careful when you lift or put it down.

（3）为婴儿旅客主动提供婴儿安全带。

May I bring you an infant seatbelt? Your baby will feel more comfortable with it and it will be safer during an emergency.

（4）为其提供餐饮服务时，可以向旅客介绍餐食预订服务。

If you would like to, you may reserve a baby meal 24 hours before departure by dialing the hotline.

（5）如果执飞的是只提供小吃的国内短途航线，不为宝宝们提供任何水溶性食品，以防气道异物梗阻，同时也不建议家长在飞机上喂宝宝食用容易卡喉的食物。

Excuse me, Sir. We have prepared biscuits instead of cheese peanuts for your baby just in case of being choked. Meanwhile, for the safety, we don't advise you to offer water-insoluble food for your baby.

（6）家长需要协助冲泡，询问用量。How much warm water do you need？按照旅客需求冲泡，置于掌心来回摇动直到奶粉溶解，提示家长确认好温度再喂宝宝，以防烫伤。

（7）起飞下降过程中系好婴儿安全带。使用机载摇篮的注意事项：婴儿需出生已满14天，未满24个月，身高75厘米以内，体重11公斤（25磅）以内，所以要记得询问带婴儿的旅客其宝宝的年龄和身高体重。

Your baby needs to be seated on your lap during take-off and landing and fastened to your seatbelt with a special baby belt. I will go and get one for you and show you how it works.

2. Talk with pregnant passengers 机上与孕妇旅客交谈

（1）怀孕中 be pregnant/ be expecting a baby

How long have you been pregnant/ been expecting a baby?

（2）怀孕后期/临产 be heavily pregnant

It seems that you are heavily pregnant. I wonder if you have a certificate from a doctor to prove you are safe for an air trip.

（3）Morning sickness 指的就是"孕妇晨吐"，是孕妇怀孕初期的一种常见反应。当然并不是所有孕妇都在早晨孕吐，许多孕妇在下午或晚上 have pregnancy sickness（孕吐）。

She is spending a second day in hospital being treated for a morning sickness condition.

（4）孕妇需要定期做 prenatal screening（产前筛查）

尤其是 expectant mothers of older ages（高龄孕妇），随着肚子逐渐变大，有些孕妇发现自己的肚子上开始长出 stretch marks（妊娠纹），行动也日渐不便。在经历了十个月的艰辛后，孕妇还要面临 natural/ spontaneous delivery（自然分娩）和 cesarean section（剖宫产）两种选择。不过大多数孕妇的分娩日期都不是在 due date（预产期）那天，而是在那天前后。

（5）产子后产妇都会享有 maternity leave（产假），有时候，产妇的丈夫也能休 paternity leave，陪产假，也称作"父亲假"，就是男性在配偶产子后享受的假期。

（6）maternity leave 和 paternity leave 合称 parental leave（育婴假）。产妇在产后还可享受 breastfeeding breaks（哺乳假）。

3. Don't worry. How may I best assist you? (1) 为行动障碍旅客服务

（1）自我介绍：Hi, Mrs. Li. I am Lin, your flight attendant today. Welcome aboard! This is my partner, Tang. We will assist you to transfer from the aisle chair to your seat.

（2）询问病情，敏感或文化方面的问题：Before we start, may I ask whether we can touch your body during the process? Or whether there is any part we should pay extra attention to when we do the transferring?

（3）解释转移步骤：Let me explain the procedure for you. First, I will count 1, 2, 3 and then lift you a little bit to let you feel whether it is comfortable for you; and after that, I will count 1, 2, 3 again, then transfer you to your seat indeed. Is this procedure OK for you?

（4）询问旅客感受：Mrs. Li, how is it? Do you feel uncomfortable?

（5）将旅客转移到座位上之后，搭档乘务员就可以将轮椅推离，留下一名乘务员对旅客简单地做一下客舱设备及环境介绍：Mrs. Li, may I put down the armrest for you? And please fasten the seatbelt. Well, this is the call button. If you need anything or any help, please press this one. We will come here to assist you. This button is the reading light switch. The nearest lavatory is located at the front cabin, two rows in front of your seat. And the nearest exit is also in the front cabin, which is the door we just pass through, just behind the lavatory. Is there anything else you need right now?

4. Don't worry. How may I best assist you? (2) 为视力障碍旅客服务

（1）自我介绍：轻轻拍一下旅客的肩部，然后称呼旅客的名字：Mr. Smith, I'm Lin, the cabin crew today. I will lead you to your seat. Here is my elbow.

（2）直线行进：Mr. Smith, are you ready to go now? ... Is this speed OK for you? 根据旅客反馈做出调整。对环境做简单描述 There is no one in the cabin right now... We need to pass through the business class first, then reach the economy class. And your seat is 32C, in the second row of the economy class, which is an aisle seat at our right side.

（3）通过狭窄通道：此时需要与旅客纵列行走，并需告知旅客：Now we are going into the aisle, please stand behind me and grasp my wrist.

（4）换边：要告知旅客，需要换边。以旅客左手抓握手肘换到右手抓握为例：Mr. Smith, I need to change to your right side. Please don't move, I will move. And please take my left elbow.

（5）掉头往回走：告诉旅客要转弯，面对对方，旅客用空着的一只手抓住乘务员空着的手肘，然后放开刚才抓着的另一手肘。Mr. Smith, we are going to turn back. I will face to you , and please take my other elbow.

（6）上楼梯：在楼梯底部停下，告诉旅客将要上楼梯。Mr. Smith, now we need to go upstairs to get your boarding pass. 如果有楼梯扶手，让旅客站在扶手的一侧，并指导旅客握住扶手。The handrail is on your left, you may hold it. 然后，让旅客抬脚感受一下楼梯第一阶的高度，再开始往上走。You may feel the height of the first step, shall we go? Don't worry, just follow me, we are safe. Don't be afraid. Mr. Smith, this is the last step now.

（7）下楼梯：靠近楼梯时减慢速度，在楼梯顶部停下。Please slow down, Mr. Smith, we are now on the top of the stairs. Please move a little bit to find the edge of the first stair. Are you ready?

（8）路沿：如果前方有路沿或门槛，稍做停顿，让旅客感受一下，再一起迈过。There is a curb, you may feel the height of it, and we can go across together.

（9）入座：靠近座位中央，告诉旅客座位是正对还是背对着他：Mr. Smith, we have reached your seat 32C, and it is face to you. There are two more seats beside it. 然后用自己引路的手摸椅背，旅客可以顺着这条手臂摸到座椅，并确认座椅位置，感受座位边缘及检查座位。

（10）客舱设备及环境介绍：待旅客坐下后，也同样需要做客舱设备及环境介绍，介绍方式同前面的介绍一样。需要注意的是，千万不要介绍阅读灯和娱乐系统中电影之类的功能。

VI. Supplementary Reading

1. Special/ Incapable Passengers 特殊/ 限制性旅客

Special passengers not only include the passengers who need special courteous reception and protection during the flight, such as very important passengers, confidential traffic personnel, diplomats and secrecy passengers, also include the incapable passengers who need special assistance or need to comply with the transport condition, such as infants accompanied by adults, unaccompanied minors, pregnant women, disabled passengers, invalid passengers, inadmissible passengers, deportees and criminal suspects under escort, etc.

2. 4-Charactor code 四字代码

4-Charactor Code	Meaning	释义
BLND	Blind Passenger	视觉残疾的旅客
BSCT	Bassinet	婴儿摇篮服务
DEAF	Deaf Passenger	听觉残疾的旅客
DNPA	Disabled Passenger without Wheelchair	肢体残疾但无需轮椅的旅客
DPNA	Disabled Passenger Needs Assistance	智力残疾或精神残疾的旅客
INAD	Inadmissible Passenger	被拒绝入境旅客

4-Charactor Code	Meaning	释义
LEGL	Leg Damage-Left	左腿受损的旅客
LEGR	Leg Damage-Right	右腿受损的旅客
INFT	Infant	婴儿旅客
MEDA	Medical Case	伤病旅客
MAAS	Meet and Assist	需要引导和协助办理手续的旅客
PETC	Pet in Cabin	客舱运输服务犬
STCR	Stretcher	担架服务
UMNR	Unaccompanied Minor	无成人陪伴儿童
WCHC	Wheelchair-cabin seat	机上轮椅服务
WCHR	Wheelchair-ramp	地面轮椅服务
WCHS	Wheelchair-steps	登机轮椅服务

Ⅶ. Exercises

1. Could you list different types of special passengers?

(1)

(2)

(3)

(4)

2. Translate the following words and phrases into Chinese or English.

infant	婴儿摇篮
pregnant	婴儿车
adult	婴儿安全带
elderly	加长安全带
blind	无成人陪伴儿童
deaf	伤病旅客
disabled	轮椅旅客

3. Translate the following sentences into Chinese or English.

(1) Here is the infant seatbelt specially for your baby. Please allow me to show you how to use it.

(2) What's the baby's weight and height? Let me check whether the baby bassinet suitable for your baby or not.

(3) I'll keep your traveling documents and the ticket. When you disembark, I'll give them to the ground staff.

(4) Don't worry. How may I best assist you?

(5) 您可以去卫生间给婴儿换尿布。

(6) 我可以为您拿一条婴儿安全带吗？系上婴儿安全带，您的宝宝会更舒服。紧急情况下也会更安全。

(7) 飞机到达平飞高度后，我将为您安装婴儿摇篮。

4. Group work: choose one topic to start a conversation. (TIME LIMIT: 10 minutes)

(1) Explain the use of in-flight facilities to unaccompanied passengers.

(2) Look after the pregnant during international flights.

(3) Look after infants during international flights.

(4) Provide service for deaf passengers on board.

Civil Aviation

Task 9   Special Cases 特殊情况说明

Ⅰ. Warm-up Questions

1. Is it necessary to show all passengers the whole safety demonstration video before take-off?

2. During taxiing, what will you do if a passenger press the call button and ask for a glass of orange juice?

3. Why should flight attendants introduce emergency exits to the passengers involved specifically?

Ⅱ. Dialogues

Dialogue 1: The Emergency Exit Seat

Situation: Flight attendants point to the positions of all exits. A flight attendant may ask the passengers who are sitting next to an exit if they are confident and able enough to open the exit in an emergency.

音频扫一扫

Principle: The flight attendant should make sure that the passenger fully understand the situation and is willing to take the responsibility in case of an emergency.

Example

FA: Madam, you are sitting next to the emergency exit. Please allow me to introduce some necessary information to you.

PAX: Sure.

FA: This is the operating handle of the emergency exit. Under normal circumstances, please do not touch it and help us supervise. Don't let other passengers touch it. In case of an emergency, please obey the command of the crew as our aid to open the emergency exit door.

PAX: OK.

FA: Please read the *Safety Instruction* to know the emergency evacuation route and ways, and read the *Notice to Passengers in Exit Seats* carefully to know the relevant responsibilities. Do not put any luggage near the exit. Also please do not change seats at will. If you don't want to sit here, or cannot perform the duties for an emergency, please tell us. We will change the seat for you. Madam, do you get what I said? Would you like to sit in this position?

(If the passenger agrees...)

PAX: No problem.

FA: Thank you for your time. We will play the video of safety demonstration later. Please watch carefully, thank you.

(If the passenger doesn't want to sit here...)

PAX: Oh, I don't want to sit here.

FA: It doesn't matter. I will try to arrange another seat for you.

情景会话1：应急出口座位

乘务员：女士，您的座位在应急出口旁边。请让我给您介绍一些须知的内容。

旅客：你说吧。

乘务员：这是应急出口的操作手柄，正常情况下，请您不要触碰，并帮助我们监督其他旅客不触碰。在紧急情况下，请听从机组人员的指挥，协助我们打开应急出口门。

旅客：好。

乘务员：请您仔细阅读《安全须知》，知道紧急撤离的路线和方式。仔细阅读《出口座位须知》，知道相关的职责。出口附近不要放任何行李。也请您不要随意调换座位。如果您不愿意坐在这里，或是不能履行紧急情况时的职责，请您通知我们，我们会为您调换座位。女士，我所说的内容，您完全理解了吗？请问您愿意坐在这个位置吗？

（如果旅客同意……）

旅客：没问题。

乘务员：耽误您的时间了。稍后我们将播放安全演示的录像，请您认真观看，谢谢。

（如果旅客不愿意坐在应急出口座位……）

旅客：哦，我还是不坐这里了。

乘务员：没关系，我重新给您安排个座位。

音频扫一扫

Dialogue 2: Emergency Exit Qualification Confirmation

Situation: The flight attendant asks the passengers sitting next to emergency exits if they're willing to sit at their positions and instruct them.

Principle: The flight attendant should make sure that the passengers understand the situation completely and are willing to take the responsibilities in case of an emergency.

Example

FA: Excuse me, Sir. I am the flight attendant of this flight. You are sitting in the emergency exit seat. In normal situation, please do not touch this handle. In an emergency, would you like to help us by opening this exit door and help other passengers evacuate?

(If the passenger says yes)

PAX: Yes, I would like to.

FA: Thank you. The *Safety Instruction Card* is in the seat pocket in front of you. You can find the way to open the exit and other related information. Please read it carefully. If you have any questions, please contact us.

PAX: I will. Thank you.

FA: Sorry, Sir. Is this your bag?

PAX: Yes, it's mine.

FA: I am afraid you have to remove your bag away from the emergency exit as we require access to the exit at all times. Let me help you put it in the overhead compartment.

PAX: OK.

(If the passenger says no)

PAX: Sorry, I am afraid I don't want to do that.

FA: Never mind. If so, I have to find one who is willing and able to assist us. Then could you please change seats with others? Your cooperation will be appreciated.

情景会话2：应急出口座位确认

乘务员：您好，先生，我是本次航班的乘务员。您坐的是应急出口座位。在正常情况下，请勿触动出口手柄。在紧急情况下，您愿意协助我们打开应急出口门并帮助其他旅客撤离吗？

（如果旅客愿意）

旅客：好的，我愿意。

乘务员：谢谢您。《安全须知卡》在您前方座椅口袋里。您可以在上面找到打开出口门的方法和相关信息。请您仔细阅读，如有疑问，随时与我们联系。

旅客：我会的，谢谢。

乘务员：抱歉，先生，这是您的包吗？

旅客：对，是我的。

乘务员：抱歉，应急出口区域需要始终保持畅通，您需要将行李移开，我帮您放进行李架里，您看可以吗？

旅客：可以的。

（如果旅客不愿意）

旅客：不好意思，恐怕我做不了。

乘务员：没关系的。如果这样，我需要找位愿意的旅客协助我们，那么您能跟别的旅客换座位吗？谢谢您的配合。

Dialogue 3: Safety Demonstration

Situation: Generally, flight attendants show the safety demonstration before take-off. The safety demonstration includes the use of oxygen masks, seatbelts, life vests and emergency exits in emergency situations.

Principle: Flight attendants should remind passengers of watching the safety demonstration.

Example

音频扫一扫

PS: (Announcement) Ladies and gentlemen, our flight attendants will demonstrate the use of the life vest, oxygen mask and seatbelts, and show you the locations of emergency exits.

(1) Your life vest is located in the pocket under your seat. Take it out as necessary. Slip the life vest over your head. Bring the waist strap around your waist. Fasten the buckle and tighten it by pulling it outwards. To inflate your life vest, pull firmly on the red cord, only when leaving the aircraft. To inflate further, blow into these mouthpieces.

(2) Your oxygen mask is located in a compartment above your seat. It will drop automatically in case of decompression. Pull the mask down sharply to activate the flow of oxygen. Place the mask over your nose and mouth. Pull the elastic strap over your head and tighten it by pulling the end of the strap. In a few seconds, the oxygen will begin to flow.

(3) Your seatbelt contains two pieces. To fasten the belt, slip one piece into the buckle and tighten them. Please keep your seatbelt securely fastened when seated.

(4) There are 8 emergency exits on this aircraft. They are located in the front, the rear and the middle of the main cabin (and on the upper deck). Please do not touch the emergency operating handles unless specifically instructed by our crew members in emergency situations.

(5) The emergency indication lights are located along the aisle and at the exits. In the unlikely event of an evacuation, please follow the emergency indication lights to the nearest exit, and do not carry any hand luggage with you.

(6) The safety instruction card is located in your seat pocket. Please read it carefully. Thank you!

PAX: Excuse me, Miss? Where is the nearest exit to me?

FA: As you can see, your seat number is 15J and it is in the middle of the cabin. That means the nearest exit to you is the emergency exit on your right.

情景会话3：安全演示

乘务长：（广播）女士们、先生们，你们好！我们的客舱乘务员将向您介绍救生衣、氧气面罩和安全带的使用方法以及应急出口的位置。

（1）救生衣在您座椅下面的口袋里，需要时取出，经头部穿好。将带子从后向前绕在腰上，扣好带扣，向外用力拉紧。拉开充气阀门充气，但在客舱内不要充气。充气不足时，用嘴向人工充气管里吹气。

（2）氧气面罩储藏在您座椅上方，发生紧急情况时面罩会自动脱落。氧气面罩脱落后，请用力向下拉面罩。将面罩罩在口鼻处，把带子套在头上，几秒后，就会有氧气逸出。

（3）在您座椅上有两条可以对扣起来的安全带，将带子插进带扣，然后拉紧。当您就座时，请系好安全带。

（4）本架飞机共有8个应急出口，分别位于前部、后部、中部（及上舱），除非紧急情况下，有我们的机组人员专门指导，否则请不要随意拉动应急出口手柄。

（5）客舱通道及出口处有应急照明指示灯，在应急撤离时请按照应急指示灯的指示从最近的出口撤离，撤离时禁止携带任何行李。

（6）在您座椅口袋里备有安全须知卡，请仔细阅读。谢谢！

旅客：你好，请问离我最近的出口在哪里？

乘务员：正如您所见，您的座位号码是15排J座，位于客舱中部，这表示离您最近的出口是您右侧的应急出口。

Dialogue 4: Life Vests

Situation: Sometimes aircraft have to fly over large areas of water. Therefore, life vests and the emergency life raft is necessary. Upon ditching or similar situations, everyone needs to wear a life vest before getting on the raft.

Principle: Flight attendants should remind passengers not to inflate the adult life vests inside the cabin.

Example (A passenger pressed the call button.)

FA: May I help you, Madam?

PAX: Where can I find a life vest for my baby?

FA: Please remain seated and keep your seatbelt fastened. I'll take the life vest from the locker for you. Here it is.

PAX: Thank you. And where's mine?

FA: It's under your seat.

PAX: OK. (The passenger tries to unfold and inflate the life vest...)

FA: Please don't inflate it inside the cabin.

PAX: Oh, I see.

FA: Thank you for your cooperation. Pull the tab down as soon as you are out of the cabin in case of ditching.

PAX: Got it.

情景会话4：救生衣

（客舱中一位旅客按了呼唤铃。）

音频扫一扫

民航空乘英语实用口语教程　第三版

乘务员：您好，女士，请问需要帮忙吗？

旅客：我在哪儿能给我宝宝找到婴儿救生衣呢？

乘务员：请您在原位坐好并系好安全带。我马上去柜子里给您拿。给您。

旅客：谢谢。那我的救生衣在哪儿？

乘务员：在您的座位底下。

旅客：好的。（旅客试图展开救生衣并充气……）

乘务员：请您不要在客舱内充气。

旅客：好吧，我知道了。

乘务员：谢谢您的配合。水上迫降时，需要穿救生衣，一离开客舱拉下这个扣环，救生衣就立刻充气了。

旅客：明白了！

Dialogue 5: Could you please return to your original seat?

音频扫一扫

Situation: During the safety check, a flight attendant finds that some passengers changed their seats.

Principle: The flight attendant should communicate with those passengers. Due to the need of maintaining the balance, passengers should be seated in accordance with the boarding pass to prevent the imbalance and avoid accidents.

Example

PS: (Announcement) Ladies and gentlemen, in order to keep the aircraft in balance, please stay in your original seats. Thank you for your cooperation!

FA: Excuse me, Sir. Could you please return to your original seat?

PAX: My seat is in the middle of the cabin. But I've got a headache. I really need a seat by the window and have a good sleep. Would it be possible for me to sit here?

FA: I see. But for the safety's reason, you should be seated in the assigned seat.

PAX: I don't understand. Can you explain it to me?

FA: OK. The plane should be kept proper weight and balance when it takes off.

PAX: Well. I'll go back to my seat.

FA: You may return to this seat after we reaching the cruising altitude.

情景会话5：请您回到原位坐好。

乘务长：（广播）女士们、先生们，为了保持飞机配载平衡，请您在原位坐好，谢谢合作！

乘务员：打扰一下，先生，请您回到原位坐好。

旅客：我的座位在客舱中部，但是我头疼，非常需要一个靠窗的座位，好好睡一觉。我能坐在这里吗？

乘务员：我理解。但是为了确保安全，您应坐在指定的座位。

旅客：我不明白，能给我解释一下吗？

乘务员：好的，飞机起飞时需要保持配载平衡。

旅客：好吧，那我回原来的座位吧。

乘务员：您可以在飞机平飞后回到这个座位上休息。

Dialogue 6: This is a non-smoking flight.

音频扫一扫

Situation: In accordance with the *Security Administration Punishment Act of the People's Republic of China* and *Regulation on the Security of China Civil Aviation*, passengers may be subject to penalty, security detention or even criminal punishment if they have the following behaviors: damaging on-board facilities and equipment, smoking and so on.

Principle: Flight attendants should explain the regulations patiently to passengers if they couldn't understand.

Example

SF: (Announcement) Ladies and gentlemen, may I have your attention please! I am the safety officer of this flight. According to the requirements of Civil Aviation Administration of China, I am reminding you to pay special attention to cabin security. In accordance with the *Security Administration Punishment Act of the People's Republic of China* and *Regulation on the Security of China Civil Aviation*, you may be subject to penalty, security detention or even criminal punishment if you have the following behaviors: damaging on-board facilities and equipment, smoking, using the mobile phone or other electronic equipment, grabbing seats or luggage racks, interfering with flight attendants' work and other behaviors that disturb the normal order of the cabin. In accordance with relevant laws and regulations of People's Republic of China, the passenger cabin, as a public space, subjects to audio and video collection. Your support and cooperation is greatly appreciated. We will try our best to ensure your safety, please cooperate with us. Thank you!

FA: Excuse me, Sir. Please put out your cigarette immediately. Smoking is not allowed here.

PAX: Okay. By the way, is there any smoking section on board?

FA: No, there isn't, because smoking is forbidden on all flights according to the airline's regulations. After take-off, we can offer you some snacks.

PAX: Erm... I should have tried some cigarettes before boarding.

FA: By the way, may we remind you that this is a non-smoking flight and smoking is not allowed in the lavatories, either, including e-cigarettes.

PAX: Oh...Vaping is also prohibited? I see.

FA: Thank you for your cooperation.

情景会话6：本次航班全程禁烟

安全员：（广播）女士们、先生们，大家好！我是本次航班的安全员。根据中国民用航空局的统一要求，提醒各位旅客注意客舱安全。根据《中华人民共和国治安管理处罚法》和《中华人民共和国民用航空安全保卫条例》的有关规定，损坏机上设施设备、吸烟、使用手机和其他电子设备、抢占座位和行李架、干扰乘务组正常工作等扰乱客舱秩序的行为将会被处以罚款、治安拘留等处罚，严重者会被追究刑事责任。同时，依据国家相关法律规定，飞机客舱为音视频采集公共区域。请您支持配合。为了您和本次航班全体旅客的安全，我和我的组员及全体机组成员将认真履行安全职责，请您配合！谢谢！

乘务员：先生，您好，请您将烟立刻灭掉。这里不允许吸烟。

旅客：好吧，那问一下，飞机上有吸烟区吗？

乘务员：飞机上没有吸烟区，根据航空公司的规定，所有航班上都禁止吸烟。起飞后，我们可以为您提供小吃解乏。

旅客：呃……我本该在登机前抽些烟。

乘务员：在这里再提醒您一下，本次航班全程禁烟，在卫生间里也不允许吸烟，包括电子烟。

旅客：噢……电子烟也不行啊。明白了。

乘务员：谢谢您的配合。

Ⅲ. Popular Words and Phrases

CAAC（Civil Aviation Administration of China） 中国民用航空局

inspection [ɪnˈspekʃn] *n.* 检查

safety inspection/ check 安全检查

Flight/ Airplane Mode (function) 飞行模式

set on 开启，设置

laptop [ˈlæptɑp] 便携式电脑

lithium battery [ˈlɪθiəm ˈbætəri] 锂电池

turn/ switch off 关掉（开关）；切断（电源）

electronic device 电子设备

mobile phone/ cell phone 移动电话；手机

portable [ˈpɔːrtəbl] *adj.* 轻便的；手提的

electronic [ɪˌlɛkˈtrɑnɪk] *adj.* 电子的

device [dɪˈvaɪs] *n.* 装置，设备

power [ˈpaʊə] *v.* 供以动力

ensure [ɪnˈʃʊr] *v.* 确保

mobile [ˈməʊbaɪl] *adj.* 可移动的

switch [swɪtʃ] *v.* 转换；*n.* 开关

mode [məʊd] *n.* 方式，风格，模式

set...mode 设置……的模式

prohibit [prəˈhɪbɪt] *v.* 禁止，阻止

Intranet [ˈɪntrənet] *n.* 内联网，局域网

charge [tʃɑrdʒ] *v.* 使充电

socket [ˈsɑkɪt] *n.* 插座；灯座

taxi [ˈtæksɪ] *v.* 滑行

distribute [dɪˈstrɪbjuːt] *v.* 发放

initial [ɪˈnɪʃl] *adj.* 初始的，原始的

upright [ˈʌpraɪt] *adj.* 垂直的

position [pəˈzɪʃn] *n.* 位置

fasten [ˈfæsn] *v.* 使固定；扣紧

indicate [ˈɪndɪkeɪt] *v.* 指出

lock [lɔk] *v.* 锁上

proper [ˈprɔpə] *adj.* 适当的

patience [ˈpeʃəns] *n.* 耐心，耐性

demonstrate [ˈdɛmənˌstret] *v.* 证明，演示，说明

specifically [spəˈsɪfɪkli] *adv.* 明确地

modify [ˈmɒdɪfaɪ] *v.* 修改

overhead locker/ compartment 头顶上方的行李架

window shade/ blind 遮光板

stow [stəʊ] *v.* 装载、收藏

seat back 椅背

adjust [əˈdʒʌst] *v.* 调节

critical [ˈkrɪtɪkl; ˈkrɪtɪkəl] *adj.* 关键的，至关重要的

forbidden	[fə'bɪd(ə)n]	*adj.* 禁止的
potential	[pə'tenʃl]	*adj.* 潜在的
no smoking sign		禁止吸烟标志
navigation	[ˌnævɪ'geɪʃən]	*n.* 导航，航行
communication	[kəˌmjunɪ'keɪʃən]	*n.* 交流，通讯
interrupt	[ˌɪntə'rʌpt]	*v.* 打断（别人的话等）；阻止
interfere	[ˌɪntə'fɪə(r)]	*v.* 妨碍，阻扰，干涉
signal	['sɪgnəl]	*n.* 信号
condition	[kən'dɪʃən]	*n.* 状态；环境

IV. Practical Expressions

1. Excuse me, the seat you are taking is in the emergency exit area. Please don't touch the red handle. And read the instruction carefully, for we might need your help in case of an emergency. Thank you!

您好，您坐的是应急出口的位置，请您仔细阅读《出口座位须知卡》，不要触碰红色手柄。在紧急情况下，请您协助我们的工作。谢谢！

2. Excuse me, Sir, the seat you are taking today is the emergency exit seat on this aircraft. Please do not touch the operating handle in normal situations. Here is the *Emergency Exit Safety Instruction Card*. Could you please read it carefully? If you have any questions, please let us know. Thank you!

先生，您好，您乘坐的是本架飞机上应急出口的座位，这是《出口座位须知卡》请您仔细阅读，正常情况下请勿触动操作柄，如有疑问，请及时和我们联系，谢谢！

3. Excuse me, Madam. You are sitting in the emergency exit seat. Please allow me to introduce the precautions of emergency exits.

女士，您好！您现在就座的是应急出口的座位，请允许我为您介绍一下应急出口的注意事项。

4. This is the operating handle of the emergency exit. Under normal circumstances, please do not touch it and help us supervise not let other passengers touch it. In case of an emergency, please obey the crew's command as our aid to open the emergency exit door.

这是应急出口的操作手柄，正常情况下，请您不要触碰，并帮助我们监督，不要让其他旅客触碰；在紧急情况下，请听从机组人员指挥，协助我们打开应急出口门。

5. Please open the cover plate and then open the door by pulling down the handle; when evacuate on to the ground, please direct passengers to sit towards the aircraft tail and slide off the plane, get away from the plane quickly. To be safe, please remind passengers not to jump down from the aircraft.

请您打开盖板，向下拉动手柄就可以打开此出口；陆地撤离时，请您指挥旅客从这里出去，沿机翼上的箭头向机尾方向坐滑下机，并快速远离飞机。为了避免受伤，请注意提示旅客不要跳下飞机。

6. Please read the emergency evacuation route and ways in the *Safety Instruction*, as well as the relevant responsibilities in the *Notice to Passengers in Exit Seats* carefully.

请您仔细阅读《安全须知》中紧急撤离时的路线和方式，及《出口座位须知》中的相关职责。

7. Please do not put any luggage near the exit. And please do not change seats randomly.
请不要在出口附近放任何行李，也请您不要随意调换座位。

8. If you don't want to sit here, or can not perform the duties for an emergency, please tell us. We will change the seat for you.

如果您不愿意坐在这里，或是不能履行紧急情况时的职责，请您告知我们，我们会为您调换座位。

9. Madam, do you get what I said? Would you like to sit in this seat?

女士，我所说的内容，您都理解吗？请问您愿意坐这个座位吗？

V. Tips

Expressions in terms of introducing emergency exits 应急出口介绍用语

Excuse me, Sir/ Madam. You are sitting in the emergency exit seat; please allow me to introduce the precautions of emergency exits. This is the emergency exit. Please read the instruction carefully and do not hesitate to ask me if you have any questions. Do not put any luggage near the exit and do not touch the red handle. Also please do not change seats at will. If you don't want to sit here, or can not perform the duties for an emergency, please tell us. We will change the seat for you. Sir/ Madam, do you get what I said? Would you like to sit here?

VI. Supplementary Reading

The Emergency Exit 应急出口

An emergency exit in a structure is a special exit for emergencies such as a fire: the combined use of regular and special exits allows for faster evacuation, while it also provides an alternative if the route to the regular exit is blocked by fire, etc.

In aircraft terms, an "exit" is any one of the main doors (entry doors on the port side of the aircraft and service doors on the starboard side) and an "emergency exit" is defined as a door that is only ever used in an emergency (such as over-wing exits and permanently armed exits). The number and type of exits on an aircraft is regulated through strict rules within the industry, and is based on whether the aircraft is single or twin-aisled; the maximum passenger load; and the maximum distance from a seat to an exit. The majority of aircraft has 2 passenger doors on the left of the cabin and 2 service doors on the right side of the cabin and a minimum of 2 over-wing emergency exits. But the larger the aircraft is, the more exits it will have.

Passengers seated in exit rows may be called upon to assist and open exits in the event of an emergency. Emergency exit seat is the seat from which passengers can reach the exit door directly without walk around obstacles and each seat in rows, passengers must pass from the nearest aisles to emergency exits (the emergency exit window seat cannot incline).

VII. Exercises

1. Answer the following questions according to the dialogues.

(1) How to confirm the qualifications of the passengers at emergency exits?

(2) Where can passengers find their life vests on board?

(3) Is there any smoking section on board?

2. Translate the following words and phrases into Chinese or English.

安全检查	mode
飞行模式	electronic device
锂电池	upright

轻便的，手提的	fasten
转换（v.）；开关（n.）	indicate
信号	demonstrate
禁止，阻止	forbidden

3. Translate the following sentences into Chinese or English.

(1) 您好，您坐的是应急出口的座位，请您仔细阅读《出口座位须知卡》，不要触碰红色手柄。在紧急情况下，请您协助我们的工作。谢谢合作！

(2) 如果您不愿意坐在这里，或是不能履行紧急情况时的职责，请您告知我们，我们会为您调换座位。

(3) Please read the emergency evacuation route and ways in the *Safety Instruction* as well as the relevant responsibilities in the *Notice to Passengers in Exit Seats* carefully.

(4) Please do not put any luggage near the exit. And please do not change seats randomly.

(5) Madam, do you get what I said? Would you like to sit in this seat?

4. Group work: choose one topic to conduct the dialogue. (TIME LIMIT: 15 minutes)

(1) Emergency exit qualification confirmation

(2) Safety demonstration

(3) The use of life vests

Task 10　Cabin Safety Check 客舱安全检查

Ⅰ. Warm-up Questions

1. What's the content of safety check in the cabin?

2. What are the principles of safety check before taking off？

3. What will you say when you are conducting safety check while a passenger is constantly making phone calls?

4. How to make sure that the whole cabin is ready for taking off？

5. Why must passengers keep their seat-backs to the upright position during the critical period？

Ⅱ. Dialogues

音频扫一扫

Dialogue 1: You may use your cellphone during this flight (1)

Situation: Before taking off, flight attendants should conduct safety check. With the rapid development of the society, many airlines allow passengers to use cellphones in flying mode during flights.

Principle: Flight attendants should be patient and conscientious when explaining the policy.

Example

PAX：Excuse me, Miss. Can I use my cellphone during this flight？

FA：Sure. Our airline is one of the first several companies which allow passengers to use their mobile phones on board. But please do set your mobile phone on airplane mode.

PAX：Sounds great. By the way, is there a Wi-Fi system on board？

民航空乘英语实用口语教程　第三版

FA: Yes, we have it. You may use your personal information to connect the Wi-Fi on your mobile phone. If you don't mind, I can connect it for you.

PAX: I really appreciate it.

FA: It's my pleasure.

情景会话1：您可以在今天的航班上使用手机（1）

旅客：你好，请问我可以在今天的航班上使用手机吗？

乘务员：当然可以了。我们公司是国内几家首批允许旅客在航班中使用手机的航空公司之一。但是，您需要将手机调至飞行模式。

旅客：那太好了。那请问今天的飞机上有无线网络吗？

乘务员：是的，我们有机上无线网络。您可以在手机上用您的个人信息登录机上无线网。如果您不介意的话，我可以为您连接。

旅客：那再好不过了，非常感谢。

乘务员：不客气。

Dialogue 2: You may use your cellphone during this flight (2)

Situation: Before taking off, flight attendants should conduct safety check. Many Chinese airlines allow passengers to use cellphones in flying mode during flights.

Principle: Flight attendants should be patient and conscientious when explaining the policy.

Example

PAX: Excuse me, Miss, may I use my cellphone on board?

FA: Yes, Sir, you can use your cellphone on board, but please don't forget to switch your cellphone to the flight mode.

PAX: Miss, do you have free Wi-Fi on board?

FA: Sorry, Sir, we don't have Wi-Fi on board because of the aircraft type limitation.

PAX: OK.

FA: Sir, would you please remove your earphones? We will take off soon.

PAX: This is my cellphone, and I have turned it into flight mode.

FA: I see, Sir, during take-off and landing, for the safety reason, please remove the earphones that you can hear the instructions of the cabin crew and evacuate without hindrance while in an emergency.

音频扫一扫

情景会话2：您可以在今天的航班上使用手机（2）

旅客：您好，我可以在飞机上使用手机吗？

乘务员：是的，先生，您可以在飞机上使用手机，但请别忘了将手机调到飞行模式。

旅客：请问飞机上有免费的无线网络吗？

乘务员：对不起，先生，由于执飞机型的限制，我们的航班目前没有无线网络。

旅客：好吧。

乘务员：先生，飞机马上起飞了，请您取下耳机。

旅客：这是我的手机，我已经调到飞行模式了。

乘务员：我知道，先生，在飞机起飞和下降过程中，出于安全考虑，您需要取下耳机以确保在紧急情况下能够清楚听到机组人员发出的指令并在没有阻碍物的情况下迅速撤离。

Dialogue 3: Please switch off your cellphone

Situation: Before taking off, flight attendants should play the safety demonstration video and conduct safety check.

音频扫一扫

Principle: Flight attendants should be patient and conscientious.

Example

FA: Excuse me, Sir. I'm afraid you should turn off your cellphone. We are going to take off soon.

PAX: Why? My mobile phone is in flight-mode.

FA: Because flight-mode is also against the regulation of CAAC. I'm afraid the mobile phone must be turned off during the whole flight.

PAX: It is said that passengers can use cellphones during domestic flights and I watched the news several days ago.

FA: It is right only to some degree. However, our company hasn't got the document so far and the news you mentioned was the right that leaves to airline companies to decide.

PAX: Oh, I see. I will use my laptop to do some work.

FA: Sorry, Sir. Electronic devices can only be used when we reach the cruising altitude. Thank you for your understanding.

PAX: Fine. Thanks for reminding me.

FA: Thanks for your cooperation.

情景会话3：请关掉您的手机电源

乘务员：打扰一下，先生。请您关掉手机。我们马上就要起飞了。

旅客：为什么？我的手机是处于飞行模式的。

乘务员：因为飞行模式同样违反了民航局的规定。手机必须全程关机。

旅客：据说现在国内航班上旅客是可以使用手机的，而且我前些天也看到了相关的新闻报道。

乘务员：某些程度上是这样的。但是，到目前为止我们还没有收到上级文件指示，并且您提到的新闻中说的是现在把这个权力交给航空公司来评估。

旅客：哦，明白了。那我将用笔记本处理一些工作。

乘务员：抱歉，先生。电子设备需要在我们达到平飞高度之后才可以使用。感谢您的理解。

旅客：好的。谢谢提醒。

乘务员：谢谢您的合作。

Dialogue 4: Out of power

Situation: Lithium power bank can't be used during the whole flight. If a passenger would like to use power bank, flight attendants can provide possible solutions instead.

Principle: Flight attendants should be patient and conscientious.

Example

FA: Excuse me, Madam. Could you please turn off your power bank? It's prohibited during the whole flight. Thanks.

PAX: I know. But my mobile phone is out of power. I have to contact with my friend after landing.

FA: There is a socket under your seat/ in the first class. If you don't mind, you may charge your phone there after 20 minutes taking off.

PAX: Great. Thank you.

FA: You're always most welcome.

情景会话4：手机没电了

乘务员：打扰下，女士，请您关掉充电宝。充电宝全程禁止使用。谢谢。

旅客：我知道。但是我的手机没电了。落地后我还要跟我的朋友联系呢。

音频扫一扫

乘务员：在您的座椅下方/头等舱里有充电插座。如果您不介意的话，飞机起飞20分钟后，可以在那里充电。

旅客：太好了。谢谢你。

乘务员：不客气。

Dialogue 5: Safety Check: Please return your seat back to the upright position

音频扫一扫

Situation: While cabin doors have been closed, one of the safety announcements is made by the purser.

Principle: At the same time, flight attendants will start safety check.

Example

PS: (Announcement) Ladies and gentlemen, please make sure your seat backs and tray tables are in their full upright position and that your seatbelt is correctly fastened. Also, your portable electronic devices must be set on "airplane" mode until an announcement is made upon arrival. Thank you!

FA: Excuse me, Madam, would you please put your seat back to the upright position? Our plane is about to take off.

PAX: I'm fine. I feel comfortable this way.

FA: But it's not safe for you.

PAX: Why? I can't understand.

FA: Madam, take-off is a very critical period. If you don't put your seatback to the upright position, you may easily get hurt by the powerful impact in case of an emergency. It'll also block the way of the passengers behind you to escape from the aircraft quickly.

PAX: Oh, I see. I'll do it right now. Thank you for reminding me.

FA: You're welcome. Please also keep your seat belt securely fastened.

情景会话5：安全检查：请您将座椅靠背调直

乘务长：（广播）女士们，先生们，请确认调直座椅靠背、收起小桌板，确认您的安全带扣好系紧。请确保您的手机处于"飞行"模式直到落地广播。谢谢！

乘务员：打扰了，女士。请您将座椅靠背调直。我们很快就要起飞了。

旅客：我这样挺舒服的。

乘务员：但是，这样是不安全的。

旅客：为什么？我不理解。

乘务员：女士，起飞是飞行的关键阶段。如果不将座椅靠背调直的话，一旦发生紧急情况，您可能很容易在强烈冲撞下受伤，而且这也挡住了您后排旅客的逃生通道。

旅客：哦，我知道了。我现在就调。感谢你提醒了我。

乘务员：不客气。还请您系好安全带。

Dialogue 6: Safety Check: Please don't put any luggage in the emergency exit area

音频扫一扫

Situation: In terms of safety check, a flight attendant finds that a passenger put her luggage at the emergency exit area.

Principle: The emergency exit area should be clear of luggage. The flight attendant should explain patiently when communicating with the passenger.

Example

FA: Excuse me, Madam? Would you mind putting your luggage in the overhead bin because it's the emergency exit?

PAX: Can I put it under the seat in front of me?

FA: I'm sorry. You can't. If you put your luggage around this area, it will be an obstacle. In case of an emergency, it will block the way of the passengers behind to evacuate from the aircraft quickly.

PAX: Well, fine.

FA: Thank you for your cooperation.

情景会话6：安全检查：请勿在应急出口处放行李

乘务员：女士，您好，可以将您的行李放在行李架上吗？因为这里是应急出口。

旅客：我能把它放在前面座椅底下吗？

乘务员：抱歉，不可以的。如果您把行李放在此区域，在紧急情况下，它就成了障碍物，阻挡了后面旅客快速撤离。

旅客：那好吧。

乘务员：谢谢您的合作。

音频扫一扫

Dialogue 7: May I take your glass and snack bowl away?

Situation: In first and business class, passengers will be served welcome drinks and snacks. Before finishing safety check, flight attendants usually take the items away and secure tray tables for passengers.

Principle: A flight attendant should ask the passengers before taking the items away.

Example

FA: Excuse me, Sir, we are going to take off. May I take your glass and snack bowl away?

PAX: Sure, thank you.

FA: My pleasure. Would you like something to drink after take-off?

PAX: Champagne, thanks.

FA: Sure, it's my pleasure.

情景会话7：可以为您收一下水杯和小吃碗吗？

乘务员：打扰了，先生，飞机马上就要起飞了，我为您把水杯和小吃碗收走，好吗？

旅客：好的，谢谢。

乘务员：不客气。起飞后您想喝点儿什么？

旅客：香槟，谢谢。

乘务员：好的，不客气。

音频扫一扫

Dialogue 8: During Taxiing

Situation: During taxiing, a passenger would like to use the lavatory.

Principle: Flight attendants should explain patiently and let the passenger stay in the seat.

Example

FA: Excuse me, Sir? Please stay in your seat.

PAX: I just want to use the lavatory.

FA: As we are taxiing, it's dangerous to use the lavatory. Could you please remain seated until we get to the cruising level?

PAX: Okay... How long do I have to wait?

FA: Usually after 20 minutes taking off.

情景会话8：飞机滑行期间

乘务员：先生，请您在原位坐好。

旅客：我就想用下洗手间。

乘务员：飞机正在滑行，这时候使用卫生间是非常危险的。请您在飞机平飞之后再使用好吗？

旅客：好吧……那我还要等多久呀？

乘务员：通常起飞后二十分钟的样子。

Ⅲ. Popular Words and Phrases

Safety Instruction		《安全须知》
play the video		播放录像
demonstrate	['demənstreɪt]	*v.* 示范，演示
demonstration	[ˌdemən'streɪʃn]	*n.* 示范，演示
safety demonstration		安全演示
Safety Demonstration Kit		安全演示包
life vest		救生衣
oxygen mask		氧气面罩
slide	[slaɪd]	*n.* 滑梯
Emergency Light Switch		应急灯开关
engine	['endʒɪn]	*n.* 发动机
Emergency Exit		紧急出口
precaution	[prɪ'kɔːʃn]	*n.* 预防措施，注意事项
caution	['kɔːʃn]	*n.* 小心，谨慎
operating handle		操作手柄
operate	['ɒpəreɪt]	*v.* 操作，操纵
circumstance	['sɜːkəmstəns]	*n.* 情况，情形
under normal circumstance		在通常情况下
supervise	['sjuːpəvaɪz]	*v.* 监督，监控
supervisor	['sjuːpəvaɪzə(r)]	*n.* 督导，监督者，管理者
in case of		在……情况下
in case of an emergency		在紧急情况下
obey	[ə'beɪ]	*v.* 服从，遵守
aid	[eɪd]	*v.* 帮助，援助
cover	['kʌvə(r)]	*v.* 遮盖，覆盖；*n.* 封面，盖子
plate	[pleɪt]	*n.* 牌子，盖板
direct	[də'rekt]	*v.* 指导，引导
relevant	['reləvənt]	*adj.* 有关的，切题的
Notice to Passengers in Exit Seats		《出口座位须知》
at will		随意，任意
perform	[pə'fɔːm]	*v.* 执行，履行
be willing to do		愿意做某事
nose	[nəʊz]	*n.* 鼻子；机头
tail	[teɪl]	*n.* 尾巴；尾翼
wing	[wɪŋ]	*n.* 翅膀；机翼

ambulance	['æmbjʊləns]	*n.* 救护车
bandage	['bændɪdʒ]	*n.* 绷带
megaphone	['megəfəʊn]	*n.* 扩音器
life raft		救生筏

Ⅳ. Practical Expressions

1. We will conduct safety demonstration later. Please watch carefully, thank you!

稍后，我们将做安全演示，请认真观看，谢谢！

2. Excuse me, Sir. We are going to play the safety instruction video. For your safety, please pay attention to it.

打扰您了，先生。我们将为您播放安全须知录像，为了您的安全，请您注意观看！

/ We are playing the safety instruction video. Please pay attention to it.

我们正在播放安全须知录像，请您注意观看！

3. We're taking off soon. For your safety, please open the window shade.

飞机马上要起飞了，为了您的安全，请把遮光板打开。

4. Would you please fasten your seat belt, stow your tray table, return your seat back to the upright position and pull up the window shade?

请您系好安全带，收起小桌板，调直座椅靠背，打开遮光板。

5. Excuse me, could you please fasten your seatbelts and put your seat back upright?

打扰一下，请您系好安全带并调直座椅靠背。

/ Please fasten your seatbelts and adjust your seat back to the upright position.

请系好安全带，将座椅靠背调直。

6. We are taking off soon, please return your seat back to the upright position and secure your table and footrest.

请您调直座椅靠背；收起小桌板；把脚踏板收起，我们的飞机马上就要起飞了。

7. We will take off shortly. Please stow your footrest. Thank you for your cooperation!

我们的飞机马上就要起飞了，请您收起脚踏板。 谢谢您的合作！

8. Please stow your footrest and the video screen.

请您收起脚踏板和娱乐小屏幕。

9. The aircraft is taking off immediately, may I help you store your personal video?

飞机马上要起飞了，我帮您把小屏幕收起来，好吗？

/ May I help you stow your personal video?

我可以帮您把小屏幕收起来吗？

10. The take-off period is critical. If you don't put your seat back to the upright position, in case of an emergency, you may easily get hurt by the powerful impact. It'll also block the way for the passengers behind you to escape from the aircraft quickly.

起飞是飞行的关键阶段。如果不将座椅靠背调直的话，一旦发生紧急情况，您很容易在强烈冲撞下受伤，同时椅背也挡住了您后排旅客的逃生通道，使他们不能很快从飞机上逃生。

11. Would you please switch off your mobile phone/ electronic device/ portable charging device?

请您关掉手机电源/电子设备/充电宝。

12. Sir, our plane is taxiing. I understand that this call may be very important. But for flight safety, please switch your cellphone off.

先生，飞机正在滑行，我知道这个电话可能对您非常重要。但是为了飞行安全，请关掉您的手机电源。

/ Excuse me, Sir, our plane is taxiing now. Could you please switch off your mobile phone at all times?

打扰一下，先生，我们的飞机正在滑行，请您全程关掉您的手机电源。

13. Flight-mode is also against the regulation of CAAC (Civil Aviation Administration of China). I'm afraid the mobile phone must be turned off during the whole flight.

飞行模式同样违反了民航局的规定。手机必须全程关机。

14. Our airline is one of the first several companies which allow passengers to use their mobile phones on board. But please do set your mobile phone on airplane mode.

我们公司是国内几家首批允许旅客在航班中使用手机的航空公司之一。但是，您需要将手机调至飞行模式。

15. During take-off and landing, for the safety reason, please remove the earphones that you can hear the instructions of the cabin crew and evacuate without hindrance while in an emergency.

在飞机起飞和下降过程中，出于安全考虑，您需要取下耳机以确保在紧急情况下能够清楚听到机组人员发出的指令并在没有阻碍物的情况下迅速撤离。

16. There are some differences on the regulation among countries.

每个国家的规定会有一些区别。

17. Electronic devices can only be used when we reach the cruising altitude.

电子设备需要在我们达到平飞高度之后才可以使用。

18. I'm afraid smoking is not permitted during the whole flight.

飞机上全程禁止吸烟。

19. As we are going to take off, may I take your cup and snack bowl away?

我们的飞机马上就要起飞了，我可以为您收一下水杯和小吃碗吗？

20. The aircraft will take off soon. May I take it away? I'll serve you another after take-off.

飞机马上要起飞了，我可以将它拿走吗？起飞后我再给您送一杯。

21. We will offer you the beverages and meals soon after take-off.

起飞之后会很快给您提供餐饮。

22. Please stay in your seat and keep your seat belt fastened until the sign has been turned off. The plane is about to take off. Please don't walk around in the cabin.

飞机马上要起飞了，请不要在客舱内走动。请在安全带信号灯关闭前坐在座位上，系好安全带。

23. Sir/ Madam, the plane is taking off. For your safety, please return to your seat and fasten your seat belt.

先生/女士，我们的飞机马上就要起飞了，为了您的安全，请您马上回到座位上坐好，并系好安全带。

/ The plane is still taxiing. For your safety, could you please remain seated with your seatbelt fastened?

飞机正在滑行，为了您的安全，请您在座位上坐好并系好安全带。

24. Excuse me. Would you please return to your seat? We are taking off soon, and the lavatory has been suspended.

对不起，请回到座位上，飞机马上起飞，卫生间暂时停用。

25. As we are taking off shortly, it's dangerous to use the lavatory now. Could you please remain seated until we get to the cruising level?

飞机马上要起飞了，这时候使用卫生间是非常危险的。请您在飞机平飞之后再使用好吗？

26. Excuse me, this is the crew seat. May I kindly ask you to return to your original seat? Thank you for your cooperation.

您好，这里是机组座位，请您回到原位。谢谢您的合作。

27. Excuse me, Sir/ Madam, in order to keep the aircraft in balance, could you please return to your original seat? Thank you.

您好，先生／女士，为了使飞机保持配载平衡，请您回到原来的座位上坐好。谢谢。

28. Cabin attendants, please return to your seats for take-off.

飞机马上就要起飞，请乘务员回座位坐好。

V. Tips

1. Cabin safety check procedures 客舱安检步骤

Step 1: Make sure the overhead compartment is properly locked.

Please put your luggage in the overhead compartment.

Step 2: open window shades.

Please open the window shade.

Step 3: Stow tray tables.

Please stow your tray table.

Step 4: Fasten seatbelts.

Please keep your seatbelts securely fastened.

Step 5: Return seat backs to the upright position.

Please adjust your seat back to the upright position. Take-off/ Descending is a very critical period. If you don't put your seat back to the upright position, in case of an emergency, you may easily get hurt. It'll also block the way and the passengers behind you cannot get out quickly.

Step 6: Emergency exit safety check

Please do not put anything in the vacant seats.

Everything has to go in the overhead locker so that nothing will block the aisle.

Step 7: Turn/ Switch off electronic devices and mobile phones.

2. In-flight announcements in terms of "cellphone" 手机等便携式电子设备管理广播词

Ladies and gentlemen, please note that mobile phones and other portable electronic devices are switched off or switched to the "flight mode" function throughout the flight. Lithium battery chargers must be turned off for the duration of this flight. Thank you for your cooperation.

VI. Supplementary Reading

Lithium batteries carried by passengers and crew 旅客和机组锂电池运输

No spare lithium battery may be carried in checked baggage. Lithium battery mobile power bank is considered as spare lithium battery. A maximum of two charger babies each not exceeding 160Wh may be carried by a passenger or a crew member. It will ensure the lithium battery mobile power with on/ off switch is OFF on board, and may not supply power to electronic equipment. Each passenger or crew member may carry spare lithium batteries specified in *Dangerous Goods Transportation Manual* up to 8, including no more than 2 lithium ion batteries with Watt-hour rating more than 100Wh but not more than 160Wh and lithium metal cells with lithium content more than 2g but not more than 8g (the approval of the airline is required); no more than 2 lithium ion batteries with Watt-hour rating more than 50Wh but not more than 100Wh and lithium metal cells with lithium content more than 1g but not more than 2g. If the company has agreed passengers use specific portable medical equipment on board in other manuals or documents, the number of spare lithium batteries of the equipment should follow the company rules on that equipment.

VII. Exercises

1. Could you list some expressions we use during safety check?

(1)

(2)

(3)

(4)

2. Translate the following words and phrases into Chinese or English.

安全须知	be willing to do
氧气面罩	operating handle
滑梯	life raft
在通常情况下	Safety Demonstration Kit
在紧急情况下	life vest
direct	

3. Translate the following sentences into Chinese or English.

(1) 我们将为您播放安全须知录像，为了您的安全，请您注意观看！

(2) 请您系好安全带，收起小桌板，调直座椅靠背，打开遮光板。

(3) 电子设备需要在我们达到平飞高度之后才可以使用。

(4) 飞机上全程禁止吸烟。

(5) Please stow your footrest and the video screen.

(6) The take-off period is critical. If you don't put your seat back to the upright position, in case of an emergency, you may easily get hurt by the powerful impact. It'll also block the way for the passengers behind you to escape from the aircraft quickly.

(7) As we are taking off shortly, it's dangerous to use the lavatory now. Could you please remain seated until we get to the cruising level?

4. Group work: choose one topic to start a conversation. (TIME LIMIT: 10 minutes)

(1) Safety Check: Please switch off your cellphone.

(2) Safety Check: Please secure your tray table.

(3) Safety Check: Please return your seat back to the upright position.

Project 5

Humanity Service
细微服务

Civil Aviation

Task 11   Providing Information and Fund-raising for Charities 回答问询与慈善募捐

I. Warm-up Questions

1. Is it necessary to adjust the cabin temperature according to passengers' feeling?

2. How to show a flight attendant's concern in a short time before catering?

3. How to introduce geography information to passengers with a route map?

4. What are the codes of in-flight donations?

5. Is it compulsory for passengers on board to make substantial donations to charity?

II. Dialogues

Dialogue 1: Asking about the cabin temperature

Situation: For the economy class, flight attendants should pay attention to the cabin temperature, providing blankets to the passengers especially who are sleeping.

Principle: Flight attendants should be considerate.

Example

FA: Excuse me, Mr. Tang. How would you like the cabin temperature now?

PAX: It seems a little bit hot.

FA: OK, I will lower the temperature right now. And after a while, you will feel better. Please wait a second.

FA: Are you feeling better now?

PAX: Erm... A little bit better!

FA: I will help you adjust the air flow knob and bring you a cup of ice water in a minute.

情景会话1：询问客舱温度

乘务员：您好，唐先生，您觉得现在的客舱温度怎么样？

旅客：好像有点儿热。

乘务员：好的，我马上把客舱温度调低一些，过一会儿，您就会感到好些。请您稍等。

乘务员：（调好后）您觉得现在的客舱温度合适吗？

旅客：呃……好一点儿了！

音频扫一扫

乘务员：我马上给您调节下通风口，稍后给您来杯冰水。

Dialogue 2: No more blankets

音频扫一扫

Situation: As is often the case, the temperature out of the cabin differs from the temperature inside. When passengers first entered the cabin, they might feel cool and comfortable. However, after a while, they might feel a little cold. Some passengers may feel cold during the flight and ask for blankets. Due to the limited in-flight resources, blankets are not enough occasionally.

Principle: Flight attendants should find available resources for passengers (if necessary, use the first class and business class resources to meet passengers' needs). If there's no more blanket, flight attendants should apologize sincerely and tell them that the cabin temperature will be adjusted immediately.

Example

FA: Excuse me, Madam. What can I help you with?

PAX: Oh, nothing. I just want to relax and stretch myself here.

FA: Sorry, Madam. We may encounter turbulence from time to time. Passengers are not allowed to stay in the galley area for a long time. But such a long journey makes people very tired, and you may do some exercises here for several minutes. Please return to your seat when you feel better. Is that okay?

PAX: OK. I will leave in a minute. By the way, may I have one more blanket? It's cold.

FA: Sure, Madam. I will bring you an extra.

(After a while...)

FA: Thank you for your waiting, Madam. I'm sorry. There's no more blanket. Let me bring you a cup of hot tea.

PAX: OK.

FA: If you have thick clothes in the overhead locker, may I help you take them out？

PAX: That's fine. Thanks.

(After a while...)

FA: Are you feeling better now?

PAX: No, I still feel cold. Can you turn up the cabin temperature a little bit?

FA: I apologize that you are not feeling comfortable in this part of the cabin. Let me see if we can adjust the cabin temperature.

PAX: Thanks.

FA: You're welcome.

情景会话2：毛毯发完了

乘务员：您好，女士。我能帮您做点儿什么吗？

旅客：哦，不用，没什么。我只是在这里放松舒展一下。

乘务员：不好意思，女士。因为随时会有颠簸，所以旅客不可以长时间逗留在厨房服务区内。不过，这么久的航程确实令人非常疲惫，您可以在这里做些运动放松一会儿。等您感觉好些了，就请回到座位上。这样可以吗？

旅客：好的，我一会儿就回去。顺便问一下，我能再要一条毛毯吗？好冷啊。

乘务员：可以的，女士。我马上为您拿一条。

（过了一会儿……）

乘务员：女士，让您久等了。我很抱歉，机上毛毯发完了。我为您倒杯热茶吧！

旅客：好的。

乘务员：如果您的行李里有厚衣服，我帮您从行李架里取出来好吗？

旅客：就这样吧。谢谢你。

（过了一会儿……）

乘务员：现在您感觉好点儿了吗？

旅客：没有，我还是觉得冷。客舱温度能调高一点儿吗？

乘务员：我很抱歉客舱温度使您感觉不舒服了。我看看能不能调节一下客舱温度。

旅客：谢了。

乘务员：不客气。

音频扫一扫

Dialogue 3: Have a nap

Situation: After the aircraft reaching the cruising altitude, flight attendants walk in the cabin and provide courteous and attentive service.

Principle: Flight attendants should communicate with passengers and answer their questions patiently.

Example

FA: Excuse me, Sir. Would you like to read some newspapers or magazines?

PAX: No, thank you. I prefer to have a nap.

FA: May I lower the window shade for you? It is adjustable. The sunlight is so bright that it may disturb your sleeping.

PAX: Thank you so much. I can lower it by myself later. By the way, I'd like to listen to music to help me go to sleep. Do you have music channels?

FA: Yes. Here you can see the channel selection buttons. Folk songs, classical music, pop music, light music and Chinese operas are available in our in-flight entertainment system. You can select any one you like. The channel you select can be seen on the channel display. And there are volume adjusting buttons. You can adjust the volume. Besides, you can select languages as you like by pressing these buttons.

PAX: Yes, that's convenient. Light music is my favorite. Which channel shall I select?

FA: Channel 2 is for light music. Just press the button on your armrest, please.

PAX: Got it. Thank you.

FA: It's okay. Hope you enjoy the music.

情景会话3：睡一会儿

乘务员：您好，先生，请问您想看报纸或杂志吗？

旅客：不用了，谢谢。我想睡一会儿。

乘务员：我帮您拉下遮光板吧？它是可以调节的，光线这么强可能会影响您休息。

旅客：非常感谢你，我一会儿自己来。顺便问下，我想听着音乐入睡，你们有音乐频道吗？

乘务员：有的。这里，您可以看到频道选择键。我们的机上娱乐系统里有民谣、古典音乐、流行音乐、轻音乐以及中国戏剧。您可以选择任意一种您喜欢的，通过显示屏可以看到您选择的频道。这里还有音量调节按钮，您可以调节音量。此外，您还可以通过按这些按钮根据自己的喜好选择语言。

旅客：嗯，挺方便的。我最喜欢轻音乐，那我选择哪个频道呢？

乘务员：频道2是轻音乐。只需要按您座椅扶手上这个按钮即可。

旅客：懂了，谢谢。

乘务员：不客气。希望您能喜欢。

Dialogue 4: The route map

Situation: After the aircraft reaching the cruising altitude, flight attendants walk in the cabin and provide courteous and attentive service.

音频扫一扫

Principle: Flight attendants should communicate with passengers and answer their questions patiently.

Example

PAX: Excuse me, where are we right now?

FA: You may refer to the flight map in your screen, Sir.

PAX: OK, I've got it. This is my first time to travel by air. I'm so curious about your job.

FA: Oh, I see. Let me make a brief introduction about our air crew.

PAX: Wow, if not presumptuous.

FA: On this plane, we have the captain in charge of the plane. He works in the cockpit, as you may know. We have a purser in charge of the cabin and four flight attendants serving our passengers. I'm one of them.

PAX: Oh, I see. You are so nice. How long have you been flying?

FA: I've been flying as an international flight attendant for almost 5 years.

PAX: Do you like your job?

FA: Yes, I like flying around the world. It makes me feel full and excited.

PAX: Thank you. Nice to have a talk with you.

FA: My pleasure.

情景会话4：航路图

旅客：您好，请问我们现在飞到哪儿了？

乘务员：先生，您可以看看屏幕，上面有飞行地图。

旅客：好的，我知道了。这是我第一次乘飞机旅行，对你们的工作很好奇呀。

乘务员：哦，这样啊。我来给您简单介绍一下我们的机组成员吧。

旅客：哇，如果不冒昧的话。

乘务员：在这个航班上，机长对整架飞机负责。您可能知道，他在驾驶舱工作。机上还有一位负责整个客舱的乘务长和四名负责旅客服务工作的乘务员，我是其中之一。

旅客：哦，我知道了。你人真好。你飞行多久啦？

乘务员：作为国际乘务员，我已经飞行快五年了。

旅客：你喜欢自己的工作吗？

乘务员：是的，我喜欢全世界四处飞。飞行让我感到充实和兴奋。

旅客：谢谢你。和你聊天挺开心的。

乘务员：是我的荣幸。

Dialogue 5: "May I use the restroom now?"

Situation: After the aircraft reaching the cruising altitude, flight attendants walk in the cabin. A passenger would like to know the location of the lavatory on board. And later the passenger finds that the lavatory is in a mess.

音频扫一扫

Principle: Flight attendants should communicate with passengers and answer their questions patiently. If the passenger complains about the cabin service to a flight attendant, the flight attendant should apologize sincerely and thank the passenger for his or her feedback.

Example

PAX: May I use the restroom now?

FA: Yes, the "fasten seatbelts" sign is off. You may use the lavatory now.

PAX: Where is the restroom?

FA: Walking along the aisle and the restroom is at the end of it. The lavatory is vacant.

(After a while...)

PAX: Excuse me, it's a little dirty there. Could you come and have a look?

FA: I do apologize for the condition of the lavatory. I will clean it immediately. Thank you for drawing this to our attention.

情景会话5："现在可以使用卫生间吗？"

旅客：（平飞后）现在可以用卫生间吗？

乘务员：可以的，"系好安全带"信号已经解除，您现在可以使用洗手间。

旅客：请问洗手间在哪儿呢？

乘务员：沿着这条过道往前走，走到头就是了。洗手间现在没人使用。

（过了一会儿……）

旅客：你好，里面有点儿脏。你能来看一下吗？

乘务员：对洗手间的状况我感到非常抱歉，我立刻为您打扫，谢谢您把这个信息反馈给我们。

音频扫一扫

Dialogue 6: Communication in the first class and business class

Situation: Flight attendants should pay attention to the details in terms of providing service. In the first and business class, flight attendants should offer service according to the passengers' requests.

Principle: Flight attendants should observe and communicate willingly.

Example

PAX: Excuse me, Miss. I want to know what's the time difference between Beijing and Seattle.

FA: For winter time, Beijing is 16 hours earlier than Seattle time.

PAX: That means we will arrive in Seattle at Beijing time... Erm...

FA: At Beijing time 2:35 a.m. on the next day.

PAX: Alright! I just want to confirm whether I should call my wife when we land. Thank you.

FA: My pleasure.

FA: By the way, if you would like to have a rest now, please let me know. I'll prepare the bed for you.

PAX: Well, I'm just about to sleep. Thank you!

FA: Wish you a good dream!

情景会话6：两舱服务沟通

旅客：你好，请问一下北京和西雅图的时差是多少？

乘务员：对于冬令时来说，北京比西雅图早16个小时。

旅客：那意思是我们到达西雅图在北京时间……嗯……

乘务员：在北京时间第二天的凌晨2:35。

旅客：好的！我只是想确认下落地后是不是应该给我妻子打个电话。谢谢！

乘务员：不客气。

乘务员：顺便说一下，如果您现在想休息一会儿，请告诉我。我将为您提供铺床服务。

旅客：嗯，我刚好想先休息了。谢谢你！

乘务员：祝您好梦！

Dialogue 7: Fund-raising for charities on board

音频扫一扫

Situation: After the aircraft reaching the cruising altitude, the purser makes an announcement about fund raising and flight attendants provide courteous and attentive service.

Principle: Flight attendants should communicate and answer questions patiently and willingly.

Example

FA: (Making the announcement) Ladies and gentlemen, welcome aboard our Airline. We wish you a pleasant journey. Since its establishment, our Airline has participated actively in public charity and conveyed true love with sincerity. Our Airline has become the first mainland airline to support Change for Good activity of United Nations Children's Fund, and has launched the Change for Good fund raising activities on board for many times to improve the lives of poor children all over the world. Now, we sincerely invite you to join in the fund-raising activity to dedicate your love by donating your change voluntarily.

FA: Excuse me, Sir. Did you just press the call button, and what can I do for you?

PAX: Yeah, I was quite interested in the activity that was told in the announcement. Would you mind introducing anything more about it?

FA: Sure, that's my honor. It's the first time that Change for Good fund raising activity is brought to China.

FA: Their donations have improved the lives of poor children in more than 150 developing countries. The donation, even if it is 1 Yuan, 5 Yuan, or 10 Yuan, can improve the lives of children in trouble, guarantee them to receive high-quality elementary education, protect them from violence, kidnapping and AIDS, and make this world as best we can for children. If you are willing to offer your love, please put your changes into this fund raising bag. The donations will be sent to United Nations Children's Fund. We sincerely appreciate your generous support.

PAX: Of course, please count me in. I'd like to join in such a meaningful activity very much. Just like the saying goes, "one good deed a day will keep an old man gloom away". Here are the changes.

FA: It's really kind of you. Your generous act will be sincerely appreciated. And with your donation, those children will be closer to their dreams. Thank you for your trust and support. Enjoy your flight!

情景会话7：机上慈善募捐活动

乘务员：（客舱广播）女士们，先生们，欢迎选乘我们航空公司的航班。我们祝愿您有一段愉快的旅程。自成立之初，我们航空公司便一直积极参与社会公益慈善活动，秉承赤子之心传递爱心。我们是中国第一家参与支持联合国儿童基金会 Change for Good "机上爱心零钱募捐"慈善活动的航空公司，并已举办多次机上募捐活动改善世界过低贫困儿童的生存状况。现在，我们真诚邀请您参加我们的机上捐款活动，通过自愿捐赠奉献您的爱心。

乘务员：打扰您了，先生，请问有什么可以为您效劳呢？

旅客：嗯，我对刚才广播中的活动内容很感兴趣，你介意为我介绍一下吗？

乘务员：很荣幸为您介绍这项活动。Change for Good 这项"机上爱心零钱募捐"筹款活动是第一次在中国开展。

乘务员：筹集的善款已经改善了全球 150 多个发展中国家贫困儿童的生活。只需您捐出随身携带的零钱，哪怕是 1 元、5 元、10 元不等，都能改善处于困境中的儿童的生活，保障他们接受优质的基础教育，免受暴力、拐卖和艾滋病的伤害，尽我们所能让他们的生活变得更加美好。如果您愿意献出一份爱心，请将钱币装进爱心钱袋，我们将用密封袋收集后送至联合国儿童基金会。在此，衷心感谢您的慷慨支持！

旅客：当然啊，算我一份。我非常愿意参加这样有意义的活动。正像一句谚语中所说："日行一善，可永葆无忧无虑的心情"。这是我捐赠的零钱。

乘务员：您真是个好人，非常感谢您的慷慨义举。相信您的爱心捐助，将会让孩子们离梦想更近！再次感谢您的信任和支持！祝您航程愉快！

Ⅲ. Popular Words and Phrases

cold	[kəʊld]	*adj.* 冷的
freezing	[ˈfriːzɪŋ]	*adj.* 严寒的，冰冻的
chilly	[ˈtʃɪli]	*adj.* 寒冷的，严寒的，怕冷的
lavatory	[ˈlævətəri]	*n.* 厕所；盥洗室
toilet flush button		冲水钮
tissue	[ˈtɪsjuː]	*n.* 纸巾
napkin	[ˈnæpkɪn]	*n.* 餐巾（纸质或布的）
toilet paper		卫生纸，厕纸
hand sanitizer	[hænd ˈsænɪtaɪzə]	洗手液，手部消毒剂
sanitary napkin	[ˈsænɪt(ə)rɪ ˈnæpkɪn]	卫生棉（女士经期使用）
adjust	[əˈdʒʌst]	*v.* 调节
airflow knob	[ˈeəfləʊ nɒb; -nɑːb]	通风口
reading light		阅读灯
ascend	[əˈsend]	*v.* 上升
descend	[dɪˈsend]	*v.* 下降
cruise	[kruːz]	*v.* 巡航
altitude	[ˈæltɪtjuːd]	*n.* 高度
recline	[rɪˈklaɪn]	*v.* 使躺下；使斜倚
blow	[bləʊ]	*v.* 吹风；喘气
slip	[slɪp]	*v.* 滑动；滑倒
buckle	[ˈbʌkl]	*v.* 扣住；使弯曲
armrest	[ˈɑːmrest]	*n.* 扶手；靠手
in accordance to		根据，依据
due to		由于；因为
emphasize	[ˈemfəsaɪz]	*v.* 强调
welfare	[ˈwelfeə]	*n.* 福利；幸福
responsibility	[rɪˌspɒnsəˈbɪlətɪ]	*n.* 责任；职责；责任感；责任心
commitment	[kəˈmɪtmənt]	*n.* 承诺，许诺，承担义务
orphan	[ˈɔːrfn]	*n.* 孤儿
launch	[lɔːntʃ]	*v.* 发动；开展（活动、计划等）
donation	[dəʊˈneɪʃn]	*n.* 捐赠；捐款
notify	[ˈnəʊtɪfaɪ]	*v.* 通知；布告
generosity	[ˌdʒenəˈrɒsətɪ]	*n.* 慷慨，大方

Ⅳ. Practical Expressions

1. How would you like the cabin temperature now?

您觉得现在的客舱温度怎么样？

2. I will adjust the temperature right away/ straight away/ at once/ immediately.

我马上把客舱温度调节一下。

3. I'm sorry that you are not feeling comfortable in this part of the cabin. Let me see if we can adjust the air conditioner. In the meantime, would you care for another blanket?

我很抱歉客舱温度使您感觉不舒服了。我看看能不能调节空调的温度，同时，我再给您拿一条毛毯好吗？

4. I'm sorry. I didn't get that. Could you repeat it, please? May I find another flight attendant to help you?

对不起，我没有听清。您能重复一遍吗？我能找我的同事来帮助您吗？

5. Excuse me, Sir/ Madam. What can I do for you?

您好，先生/女士，请问我能为您做些什么吗？

6. It is my pleasure/ honor to be at your service.

为您服务是我的荣幸。

7. We are pleased to help you if you have any question.

如果您有任何疑问，我们很乐意帮您。

8. Excuse me, Sir/ Madam, I'm Lee. I'm glad to be at your service. If you need any help, please do not hesitate to call me.

先生/女士，您好，我是小李。今天很高兴能为您服务，如果您有什么需要，请随时找我。

9. The flight time today is ten hours and twenty-five minutes.

我们今天整个航程大约飞行10小时25分钟。

10. The aircraft you are taking is an Airbus 330.

您今天乘坐的是空客330型飞机。

11. Excuse me, Sir/ Madam, do you need a blanket? Would you like me to put it over your body?

先生/女士，您好，请问您需要毛毯吗？我帮您盖在身上好吗？

12. I will bring you a cup of warm water and a blanket. If you have thick clothes in the overhead locker, may I help you take them out？

我将给您拿一杯热水和一条毛毯来。如果您有厚衣服，我也可以帮助您从行李架上取出来。

13. If you would like to have a rest now, I'll make the bed for you.

您现在需要休息的话，我来为您铺床。

14. If there's anything we can do for you, just press the call button.

如有任何需要，请按呼唤铃。

15. This is the call button. If you need some help, please press it, and we will come to assist you.

这是呼叫铃，如果您需要帮助，请按这个按钮，我们就会来帮助您。

16. If you need any help, please press this call button. If you want to read, you can turn on the reading light. If you'd like to have a rest, you can press this button on your armrest and lean back at the same time. Here is the air vent. You can turn the knob here in whichever direction you like, or you can turn it off by turning it tightly to the right.

如果您需要任何帮助，请按呼唤铃；如果您想阅读，可以打开阅读灯；如果您想休息，可以按住座椅扶手上的这个按钮，同时身体向后仰，放倒座椅靠背。这是通风孔，您可以把它向任意方向调节，或向右旋紧关掉。

17. You can draw down the window-shade, turn the reading light off and fasten your seat-belt so that you can take a good nap.

您可以放下遮阳板，关掉阅读灯，系好安全带，这样您能好好休息一下。

18. Sir/ Madam, may I turn on the reading light for you?

先生/女士，您好，需要我为您打开阅读灯吗？

19. Excuse me, here's the newspaper we've prepared for you. We hope you can enjoy it.

您好，这是我们为您准备的报纸，希望您能喜欢。

20. Excuse me, Sir. May I close the window shade so that the bright sunlight won't disturb you?

先生，我帮您拉下遮光板吧，以免亮光干扰您休息。

21. Excuse me, Sir/ Madam. May I help you adjust the seat to a more comfortable position so that you can have a good rest?

先生/女士，您好，我帮您把座椅调整到比较舒服的位置好吗？这样您就可以好好休息一下。

22. Please press the button on the armrest and lean against the seat back at the same time.

请您按下座椅扶手上的这个按钮，身体同时向后靠。

23. You may close the sun shade board/ sun shield/ window shade and turn off the reading light when sleeping. But don't forget to fasten your seatbelts.

休息时您可以放下遮光板，关掉阅读灯，但请系好安全带。

24. In order to ensure the normal operation of the airplane navigation and communication system, you are kindly requested not to use your cellphone.

为确保飞行和通信系统的正常操作，请您不要使用手机。

25. I understand it's tiring for such a long flight. You can move around in the cabin. However, for your safety, may I kindly remind you not to stay at the emergency exit for a long time?

我很理解您乘坐长航线的疲劳，您可以在客舱内稍微活动舒缓一下。但是为了您的安全，请您不要长时间在应急出口处停留。

26. You may stand up and walk around in the cabin when the flight is in a relatively stable condition.

如果飞机飞行状态相对平稳，您可以站起来在机舱内走动走动。

27. Excuse me, Sir. It is not safe lying on the floor. It might bruise you in case of turbulence and threaten others. Please be seated and fasten your seatbelts.

先生，躺在地板上休息很危险，一旦遇到颠簸会伤到您，对其他旅客也不安全。请回到座位上坐好并系好安全带。

28. The aircraft has met with turbulence. Please return to your seat and fasten the seatbelts. Passengers, please do not use the lavatory for this moment.

飞机现在遇有不稳定气流，请您回原位坐好并系好安全带，暂时不要使用卫生间。

29. The "fasten seatbelts" sign has been turned off. You may use the lavatories at the middle or the rear of the cabin.

"系好安全带"信号已经解除，您可使用客舱中部或后部的洗手间。

30. The restroom for the first class passengers is located in the front of the cabin and the one for other passengers in the rear.

头等舱旅客的卫生间位于前舱，其他旅客的在后舱。

31. The lavatory is occupied./ The lavatory is vacant.

卫生间有人/没人。

32. The different color uniforms represent different ranks of flight attendants.

不同颜色的制服代表乘务员的不同级别。

33. I'm sorry. I will let you know after I confirm our exact location. You may also check the flight map on the PTV.

对不起，让我确认一下我们的确切位置再告诉您。您也可以查看个人电视上的航路图。

34. How long are you going to stay in Beijing?

您打算在北京停留多久呢？

35. It's the first time that Change for Good fund raising activity brought to China.

这项筹款活动是第一次在中国开展。

36. We sincerely appreciate your generous support.

我们衷心感谢您的慷慨支持！

V. Tips

Chat with passengers 细微服务：与旅客聊天

(1) About flights

We have flights from Beijing to Paris. There are a lot of places of interest in Beijing and Beijing is a capital city. It's a place worth visiting as well. I think you may start off from Beijing and have a good time there.

(2) About temperature

It could get nippy in the cabin. We will adjust the cabin temperature.

We will help you adjust the air flow knob.

I will bring you a cup of warm water and a blanket.

If you have thick clothes in the overhead locker, may I help you take them out？

(3) About uniforms

The different color uniforms represent different ranks of flight attendants.

It is a cheongsam with some Chinese style prints on it.

The shape of these uniforms makes us feel free and comfortable when we work.

It's really a perfect fusion of western and oriental beauty.

VI. Supplementary Reading

United Nations International Children's Emergency Fund (UNICEF) 联合国儿童基金会	

Established: December 11, 1946 (at 12：01 p.m. Eastern Time Zone)

Headquarters: New York City, Geneva

The United Nations Children's Fund (UNICEF) is a United Nations (UN) program headquartered in New York City that provides humanitarian and developmental assistance to children and mothers in developing countries. It is a member of the United Nations Development Group. UNICEF's programs emphasize developing community-level services to promote the health and well-being of children. UNICEF was awarded the Nobel Peace Prize in 1965 and the Prince of Asturias Award of Concord in 2006.

UNICEF's work: for 70 years, across 190 countries and territories, UNICEF defends the rights of every child.

VII. Exercises

1. Answer the following questions according to the dialogues.

(1) Is it necessary to adjust the cabin temperature according to passengers' feeling?

(2) How to introduce geography information to passengers?

(3) Is it compulsory for passengers to make substantial donations to charity?

2. Translate the following words and phrases into Chinese or English.

adjust	航路图
airflow knob	巡航
reading light	捐款
ascend	慷慨，大方
altitude	福利
responsibility	

3. Translate the following sentences into Chinese or English.

(1) 您觉得现在的客舱温度怎么样？

(2) 我很抱歉，客舱温度使您感觉不舒服了。我们马上调节客舱温度，现在我再给您拿一条毛毯好吗？

(3) 我们今天整个航程大约飞行 10 小时 25 分钟。

(4) 如有任何需要，请按呼唤铃。

(5) Please press the button on the armrest and lean against the seat back at the same time.

(6) You may close the window shade and turn off the reading light when sleeping. But don't forget to fasten your seatbelts.

(7) We sincerely appreciate your generous support.

4. Group work: choose one topic to start a conversation. (TIME LIMIT: 10 minutes)

(1) No more blanket.

(2) About the cabin temperature.

(3) About the donation.

Task 12　Entertainment System 娱乐系统

I. Warm-up Questions

1. What are the principles of introducing in-flight entertainment system to diverse passengers?

2. Why is it necessary to pay attention to the passengers without using the entertainment system on board?

3. How to deal with the breakdown of in-flight entertainment system?

II. Dialogues

Dialogue 1: In-flight Entertainment System

Situation: After taking off about 20 minutes, the in-flight entertainment system will be turned on. Passengers would like to know everything nearby, especially the entertainment system on board. And

音频扫一扫

normally, they would love to seek assistance from flight attendants.

Principle: Flight attendants should be willing to observe and answer questions patiently.

Example

PAX: Could you help me with this device?

FA: Certainly. This is our on-board entertainment device, and you may use it for fun during the flight.

PAX: OK... How can I use it?

FA: As you can see, the touch screen makes it very convenient to operate. There are quite a lot of movies, music and games in it for you to choose. But it can only be used during the cruising period. When you finish using its handle, please put it back. And this is the entertainment system guide/ seat instruction. If you have any question, please feel free to ask me. I will be glad to help you at any time.

PAX: Got it. Thanks a lot.

FA: My pleasure, Sir. Enjoy your flight!

情景会话1：机上娱乐系统

旅客：请问您能帮我看一下这个设备吗？

乘务员：好的。这是我们的机上娱乐设备。您可以在飞行期间用它来消遣。

旅客：这样啊，那怎么用呢？

乘务员：您看，触摸屏的操作非常方便。有很多电影、音乐和游戏供您挑选。但只能在平飞期间使用（控制）手柄。用完后，请放回原处。这是娱乐系统指南/座椅使用说明。如有任何疑问，请随时找我，我将非常高兴为您提供帮助。

旅客：我知道了。谢谢你。

乘务员：很乐意为您服务，先生。祝您航程愉快！

Dialogue 2: Something wrong with the headset

Situation: The in-flight entertainment system has been turned on. A passenger asks a flight attendant for help in terms of the headset.

Principle: The flight attendant should apologize first and change the headset immediately. When the new one still not working, check the socket of the armrest headset. If something wrong with it, help the passenger with changing his/ her seat.

音频扫一扫

Example

PAX: Excuse me, my headset doesn't seem to be working. Can you give me a hand?

FA: OK. Don't worry. Let me check it for you.

PAX: I've been trying for several minutes.

FA: The headset is probably broken. I'm sorry about the problem with the headset. Let me get you a new one. Please wait a moment.

PAX: Thank you.

FA: You are welcome, Sir.

情景会话2：耳机坏了

旅客：打扰了，我的耳机好像不好使了。你能帮我看看吗？

乘务员：好的，您别着急，我来帮您检查一下。

旅客：我都试了好几分钟了。

乘务员：这个耳机可能坏了，非常抱歉这个耳机不能使用了。我马上为您更换一个新的，请稍候。

旅客：谢谢。

乘务员：不客气，先生。

Dialogue 3: "My entertainment device doesn't seem to work."

Situation: The in-flight entertainment system has been turned on. A passenger asks a flight attendant for help.

Principle: Flight attendants need pay attention to the in-flight entertainment system. If something wrong, flight attendants ought to find out the reasons and help passengers restart the entertainment system. If it doesn't work, flight attendants should apologize immediately. A responsible flight attendant should also pay attention to the restart of the entertainment system.

Example

FA: Excuse me, Miss. What can I do for you?

PAX: Yes. My entertainment device doesn't seem to work.

FA: I'm sorry, Madam. Wait a moment, please. Let me restart it for you. It usually takes 8 to 10 minutes. I'll be back and confirm it for you soon.

(After resetting several times...)

FA: I'm terribly sorry, Miss. The system cannot work after a restart. Would you mind taking another seat? Let me see if there are vacant seats.

PAX: That's OK.

FA: Miss, there is a vacant seat 36A. The entertainment system works there. You may sit there. Please take your belongings and follow me.

PAX: Thanks a lot.

FA: Thank you for your understanding. We do apologize for this inconvenience.

PAX: By the way, do you have any recommendations on the program?

FA: There are several kinds of movies, TV plays, music and games in our entertainment system. The recommended movies are *The Wandering Earth* and *Crazy Alien*. They are among the most popular movies.

PAX: Thanks a lot.

FA: My pleasure.

情景会话 3："我的娱乐系统好像死机了"

乘务员：女士，打扰您了，请问有什么可以帮您吗？

旅客：是的，我的娱乐设备好像死机了。

乘务员：非常抱歉，女士。请稍等，我来为您重启一下，通常需要 8 到 10 分钟，等下我会过来帮您确认。

（重启几遍之后……）

乘务员：女士，真是对不起，这个娱乐系统重启之后还是不能正常使用。您是否介意换个座位？我来看看是否还有空位。

旅客：好的，没关系。

乘务员：女士，36 排 A 座位没有人坐，而且娱乐系统可以正常使用。您可以坐在那里。请带好您的随身物品跟我来。

旅客：非常感谢。

乘务员：感谢您的理解，为此带来的不便我们感到很抱歉。

旅客：有什么好节目推荐吗？

乘务员：我们的机上娱乐系统有好几种电影、电视剧、音乐和游戏。推荐的影片有《流浪地球》和《疯狂的外星人》，这两部都是最受欢迎的影片。

旅客：多谢啦。

乘务员：不客气的。

Ⅲ. Popular Words and Phrases

entertainment	[ˌentəˈteinmənt]	*n.* 娱乐，消遣
in-flight entertainment system		客舱娱乐系统
homepage	[ˈhəumpeidʒ]	*n.* 主页，主菜单
screen brightness		屏幕亮度
TV feature	[ˈfiːtʃə]	电视短片
movie	[muːvɪ]	*n.* 电影（film *n.* 电影）
cartoon	[kɑːˈtuːn]	*n.* 动画片
route map		航路图
transfer	[ˈtrænsfɜː]	*n.* 转机信息
tablet	[ˈtæblɪt]	*n.* 平板电脑
laptop	[ˈlæpˈtɒp]	*n.* 笔记本电脑
USB connector	[kəˈnektə(r)]	USB接口
headset plug		耳机插孔
headset socket		耳机插口
headset	[ˈhedset]	*n.* 耳麦，耳机
remote control		遥控器
channel display		频道显示
channel selector		频道选择器
channel up/ down		上/下调频道
AVOD control（Audio and Video on Demand）		音视频点播控制
volume	[ˈvɒljuːm]	*n.* 音量
mute	[mjuːt]	*n./adj.* 静音
display on/ off		*n.* 显示屏开/关
touch screen		触摸屏
channel selection button		频道选择按钮
control panel		控制面板
armrest	[ˈɑːmrest]	*n.* 扶手
audio	[ˈɔːdiəu]	*n.* 音频
video	[ˈvɪdiəu]	*n.* 视频
dim	[dɪm]	*v.* 调暗
image	[ˈɪmɪdʒ]	*n.* 图像
insert	[ɪnˈsɜːt]	*v.* 插入
mode	[məud]	*n.* 模式
plug	[plʌg]	*n.* 插头
portable multimedia device		手持机上娱乐设备
rating	[ˈreɪtɪŋ]	*n.* 电影分级
cast	[kɑːst]	*n.* 演员表
costume	[ˈkɒstjuːm]	*n.* 服装

keen	[kiːn]	*adj.* 渴望的；强烈的	
taste	[teɪst]	*n.* 喜好	
gunfight	['gʌnfait]	*n.* 枪战	
iceberg	['aisbɜːg]	*n.* 冰山	
legend	['ledʒənd]	*n.* 传说	
myth	[miθ]	*n.* 神话	
track	['træk]	*v.* 追踪	
locate	[ləu'keit]	*v.* 位于；定位	
treasure	['treʒə]	*n.* 金银财宝；财富	
masterpiece	['mɑːstəpiːs]	*n.* 杰作，名作，杰出的作品	
fantastic	[fæn'tæstik]	*adj.* 极好的，极出色的	
blockbuster	['blɒkbʌstə(r)]	*n.* 大片	
criticism	['kritisizəm]	*n.* 评论	
critic	['kritik]	*n.* 评论家，批评家	
OVA (Original Video Animation)		剧场版	
subtitle	['sʌbtaitl]	*n.* 字幕	
release date		上映日期	
producer	[prə'djuːsə(r)]	*n.* 制片人	
director	[daɪ'rektə(r)]	*n.* 导演	
script	[skript]	*n.* 剧本	
soundtrack	['saundtræk]	*n.* 电影配音、配乐	
hero/ chief actor		男主角	
heroine/ chief actress		女主角	

Ⅳ. Practical Expressions

1. Excuse me, Sir. Here's the entertainment system instruction card. If you have any question, please tell me. I'll be very happy to help you.

先生，您好，这是娱乐系统指南，如有疑问，请随时找我，我将非常高兴为您提供帮助。

2. Excuse me, Madam, the movies we have on board include comedy, action, romance and horror. ×× is a latest released movie. Here's the entertainment guide. Enjoy your time.

女士，您好，今天我们为您准备了喜剧片、动作片、爱情片和恐怖片，其中××是最新的影片。这是娱乐指南，祝您观看愉快。

3. The headset socket is in the armrest. You may enjoy the audio programs at your preference by selecting channels.

耳机插孔在座椅扶手上，选择频道后，您就能听到自己喜欢的音乐节目。

4. The movie audio is usually on channel 1 or 2.

电影的配音通常在 1 或 2 频道。

5. Folk songs, classic music, pop music and Chinese opera are available in our in-flight audio system. You can choose what you like.

飞机上的音频系统播放民歌、古典音乐、流行音乐和中国戏剧，您可以选择您喜欢的频道。

6. The headset/ earphone is probably broken. Let me get you a new one. Please wait for a moment.

这个耳机可能是坏了，我来给您取一个新的，请稍等一下。

/ I'm sorry about the problem with the headset. I'll replace it for you straight away.

非常抱歉这个耳机不能使用了，我马上为您更换一个。

7. I'll show you how to use it.

让我给您示范一下怎么使用。

8. As you can see, the touch screen makes it very convenient to operate. There are quite a lot of movies, music and games for you to choose.

正像您所看到的，触摸屏的操作非常方便。里面有很多电影、音乐和游戏供您挑选。

9. I'm terribly sorry about the condition of your personal TV. Please allow me a moment to see if we can have it reset for you.

非常抱歉您的个人娱乐系统出现问题，请您稍等让我看看能否为您重启系统。

10. Let me restart it for you. It usually takes 10 minutes. I'll be back and confirm it for you later.

我来为您重启一下，通常需要10分钟，稍等我会过来帮您确认。

11. I'm sorry about the problem with the television. I'll ask my colleague to reset it for you straight away. It will take about 5-10 minutes.

我很抱歉您的电视出现了故障，我马上让我的同事为您重启，系统重启大概需要5至10分钟的时间。

/ I'm terribly sorry about the condition of your personal TV. Please allow me a moment to see if we can reset it for you. It'll take about 5 minutes, and during the waiting time, please do not touch any button. Thank you for your cooperation.

非常抱歉您的个人娱乐系统出现问题，请您稍等，我马上为您重启系统，需要5分钟左右的时间，在此期间，请您不要触碰任何按键，谢谢合作。

12. Sir/ Madam, I do understand that you are feeling disappointed with the facilities in this flight. Please do accept my apology. I will check if we can reset your personal TV or alternatively I can check if we have another seat available.

先生/女士，我非常理解您不能正常使用设备的失望，非常抱歉。我马上去为您重启系统，或者为您调换其他空座。

13. If you have any other question, please don't hesitate to contact us.

如有其他问题请随时与我们联系。

14. Mr. Smith, there are several kinds of movies, TV plays, music and games in our entertainment system. The recommended movies are *The Battle at Lake Changjin* and *NeZha* 2. They are the latest movies.

史密斯先生，我们的机上娱乐系统有好几种电影、电视剧、音乐和游戏。推荐的影片有《长津湖》和《哪吒之魔童闹海》，这两部都是最新上映的影片。

Ⅴ. Tips

Talking about films 讨论电影

What's playing?

What's your favorite movie? Cartoon is my favorite.

Which do you prefer, comedy or romance? I like comedy better.

What's your preference? I prefer comedy to romance.

What kind/ sort of movies do you like? I enjoy cartoon.

I'm very interested in cartoon. Yes, me too.

I'm not keen on action movies. Neither am I.

Action movies are not to my taste. Neither do I.

I don't like action movies. Neither do I.

VI. Supplementary Reading

1.Inflight Entertainment Systems 机上娱乐系统

Inflight entertainment (IFE) system, usually with remote control capability and video display synchronization. Remote control capability and video display synchronization are used to extend the advantages of touch screen IFE passenger controls. This advantage is realized through the expedient of a passenger control unit (PCU) touch screen video display that is synchronized with a VDU video display. When the passenger makes a selection by touching the PCU touch screen video display, the VDU video display reflects the selection. The inflight entertainment system gives passengers access to the latest movies as well as game, in addition to a wide variety of audio content ranging from the latest pop music to audio books. Passengers personal screens let them start watching a variety of programs.

2.The film awards 电影奖项

（1）Cannes International Film Festival 戛纳国际电影节

Location: Cannes, France

Founded: September 20, 1946

Awards: *Palme d'Or*, Grand Prix

The Cannes Festival is an annual film festival held in Cannes, France, which previews new films of all genres, including documentaries, from all around the world. Founded in 1946, the invitation-only festival is held annually (usually in May) at the Palais des Festivals et des Congrès.

On July 1, 2014, co-founder and former head of French pay-TV operator Canal, Pierre Lescure, took over as President of the Festival, while Thierry Fremaux became the General Delegate. The board of directors also appointed Gilles Jacob as Honorary President of the Festival.

Palme d'Or 金棕榈奖（最高奖项）

Grand Prix 评审团大奖

（2）Berlin International Film Festival 柏林国际电影节

Location: Berlin, Germany

Founded: 1951

Awards: Golden Bear, Silver Bear

The Berlin International Film Festival, also called the Berlinale, is one of the world's leading film festivals and most reputable media events.

Founded in West Berlin in 1951, the festival has been celebrated annually in February since 1978. With around 300,000 tickets sold and 500,000 admissions, it is considered the largest publicly attended film festival worldwide based on actual attendance rates. Up to 400 films are shown in several sections, representing a comprehensive array of the cinematic world. Around twenty films compete for the awards called the Golden and Silver Bears. Since 2001, the director of the festival has been Dieter Kosslick. The Berlinale has established a cosmopolitan character integrating art, glamour, commerce and a global media attention.

Golden Bear 金熊奖（最高奖项）	

（3）Venice International Film Festival 威尼斯国际电影节 Location: Venice, Italy Founded: 1932 Awards: Golden Lion, Silver Lion	

The Venice Film Festival or Venice International Film Festival, founded in 1932, is the oldest film festival in the world and one of the "Big Three" film festivals alongside the Cannes Film Festival and Berlin International Film Festival. The film festival is part of the Venice Biennale, which was founded by the Venetian City Council in 1895. Since its inception the Venice Film Festival has grown into one of the most prestigious film festivals in the world.

Golden Lion 金狮奖（最高奖项）	

（4）Academy Awards/ The Oscars 奥斯卡金像奖 Awarded for: Excellence in cinematic achievements Country: United States Presented by: Academy of Motion Picture Arts and Sciences First awarded: May 16, 1929	

The Academy Awards, now known officially as The Oscars, is a set of twenty-four awards for artistic and technical merit in the American film industry, given annually by the Academy of Motion Picture Arts and Sciences (AMPAS), to recognize excellence in cinematic achievements as assessed by the Academy's voting membership. The awards ceremony was first broadcast on radio in 1930 and televised for the first time in 1953. It is now seen live in more than 200 countries and can be streamed live online. The Academy Awards ceremony is the oldest worldwide entertainment awards ceremony.

VII. Exercises

1. Can you list different types of movies?

(1)

(2)

(3)

(4)

2. Translate the following words and phrases into Chinese or English.

entertainment	客舱娱乐系统
homepage	屏幕亮度
headset	电视短片
volume	遥控器
mute	电子设备
dim	

3. Translate the following sentences into Chinese or English.

(1) 先生，您好，这是娱乐系统指南，如有疑问，请随时找我，我将非常高兴为您提供帮助。

(2) 耳机插孔在座椅扶手上，选择频道后，您就能听到自己喜欢的音乐节目。

(3) 我非常抱歉您的耳机不能使用。我马上为您更换一个。

(4) As you can see, the touch screen makes it very convenient to operate. There are quite a lot of movies, music and games for you to choose.

(5) I'm sorry about the problem with the television. I'll ask my colleague to reset it for you straight away. It will take about 5-10 minutes.

4. Group work: choose one topic to start a conversation. (TIME LIMIT: 15 minutes)

(1) Use in-flight entertainment system.

(2) Something wrong with the headset.

(3) The in-flight entertainment system doesn't work.

Project 6

Beverage and Meal Service
餐饮服务

Task 13　Beverage Service 饮料酒水服务

Ⅰ. Warm-up Questions

1. Why we need to pay attention to cups delivering, especially with hot drinks?

2. How to recommend different sorts of beverage to passengers?

3. Shall we offer passengers drunkard alcohols? If not, how to refuse their demands?

Ⅱ. Dialogues

Dialogue 1: Domestic flights

Situation: After the aircraft reaching the cruising altitude, the purser makes an announcement and flight attendants walk in the cabin providing beverage service.

Principle: Flight attendants should assist passengers with tray tables.

Example

PS: (Announcement) Ladies and gentlemen, due to the very short duration of this flight, we will not be providing meal service. In a few moments, our flight attendants will be offering you hot and cold drinks. We wish you a pleasant journey. Thank you!

FA: Would you like something to drink, Madam? We have prepared soda, fruit juice, coffee, tea and mineral water.

PAX: I'd like some juice.

FA: We have orange juice, tomato juice and apple juice. Which one would you like?

PAX: Apple juice, please.

FA: With ice?

PAX: No, thanks.

FA: Here you are.

音频扫一扫

视频扫一扫

情景会话1：国内航线提供饮料

乘务长：（广播）女士们、先生们，由于航程时间较短，本次航班不提供餐食。稍后，我们的乘务员将会为您提供多种冷热饮料，希望您能喜欢。我们愿与您共同度过一段愉快的旅程。谢谢！

乘务员：女士，我们准备了汽水、果汁、咖啡、茶和矿泉水。请问您想喝点儿什么？

旅客：给我来点儿果汁吧。

乘务员：我们有橙汁、番茄汁和苹果汁，请问您喜欢哪一种？

旅客：苹果汁吧。

乘务员：需要加冰吗？

旅客：不用了，谢谢。

乘务员：给您。

Dialogue 2: International flights

音频扫一扫

Situation: After the aircraft reaching the cruising altitude, the purser makes an announcement and flight attendants walk in the cabin providing beverage service, including alcohol.

Principle: Flight attendants should assist passengers with tray tables.

Example

FA: Sir, we have juice, soda drinks, wine, cocktail and some spirits. Which one would you like?

PAX1: You have wine! Red or white?

FA: Both.

PAX1: Which kind of grape is this red wine made from?

FA: It's made from Shiraz.

PAX1: Well, I think I would rather have some coffee. Don't you have any coffee?

FA: Sorry, Sir, we serve hot drinks during the second time beverage service, but if you want it now, I'll get it for you right away.

PAX1: Well, it doesn't matter. I'll take the coffee later. Now apple juice, please.

FA: OK. Here you are.

PAX2: What kind of spirits do you have?

FA: Madam, we have Chivas Regal, Hennessy V.S.O.P, Stolichnaya Vodka and London Gin. Which one do you prefer?

PAX2: Erm... It's hard to decide...

FA: May I recommend you our cocktail Dancing Autumn? It's made from Baileys and coconut juice and quite suitable for ladies.

PAX2: That sounds great. I'll take it!

FA: Alright.

情景会话2：国际航班/两舱提供酒水

乘务员：先生，我们今天准备了果汁、汽水、葡萄酒、鸡尾酒和一些烈酒。请问您想喝哪种？

旅客1：你们有葡萄酒！红葡萄酒还是白葡萄酒？

乘务员：两种都有的。

旅客1：请问红葡萄酒是由哪种葡萄酿成的？

乘务员：这款酒是由色拉子酿造的。

旅客1：这样啊，我想我还是喝点儿咖啡吧。

乘务员：对不起，先生，热饮我们二次发饮料时提供，但是如果您想现在喝，我马上去给您倒一杯。

旅客1：没关系，那我一会儿再要好了。现在请给我一杯苹果汁吧。

乘务员：好的。给您。

旅客2：你们都有什么烈酒呢？

乘务员：女士，我们有芝华士、轩尼诗V.S.O.P、红牌伏特加和伦敦金酒，请问您喜欢喝哪种？

旅客2：嗯……好难决定呀……

乘务员：如果您想喝点酒精饮料，请允许我向您推荐我们机上的鸡尾酒金秋之舞。它是由百利甜和椰子汁调制而成的，非常适合女士饮用。

旅客2：听起来很不错，那我就要这个了。

乘务员：好的。

Dialogue 3: Wine service

音频扫一扫

Situation: When serving in the first class and business class, flight attendants need to recommend wine for passengers according to their main courses.

Principle: If a passenger chose seafood as his/ her main course, the flight attendant should recommend white wine accordingly.

Example

FA: Mr. Lin, these are champagne and canapé for you. The canapé today is steamed dumplings with shrimp. Please enjoy them .

PAX: Thank you!

FA: My pleasure. Mr. Lin, may I present you your main course seafood spaghetti now?

PAX: Sure, hmm, it smells nice.

FA: Thank you, would you like to have some table wine? We added one exquisite white wine to our collection recently and it would make a perfect match with the spaghetti.

PAX: Oh, nice, tell me more about it.

FA: Okay, just a moment.

(The flight attendant comes back with the wine.)

FA: Mr. Lin, this is Cloudy Bay Sauvignon Blanc from Marlborough, New Zealand, 2013. It has fruit flavor and it also obtains balance from a solid structure of tannin and acidity. May I serve the wine for you now?

PAX: Yes, please.

情景会话3：推荐酒饮

乘务员：林先生，这是为您准备的香槟，同时还为您搭配了佐酒小食水晶虾饺，请您享用！

旅客：谢谢！

乘务员：不客气的。林先生，现在可以为您上主菜海鲜意面吗？

旅客：当然，嗯，闻起来不错。

乘务员：谢谢，要不要尝尝我们的佐餐酒呢？我们最近新增了一款精选的白葡萄酒，和您点选的海鲜意面是最佳搭配。

旅客：不错，跟我详细介绍一下吧。

乘务员：好的，我马上回来。

（乘务员手持葡萄酒回到客舱。）

乘务员：林先生，这是产自新西兰，2013年的云雾湾长相思干白葡萄酒，这款白葡萄酒果味芬芳，酸度较高，并带有层次丰富的水果香气。请问现在可以为您准备吗？

旅客：好的，请吧。

Dialogue 4: Recommend hot drinks

音频扫一扫

Situation: After the aircraft reaching the cruising altitude, the purser makes an announcement and flight attendants walk in the cabin providing beverage service.

Principle: Flight attendants should give passengers some recommendations, assist them with tray tables and remind them of hot drinks.

Example

PAX1: Excuse me, Miss. This is the very first time I take plane. I am wondering whether I have to pay for any of the drinks on the plane.

FA: Not necessarily, Madam. All the soft drinks are free to all passengers. However, bar service is offered to the first class and business class passengers on a complimentary basis.

PAX1: I see. What soft drinks do you serve?

FA: We have prepared mineral water, fruit juice, Coke, Sprite, tea and coffee. Which one would you prefer?

PAX1: It is quite cold now.

FA: Would you like some hot drinks? Today we have hot tea and hot coffee. Which one would you prefer?

PAX1: Would you like to give me some recommendations?

FA: Would you like a cup of coffee? It's about to land and a cup of coffee will give you a lift.

PAX1: I can't agree with you more. In that case, please give me a cup of coffee.

FA: Sure. Then how would you like your coffee, with milk and sugar?

PAX1: Black coffee will be better.

FA: Please take care. It's very hot.

(Turning towards another passenger...)

FA: How about you, Sir?

PAX2: What kind of tea do you have?

FA: We have prepared Oolong Tea, Long Jing Tea, Black Tea, Chrysanthemum Tea, Jasmine Tea and Green Tea for you. Which one would you prefer?

PAX2: Just Green Tea, please.

FA: OK. Here you are.

情景会话4：推荐热饮

旅客1：您好，这是我第一次坐飞机，想问下飞机上的饮料需要付费吗？

乘务员：女士，不用的。机上所有旅客的软饮料都是免费的。但酒类只免费提供给头等舱和商务舱的旅客。

旅客1：我知道了。那你们都有哪些软饮料？

乘务员：我们准备了矿泉水、果汁、可乐、雪碧、茶水和咖啡。您喜欢哪一种呢？

旅客1：现在感觉挺冷的。

乘务员：给您来杯热饮吧？今天我们准备了热茶和热咖啡。您看喜欢哪一种？

旅客1：要不你给我推荐下吧？

乘务员：您看咖啡怎么样？落地前喝杯咖啡可以提神。

旅客1：嗯，太对了，那就给我一杯咖啡吧。

乘务员：好的，咖啡需要加牛奶和糖吗？

旅客1：就黑咖啡吧。

乘务员：咖啡挺烫的，请您当心哦。

（转身为另一位旅客服务……）

乘务员：先生，请问您想喝点儿什么呢？

旅客2：你们都有什么茶啊？

乘务员：我们为您准备了乌龙茶、龙井茶、红茶、菊花茶、茉莉花茶和绿茶，请问您喜欢哪一种？

旅客2：就绿茶吧。

乘务员：好的。给您。

Dialogue 5: (Special Cases) "I haven't been served any drinks yet."

音频扫一扫

Situation: As is often the case, some passengers may fall asleep during beverage service.

Principle: Flight attendants should take care of those who didn't have their drinks. Be polite and patient.

Example

PAX: Excuse me, Miss. I haven't been served any drinks yet.

FA: Sorry, Sir. You were sleeping just then, so we didn't disturb you. What would you like to drink? I'll get it for you at once.

PAX: OK, thanks. Do you have anything without sugar?

FA: Let me see. Oh, I think you may choose from coffee, tea, milk and diet coke. If you like cold drinks, diet coke will fit you. It doesn't contain any sugar at all.

PAX: You have milk? That's great!

FA: Yes, we have hot milk for breakfast.

PAX: I'd like to have a cup of hot milk, please.

FA: Here you are.

PAX: Thanks.

FA: My pleasure.

情景会话5 :（特殊情况）"你们到现在还没给我提供饮料呢！"

旅客：打扰一下，女士。你们到现在还没给我提供饮料呢！

乘务员：对不起，先生，您刚才一直在睡觉，所以没有打扰您。请问您现在想喝点儿什么？我马上拿给您。

旅客：好的，谢谢。你们有无糖饮品吗？

乘务员：让我想一想。我想您可以从咖啡、茶、牛奶和健怡可乐中选择。如果您喜欢冷饮，那么健怡可乐比较适合您，它是无糖的。

旅客：你们有牛奶？太棒了！

乘务员：是的，我们早餐提供热牛奶。

旅客：那我要一杯热牛奶。

乘务员：给您。

旅客：谢谢。

乘务员：不客气。

Ⅲ. Popular Words and Phrases

mineral water		矿泉水
galley power		厨房电源
water boiler		煮水器
hot cup		烧水杯
glass	[glɑːs]	n. 玻璃

plastic cup		塑料杯
champagne flute		香槟杯
bottle	['bɒt(ə)l]	n. 瓶子
straw	[strɔː]	n. 吸管
saucer	['sɔːsə]	n. 茶托
bottle opener		开瓶器
still water		无气泡水
sparkling water		气泡水
ice water		冰水
warm water		热水
juice	[dʒuːs]	n. 果汁；果汁饮料
lemon juice		柠檬汁
orange juice		橙汁
apple juice		苹果汁
tomato juice		番茄汁
grape juice		葡萄汁
pineapple juice		菠萝汁；凤梨汁
mango juice		芒果汁
peach juice		桃汁
watermelon juice		西瓜汁
mulberry juice		桑果汁；桑葚汁
blueberry juice		蓝莓汁
raspberry juice		树莓汁
coconut juice/ coconut milk		椰子汁
green tea		绿茶
black tea		红茶
jasmine tea		茉莉花茶
chrysanthemum tea		菊花茶
herbal tea		凉茶；花草茶
tea bag		茶包
Oolong tea		乌龙茶
Puer		普洱茶
Long Jing Tea		龙井茶
soda water		苏打水；气泡水
Coke	[kəʊk]	n. 可乐
Diet Coke		健怡可乐
Coke Zero	[kəʊk 'zɪərəʊ]	零度可乐
Coca-cola	['kəʊkə'kəʊlə]	n. 可口可乐
Pepsi	['pepsi]	n. 百事可乐
Sprite	[spraɪt]	n. 雪碧
Seven-up	['sevən'ʌp]	n. 七喜 (7-up)
Fanta		n. 芬达
Tonic	['tɒnɪk]	n. 汤力水
ginger ale	['dʒɪndʒə eɪl]	干姜汁，姜汁无酒精饮料
aperitif	[ə,perɪ'tiːf]	n.（餐前）开胃酒

liqueur	[lɪˈkjʊə(r)]	n.（餐后）利口酒，烈性甜酒
spirit	[ˈspɪrɪt]	n.（威士忌、杜松子酒等）烈酒
champagne	[ʃæmˈpeɪn]	n. 香槟杯
beer	[bɪə]	n. 啤酒
wine	[waɪn]	n. 葡萄酒
cocktail	[ˈkɒkteɪl]	n. 鸡尾酒
red wine		红葡萄酒
white wine		白葡萄酒
sparkling wine		起泡葡萄酒
whisky	[ˈwɪski]	n. 威士忌
brandy	[ˈbrændi]	n. 白兰地
gin	[dʒɪn]	n. 金酒，杜松子酒（烈性酒）
rum	[rʌm]	n. 朗姆酒（烈性酒）
vodka	[ˈvɒdkə]	n. 伏特加
tequila	[təˈkilə]	n. 龙舌兰
Chinese liquor		中国白酒
liquor	[ˈlikə]	n. 酒，含酒精饮料
wheat	[hwiːt]	n. 小麦
sake	[seɪk]	n. 日本清酒
plum wine		梅子酒
neat	[niːt]	adj. 不掺水的、不加冰的
straight	[streɪt]	adj. 直饮的
double	[ˈdʌb(ə)l]	adj. 双份的
mixed	[mɪkst]	adj. 混合的
chaser	[ˈtʃeɪsə]	n. 追水
on the rocks		加冰 (with ice)
coffee	[ˈkɒfɪ]	n. 咖啡
sugar	[ˈʃʊgə]	n. 糖
rock candy	[rɔk ˈkændi]	冰糖
milk	[mɪlk]	n. 牛奶
milk power/ dried milk		奶粉
cream	[kriːm]	n. 奶油
milk tea		奶茶
muddler	[ˈmʌdlə]	n. 搅拌棒 (stick)

IV. Practical Expressions

1. Would you like something to drink?
请问您想喝点儿什么？

2. Would you like some hot drinks?
您想来点儿热饮吗？

3. May I put your drink on the table, so as not to spill it on your laptop?
我帮您把饮料放在小桌板上吧，以免酒在电脑上。

4. Which flavor do you like? We have orange and apple juice.
请问您想要哪种口味的？我们有橙汁和苹果汁。

5. Would you like a glass of champagne, Sir?

先生，您想要杯香槟吗？

6. Would you like some ice in your drink?

您想在饮料里放点儿冰块吗？

7. We have red wine, white wine, Cognac, Whisky, Gin and Vodka, and which would you like?

我们为您准备了红葡萄酒、白葡萄酒、白兰地、威士忌、金酒和伏特加。请问您喜欢哪一种？

8. This red wine is specially offered for European and American flights.

这款红葡萄酒是欧美航线的特供酒 。

9. What do you think of the wine?

酒的口感如何？

10. We have a new brand of wine on board. Would you like to have a taste?

我们机上有新品酒水，您想要尝一下吗？

11. It contains cherry, plum and strawberry aromas with a little whiff of French oak casks.

这款酒蕴含樱桃、李子和草莓的芳香，还有一丝法国橡木桶气息。

12. This is very refreshing and crispy. It is full of fresh green apple and lemon flavors. The finish is layered with yeasty aromas. It's very popular as a welcome drink. It also matches very well with starter and seafood.

这一款香槟口感清新爽脆，充满了新鲜的绿色苹果和柠檬味道，同时含有醇厚的酵母风味，层次分明。非常适合作为迎宾饮料饮用，同时也非常适合搭配前菜和海鲜。

13. This dry white wine is from Entre-Deux-Mers of Bordeaux in France. It is fruity and with refreshing acidity. A lot of flavors as lemon, grapefruit and passionfruit. It tastes very nice with either starter or fish and seafood.

这一款干白来自法国波尔多的两海之间，果味丰沛，酸度清新，有典型的柠檬、西柚以及百香果的味道，非常适合搭配前菜以及鱼肉海鲜等。

14. This dry red wine is from the left bank of Bordeaux. It has deep ruby color. The body is medium and structured. There is plenty of redberry and blackberry aromas. It matches very well with beef steak and lamb chop.

这一款来自波尔多左岸的干红，酒体呈深邃宝石红色，酒体适中有层次感，红色浆果和黑色浆果味道彰显，非常适合搭配西餐牛排和羊排。

15. Would you like to have some wine with your meal? We have wine, spirits, liquors, beer and Chinese wine.

餐中酒想要来一点儿吗？我们有葡萄酒、烈酒、利口酒、啤酒和中国酒。

16. Sir/ Madam, I am sorry about the mistake with your drink. I'll serve you a glass of white wine straight away.

先生/女士，我很抱歉给您送错了饮料。我马上给您送一杯白葡萄酒来。

17. Would you like your whisky straight or on the rocks?

您喜欢直喝威士忌还是加冰块？

18. How should I prepare your cocktail, Sir?

先生，请问需要如何调制您的鸡尾酒？

19. The cocktails and mixed drinks served in Air Bar are all invented by the flight attendant. Would you like a try?

空中酒廊的饮品都是由乘务员自行调制的。请问您要试一试吗？

20. Sir, would you like a glass of cocktail? It has pretty color and rich taste.

先生，请问您想喝一杯鸡尾酒吗？这杯酒调出来的颜色非常漂亮，口感也特别好！

21. The one has a pretty color and good taste. The base liquor is mint liquor. It's nice to drink in summer. Hope you'll like it.

这款鸡尾酒色泽诱人，口感也很好，基酒是薄荷酒，非常适合夏季饮用。希望您会喜欢。

22. The one is alcohol-free. It is quite suitable for ladies.

这款不含酒精，非常适合女士饮用。

23. The main ingredients are black tea and sprite. It tastes very good.

主要成分是红茶和雪碧，口味甜美。

24. This one can be served either with or without sugar. Which would you prefer?

这款有含糖和不含糖两种，请问您喜欢哪种？

25. Would you like some more mineral water or anything else?

我再给您添些矿泉水吗？还是喝点儿其他饮料？

26. We didn't disturb you when you were having a rest. Would you like something to drink now?

刚才您在休息，我们没有打扰您，请问您现在要喝点什么吗？

27. I do apologize, Madam. As pineapple juice is not available in this flight, may I advise another juice such as orange or apple?

非常抱歉，女士，我们的飞机上没有菠萝汁，我向您推荐橙汁或苹果汁，好吗？

28. Certainly, a glass of apple juice. I'll be right back with your drink. Would you like any ice in your juice? Please enjoy your drink.

好的，一杯苹果汁，我马上给您送过来。请问您的果汁需要加冰吗？请您慢用。

Ⅴ. Tips

Serve the wine 侍酒服务

（1）Terms used when serving the wine 侍酒时的术语

① originate （v.) 有"起源于、始于"的意思，与 from 连用，originate from 用来表达红酒的产地。

This is a 2011 Coppola Rosso originating from Napa Valley, California, USA.

② blend （n.) 融合，混合物

It's a classic Bordeaux-style blend with vanilla and black cherry.

③ note （n.) 特征，调子

Full-bodied spicy black cherry notes on the palate.

④ tannin （n.) 单宁酸

Supple tannin on the finish.

（2）Expressions in terms of serving the wine 机上"侍酒"用语举例

① This red wine is specially offered for European and American flights.

这款红葡萄酒是欧美航线的特供酒。

② What do you think of the wine?

酒的口感如何？（您满意吗？）

③ It contains cherry, plum and strawberry aromas with a little whiff of oak cask.

这款酒蕴含樱桃、李子和草莓的芳香，还有一丝橡木桶气息。

④ This dry white wine is from Entre-Deux-Mers of Bordeaux in France. It is fruity and with refreshing acidity. A lot of flavors as lemon, grapefruit and passionfruit. It tastes very nice with either starter or fish and seafood.

这一款干白来自法国波尔多的两海之间，果味丰沛，酸度清新，有典型的柠檬、西柚以及百香果的味道，非常适合搭配前菜以及鱼肉海鲜等。

⑤ This dry red wine is from the left bank of Bordeaux. It has deep ruby color. The body is medium and structured. There is plenty of redberry and blackberry aromas. It matches very well with beef steak and lamb chop.

这一款来自波尔多左岸的干红，酒体呈深邃宝石红色，酒体适中有层次感，红色浆果和黑色浆果味道彰显，非常适合搭配西餐牛排和羊排。

VI. Supplementary Reading

1. Tea 茶

Tea is an aromatic beverage commonly prepared by pouring hot or boiling water over cured leaves of the Camellia sinensis, an evergreen shrub (bush) native to East Asia. After water, it is the most widely consumed drink in the world. There are many different types of tea; some, like Darjeeling and Chinese greens, have a cooling, slightly bitter, and astringent flavour, while others have vastly different profiles that include sweet, nutty, floral or grassy notes.

Tea originated in Southwest China, where it was used as a medicinal drink. It was popularized as a recreational drink during the Chinese Tang dynasty, and tea drinking spread to other East Asian countries. Portuguese priests and merchants introduced it to Europe during the 16th century. During the 17th century, drinking tea became fashionable among Britons, who started large-scale production and commercialization of the plant in India.

2. Coffee 咖啡

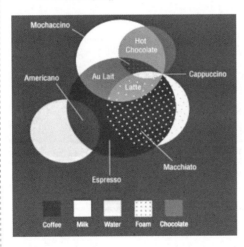

Coffee is a brewed drink prepared from roasted coffee beans, the seeds of berries from certain Coffea species. The genus Coffea is native to tropical Africa (specifically having its origin in Ethiopia and Sudan) and Madagascar, the Comoros, Mauritius, and Réunion in the Indian Ocean. Coffee plants are now cultivated in over 70 countries, primarily in the equatorial regions of the Americas, Southeast Asia, Indian subcontinent, and Africa. The two most commonly grown are C. arabica and C. robusta. Once ripe, coffee berries are picked, processed, and dried. Dried coffee seeds are roasted to varying degrees, depending on the desired flavor. Roasted beans are ground and then brewed with near-boiling water to produce the beverage known as coffee.

3. Beer 啤酒

Beer is the oldest and most widely consumed in the world, and the third most popular drink overall after water and tea. Beer is brewed from cereal grains — most commonly from malted barley, though wheat, maize (corn), and rice are also used. During the brewing process, fermentation of the starch sugars in the wort produces ethanol and carbonation in the resulting beer. Most modern beer is brewed with hops, which add bitterness and other flavours and act as a natural preservative and stabilizing agent. Other flavouring agents such as gruit, herbs, or fruits may be included or used instead of hops. In commercial brewing, the natural carbonation effect is often removed during processing and replaced with forced carbonation.

4. Wine 葡萄酒

Wine is an alcoholic beverage made from fermented grapes. Yeast consumes the sugar in the grapes and converts it to ethanol, carbon dioxide and heat. Different varieties of grapes and strains of yeasts produce different styles of wine. These variations result from the complex interactions between the biochemical development of the grape, the reactions involved in fermentation, the terroir and the production process. Many countries enact legal appellations intended to define styles and qualities of wine. These typically restrict the geographical origin and permitted varieties of grapes, as well as other aspects of wine production. Wines not made from grapes include rice wine and fruit wines such as plum, cherry, pomegranate, currant and elderberry.

(1) Terrior 风土

Wine is made from the fruit of grape vine. The main factors that determine how a wine will taste is called "Terrior". Terrior does not just simply means soil but includes, the grape variety used, the environment in which it is grown (climate and weather, soil and slope), the care with which the grapes are grown and harvested, how the wine is made, and how it is matured (including bottle-age).

(2) Rose 玫瑰花

Rose plant at the end of the rows give an early warning of mildew.

(3) Valley 河谷

The certain vineyard in a Valley make it a top class vineyard of the world. The vineyard in the Valley is usually on very steep slopes with a south facing aspect. This is because the slop receives more sunlight than the lower site and it is good for watering draining. The grape fruit is fully ripe with high sugar contain and phenolic acids contain which make the wine with complex flavors and plenty of layers.

(4) Wine glass 酒杯

Red wines are best served in larger-sized glasses. This will allow air to come into contact with a large wine surface and develop the aromas and flavors.

White and Rose wines require medium-sized glasses so that the fresh, fruit characteristics are gathered.

Sparkling wines are best served in flute glasses. This shape enhances the effect of the bubbles.

Fortified wines should be served in small glasses to emphasize the fruit characteristics rather than the alcohol.

VII. Exercises

1. Can you list different sorts of beverages on board?

(1)

(2)

(3)

(4)

2. Translate the following words and phrases into Chinese or English.

ice water	矿泉水
tomato juice	气泡水
grape juice	橙汁
chrysanthemum tea	苹果汁
whisky	红葡萄酒
vodka	

3. Translate the following sentences into Chinese or English.

(1) 请问您想喝点儿什么？

(2) 您想在饮料里放点儿冰块吗？

(3) We have red wine, white wine, Cognac, Whisky, Gin and Vodk. Which would you like?

(4) We didn't disturb you when you were having a rest. Would you like something to drink now?

(5) I do apologize, Madam. As pineapple juice is not available in this flight, may I advise another juice such as orange or apple?

4. Group work: choose one topic to start a conversation. (TIME LIMIT: 10 minutes)

(1) Provide cold drinks.

(2) Provide hot drinks.

(3) Recommend a type of red wine.

Task 14　Meal Service 餐食服务

Ⅰ. Warm-up Questions

1. Why is it so significant to calculate the total number of heated meals before catering?

2. What will you do if the whole cabin runs out of a kind of meal and only left the other that many passengers don't like?

3. How to recommend a meal that a passenger isn't sure he/ she likes or dislikes?

4. Could you please list several different kinds of special meals?

5. How to serve special meals on board?

Ⅱ. Dialogues

音频扫一扫

Dialogue 1: Snacks on short-haul flights

Situation: When providing catering service, flight attendants should actively assist passengers with tray tables, especially those hidden in the armrest in the first row of the cabin.

Principle: Flight attendants should explain to passengers patiently that in terms of short-haul flights there is no meal on board.

Example

FA: Sir, we are going to serve snacks now. May I put down your tray table?

PAX: Sure. Thanks.

FA: Here are your cookies.

PAX: Don't you serve dinners? It's already 17:30.

FA: Sorry, this is a short-haul flight. I'm afraid we only have cookies.

PAX: Well, I'm so hungry. Could you give me more?

FA: Please wait for a moment. If we have more available, I'll give them to you as soon as possible.

PAX: That's all right.

FA: What kind of drinks do you prefer? We have hot tea and coffee as well as mineral water.

PAX: Just water, please.

FA: OK, here you are.

情景会话1：短程航线上的点心餐

乘务员：先生，我们现在马上为您提供点心餐，我可以帮您打开小桌板吗？

旅客：当然，谢谢。

乘务员：这是为您准备的饼干。

旅客：难道你们不提供晚餐吗？现在都已经17:30了。

乘务员：对不起，本次航班航程时间短，我们只提供饼干。

旅客：这样啊，我很饿，你能多给我点儿吗？

乘务员：请稍等片刻，如果有富余的，我会马上给您拿过来。

旅客：好吧。

乘务员：我们为您准备了热茶、咖啡以及矿泉水。您喜欢哪种呢？

旅客：水就好了。

乘务员：好的，给您。

Dialogue 2: Breakfasts

Situation: Breakfasts are usually divided into Chinese style and Western style on board. The Chinese breakfast is usually served with mustard, porridge/congee or Chinese snacks. The Western breakfast is usually served with potato pancakes or omelette/ fried eggs with sausages.

Principle: Be careful with the hot porridge.

Example

(In the economy class)

FA1: Excuse me, Madam. Today we have Chinese dim sum and omelette with sausages for breakfast, which one would you like?

PAX1: Erm... What's in the omelette, please?

FA1: We have onion, pepper, tomato and bacon in the omelette. Would you like to have a try?

PAX1: Sounds great! I'll have the omelette then. Thanks.

FA1: OK. Here you are. It's a little bit hot. Please be careful!

(In the first class and business class)

FA2: Excuse me, Madam. Today we have Chinese dim sum and omelette with sausages for breakfast, which one would you like?

PAX2: Erm... What's in the omelette, please?

FA2: We have onion, pepper, tomato and bacon in the omelette. Would you like to have a try?

PAX2: Sounds great! I'll have the omelette then. Thanks.

FA2: Excuse me, Sir. Now we are serving breakfasts. We have omelette and Chinese dim sum. Which choice would you like?

PAX3: Um... May I know what kinds of dim sum do you have?

FA2: Of course. They are shrimp dumplings and sticky rice in lotus leaf.

PAX3: That's great. I will have this one.

FA2: Sure, here you are. Please enjoy yourself.

音频扫一扫

视频扫一扫

情景会话2：早餐

（在经济舱）

乘务员1：打扰了，女士，我们今天的早餐准备了中式点心和西式煎蛋卷配香肠，请问您喜欢哪种？

　　旅客1：呃……请问煎蛋卷里都有什么？

　　乘务员1：煎蛋卷里面有洋葱、青椒、番茄和培根，您要不要试试？

　　旅客1：听起来不错，那我就来一份西式煎蛋卷吧，谢谢！

　　乘务员1：好的，给您。有点儿烫，请当心！

　　（在头等舱与公务舱）

　　乘务员2：女士，打扰了，我们今天的早餐准备了中式点心和西式煎蛋卷配香肠，您喜欢哪种？

　　旅客2：呃……请问煎蛋卷里都有什么？

　　乘务员2：煎蛋卷里面有洋葱、青椒、番茄和培根，您要不要试试？

　　旅客2：听起来不错，那我就来一份西式煎蛋卷吧，谢谢！

　　乘务员2：先生，抱歉打扰了。我们为您准备了早餐，有煎蛋卷和中式点心，请问您喜欢哪种呢？

　　旅客3：呃……我可以问下点心具体都有哪些吗？

　　乘务员2：当然。点心是虾饺和荷叶糯米饭。

　　旅客3：太棒了，我来一份中式点心。

　　乘务员2：好的，给您。请慢用。

Dialogue 3: Dissatisfy with the meal

Situation: During meal service, a passenger is complaining about the meal because he doesn't get what he likes.

Principle: Flight attendants should explain to the passenger patiently.

Example

PAX: I have no idea. Can you recommend one for me?

FA: Sure, we have beef with rice and fish with rice.

PAX: Erm... Beef and fish again! It's the third time in a row! Can't you prepare some new dishes? Always the same！

FA: I'm sorry for your dissatification, Madam. Our menu changes every 15 days, and you must have travelled a lot recently.

PAX: Yes, I do. I should be aware of my attitude. I apologize for that. But I am so tired of these two. Oh, I miss chicken right now!

FA: Yeah, I know how you feel. Have you tried our healthy vegetarian meal? It's made of mushrooms and bean curd rolls. It's unique and delicious.

PAX: Well, I don't know. But that seems to be the best choice.

FA: Thank you for giving us a try, and you won't be disappointed. Actually, you can book your meal online next time.

PAX: Really? How should I do that?

FA: You can go on our website or simply dial our hotline.

PAX: OK, that helps, thank you.

FA: My pleasure.

情景会话3：不满意餐食

　　旅客：我不知道选什么，你能帮我推荐一款吗？

　　乘务员：好的，我们有牛肉配米饭和鱼肉配米饭。

  民航空乘英语实用口语教程　第三版

旅客：呃……又是牛肉和鱼肉，连着吃了三次了！就不能来点儿新鲜的吗？总是这两样。

乘务员：很抱歉让您不满意，女士，我们的餐谱每半个月更换一次，看来您最近经常乘坐我们航班出行。

旅客：没错，对不起，我没控制好情绪。可是这两样都吃腻了，我现在想要吃鸡肉啊！

乘务员：嗯，我能体会。您有没有尝过我们的健康素食呢？是用菌菇和腐竹做的，味道非常独特可口。

旅客：哦，我不知道。但似乎只好这样了。

乘务员：感谢您给我们机会一试，您会喜欢的。其实，您下次乘机可以预先在网上点选餐食。

旅客：真的吗？要怎么做呢？

乘务员：您可以访问我们的官网，或者拨打热线电话。

旅客：好的，我知道了，谢谢。

乘务员：不客气。

Dialogue 4: Didn't get the first choice

音频扫一扫

Situation: Flight attendants provide catering service. Occasionally, some passengers may not get their first choice of meals.

Principle: Flight attendants should actively look for alternative meals for the passengers. Ask colleagues or use the first class meals to meet the passengers' needs if possible. If the passengers are still not satisfied, flight attendants should apologize and explain patiently to them and let the passengers know that they will have the priority of choosing the second meal to avoid the complaints caused by the choice of meals.

Example

FA: Excuse me, Sir. Here is the menu we prepared for you, later we will serve you dinner, and you may read it first.

PAX1: It's nice, thank you.

FA: It's my pleasure.

FA: Sir, here is the towel for you. Take care, please. It's a little bit hot.

PAX1: You are very considerate. Thank you.

FA: You are welcome.

FA: Madam, we have prepared tomato and egg noodles, stewed beef with potato and beef with rice today. Which one do you prefer?

PAX2: Beef with rice, please.

FA: Let me put it here. The side dish is smoked salmon salad. Please be careful. It's hot. Enjoy your meal, please.

PAX2: Thank you.

FA: Sir, we have prepared tomato and egg noodles, stewed beef with potato and beef with rice today. Which one would you like?

PAX3: Beef with rice as well.

FA: Oh, sorry. That one runs out in the trolley. Let me check if there are some available in other trolleys. Wait a second, please.

(After 5 minutes...)

FA: Thank you for your waiting. Here's your meal, Sir.

/ (There's no more beef with rice) Now we have tomato and egg noodles, stewed beef with potato as well as selected salad. You may choose one you like. Thank you for your understanding. You will have the priority to make a choice for the next meal.

情景会话 4：（国际航班）选餐没选上

乘务员：先生，打扰一下，这是为您准备的餐谱，稍后我们将为您准备晚餐，请您先参阅一下。

旅客1：好的，谢谢你。

乘务员：不客气。

乘务员：先生，这是为您准备的毛巾。有点儿热，您小心。

旅客1：你们真贴心。谢谢。

乘务员：不客气。

乘务员：女士，我们为您准备了西红柿鸡蛋面、土豆炖牛肉以及牛肉米饭。请问您喜欢吃哪种？

旅客2：请给我牛肉米饭吧。

乘务员：给您放在这里了。牛肉米饭的配菜是烟熏三文鱼沙拉。小心烫，请慢用。

旅客2：谢谢。

乘务员：先生，我们为您准备了西红柿鸡蛋面、土豆炖牛肉以及牛肉米饭。请问您喜欢吃哪种？

旅客3：我也要牛肉米饭。

乘务员：对不起，这辆餐车里的牛肉米饭刚刚发完。请稍等片刻，我看看其他餐车里有没有富余的牛肉米饭。

（五分钟后……）

乘务员：先生，让您久等了，这是您的餐食。

/（客人未选择上餐食时）现在有西红柿鸡蛋面、土豆炖牛肉和我们专门为您搭配的沙拉，供您选择。感谢您的理解，下一餐我们将请您优先选择。

Dialogue 5: Special meals

Situation: Due to various reasons, some passengers need special meals. Occasionally, they can't book those meals successfully; some meals can't meet their needs; they have booked special meals, but flight attendants are unable to provide them in time.

Principle: Flight attendants should actively look for alternative meals for the passengers. Ask colleagues or use the first class meals to meet their needs if possible. If the passengers are still not satisfied, flight attendants should apologize and explain to them patiently and let them know that they will have the priority of choosing the second meal to avoid their complaints caused by the choice of meals.

Example

FA: Excuse me, Sir. We have fish rice and beef noodles. Which one do you care for?

PAX: I'm a vegetarian. Do you have a special meal for me?

(The passenger didn't book the special meal.)

FA: Sorry, I'm afraid we don't have any special meal on board. But don't worry, Sir. I'll try my best to find something instead.

PAX: OK, that would be fine.

FA: I will get some for you, Sir. If you need the special meal, you may reserve it 24 hours before departure next time.

音频扫一扫

民航空乘英语实用口语教程　第三版

PAX: OK. I will have a try. Thank you.

(The passenger has already booked the special meal.)

PAX: I have dialed your hotline to order it the day before yesterday.

FA: Really, Sir? Sorry, let me check the special meal list to the galley at once. Wait a moment, please.

PAX: That's OK.

FA: May I confirm which special meal you've ordered?

PAX: Vegetarian meal.

FA: I do apologize for the delay with your special meal, Sir. Here is your meal. Be careful, it's a little hot.

情景会话5：特殊餐食

乘务员：先生，您好，我们有鱼肉米饭和牛肉面条，您想吃哪种？

旅客：我吃素，你们有给我的特殊餐吗？

（这位旅客没有提前预订这种特殊餐食。）

乘务员：对不起，飞机上没有配备特殊餐。但请别担心，先生。我将尽量为您找一些其他的代替。

旅客：好吧，这样不错。

乘务员：我这就去给您拿，先生。如果您需要这种特殊餐的话，下次可以在航班起飞前24小时预订。

旅客：好的，我会试试的。谢谢你。

（这位旅客已预订了特殊餐食。）

旅客：我前天已经拨打你们的热线电话提前预订素食餐了。

乘务员：是吗，先生？抱歉，请稍等片刻，我马上回厨房查询特餐表。

旅客：没事。

乘务员：我可以和您确认一下特餐的种类吗？

旅客：素餐。

乘务员：非常抱歉您的特餐未能及时送来。这是您的餐。请当心，有点儿烫。

Dialogue 6: " Please don't wake me up"

Situation: A passenger would like to sleep for a while and asks the flight attendant not to wake him up.

Principle: The flight attendant should listen carefully and deliver the information to other crew working in the same area.

音频扫一扫

Example

PAX: Excuse me, Miss. Will you serve the meal later?

FA: Yes, Sir. We serve two meals during the whole flight. Next one is two hours later. And we have prepared some snacks and drinks at the bar. Please feel free to enjoy them.

PAX: Great!

FA: Have a nice sleep!

PAX: Thanks. And please don't wake me up then. I want to sleep a little longer.

FA: OK. You may tell us if you need your breakfast by then.

PAX: Thanks a lot.

FA: You're welcome.

情景会话6："请不要叫醒我。"

旅客：打扰一下，女士。请问你们稍后提供餐食吗？

乘务员：是的，先生。本次航班共提供两次餐饮服务。下一餐在两个小时以后提供。我们在吧台准备了小吃和饮料。您可以随意享用。

旅客：太棒了！

乘务员：祝您好梦！

旅客：谢谢。不过到时请不要叫醒我，我想多睡一会儿。

乘务员：好的。到时候如果您需要用早餐，您可以叫我们。

旅客：非常感谢。

乘务员：不用客气。

音频扫一扫

Dialogue 7: Serve the ordered meal (in the first class and business class)

Situation: Flight attendants of the first class and business class should offer meal service personally according to the passengers' requests.

Principle: The flight attendants should be considerate when serving meals. When providing meal service, the flight attendants should strictly follow the standards and rules of the cabin service department. The flight attendants should get familiar with all the dishes and specialties of certain route. And the purser should supervise and guide them to make sure all the services have been best performed. And the flight attendants should not forget that the service should be always personalized and alternative to meet the passengers' personal needs under standard routines.

Example

FA: Mr. Yi, we are going to serve you dinner soon. May I set your tray table now?

PAX: Sure.

FA: Here's the hot towel for you.

PAX: Thanks.

FA: Mr. Yi, we have prepared assorted bread for you, including garlic bread, baguette roll, whole-wheat bread, rye roll, pumpkin seed bread and sesame grissini. We also have butter and olive oil for you to choose.

PAX: Thank you!

FA: That's OK!

(Appetizer)

FA: Mr. Yi, this is Gravlax and Roasted Duck Breast. Hope you like it!

PAX: I can't wait...

(Soup)

FA: Mr. Yi, this is Creamy Soup of White Asparagus Puree. Please be careful, it's a little hot.

(Salad)

FA: Mr. Yi, this is the salad with Calvados dressing for you. Please enjoy it!

(Drinks during the meal)

FA: This is 2012 Parducci red wine from America. Would you like to have a try?

PAX: OK.

FA: I'll bring you Grilled Beef Fillet with Green Peppercorn Butter and Porcini Cherry Sauce right now.

(Entrée/ Main course)

FA: Mr. Yi, this is Grilled Beef Fillet for you. Would you like some pepper and salt?

PAX: Yes, please.

FA: Would you like some more baked bread?

PAX: It's fine.

(After a while...)

FA: Excuse me, Mr. Yi, may I clear your tray table?

PAX: OK, thanks.

FA: It's my pleasure. How would you like the dinner? Does the food appeal to your appetite?

/ Do you enjoy that main course? You did not take much. Would you like to try others instead?

PAX: I need to keep fit actually. It tastes delicious. The red wine is also very good!

FA: OK. I'm glad that you like it!

情景会话 7 :（两舱）提供预订餐食

乘务员：易先生，我们马上为您提供晚餐，现在为您摆桌吗？

旅客：好的。

乘务员：这是为您准备的热毛巾。

旅客：谢谢。

乘务员：易先生，我们为您准备了多种现烤面包，有蒜蓉包、法包、全麦包、黑麦包、南瓜子包和芝麻芝士起酥条，并搭配有黄油和橄榄油供您选择。

旅客：谢谢！

乘务员：不客气！

（前菜）

乘务员：这是刁草三文鱼配橙味烤鸭胸脯片，希望您会喜欢！

旅客：我等不及想尝尝了……

（汤品）

乘务员：易先生，这是白芦笋奶油汤，小心烫。

（沙拉）

乘务员：易先生，这是田园蔬菜沙拉，已为您浇好苹果白兰地汁，请您慢用。

（餐中酒）

乘务员：这是餐中酒 2012 年帕度希红葡萄酒，产自美国，您愿意品尝一下吗？

旅客：好的。

乘务员：我马上为您奉上炙烤牛排配绿胡椒黄油及牛肝菌樱桃汁。

（主菜）

乘务员：易先生，这是您点选的炙烤牛排。请问需要盐和胡椒粉吗？

旅客：好的，多谢。

乘务员：现烤的面包还需要再来点儿吗？

旅客：够了，不用了。

（过了一会儿……）

乘务员：打扰了，易先生，餐盘我可以为您收一下吗？

旅客：好的，谢谢！

乘务员：不客气！您觉得我们的餐食怎么样？符合您的胃口吗？

/ 不知今天为您提供的这道主菜是否符合您的口味呢？看您没有用多少，您要不要试试其他的选择？

旅客：其实是我最近需要保持身材。很好吃，搭配的红酒也很不错。

乘务员：好的，很高兴您喜欢。

音频扫一扫

Dialogue 8: After the meal (in the first class and business class)

Situation: Flight attendants of the first class and business class should offer meal service personally. Pay attention to the passengers' needs after main course.

Principle: The flight attendants should be considerate.

Example

FA: We've prepared cheese, fruits and desserts for you. And I will serve you right away.

(Desserts)

FA: Mr. Yi, we have Emmental cheese, Gruyere cheese, Brie cheese and fresh seasonal fruits. For sweet delight, we have Tiramisu and ice cream. Which one would you prefer?

PAX: Gruyere cheese and fruits.

(After-meal wine/ Dessert wine)

FA: We have also prepared some dessert wines, such as Baileys, Brandy and wine. Which one would you like to have a try?

PAX: A glass of Baileys on the rock, please.

FA: Sure, here we go.

PAX: Thank you.

(Coffee or tea)

FA: Mr. Yi, would you like to try some hot drinks after meal? We have Chinese tea, Western tea, hot chocolate and coffee.

PAX: Coffee, please.

FA: For coffee, we provide espresso, Americano, coffee latte and coffee cappucino. Which one would you prefer?

PAX: Americano coffee, please.

FA: OK. I'll prepare it for you at once.

FA: (After a while) Be careful. It's a little bit hot.

(Introduce the mini-bar)

FA: By the way, buffet on the middle bar is available during your rest, including fruits, cheese, nuts, crackers and chocolate. For sky snacks, we also have noodle soup with shredded chicken, instant noodle soup and baguette with sliced roasted beef.

PAX: OK, thanks.

FA: My pleasure.

情景会话8：（两舱）用餐后

乘务员：我们准备了芝士、水果和甜点，稍后我将为您提供。

（餐后甜点）

乘务员：易先生，我们今天为您准备了大孔芝士、格鲁耶尔芝士、必然芝士和时令水果。餐后甜点有提拉米苏和冰激凌。您喜欢哪一种呢？

旅客：格鲁耶尔芝士和水果。

（餐后酒/甜酒）

乘务员：餐后酒有百利甜、白兰地和葡萄酒。您喜欢来点儿什么？

旅客：一杯百利甜加冰，谢谢。

乘务员：好的，这就拿给您。

旅客：谢谢。

（餐后热饮）

乘务员：易先生，餐后热饮为您备了中式茶、西式茶、热巧克力和咖啡。请问您喜欢哪一种？

旅客：咖啡就好。

乘务员：那是想要意式咖啡、美式咖啡、拿铁咖啡还是卡布奇诺咖啡呢？

旅客：美式咖啡，谢谢！

乘务员：好的。我马上为您准备。

乘务员：（准备好后）请您小心。它有点儿烫。

（介绍自助吧台）

乘务员：另外，在您休息期间，我们自助吧台备有水果、芝士、坚果、饼干和巧克力供您选用。我们还为您提供了空中点心，包括：鸡丝面、方便面和烤牛肉三明治。

旅客：好的，谢谢。

乘务员：不客气。

Ⅲ. Popular Words and Phrases

scrambled egg		炒蛋
fried egg		煎蛋，荷包蛋
steamed egg		蒸蛋
omelette	['ɔmlɪt]	n. 煎蛋卷
shrimp dumpling		虾饺
siu mai		烧麦
salted egg yolk		咸蛋黄
recommend one for sb.		帮某人推荐一款
give sb. a recommendation		给某人个建议
breakfast	['brekfəst]	n. 早餐
lunch	[lʌn(t)ʃ]	n. 午餐
supper	['sʌpə]	n. 晚餐
dinner	['dinə]	n. 正餐
Chinese food	[ˌtʃaɪ'niːz fuːd]	中餐
Western food	['westən fuːd]	西餐
appetizer	['æpɪtaɪzə]	n. 开胃菜
cold dish	[kəʊld dɪʃ]	冷盘
menu	['menjuː]	n. 菜单
beef	[biːf]	n. 牛肉
steak	[steɪk]	n. 牛排
mutton/ lamb	['mʌtən] / [læm]	n. 羊肉
pork	[pɔːk]	n. 猪肉
chicken	['tʃikin; 'tʃɪkən]	n. 鸡肉
drumstick	['drʌmstɪk]	n. 鸡腿肉
duck	[dʌk]	n. 鸭肉
ham	[hæm]	n. 火腿
sausage	['sɒsɪdʒ]	n. 香肠
hotdog	['hɒtˌdɒg]	n. 热狗
meat ball	[miːt bɔːl]	肉丸
fish	[fɪʃ]	n. 鱼肉

Salmon	['sæmən]	*n.* 三文鱼	
shrimp	[ʃrɪmp]	*n.* 虾	
seafood	['si:fu:d]	*n.* 海鲜	
filet	['fi:leɪ; 'fɪlɪt]	*n.* 鱼片	
tuna	['tju:nə]	*n.* 金枪鱼	
codfish	['kɒdfɪʃ]	*n.* 鳕鱼	
main course	[meɪn kɔ:s]	主菜	
steamed bun	[sti:md bʌn]	馒头	
dumpling	['dʌmplɪŋ]	*n.* 饺子	
rice	[raɪs]	*n.* 米饭	
porridge	['pɒrɪdʒ]	*n.* 稀饭，粥	
congee	['kɒndʒi:]	*n.* 粥	
noodle	['nu:d(ə)l]	*n.* 面条	
noodles in soup		汤面	
spaghetti	[spə'ɡeti]	*n.* 意大利细面	
pasta	['pæstə]	*n.* 意大利面	
fried	[fraid]	*adj.* 炸的	
fried noodles		炒面	
fried rice	[fraid raɪs]	炒饭	
sandwich	['sæn(d)wɪdʒ]	*n.* 三明治	
bread	[bred]	*n.* 面包	
roll	[rəʊl]	*n.* 面包卷	
garlic bread		蒜蓉面包	
oatmeal bread		燕麦包	
milk bread roll		牛奶面包卷	
soft roll		软面包，小圆包	
Laugen roll	[rəʊl]	娄根包（德式粗盐餐包）	
French roll		法式面包	
croissant	[krwɑ:sɒŋ]	*n.* 牛角面包，羊角面包，可颂面包	
toast	[təʊst]	*n.* 吐司面包	
butter	['bʌtə]	*n.* 黄油	
jam	[dʒæm]	*n.* 果酱	
snack	[snæk]	*n.* 小吃	
dessert	[dɪ'zɜ:t]	*n.* 甜点；甜品	
refreshment	[rɪ'freʃm(ə)nt]	*n.* 点心	
cake	[keɪk]	*n.* 蛋糕	
dim sum	[ˌdɪm 'sʌm]	*n.* 点心（中国食品）	
mixed nuts	[mɪkst]	混合果仁	
nut	[nʌt]	*n.* 坚果	
yoghurt	['jɒɡət]	*n.* 酸奶	
almond	['ɑ:mənd]	*n.* 杏仁	
walnut	['wɔ:lnʌt]	*n.* 胡桃；核桃	
peanut	['pi:nʌt]	*n.* 花生	
chestnut	['tʃesnʌt]	*n.* 栗子	
cashew nut		*n.* 腰果	
biscuit	['bɪskɪt]	*n.* 饼干（英）	

cookie	[ˈkʊkɪ]	n. 曲奇；饼干（美）
cracker	[ˈkrækə]	n. 饼干（英）
candy	[ˈkændɪ]	n. 糖果
chocolate	[ˈtʃɒk(ə)lət]	n. 巧克力
ice cream		冰激凌
pudding	[ˈpʊdɪŋ]	n. 布丁
jelly	[ˈdʒelɪ]	n. 果冻
pie	[paɪ]	n. 派
pancake	[ˈpænkeɪk]	n. 薄饼
cheese	[tʃiːz]	n. 芝士
sugar	[ˈʃʊgə]	n. 糖
mushroom	[ˈmʌʃruːm]	n. 蘑菇
onion	[ˈʌnjən]	n. 洋葱
corn	[kɔːn]	n. 玉米
broccoli	[ˈbrɒkəlɪ]	n. 西蓝花
celery	[ˈselərɪ]	n. 西芹
potato	[pəˈteɪtəʊ]	n. 土豆
sweet potato	[swiːt pəˈteɪtəʊ]	红薯；地瓜
tomato	[təˈmɑːtəʊ]	n. 番茄；西红柿
cherry tomato	[ˈtʃerɪ təˈmɑːtəʊ]	小番茄；圣女果
cabbage	[ˈkæbɪdʒ]	n. 卷心菜
carrot	[ˈkærət]	n. 胡萝卜
cucumber	[ˈkjuːkʌmbə]	n. 黄瓜
garlic	[ˈgɑːlɪk]	n. 蒜
lettuce	[ˈletɪs]	n. 生菜
pea	[piː]	n. 豌豆
spinach	[ˈspɪnɪdʒ]	n. 菠菜
pumpkin	[ˈpʌm(p)kɪn]	n. 南瓜
pickle	[ˈpɪk(ə)l]	n. 泡菜；腌制食品
vegetarian	[vedʒɪˈteərɪən]	n. 素食者 adj. 素食的
bean	[biːn]	n. 豆
bean curd	[biːn kɜːd]	豆腐
tofu	[ˈtəʊfuː]	n. 豆腐
cauliflower	[ˈkɒliflaʊə(r)]	n. 花椰菜
red cabbage	[red ˈkæbɪdʒ]	紫甘蓝
okra	[ˈəʊkrə]	n. 秋葵
marrow	[ˈmærəʊ]	n. 西葫芦
lotus root	[ˈləʊtəs ruːt]	藕
tableware	[ˈteɪb(ə)lweə]	n. 餐具（包括碗、盘、刀叉等）
dinner set	[ˈdɪnə(r) set]	成套餐具
cutlery	[ˈkʌtlərɪ]	n. 餐具（特指刀、叉、勺、匙）
cutlery set	[ˈkʌtlərɪ set]	刀叉包（英式）
cup	[kʌp]	n. 杯子
dish	[dɪʃ]	n. 盘；碟；一盘菜
menu	[ˈmenjuː]	n. 餐谱；菜谱
napkin	[ˈnæpkɪn]	n. 餐巾（纸质或布的）

wet tissue	[wet ˈtɪʃuː]	湿纸巾
handkerchief	[ˈhæŋkətʃɪf]	n. 手帕
tray table	[treɪ ˈteɪb(ə)l]	小桌板
serving cart	[ˈsɜːvɪŋ kɑːt]	餐饮车
trolley	[ˈtrɒli]	n. 手推车
table cloth	[ˈteɪb(ə)l klɒθ]	桌布
bowl	[bəʊl]	n. 碗
can/ tin	[kæn]/[tɪn]	n. 罐；听
cart	[kɑːt]	n. 餐车；手推车
chopsticks	[ˈtʃɒpstɪks]	n. 筷子
knife	[naɪf]	n. 小刀；餐刀
fork	[fɔːk]	n. 叉子
spoon	[spuːn]	n. 勺
plate	[pleɪt]	n. 碟子
toothpick	[ˈtuːθpɪk]	n. 牙签
tray	[treɪ]	n. 托盘
warming cabinet	[ˈwɔːmɪŋ ˈkæbɪnət]	保温箱
electric oven	[ɪˈlektrɪk ˈʌvn]	电烤箱
air chiller	[ˈtʃɪlə]	冷风机
oven	[ˈʌv(ə)n]	n. 烤箱
steamed	[stiːmd]	adj. 蒸的
scrambled	[ˈskræmb(ə)ld]	adj. 炒的
boiled	[bɒɪld]	adj. 煮的
braised	[breizd]	adj. 红烧的
fried	[fraɪd]	adj. 炸的
smoked	[sməʊkt]	adj. 烟熏的
stewed	[stjuːd]	adj. 炖的
stir fried	[stɜː fraɪd]	煸炒
poached	[pəʊtʃt]	adj. 水煮的
marinated	[ˈmærɪneɪtɪd]	adj. 浸泡于腌泡汁中的，腌制的
shredded	[ʃreddɪd]	adj. 切碎的
grilled	[grɪld]	adj. 烧烤的，炙烤过的
roast	[rəʊst]	v. 烘烤
ingredient	[ɪnˈgriːdɪənt]	n. 原料
salt	[sɔːlt; sɒlt]	n. 盐
sugar	[ˈʃʊgə]	n. 糖
pepper	[ˈpepə]	n. 胡椒粉
curry	[ˈkəːri]	n. 咖喱
soy sauce	[sɔi sɔːs]	n. 酱油
sauce	[sɔːs]	n. 酱汁
vinegar	[ˈvɪnɪgə]	n. 醋
olive	[ˈɒlɪv]	n. 橄榄油
spice	[spaɪs]	n. 调味料
chili sauce	[ˈtʃɪlɪ sɔːs]	辣椒酱
ketchup	[ˈketʃəp; —ʌp]	n. 番茄酱

dressing	['dresɪŋ]	n. 沙拉酱
French dressing		法汁
Thousand Island dressing		千岛汁

Ⅳ. Practical Expressions

1. May I take your order now, Sir?

现在可以为您点餐吗，先生？

2. Sir, it's 6 p.m. now. Shall we serve dinner for you?

先生，现在是下午6点钟，现在为您开餐可以吗？

3. We have prepared dinner for you. When would you like to have the meal?

我们为您准备了正餐，您想什么时候用餐呢？

4. This is the second meal menu. When would you like to have your breakfast?

这是二餐的餐谱，您大概想什么时候用早餐？

5. I will be at service any time when you would like to have the meal.

当您想用餐时，请随时叫我。

6. In order to make you feel more at ease, you may have flexible dinner time either at 30 minutes take-off or one and a half hours before landing.

为了给您创造良好的休息环境，你可以选择在起飞后30分钟或下降前一个半小时用餐。

7. We have renewed our service procedure in order to offer meals in a short time and let our guests have more time to rest. Hope you will like it. Wish you have a good appetite!

为了让您能够方便快捷地享用美食，同时能够有更加充裕的休息时间，我们对服务方式进行了更新，希望您会喜欢。祝您用餐愉快！

8. We have prepared fish ball with rice and beef with rice, which one would you prefer?

今天我们为您准备了鱼丸米饭和牛肉米饭，请问您喜欢哪一种？

9. We have a selection of dishes for you. Our meals on board are designed to meet both Chinese and Western tastes.

我们有多种菜品供您选择。我们机上配备的餐食既有中式口味也有西式口味。

10. We have prepared tomato and egg noodles, stewed beef with potato and beef with rice today. Which one would you like?

我们今天为您准备了西红柿鸡蛋面、土豆炖牛肉以及牛肉米饭。请问您喜欢吃哪种？

11. Here is the menu, Sir. On today's flight, we have prepared a dinner and a breakfast rich in variety and nutrition.

先生，这是今天航班的餐谱，在今天的航班中我们为您准备了一顿丰盛的晚餐和一顿营养充足的早餐。

12. Excuse me, Sir/ Madam, we provide two meals for you on this flight. When would you like to take them? How about 12 o'clock for the lunch service?

您好，先生/女士，本次航班我们为您准备了两顿餐食。请问您想在什么时间用餐？ 12点用午饭可以吗？

13. We are going to serve you meals. May I put down your tray table?

现在我们要为您提供餐食。我可以为您把小桌板放下来吗？

14. We'll get it done soon! Sir, may I set the table for you?

我们马上为您准备好！先生，我可以为您摆好餐具吗？

15. Let me make up your seat while you leave. When you come back, we'll be ready to serve dinner.

您离开的时候，我来帮您把座位整理一下，您回来后，我们马上为您提供晚餐。

16. We have prepared appetizer, soup, salad, main dish and dessert for you. Is there any food you are allergic to/ don't eat?

我们为您准备了前菜、汤、沙拉、主菜，之后还有甜点。请问您有过敏/不吃的吗？

17. Would you like to have a try with seafood rice? It's worth tasting.

您愿意尝一下海鲜配米饭吗？它值得一尝。

18. Would you like something spicy? Do you have any other eating habits?

您吃辣椒吗？您还有什么其他用餐习惯吗？

19. When would you like to have your fruits, before or after the main dish?

对于水果，您喜欢在主菜之前还是之后用呢？

20. If you don't need the main course, how about some fruit?

如果您不需要用主菜了，那么来点儿水果如何？

21. How do you like your steak done? Rare, medium or well-done?

您想要什么样的牛排呢？嫩点儿的、适中的、还是老点儿的？

22. Today's special is seafood pasta. This dish is a popular choice among our passengers.

今天的特色菜是海鲜意面。这是我们的客人很喜欢的一道菜。

23. May I suggest / recommend this one? It is very nice.

我可以推荐这一款给您吗？这道菜味道很好。

24. We have prepared assorted bread for you, including garlic bread, baguette roll, whole-wheat roll, rye roll, pumpkin seed bread and sesame grissini.

我们为您准备了多种面包，有蒜蓉包、法包、全麦包、黑麦包、南瓜子包和芝麻芝士起酥条。

25. Here is the meal/ hot drink. Please be careful.

这是您的餐食/热饮，请小心烫手。

26. Madam, here is the vegetable salad, and we have Thousand Island dressing and Italian Balsamic dressing. Which one would you prefer? Would you like some more?

女士，这是蔬菜沙拉，我们配有千岛汁和意大利香醋汁，请问您喜欢哪种口味？要不要再加一些？

27. Excuse me, Sir/ Madam, we have also prepared pickled vegetables and chili sauce. Would you like some of them?

打扰一下，先生/女士，我们还准备了榨菜和辣酱，您需要品尝一下吗？

28. Does the meal taste good? Would you like some more bread?

我们今天为您准备的餐食还可口吗？您还需要再加些面包吗？

29. I am glad that you enjoy Chinese cuisine.

很高兴您喜欢中国美食。

30. What flavor of food do you like best?

您最喜欢吃什么口味的食物？

/ What's your favorite flavor?

您最喜欢的口味是什么？

31. We will be showing an exercise video, and breakfast will be served right after that.

稍后我们将播放健身操视频。健身操后，我们将为您提供早餐。

32. I am so sorry. Roast Duck is not available. However, may I suggest today's fried fish and beef steak which also taste delicious? Would you like a try?

实在抱歉，烤鸭没有了，不过，今天的炸鱼和牛排的味道还不错，您愿意尝一尝吗？

33. I am sorry but there is no extra meal today. Is it alright that I bring you some bread or peanuts?

很抱歉，今天的餐食没有多余的了，我给您拿一些面包或花生好吗？

34. Let me check if there are some available in other trolleys. I'll bring it here if we have an extra.

我看看其他餐车里有没有富余的。如果有富余的，我会给您拿过来。

35. Thank you for your understanding. You will have the priority to make a choice for the next meal.

（客人未选择上餐食时）感谢您的理解，下一餐我们将请您优先选择。

36. Sir, I understand you are feeling frustrated because your vegetarian meal is not available in the flight. I fully appreciate how important the special meal is for you. I will do my best to arrange an alternative vegetarian meal for you.

先生，我很理解您很不满意飞机上没有您预订的素食，我完全懂得这份特殊餐食对您有多么重要。我会尽我所能给您准备一份素食代替。

37. Sorry, we don't have any special meal on board. But don't worry, Sir. I'll try my best to find something instead. We also have some fruits and desserts. Would you like some?

对不起，飞机上没有配备特殊餐。但请别担心，先生。我会尽量为您找一些其他的代替。我们还准备了水果和点心，请问您需要来点儿吗？

38. We have prepared some snacks and drinks at the mini-bar.

我们在小吧台准备了一些小吃和饮料。

39. We serve two meals during the whole flight. Next one is two hours later.

本次航班共提供两次餐饮服务。下一餐在两个小时以后提供。

40. You were sleeping just then, so we didn't interrupt you.

您刚才正在睡觉，所以我们没有打扰您。

41. Please don't worry, we will try to meet your need. However, please reserve the special meal next time when you book a ticket and confirm it 24 hours before departure.

您别担心，我们会尽力满足您的要求。但请您在下次订票时预订，并于乘机前 24 小时再次确认餐食。

42. Here is the special meal you ordered/ reserved.

这是您预订的特殊餐食。

43. May I confirm it with you? Did you order the special meal?

我能和您核实一下吗？您预订了特殊餐，对吗？

44. I'm sorry about the delay with your special meal, Sir/ Madam. May I confirm which special meal you've ordered? I'll check the galley for you straight away.

先生/女士，我非常抱歉您的特餐未能及时送来。我可以和您确认一下特餐的种类吗？我马上回厨房为您查询特餐情况。

45. Let me check the special meal list. Sorry for the mistake.

让我去查一下特殊餐单。对于失误，我向您道歉。

46. This dish really tastes good, and it is very popular among the passengers.

这道菜味道很不错，很多旅客都赞不绝口。

47. I'm sorry to hear that you are not enjoying your meal. We are also serving fruit, cheese and cake. Would you like to have a try?

（旅客对餐食不满时）我非常抱歉您对餐食不满意。我们还为您准备了水果、奶酪和蛋糕，您愿意品尝一下吗？

48. Thank you for giving us a try, you won't be disappointed. Actually, you can book your meal online next time. If you are departing from Shanghai, you can have up to 24 choices of the main course

for the first class passengers, and 16 for the business class.

感谢您给我们机会尝试，您一定不会失望的。其实，您下次乘机可以预先在网上点选餐食，上海始发的航班，头等舱有多达 24 种可点选的餐食，商务舱也有 16 种可供选择的。

49. This is a short-haul flight. I'm afraid we only have snacks.

本次航班是短程航线，我们只提供小吃。

50. Please enjoy your meal!/ Good appetite!

祝您用餐愉快！

51. What do you think of the dinner? Does the food appeal to your appetite?

您觉得晚餐口味如何？还合您的口味吗？

52. How do you like the meal?

您觉得这顿饭怎么样？

/ Did you enjoy your meal, Sir?

用餐愉快吗，先生？

53. Here is the hot towel for you. Did you have a good rest? You look full of energy.

这是为您准备的毛巾。您休息得还好吗？您看起来很精神。

54. Would you like something more, Sir? Please feel free to enjoy.

先生，您还要别的什么吗？您可以随意享用。

55. May I get you a new set of cutlery?

让我为您换一副干净的刀叉吧？

56. Would you pass me your tray and meal box please, Madam? Thank you.

女士，请将您的托盘和餐盒递给我。谢谢。

57. Would you mind me taking these away?

您介意我把这些东西拿走吗？

58. Have you finished? May I clear up your tray table now?

您用完了吗？现在我可以为您收拾一下餐桌吗？

59. No problem. I will take away your tray in a minute.

没问题，我马上为您收走餐盘。

60. Excuse me. Please be careful of the trolley.

打扰一下，餐车经过，请小心。

Ⅴ. Tips

1. Flavour "口味" 的表达方式

（1）acidic/ sour 酸的

Erm, the soup tastes acidic, what did you put in it besides tomato?

（2）brackish/ salty 有点儿咸的

Unlike other bread, this one is a bit brackish, interesting.

（3）mild 清淡的

I got inflamed for eating the hot pot, I need some mild food today.

（4）seasoned 调过味的

This salad isn't seasoned so that it tastes like nothing.

（5）syrupy 过甜的

The reason why I don't eat this cake is that it's so syrupy.

2. How do you like your steak cooked? 你的牛排要几分熟?

（1）牛排种类

通常在菜单上会出现关于牛排（Steak）的项目，大都是牛肉的种类（牛身上的部位），但是除了牛肉的种类、等级（Grade）以外，还会被问到烹调牛排的生熟度、调味料、配料等问题。首先了解一下牛排各个部位的说法。以右图的美式切法为例：

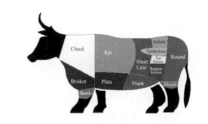

虽然一头牛可以被切割为这么多部位，但是并不需要全部记住。我们只需要了解在菜单上出现的名称和其对应的部位就可以了。在西餐厅常见的牛排种类一般有以下几种：

① filet mignon 也可以简称为 filet，中文名为"菲力"，来自牛的 tenderloin（牛柳）部位，整块的 tenderloin 是如右上图的长条形状。tenderloin 是整头牛中最嫩的部位，口感柔软多汁，价格也是最贵的。

② rib-eye 中文名为"肋眼"，来自 rib（牛肋）中央去骨的部分。肉质嫩且脂肪较多，油油嫩嫩的肉中夹着弹性有劲的油筋，比沙朗耐嚼，比菲力够味，而且油花十分丰郁，红白相间像大理石一样，鲜嫩多汁。

③ sirloin 在表示牛排的种类时叫做"西冷"或"沙朗"，顾名思义来自 sirloin（牛里脊）部位，也包括 top sirloin 和 bottom sirloin 两个部位。这几个部位的油脂介于 tenderloin 和 rib-eye 之间，是很多食客的最爱。此外，short loin（腰脊肉）这一部位的牛排被称为 New York strip（纽约客），或简称为 strip steak，肉质和形状与 sirloin 较类似。

④ T-bone 又被称为 poterhouse，来自 short loin 和 tenderloin 相接的部位，切割后保留了 T 字形的骨头，故而得名。中文名为"T 骨牛排"，T 形骨头的一边是菲力，另一侧则是纽约客（西冷），肉质一侧细嫩一侧粗犷，可以同时品尝牛的两个不同部位。

（2）几分熟的问题

知道想要的牛排种类后，服务人员会询问"How do you like your steak done?/How do you like it cooked?"（您想要几成熟的牛排？）肉熟程度不同，口感也不一样。中文一般会使用单数数字来表示牛排的烹饪熟度，例如：一成熟、三成熟、五成熟、七成熟、全熟，但是英语中却不是用数字来表示，而是有约定俗成的表达方法。一般来说，大部分的牛排做成 medium rare 的熟度是最适合的。当然，想要几成熟的牛排最后还是取决于个人的喜好和接受程度。

rare 可以对应汉语中的一成熟。只将牛排的表面煎成褐色，内部的肉呈血红色。

medium rare 可以对应汉语中的三成熟。中间虽然仍呈现红色，但是外围的肉为褐色。

medium 可以对应汉语中的五成熟/半熟。内部呈粉红色，中间还会保留一丝血红。

medium well 可以对应汉语中的七成熟。除中心部位呈粉红色外，其余部分为烧烤过的褐色。

well done 可以对应汉语中的全熟。从内到外都已经熟透，无血水，只有肉汁。

（3）牛排酱汁

询问"Any condiment?"（需要调味料吗？）如果不想要酱汁，可以回答："No, thank you, I prefer the original taste of the steak."（不，我喜欢原味牛排，谢谢！）

一般有以下几种常见的牛排酱汁：

① 黑胡椒酱汁（peppercorn sauce）为最经典的牛排搭配，由黑胡椒洋葱末及奶油熬制，口味鲜咸，略辛辣。

② 红葡萄酒酱汁（red wine reduction sauce）为糖渍的红酒与葱段做成的酱汁。

（4）其他的常见表达

①"肉太老"：不是"The meat is old"；英文表示"太老、很难嚼、咬不动"，正确的形容词是"tough". The steak is so tough and it's hard to cut. 这牛排太老了，我切都切不开。

② "肉要嫩一些"：我们吃西餐，当然都不希望吃到很老、咬不动、切不开的肉，那么要嘱咐厨师把牛排煎嫩一些，可以说"tender"，表达软嫩、有弹性的感觉。

I prefer my steak a little more rare and tender. 我的牛排要生一点儿，保持口感软嫩的那种。

③ 介绍口感：在点选主菜时，要怎样介绍牛排呢？可以用 tender，juicy 和 succulent。

tender 肉质嫩的

It is a beautiful meat, very lean and tender. 这块肉很棒，肉质既瘦又嫩。

juicy/ succulent 多汁的

Cook pieces of succulent chicken with ample garlic and a little sherry. 用很多大蒜和一点儿葡萄酒烹制这些鲜嫩多汁的鸡片。

VI. Supplementary Reading

1. Special Meals 特殊餐食

Except for Kosher meals, passengers can make special meals reservations 24 hours (inclusive) before flight departure. If flights are delayed or cancelled, the meals ordered might be affected. If a passenger makes a request for a special meal which is not included in the special meal choices listed, (for health or other special reasons), he or she shall provide accurate, detailed and clear information to the sales person, so that the sales person can record the information correctly and that the catering company can understand the special meal requirement correctly.

特餐四字代码	英文全称	中文全称
AVML	Vegetarian Asian (Hindu) Meal	亚洲素餐
BBML	Baby (Infant) Meal	婴儿餐
BLML	Bland Meal	清淡餐
CHML	Child Meal	儿童餐
DBML	Diabetic Meal	糖尿病餐
FPML	Fruit Platter Meal	水果餐
GFML	Gluten Free (Intolerant) Meal	无麸质餐
HNML	Hindu Meal	印度教餐
KSML	Kosher Meal	犹太教餐
LCML	Low Calorie Meal	低卡路里餐
LFML	Low Fat Meal	低脂肪餐/低胆固醇餐
LSML	Low Salt Meal	低盐餐
MOML	Moslem Meal	穆斯林餐
NLML	(Non) Low Lactose Meal	低乳糖餐

特餐四字代码	英文全称	中文全称
RVML	Raw Vegetarian Meal	生蔬菜餐
SFML	Seafood Meal	海鲜餐
VGML	Vegetarian Vegan Meal	纯素餐
VJML	Vegetarian Jain Meal	耆那教餐
VLML	Vegetarian Lacto-Ovo Meal	西式素餐
VOML	Vegetarian Oriental Meal	东方素餐

2. Omelette 煎蛋卷，鸡蛋饼

In cuisine, an omelette or omelet is a dish made of beaten eggs fried with butter or oil in a frying pan (without stirring as cooking a scrambled egg). It is quite common for the omelette to be folded around a filling such as cheese, chives, vegetables, mushrooms, meat (often ham or bacon) or some combination of the above. Whole eggs or sometimes only egg whites are beaten with a small amount of milk, cream or even water.

VII. Exercises

1. Can you list different types of special meals on board?

(1)

(2)

(3)

(4)

2. Translate the following words and phrases into Chinese or English.

scrambled egg   中餐

porridge   主菜

congee   炒面

pasta   黄油

omelette   果酱

ice cream   吐司面包

vegetarian   酸奶

3. Translate the following sentences into Chinese or English.

(1) 我们为您准备了正餐，您想什么时候用餐呢？

(2) 今天我们为您准备了鱼丸米饭和牛肉米饭，请问您喜欢哪一种？

(3) 我们为您准备了前菜、汤、沙拉、主菜，之后还有甜点。请问您有忌口吗？

(4) We have a selection of dishes for you. Our meals on board are designed to meet both Chinese and Western tastes.

(5) We are going to serve you the meal. May I put down your tray table?

(6) Let me check if there are some available in other trolleys. I'll bring it here if we have an extra.

(7) Sorry, we don't have any special meal on board. But don't worry, Sir. I'll try my best to find something instead. We also have some fruits and desserts. Would you like some?

4. Group work: choose one topic to start a conversation. (TIME LIMIT: 10 minutes)

(1) Short-haul flights and snacks.

(2) Provide a special meal.

(3) Serve the ordered meal in the business class.

International Flights
国际航班

Task 15　Duty-free Sales 免税品销售

Ⅰ. Warm-up Questions

1. What's the in-flight duty free product?

2. Why do passengers need to keep the receipt when buying in-flight products?

3. How many ways of paying are there for the duty free products on board?

4. What will you say to a passenger when he / she wants to buy a duty-free item that has been sold out?

5. During the flight, how to give passengers suggestions in terms of selling duty free products or calculating the exchange rate of US dollars to RMB?

6. What's the in-flight promotion?

Ⅱ. Dialogues

音频扫一扫

Dialogue 1: Give recommendations

Situation: During duty-free sales, some passengers ask about the duty-free items.

Principle: When providing our service products, flight attendants should strictly follow the standards and rules of the airline. Flight attendants should get familiar with all on-board service products and specialties of a certain route.

Example

FA: Excuse me, Madam. What can I do for you? You just pressed the call button.

PAX1: I'm looking for a facial cream.

FA: What is your skin type?

PAX1: It's a little bit oily.

FA: These three creams all suit you. But if your skin is sensitive, I would recommend you to choose the first one.

PAX1: Thanks a lot. I will go through the *Duty Free Shopping Guide*.

FA: Take your time.

PAX2: Excuse me? It really smells good on board. What's it?

FA: Well, it's our special fragrance which is emitted by our fragrance diffuser.

PAX2: Oh, great.

FA: Yes. A scent has the ability to influence behavior and trigger memories almost instantaneously. Scent receptors in the nose connect directly to the section of the brain that is responsible for memory and emotion. This is why a smell has the ability to transport you to a certain time and place, linking back to a particular memory or feeling.

PAX2: What is the brand of it?

FA: It's Sky Aroma, a well-known aroma brand overseas.

PAX2: Wow, that sounds good. Can I buy it in retail stores or on the Internet?

FA: Sorry, Sir, it is customized for our airlines, one of a kind. If you really like it, you may purchase it on board.

PAX2: OK! I'll take one.

FA: No problem.

情景会话1：给予建议

乘务员：您好，女士，请问您刚才按呼唤铃，有什么需要帮助的吗？

旅客1：我想买一款面霜。

乘务员：您的肤质是什么样的呢？

旅客1：有点儿油性肤质。

乘务员：这三款面霜都适合您，但是如果您是敏感肌，最好选第一款。

旅客1：太感谢了，我要看看《免税品购物指南》。

乘务员：好的，您慢慢看。

旅客2：您好，客舱里闻起来很香，请问是什么气味呀？

乘务员：哦，是由我们的香氛喷雾散发出来的专属香味。

旅客2：哦，真好。

乘务员：是呢。香味会影响我们的行为方式，也会唤起我们即刻的记忆。我们鼻子内的香味接收器与我们大脑中负责记忆与情绪的部分直接相连。这就是为什么一种味道会把你带到一个特定的时间和地点，使你产生独特的感觉并唤起你的记忆。

旅客2：请问这是什么牌子的？

乘务员：是天空香氛，一个海外的著名香氛品牌。

旅客2：哇，听起来很不错呀。请问我能从零售店或网上买到这种香氛吗？

乘务员：抱歉，先生，这是我们飞机上专卖的香氛。如果您真的喜欢这种香氛，可以在飞机上购买。

旅客2：好的。我要买一个。

乘务员：没问题。

Dialogue 2: Pay in cash

Situation: During duty free sales, some passengers would like to buy certain duty free items.

Principle: When providing our service products, flight attendants should strictly follow the standards and rules of the airline. Flight attendants should get familiar with all on-board service products and specialties of acertain route.

Example

FA: Sir, this is the *Duty Free Shopping Guide*. If there is any duty free item you'd like to purchase, please let me know.

PAX: I want to buy some cigarettes.

FA: Sure. According to the entry requirements of America, each passenger can carry 200 cigarettes

音频扫一扫

into America. So you can buy 1 carton of cigarettes.

PAX: OK, 1 carton. I also want to buy something for my wife. Which one is suitable for a lady?

FA: Perfume and cosmetics will be good choices for ladies, such as Christian Dior, Chanel, Estēe Lauder and Lancôme. All of these brands are popular. Watches and ornaments are also well sold.

PAX: OK. Maybe she likes this Miss Dior Cherie. I'd like to buy some liquor as well. Three bottles of whiskey, please. Oh, how much do they cost?

FA: 29 US dollars for each. But sorry, Sir. Visitors to the United States are allowed to buy one liter a person at most.

PAX: Alright. Just one bottle. Can I have a discount?

FA: Sorry. All the items offered on board are sold at marked prices. Your total price is $154.

PAX: OK. Can I pay it by cheque?

FA: I am afraid not. We only accept cash and credit card. For cash, we only accept US dollars, Euros and RMB. And the credit cards of VISA, JCB and MasterCard are acceptable.

PAX: OK. I'll pay in cash by US dollars. Here is $200.

FA: I'm sorry. I don't have the change right now. Do you have some changes?

PAX: No, I don't.

FA: May I come back later? I will see if I can get some changes from other passengers' purchases.

PAX: That's fine.

FA: Thank you for your support and understanding.

情景会话2：用现金付款

乘务员：先生，这是《免税品购物指南》，如果您有什么需要，请与我联系。

旅客：我想买些香烟。

乘务员：好的。根据美国入境要求，每位旅客可以携带200支香烟入境，因此，您可以购买一条。

旅客：好的，我买一条。我还想为我太太买一些东西，哪一种比较适合女士？

乘务员：香水和化妆品都是非常好的选择，比如迪奥、香奈儿、雅诗兰黛和兰蔻，这些都是知名品牌。手表和配饰也不错！

旅客：好的，或许她会喜欢这款迪奥甜心系列香水。我还想买一些酒。请给我三瓶威士忌，一共多少钱？

乘务员：29美元一瓶。不过，抱歉，先生，去美国的游客每人最多允许购买一升。

旅客：好吧，那就买一瓶吧。有折扣吗？

乘务员：抱歉，机上所有商品都是明码标价的。一共是154美元。

旅客：好的。我能用支票支付吗？

乘务员：恐怕不能，我们只收现金和信用卡。现金方面，我们接受美元、欧元和人民币。至于信用卡，您可以用VISA、JCB或者MasterCard的信用卡。

旅客：好的，我知道了。我用美元付款。这是200美元。

乘务员：抱歉，目前我找不开200美元。请问您有零钱吗？

旅客：没有呢。

乘务员：我一会回来好吗？我看看其他旅客购买时会不会有些零钱。

旅客：好的。

乘务员：谢谢您的支持和理解。

Dialogue 3: The exchange rate

Situation: During duty free sales, a passenger would like to buy certain duty free items and ask about the exchange rate on board.

Principle: When providing our service products, flight attendants should strictly follow the standards and rules of the airline. Flight attendants should get familiar with all on-board service products and specialties of a certain route.

Example

PAX: Miss, I feel like some alcoholic drinks. Can you give me some suggestions?

FA: Yes, Sir. We have Remy Martin, Johnnie Walker Black Label and Martell. Which one would you prefer?

PAX: Can I have a bottle of Johnnie Walker Black Label?

FA: I'm sorry, Sir. We sold it out just now. We can only carry a limited stock of each item and this one has been very popular today.

PAX: That's OK. Can you recommend a perfume for a lady? She is my fiancée.

FA: Do you care about the price?

PAX: About $120.

FA: This French perfume, Chanel No. 5 costs $115. Do you like it?

PAX: Can I have a try?

FA: Yes, try this one, please.

PAX: Oh, nice. I will take one.

FA: Anything else, Sir?

PAX: No, thank you. May I pay in Euros?

FA: Of course, Sir. You may pay in US dollars, Euros, UK pounds, Japanese *yen* or Chinese *yuan*.

PAX: What's the exchange rate between US dollars and Euros?

FA: The exchange rate today makes 100 US dollars equal to 75 Euros. So it comes to 90 Euros, Sir.

PAX: I see. Here you are.

FA: 100 Euros. I haven't got enough changes for you, Sir. Please wait for a moment. I will be back soon.

情景会话 3：汇率

旅客：女士，我想买几瓶酒，能帮我推荐下吗？

乘务员：好的，先生。我们有人头马、尊尼获加黑方和马多利这样的世界名酒。您看您喜欢哪一种？

旅客：来瓶尊尼获加黑方吧。

乘务员：抱歉，先生，这种酒刚刚卖完。每趟航班上，我们所配的商品数量有限，而且今天这个品牌挺畅销的。

旅客：没事。那你能帮忙推荐一款香水给我未婚妻吗？

乘务员：价格上有什么考虑吗？

旅客：120美元左右的。

乘务员：这是香奈儿五号，一款法国香水，标价115美元。您喜欢吗？

旅客：我能试一下吗？

乘务员：好的，您可以试试这个。

旅客：哇，不错。我买一瓶。

乘务员：先生，请问还需要些别的吗？

旅客：不用了，谢谢。我能用欧元付款吗？

乘务员：当然，可以的。您可以用美元、欧元、英镑、日元或人民币付款。

旅客：请问美元和欧元之间的汇率是多少呢？

乘务员：今日机上100美元合75欧元。所以，先生，您需要支付90欧元。

旅客：好的，给你。

乘务员：100欧元，我现在没有足够的零钱找您。请稍等一下，我马上回来。

音频扫一扫

Dialogue 4: Pay by credit card

Situation: During duty free sales, a passenger would like to buy certain duty free items.

Principle: When providing our service products, flight attendants should strictly follow the standards and rules of the airline. Flight attendants should get familiar with all on-board service products and specialties of a certain route.

Example

FA: Ladies and gentlemen, we're selling duty free items now. We have perfumes, cigarettes, cosmetics, alcohol, watches, and so on. And this is our *Duty Free Shopping Guide*. You can find them on it. If there is something you need, please take down the article number and let me know.

PAX: I want to buy a gift for my wife. Do you have any recommendation? Which one is suitable for her?

FA: Perfume and cosmetics would be good for ladies, such as Christian Dior, Chanel. All of these brands are popular around the world.

PAX: Maybe she likes this Miss Dior Cherie. How much does it cost? Can I have a discount?

FA: Sorry, all the items offered on board are sold at marked prices. Your total price is 80 dollars.

PAX: How can I pay for it? Can I pay it by check?

FA: I'm afraid not. We only accept cash and credit card.

PAX: Then... I'll pay by credit card. VISA, is that okay?

FA: Sure. Please enter your PIN.

PAX: Here you go.

FA: Please sign here. Thanks!

情景会话4：用信用卡付款

乘务员：女生们，先生们，我们正在出售免税品，有香水、香烟、化妆品、酒类、手表等。您可以看看这份《免税品购物指南》，如果有需要的商品，您可以记录下商品编号随时告诉我。

旅客：我想为我妻子买个礼物。你有什么建议吗？哪一款适合她呢？

乘务员：像迪奥、香奈儿这些品牌的香水和化妆品都挺适合女士的，这些都是全球知名品牌。

旅客：估计她喜欢这款迪奥甜心系列香水。这款多少钱？有折扣吗？

乘务员：抱歉，先生，机上销售的产品都是明码标价的。总共是80美元。

旅客：我怎么支付呢？可以用支票支付吗？

乘务员：恐怕不行，只能用现金或者刷信用卡。

旅客：好吧，我刷卡吧。VISA信用卡可以吗？

乘务员：可以的。请您输入密码。

旅客：好了。

乘务员：请您在这里签名，谢谢！

Dialogue 5: "Your credit card has expired."

Situation: During duty free sales, a passenger would like to buy some duty free products but he/she can't pay by credit card successfully.

Principle: When providing our service products, flight attendants should strictly follow the stan-

音频扫一扫

dards and rules of the airline. Flight attendants should get familiar with all on-board service products and specialties of a certain route.

Example

FA: Hello, would you like to buy some duty-free goods? We have a fine selection on board today.

PAX: What kind of perfumes do you have?

FA: We have Chanel No. 5, YSL Mon Paris and Gucci Bloom.

PAX: Gucci Bloom, please.

FA: OK, (50ml)115 dollars, please. How would you like to pay, Madam?

PAX: May I pay by credit card?

FA: Of course. Just a moment, please... I'm sorry. Your credit card has expired. I'm afraid we can't accept it. Would you like to pay in cash?

PAX: Expired? I didn't realize. In that case, I'll pay in cash. And I've only got 120 dollars.

FA: OK. Here is your change, 5 dollars. Thank you very much. Enjoy the rest of your flight.

情景会话5："您的信用卡已经过期了。"

乘务员：您好，您想买些免税商品吗？今天机上配备的商品都不错呢。

旅客：你们有什么香水？

乘务员：我们有香奈儿五号，圣罗兰反转巴黎和古驰花悦绽放香水。

旅客：就古驰的吧。

乘务员：好的，（50毫升）115美元。女士，请问您如何支付呢？

旅客：能刷信用卡吗？

乘务员：可以的。请稍等一下……很抱歉，您的信用卡过期了，无法完成支付。您想用现金付款吗？

旅客：过期了？我没注意。那我付现金吧，但我只有120美元了。

乘务员：好的，找您5美元零钱。非常感谢。祝您旅程愉快！

Dialogue 6: "Thanks! But we don't accept tips."

Situation: During duty free sales, a passenger would like to buy duty free products.

Principle: When providing our service products, flight attendants should strictly follow the standards and rules of the airline. Flight attendants should get familiar with all on-board service products and specialties of a certain route.

音频扫一扫

Example

(A flight attendant comes with a trolley along the aisle...)

PAX: Miss! Could you come here, please?

FA: May I help you, Sir?

PAX: I'd like to buy something as a gift for my wife. Could you do me a favor?

FA: Certainly. We have lipsticks, perfumes and silk scarves.

PAX: Have you got anything... brighter? Something more Chinese?

FA: How about this silk scarf with floral design? It's a traditional design and the colors are bright.

PAX: Oh, it's nice and very Chinese. Is it pure silk?

FA: Yes, guaranteed pure silk.

PAX: Where was it made?

FA: It was made in Hangzhou.

PAX: I know that Hangzhou is famous for silk. That's just what I need. How much is it?

FA: Only 17 US dollars.

PAX: Plus tax?

FA: All the items sold on board are tax free.

PAX: I'll take it. Can I pay for it in check?

FA: I'm afraid you can't.

PAX: Here's 20 dollars. Keep the change.

FA: No, thanks. We don't accept tips. It's my pleasure to serve you. Here is your change.

情景会话6："谢谢！我们不接受小费哟。"

（乘务员在过道推着免税品车……）

旅客：乘务员，你能过来一下吗？

乘务员：先生，有什么可以帮您的呢？

旅客：我想给我妻子买份礼物。你能帮忙推荐下吗？

乘务员：当然可以。我们有口红、香水和丝巾。

旅客：你们有鲜亮一点儿、更中国风些的东西吗？

乘务员：这条有花卉图案的丝巾怎么样？这个设计就是传统的中国风，并且颜色也很鲜亮。

旅客：嗯，很漂亮，也很中国风。是纯丝质的吗？

乘务员：是的，保证纯丝。

旅客：哪儿生产的呢？

乘务员：是在杭州生产的。

旅客：我知道杭州丝绸很有名。这正是我想要的，多少钱呢？

乘务员：只需要17美元。

旅客：含税吗？

乘务员：飞机上所售的商品都是免税的。

旅客：那我来一条。我能用支票付款吗？

乘务员：抱歉，不可以哦。

旅客：这是20美元，剩下的是小费。

乘务员：谢谢，您太客气了。我们不收小费。这是找您的零钱。很高兴为您服务。

Dialogue 7: "The lipstick you want was sold out."

Situation: During duty free sales, a passenger would like to buy some duty free products, but her favorite one was sold out.

Principle: When providing our service products, flight attendants should strictly follow the standards and rules of the airline. Flight attendants should get familiar with all on-board service products and specialties of a certain route.

Example

FA: Today, we've prepared perfumes, cigarettes, cosmetics, ornaments, alcohol, watches, chocolates, and so on. Some products are 20% off.

PAX: Excuse me, Miss? I'd like this lipstick in the *Duty Free Shopping Guide*.

FA: I'm so sorry, Madam. The lipstick you want has been sold out on board. How about other brands? They are also of good quality.

PAX: Well... Never mind.

FA: You can fill out the order form of the duty-free items you like or reserve them on our official website next time.

音频扫一扫

PAX: I will. By the way, I want to buy something for my boyfriend. And he doesn't have the habit of smoking or drinking.

FA: Let me see… How about this silk tie?

PAX: That looks great. How much is it?

FA: After 20% discount, it's $48.

PAX: May I pay by traveler's cheque?

FA: I'm afraid you can't, Madam. You may pay in cash.

PAX: Okay. Here you are.

FA: Thank you for your understanding. Enjoy your flight!

情景会话7："您喜欢的口红卖完了。"

乘务员：今天，我们有香水、香烟、化妆品、首饰、酒类、手表、巧克力等商品。免税化妆品八折优惠。

旅客：乘务员？我想要《免税品购物指南》上的这款口红。

乘务员：很抱歉，女士，您想要的这款口红已经卖完了，您再看看其他品牌的口红怎么样？它们的品质也很好。

旅客：好吧，没关系。

乘务员：下次您可以通过填写免税品预订单预订喜欢的商品，或者从我们的官方网站上预订您喜欢的免税商品。

旅客：我会的。另外，我想给我男朋友买些东西，他不抽烟也不喝酒。

乘务员：让我想想看……这条丝质领带怎么样？

旅客：看起来不错。价格是多少呢？

乘务员：打完八折后是48美元。

旅客：可以用旅游支票支付吗？

乘务员：不可以哦，女士。您可以用现金付款。

旅客：好的，给你。

乘务员：谢谢您的理解。祝您旅途愉快！

Ⅲ. Popular Words and Phrases

euro	['juərəu]	n. 欧元
floral	['flɔːrəl]	adj. 花的，用花装饰的
conventional	[kən'venʃənəl]	adj. 符合习俗的，传统的
guaranteed	[ˌɡærən'tiːd]	adj. 有保证的，有人担保的
alcoholic	[ˌælkə'hɒlɪk]	adj. 酒精的，含酒精的
brand	[brænd]	n. 品牌，牌子
spirit	['spɪrɪt]	n. 烈酒；精神
liter	['liːtə]	n. 升（容量单位）
credit	['kredɪt]	n. 信用，信誉
expire	[ɪk'spaɪə]	v. 期满，终止
cosmetic/ makeup	[kɒz'metɪk] / [meɪkʌp]	n. 化妆品
accessory/ ornament	[ək'sesərɪ] / ['ɔːnəmənt]	n. 饰品
perfume	[pə'fjuːm]	n. 香水
fragrance	['freɪɡr(ə)ns]	n. 香氛，香味
feminine	['femɪnɪn]	adj. 女性的

intoxicating	[ɪn'tɒksɪkeɪtɪŋ]	adj. 令人迷醉的
subtle	['sʌtl]	adj. 不明显的；微妙的
cleansing cream		洗面奶
skin care		护肤
essence	['es(ə)ns]	n. 精华
toner / smoothing toner（facial mist/ facial spray/ complexion mist）	['təʊnə]	n. 柔肤水；爽肤水
lotion	['ləʊʃ(ə)n]	n. 乳液，露
moisturizer	['mɔɪstʃəraɪzə(r)]	n. 润肤霜，保湿霜
facial cream		面霜
whitening cream		美白面霜
eye cream		眼霜
facial mask/ masque		面膜
moisture	['mɔɪstʃə]	n. 保湿；湿度
brightening	['braɪtənɪŋ]	adj. 提亮肤色的
hydrating	['haɪdreɪtɪŋ]	adj. 保湿的
SPF（Sun Protect Factor）	[ˌes piː 'ef]	防晒系数，防晒指数
gentle	['dʒent(ə)l]	adj. 温和的
sensitive	['sensɪtɪv]	adj. 敏感的
normal	['nɔːm(ə)l]	adj. 中性的（肤质）
oily	['ɒɪlɪ]	adj. 油性的（肤质）
dry	[draɪ]	adj. 干性的（肤质）
combination	[ˌkɒmbɪ'neɪʃ(ə)n]	n. 混合性（肤质）
body wash	['bɒdɪ wɒʃ]	沐浴液
shower gel	['ʃaʊə dʒel]	沐浴液
hand lotion/ hand cream		护手霜
catalogue	['kæt(ə)lɒg]	n. 目录
primer	['praɪmə]	n. 妆前乳
foundation	[faʊn'deɪʃ(ə)n]	n. 粉底
concealer	[kən'siːlə]	n. 遮瑕膏，遮瑕产品
eye shadow	[aɪ 'ʃædəʊ]	眼影
mascara	[mæ'skɑːrə]	n. 睫毛膏
lipstick	['lɪpstɪk]	n. 口红
blush / rouge	[blʌʃ] / [ruːʒ]	n. 腮红
hair product		护发产品
shampoo	[ʃæm'puː]	n. 洗发水
conditioner	[kən'dɪʃənə(r)]	n. 护发素
mousse	[muːs]	n.（头发定型）摩丝
umbrella	[ʌm'brelə]	n. 伞
swimming suit	['swɪmɪŋ sjuːt]	泳衣
bikini	[bɪ'kiːnɪ]	n. 比基尼泳装
belt	[belt]	n. 皮带
purse	[pɜːs]	n.（女士）皮夹，女手提袋
wallet	['wɒlɪt]	n. 钱包，皮夹
scarf	[skɑːf]	n. 围巾
tie	[taɪ]	n. 领带

brooch	[brəʊtʃ]	n. 胸针
earring	['ɪərɪŋ]	n. 耳环
bracelet	['breɪslɪt]	n. 手镯
necklace	['neklɪs]	n. 项链
travel plug adaptor	['trævl plʌg ə'dæptə]	旅行插头转换器
fridge magnet	[frɪdʒ 'mægnɪt]	冰箱贴
cigarette	[ˌsɪgə'ret]	n. 香烟
cigar	[sɪ'gɑː]	n. 雪茄
tobacco	[tə'bækəʊ]	n. 烟草
boutique	[buː'tiːk]	n. 精品；精品店
change	[tʃeɪn(d)ʒ]	v. 找零 n. 零钱
cash	[kæʃ]	n. 现金
debit card	['debɪt kɑːd]	借记卡
credit card	['kredɪt kɑːd]	信用卡
UnionPay	['juːnjən peɪ]	n. 银联卡
discount	['dɪskaʊnt]	n. 折扣
slash prices		大减价

IV. Practical Expressions

1. Here is the *Duty Free Shopping Guide*. Please tell the flight attendant if you need any help.
这是《免税品购物指南》，如果您需要什么商品可以随时告诉乘务员。

2. You'd better read the shopping guide carefully before making the purchase.
请您在购买免税商品之前，一定要仔细阅读这份购物指南。

3. May I recommend some duty-free items for you?
我可以为您推荐几款免税商品吗？

4. All the items offered on board are sold at marked prices.
机上所有商品都是明码标价的。

5. According to the entry requirements of America, each passenger can carry 200 cigarettes into America. So you can buy 1 carton.
根据美国入境要求，每个旅客可以携带200支香烟入境。所以，您可以购买一条。

6. Visitors to the United States are allowed to buy one liter a person at most.
去美国的游客每人最多允许购买一升。

7. The color of this lipstick is quite fit for beautiful ladies like you.
这款口红的颜色非常适合像您一样的漂亮女士。

8. We have perfumes, cigarettes, cosmetics, ornaments, alcohol, watches, chocolates and so on.
我们有香水、香烟、化妆品、首饰、酒类、手表和巧克力等商品。

9. We only accept cash and credit card. For cash, we only accept US dollars, Euros and RMB. And the credit cards of VISA, JCB and MasterCard are also acceptable.
我们只接受现金和信用卡付款。现金的话，我们只接受美元、欧元和人民币。信用卡呢，您可以用 VISA、JCB 或者 MasterCard 的信用卡。

10. Would you like to pay in cash or credit card?
请问您是用现金还是用信用卡支付？

11. In which way you'd like to pay?
请问您想通过哪种方式支付？

12. If you pay by the credit card, we may need your passport as well.

如果您使用信用卡付款，我们还需要您的护照。

13. This credit card has expired. Would you please pay in other ways or by another card?

这张信用卡已经过期了，请您选择其他的付款方式或者换另外一张信用卡好吗？

14. Have you got any small change?

请问您有零钱吗？

15. This is your change, please check it up.

这是找您的钱，请点清拿好。

16. I don't have the change right now. May I come back later? I will see if I can get some changes from other passengers.

我现在没有零钱。我一会儿回来好吗？我看看其他旅客购买时会不会有些零钱。

17. The perfume you want is sold out. How about other brands? They are also of good quality.

您想要的香水已售完，您再看看其他品牌的香水怎么样？它们的品质也很好。

18. You can fill out the order form if you want to order the duty-free items.

您可以通过填写免税品预订单预订想要的免税商品。

19. You can reserve the duty free items you like on our official website.

您可以从我们的官方网站上预订您喜欢的免税商品。

20. Here are the duty free items you have bought. Please check them up.

这是您购买的免税商品，请您核对一下。

21. If you need a transfer, please put the liquid items you have bought on board into this transparent plastic bag, keep it sealed and have the boarding pass ready when going through the security check.

如果您需要转机，请把在飞机上购买的液体免税品放在这个透明的塑料袋内，封好，通过安检时，出示这段航程的登机牌。

22. I am afraid only some of the duty-free items have discounts during the sales promotion.

真不好意思，在这次促销活动期间只有部分免税商品可以打折。

23. We have a special offer for some selected duty free products on board. Cosmetics, skin care products and perfumes are 20 percent off.

机上部分免税商品特价活动。免税化妆品、护肤品及香水均享有八折优惠。

V. Tips

About perfume 香水

(1) Jo Malone Blackberry & Bay 祖玛珑黑莓与月桂叶

Jo Malone Blackberry & Bay is a floral fruity fragrance for women. It was launched in 2012. The fragrance features grapefruit, floral notes, vetiver, cedar, blackberry and bay leaf. This is a pretty and non-offensive citrus-blackberry scent. In the opening, you will get only a small whiff of the bay leaf and then it's tart and kind of sour. As it's mellowing, the blackberry starts coming through, followed by grapefruit nuances.

(2) Marc Jacobs Daisy for Women 莫杰雏菊女士香水（又名：马克·雅克布雏菊女士香水）

Daisy is a sparkly floral-woody fragrance, fresh and feminine at the same time. It is devoted to a sophisticated, seductive and dazzling woman, which at the same time strives to simplicity. It is captured in a lovely bottle decorated with daisy flowers on the top. Charming Daisy fragrance caresses with the fruity strawberry notes, intensive green aroma of violet leaf and sparkling spicy pink grapefruit. Its heart beats in floral rhythm, composed of silky and intoxicating gardenia, delicate violet and jasmine petals.

VI. Supplementary Reading

1.Duty Free 免税

Duty Free is the term commonly used to products that are exempt of excise duty (& tax); these are exclusively available to international passengers who are travelling abroad. These items include a wide range of perfumes, cosmetics, cigarettes, machine-made cigars, rolling tobacco and a range of selected spirits.

Duty-free shops (or stores) are retail outlets that are exempt from the payment of certain local or national taxes and duties, on the requirement that the goods will be sold to travelers who will take them out of the country. Which products can be sold duty-free vary by jurisdiction, as well as how they can be sold and the process of calculating the duty or refunding the duty component.

Duty-free shops are often found in the international zone of international airports, sea ports, and train stations. Goods can also be bought duty-free on board airplanes and passenger ships. They are not as commonly available for road or train travelers.

In some countries, any shop can participate in a reimbursement system, such as Global Blue and Premier Tax Free, wherein a sum equivalent to the tax is paid, but then the goods are presented to customs and the sum reimbursed on exit.

【背景阅读】

一般来说，免税免的是进口关税（duty, tariff），税率集中在20%~100%，比如在国际机场免税店的购物消费，免税店品类主要是香水、化妆品、烟酒、首饰、食品等，通常为国外品牌。

2.Tax Free 退税

Tax-free shopping (TFS) is the buying of goods in a foreign country and obtaining a refund of the sales tax which has been collected by the retailer on those goods. These items include a wide range of clothes, watches, electronic devices and so on.

The sales tax may be variously described as a sales tax, goods and services tax (GST), value added tax (VAT), or consumption tax.

Promoting tax-free shopping and making it easier for tourists to claim the refund back has helped to attract travellers to many countries. TFS is subject to national regulations, such as minimum spend and restrictions on the types of products on which it can be claimed. Refunds can only be claimed on goods which are exported. However, buying goods tax free does not mean travellers are exempt from paying applicable taxes on their purchases when they get home.

【背景阅读】

一般来说，退税指的是退税购物（tax free shopping），退的是增值税和消费税，税率集中在5%～20%，通常是"离境"退税，退税的物品主要包括服装、鞋帽、钟表、首饰、电器等。

VII. Exercises

1. Can you list different ways of paying for duty free products on board?

(1)

(2)

(3)

2. Translate the following words and phrases into Chinese or English.

brand	necklace
expire	借记卡
accessory	信用卡

facial cream	银联卡
lipstick	化妆品
purse	香水
bracelet	香烟

3. Translate the following sentences into Chinese or English.

(1) 女士，这是《免税品购物指南》，如果您需要什么商品可以随时告诉我们。

(2) 我们可以向您推荐几款适合您的免税商品吗？

(3) 机上所有免税品都是明码标价。

(4) 我们只接受现金和信用卡付款。现金的话，我们接受人民币、美元和欧元；信用卡，您可以用 VISA、JCB 或者 MasterCard 的信用卡。

(5) Would you like to pay in cash or credit card?

(6) I don't have the change right now. May I come back later? I will see if I can get some changes from other passengers.

(7) You can fill out the order form if you want to order duty-free items.

(8) We have a special offer for some selected duty free products on board. Cosmetics, skin care products and perfumes are 20 percent off.

4. Group work: choose one topic to start a conversation. (TIME LIMIT: 5 minutes)

(1) Duty free sales: Pay in cash.

(2) Duty free sales: Pay by credit card.

(3) A passenger's favourite duty-free item has been sold out.

Task 16　CIQ Forms Filling 表单填写
（入境卡、海关申报单、检验检疫/健康卡）

Ⅰ. Warm-up Questions

1. What does CIQ represent?

2. How would you say to a passenger when he/she is wondering what the entry forms or declaration forms are used for?

3. How would you say to a passenger when he/she is not sure to fill in the entry form?

4. How to fill in entry cards and customs declaration forms correctly?

5. Due to the differences in legislation of different countries, some items which are legal in other countries may be considered illegal in the country arrived. What should passengers take notice of when going through Customs, Immigration and Quarantine?

Ⅱ. Dialogues

Dialogue 1: The entry card

Situation: The cabin crew will assist passengers in filling out the forms on international flights.

Principle: Flight attendants should understand the laws and regulations of the destination and

音频扫一扫

民航空乘英语实用口语教程　第三版

answer passengers' questions patiently.

Example

PS: (Announcement) Ladies and gentlemen, we've prepared the entry cards and the customs declaration forms of the United States. Please fill them out before landing. Thank you!

FA: This is the entry card for you. Please fill out the form before arrival.

PAX: OK. Does everybody need to fill it out?

FA: American citizens, Canadian citizens and green card holders don't have to fill out the entry cards.

PAX: May I fill out the form in French?

FA: No, you may fill out the form in Chinese or English and keep it with your passport together.

PAX: OK. Do I need to give it back to you after I complete it?

FA: No, Sir. You'll need it when you go through Customs, Immigration and Quarantine. Please submit it to the immigration officers. In order to save your time, you'd better finish it on board.

PAX: I see. Thanks.

FA: If you have any questions about completing it, please don't hesitate to call us. By the way, don't forget the signature.

PAX: You're so considerate.

FA: My pleasure. Take your time.

情景会话1：入境卡

乘务长：（广播）女士们、先生们，我们准备了美国的入境卡和海关申报单。请在落地之前填写好。谢谢！

乘务员：这是您的入境卡。请您在飞机落地前填好。

旅客：好的。每个人都需要填写吗？

乘务员：美国籍公民、加拿大籍公民和持绿卡者可以不用填写入境卡。

旅客：我可以用法语填吗？

乘务员：不可以，请用中文或者英文填写，注意与您的护照放在一起。

旅客：好的。我填写完要交回给你吗？

乘务员：不用，先生。您通过海关、入境检查处和检疫处的时候需要用到。入境卡落地后请交给移民局官员。为了节省您的时间，您最好在机上填写完毕。

旅客：我知道了。谢谢。

乘务员：如果填写时有任何问题，请及时叫我们。顺便说一下，不要忘记签名。

旅客：你真细心。

乘务员：不客气的。您慢慢填。

Dialogue 2: The customs declaration form

Situation: The cabin crew will assist passengers in filling out the forms on international flights.

Principle: Flight attendants should understand the laws and regulations of the destination and answer passengers' questions patiently.

Example

PAX: Excuse me, Miss. Is this the customs declaration form?

FA: Exactly. By the way, a family only needs to fill in one form.

PAX: OK. But I don't know whether I should declare my pearls.

FA: Generally speaking, you need to declare them only when they exceed the limit.

音频扫一扫

PAX: I know the rule. The truth is that I bought a lot of fake pearls which are very cheap, but they look like the real ones. Don't I need to declare them? If the customs officers don't trust me, will I get myself into trouble?

FA: Don't worry. Keep your receipts with you in case they need them. What's more, they will send a specialist to identify your pearls.

PAX: You are so helpful. I'll take your advice.

FA: Don't mention it. Enjoy the rest of the flight.

情景会话 2：海关申报单

旅客：乘务员，这个是海关申报单吗？

乘务员：是的。另外，一个家庭只需要填一张就可以了。

旅客：好的，但我不知道我的珍珠是否需要申报。

乘务员：通常来说，只有超过限额时才需要申报。

旅客：我知道这个规定。但事实是，我买了很多假珍珠，它们很便宜，但看起来却非常像真的。难道我不需要申报吗？如果海关官员不相信我，我会有麻烦吗？

乘务员：别担心。请把收据带好以防海关需要查看。另外，他们还会派专业人员来鉴别你的珍珠。

旅客：谢谢你。我会接受你的建议。

乘务员：不客气。祝您接下来的旅程愉快！

Dialogue 3: The quarantine regulations

音频扫一扫

Situation: The cabin crew will assist passengers in filling out the forms on international flights.

Principle: Flight attendants should understand the laws and regulations of the destination and answer passengers' questions patiently.

Example

PS: (Announcement) (Australia) Ladies and gentlemen, Australia has strict biosecurity laws that may affect you. You must mark "yes" on your card if you have certain food, plant or animal products, or equipment or shoes used in rivers and lakes or with soil attached. Food supplied on-board must be left on board. After any international travel, there may be a small chance that you have been exposed to a communicable disease. If you are feeling unwell, particularly with fever, chills or sweats, it is important for your own health and for the protection of others, that you bring these to the attention of a member of the crew. Please pay attention to the *Quarantine for Air Travelers* video which will be shown shortly. Thank you!

PAX: Excuse me, can I bring these fruits with me?

FA: According to the quarantine requirements of the local government, passengers are not allowed to bring fresh fruits into the country.

PAX: OK. What about this pair of sneakers? With a little bit soil or ash.

FA: Then you need to mark "yes" on your card.

PAX: I will. Thanks!

FA: My pleasure.

情景会话 3：检疫规定

乘务长：（广播）（澳大利亚）女士们，先生们，澳大利亚有严格的生物安全法规，如您携带了某些食物、动植物制品，设备或鞋子在水中使用过或携带泥土，请您务必在卡中选择

"是"。所有机上供应的食物必须留在飞机上。任何一次国际旅行后，您都有可能感染上传染性疾病。为了您和他人的健康，如您在旅途中有发热、受寒或发汗等症状，请务必将这些情况告知乘务员。我们还将为您播放一段澳大利亚《航空旅行检疫》录像片，请您注意收看。谢谢！

旅客：打扰一下，那这些水果我能带吗？

乘务员：根据当地检疫规定，旅客不能携带新鲜水果入境。

旅客：好的。那我这双运动鞋呢？沾了点儿土要么是灰。

乘务员：这样，您需要在卡上选择"是"。

旅客：我会的，谢谢！

乘务员：很乐意为您服务。

Ⅲ. Popular Words and Phrases

security check	[sɪ'kjʊərətɪ tʃek]	安检
customs	['kʌstəmz]	n. 海关；关税
immigration	[,ɪmɪ'greɪʃn]	n. 移民；入境检查处
quarantine	['kwɒrəntiːn]	n. 检疫　v. 对……进行检疫隔离
declaration form	[,deklə'reɪʃ(ə)n fɔːm]	申报单
entry card	['entrɪkaːd]	入境卡
entry formality	['entrɪ fɔː'mælɪtɪ]	入关手续
entry	['entrɪ]	n. 进入
nationality	[,næʃə'nælɪtɪ]	n. 国籍
document	['dɑkjumənt]	n. 文档；文件
government	['gʌvənmənt]	n. 政府；政体
authority	[ɔː'θɒrɪtɪ]	n. 当局；权力；权威
organization	[,ɔːgənaɪ'zeɪʃn]	n. 组织；机构；团体
signature	['sɪgnətʃə]	n. 签名
be required to		被要求……
prohibit	[prə'hɪbɪt]	v. 阻止，禁止
accept	[ək'sept]	v. 接受
adhere to	[əd'hɪr tu]	遵循，依附，坚持
against	[ə'geɪnst; ə'genst]	prep. 违反
outbound	['aʊt,baʊnd]	adj. 出境的
inbound	['ɪn,baʊnd]	adj. 入境的
destination	[,destɪ'neɪʃn]	n. 目的地，终点
port of departure		始发地
date of departure		离港日期
in compliance with		符合，顺从
subject to	['sʌbdʒekt tu]	服从，受……管制
eligible	['elɪdʒəbl]	adj. 合适的；合格的；适用的
shuttle bus		机场巴士
on schedule		（时间表）按时
liquid	['lɪkwɪd]	n. 液体　adj. 液体的
aerosol	['eərəsɒl]	n. [化]气溶胶，喷雾剂　adj. 喷雾的
carton	['kaːt(ə)n]	n. 条（香烟）
liter	['liːtər]	n. 升
ml (milliliter)	['mɪlɪ,liːtə]	n. 毫升

seed	[siːd]	*n.* 种子
pest	['pest]	*n.* 有害的人或物；害虫
straw	[strɔː]	*n.* 稻草；麦秆
paddy	['pædɪ]	*n.* 稻；谷
avian	['eɪvɪən]	*adj.* 鸟的，鸟类的
herb	[hɜːb]	*n.* 草，草本植物
monitor	['mɒnɪtə(r)]	*n.* 显示器；监测仪
proceed	[prə'siːd]	*vi.* 进行；（沿特定路线）行进
domestic	[də'mestɪk]	*adj.* 家的；国内的
inspection	[ɪn'spekʃən]	*n.* 检查；检验
belonging	[bɪ'lɔːŋɪŋ]	*n.* 财物，所属物品
dried	[draɪd]	*adj.* 干燥的，干缩的
message	['mesɪdʒ]	*n.* 信息；消息
biosecurity	[ˌbaɪəusə'kjʊrəti]	*n.* 生物安全
truthfully	['truːθfəli]	*adv.* 诚实地，如实地
false	[fɔːls]	*adj.* 虚伪的，假造的
penalty	['penəlti]	*n.* 惩罚；刑罚
livestock	['laɪvˌstɑk]	*n.* 家畜，牲畜
technical	['teknɪkəl]	*adj.* 技术（性）的
unfavorable	[ʌn'feɪvərəbl]	*adj.* 不利的，不好的
Pre-clearance	[prɪ'klɪrəns]	*n.* 预检，预查
currently	['kʌrəntlɪ]	*adv.* 当前，目前
claim	[kleɪm]	*v.* 需要；索取；提取
merchandise	['mɜːtʃəndaɪs]	*n.* 商品；货物
access	['ækses]	*v.* 接近，进入，使用
dispose	[dɪ'spəuz]	*v.* 处理，处置；安排
distribute	[dɪ'strɪbjuːt]	*v.* 分配，分发
submit	[səb'mɪt]	*v.* 提交，呈送
official	[ə'fɪʃl]	*n.* 行政官员
resident	['rezɪdənt]	*n.* 居民
count	['kaunt]	*v.* 数，计算
refrain from	[rɪ'fren frʌm]	忍住，克制不要
proper	['prɒpə(r)]	*adj.* 适当的，合适的
weight	[weɪt]	*n.* 重量

Ⅳ. Practical Expressions

1. This is the entry card for you. Please fill out the form before arrival and submit it to the immigration officers.

这是您的入境卡。请您在飞机落地前填好，落地后交给移民局官员。

2. These are the arrival card and customs declaration form of China. Please fill in them before landing.

这是中国的入境卡和申报单，请您在落地之前填写。

3. You are required to show these forms to the officers when going through immigration, customs and quarantine procedures.

当您办理入境、海关和检疫手续时需要出示这些表格给官员。

4. In order to save your time, you'd better finish them on board.

为了节省您的时间，您最好在机上填写完毕。

5. Please complete these forms before arriving in Beijing and have them together with your passport.

请您在到达北京之前填写好这些表格，并和护照放在一起。

6. Here are the customs declaration form and the entry card. You may fill out the forms in Chinese or English and keep them with your passport together. It'll be convenient for you to go through the entry formalities in the terminal building.

这是您的海关申报单和入境卡。请用中文或者英文填写，并与护照放在一起。到达候机楼时可以方便您办理入境手续。

7. Please use English capital letters to complete the entry card and the customs declaration form.

请您用英文大写字母填写入境卡和海关申报单。

8. A family only needs to fill in one form.

一个家庭只需要填写一份海关申报单。

9. You'll need them when you go through Customs, Immigration and Quarantine.

您通过海关、入境和检疫处的时候需要用到它们。

10. American citizens, Canadian citizens and green card holders don't have to fill out the entry card. By the way, don't forget the signature.

美国籍公民、加拿大籍公民和持绿卡者可以不用填写入境卡。另外，请不要忘记签名。

11. Could you please stow your tray table after filling out the form?

请您填好表格后将小桌板收好。

12. Could you please have your passport ready? The immigration officer will check it when you disembark.

请将您的护照准备好，下机后将有移民局官员进行检查。

13. According to the quarantine requirements of the local government, passengers are not allowed to bring fresh fruits into the country.

根据当地检疫规定，旅客不能携带新鲜水果入境。

14. Chinese Customs permits 2 cartons of cigarettes into the country, so you'd better not exceed the limit.

中国海关只允许旅客携带两条香烟入境，所以您别超出这个限额。

15. Generally speaking, you need to declare them only when they exceed the limit.

通常来说，只有超过限额时才需要申报。

16. Keep your receipt with you in case the customs asks for it.

请把收据带好以备海关需要查看。

17. As the Immigration/ Customs/ Quarantine forms of Japan are not available on this flight, please get the forms at the relevant counter after arriving at the terminal building. Thank you!

由于本次航班没有配备日本入境卡/海关申报单/检疫申明卡，所以我们无法为您提供。请您在到达候机楼后，前往办理相应手续的柜台索取。谢谢！

18. You may consult the information counter. They'll help you.

您可以咨询机场问讯处。他们会帮您的。

V. Tips

Cabin Announcements: CIQ Regulations 客舱广播：海关、入境及检疫规定

（1）Customs Regulations 海关规定

(U.S.A. Customs) Ladies and gentlemen, all passengers are required to complete a U.S. customs declaration form. A Chinese version of this form is available; however, you are required to use English capital letters to complete the Chinese form and just one letter is allowed in each blank space. For a family traveling together, only one completed form is required. The United States Government requires that the form be completed by all passengers before arrival. Meanwhile, we will be showing a video to help you fill out the form. Please don't hesitate to contact us if you have any questions. Thank you!

（2）Immigration Regulations 入境规定

(Germany Immigration) Ladies and gentlemen, according to German Immigration regulations, all incoming passengers must have signed passports. For your convenience, we'll be showing a video to help you complete the immigration form. Thank you!

（3）Quarantine Regulations 检疫规定

(Japan General) Ladies and gentlemen, in compliance with Japanese Quarantine regulations, soil, plants with soil, pests, rice, straws, paddies, fresh fruits and vegetables are not allowed to be brought into the country. If you have any of these products onboard, please dispose of it before arrival. Please pay attention to the "Quarantine for Air Travelers" video which will be shown shortly. Thank you!

VI. Supplementary Reading

1. Customs 海关

Customs is an authority or agency in a country responsible for collecting tariffs and for controlling the flow of goods, including animals, transports, personal effects and hazardous items into and out of a country. The movement of people into and out of a country is normally monitored by immigration authorities under a variety of names and arrangements. The immigration authorities normally check for appropriate documentations to verify that a person is entitled to enter the country, apprehend the people wanted by domestic or international arrest warrants and impede the entry of the people deemed dangerous to the country.

Each country has its own laws and regulations for the import and export of goods into and out of a country, which its customs authority enforces. The import or export of some goods may be restricted or forbidden. In most countries, customs are attained through government agreements and international laws. A customs duty is a tariff or tax on the importation (usually) or exportation (unusually) of goods. Commercial goods not yet cleared through customs are held in a customs area, often called a bonded store, until processed. All authorized ports are recognized customs areas. At airports, customs is the point of no return for all passengers, once a passenger has cleared customs, they cannot go back.

2. Immigration 移民；入境

Immigration is the international movement of people into a destination country of which they are not natives or where they do not possess citizenship in order to settle or reside there, especially as permanent residents or naturalized citizens, or to take up employment as a migrant worker or temporarily as a foreign worker.

As for economic effects, research suggests that migration is beneficial both to the receiving and sending countries. Research, with few exceptions, finds that immigration on average has positive economic effects on the native population, but is mixed as to whether low-skilled immigration adversely affects low-skilled natives. Studies show that the elimination of barriers to migration would have profound effects on world GDP, with estimates of gains ranging between 67 and 147 percent. Development economists argue that reducing barriers to labor mobility between developing countries and developed countries would be one of the most efficient tools of poverty reduction.

The academic literature provides mixed findings for the relationship between immigration and crime worldwide, but finds for the United States that immigration either has no impact on the crime rate or that it reduces the crime rate. Research shows that country of origin matters for speed and depth of immigrant assimilation, but that there is considerable assimilation overall for both first- and second-generation immigrants.

3. Quarantine 检疫隔离

A quarantine is used to separate and restrict the movement of people; it is a "state of enforced isolation". This is often used in connection to disease and illness, such as those who may possibly have been exposed to a communicable disease. The term is often erroneously used to mean medical isolation, which is "to separate ill persons who have a communicable disease from those who are healthy". The word comes from an Italian variant (seventeenth-century Venetian) of "quaranta giorni", meaning forty days was the period that all ships were required to be isolated before passengers and crew could go ashore during the Black Death plague epidemic. Quarantine can be applied to humans, but also to animals of various kinds and both as part of border control as well as within a country.

VII. Exercises

1. Answer the following questions according to the dialogues.

(1) What is "CIQ"?

(2) How to fill out the customs declaration form?

(3) What should passengers take notice of when going through Customs, Immigration and Quarantine?

2. Translate the following words and phrases into Chinese or English.

immigration	海关，关税
quarantine	检查，检验
government	申报单
organization	入境卡
prohibit	国籍
subject to	签名
seed	违反
pest	

3. Translate the following sentences into Chinese or English.

(1) 这是您的入境卡。请您在飞机落地前填好，落地后交给移民局官员。

(2) 为了节省您的时间，您最好在机上填写完毕。

(3) 请您用英文大写字母填写入境卡和申报单。

(4) A family only needs to fill in one form.

(5) According to the quarantine requirements of the local government, passengers are not allowed to bring fresh fruits into the country.

(6) Generally speaking, you need to declare them only when they exceed the limit.

(7) Please complete these forms before arriving in Beijing and have them together with your passport.

4. Group work: choose one topic to start a conversation. (TIME LIMIT: 10 minutes)

(1) Fill out the entry card.

(2) Fill out the customs declaration form.

(3) The Quarantine regulations.

Task 17   Transfer and Culture Diversity 转机与文化多样性

Ⅰ. Warm-up Questions

1. What is the difference between "connecting flight" and "transfer flight"?

2. How would you say to a passenger when he/ she is worried about the connecting flight?

3. What suggestions would you give to a passenger with a transfer flight and running out of time for the next flight?

4. What are the places of historic interest and scenic beauty in China?

5. When talking about transfer flights, is it reasonable to give a brief introduction to all the in-flight passengers of the city arrived?

6. How to describe the famous spots and culture background of the destination?

7. What should be taken into consideration when conducting the procedure of spraying insecticides/ spraying against insects?

8. What's the difference between regular flights and Hajj flights?

Ⅱ. Dialogues

Dialogue 1: "I'm afraid I will miss my transfer flight."

音频扫一扫

Situation: Sometimes, due to a heavy thunderstorm on route, we may fly around it. And under this situation, some passengers with limited transferring time may not catch the transfer flight.

Principle: Flight attendants should be considerate.

Example

PAX: Excuse me, may I ask you some questions?

FA: Yes, of course. What can I do for you?

PAX: Well, it seems that we will be late for Beijing.

FA: Yes, I am afraid so. There is a heavy thunderstorm ahead of us. We have to fly around it and we may arrive at Beijing Capital International Airport one hour behind schedule.

PAX: One hour?

FA: Yes, I am sorry for the delay.

PAX: I am afraid I will miss my transfer flight to Pairs.

FA: Could you please show me your boarding pass? Or give me your flight number and departure time?

PAX: AF381 to Pairs. The departure time is 8:00 in the evening, Beijing time.

FA: Don't worry, Sir. If you miss the flight, you can go to the transfer counter and our ground staff will help you reschedule. I can reseat you towards the front, so you can get off earlier and save some time.

PAX: Great! And I also have a checked baggage. How can I get it?

FA: We'll arrive at Terminal 2. You can get your baggage at the baggage claim area there, and then go to Terminal 3 to check in for your next flight. There is a shuttle bus on the first floor for free. And it usually takes about half an hour from Terminal 2 to Terminal 3.

PAX: I see. Thank you very much.

FA: It's my pleasure.

情景会话1："我恐怕要赶不上下一段航班了。"

旅客：打扰一下，可以问你几个问题吗？

乘务员：当然可以。我能为您做些什么呢？

旅客：呃，我们好像到北京的时间晚了点。

乘务员：是的。航路上有雷雨，我们得绕飞，预计会比计划晚一小时到达北京首都国际机场。

旅客：晚一个小时？

乘务员：是的，很抱歉延误了呢。

旅客：那我转机去巴黎的航班恐怕赶不上了。

乘务员：可以给我看下您下一段航班的登机牌吗？或者告诉我航班号和起飞时间。

旅客：AF381航班北京飞巴黎。起飞时间是北京时间晚上八点。

乘务员：先生，别担心。如果赶不上下一段航班，您可以去转机服务柜台，地面工作人员会帮您改签的。此外，我帮您调个靠前些的座位，这样您可以节约时间，早些下飞机。

旅客：太好了！可我还有托运行李，怎么取呢？

乘务员：我们会降落在2号航站楼。您需要在2号航站楼的行李提取处取行李，然后您要去3号航站楼办理下一段航班的手续。落地后，一楼有免费的摆渡车。通常从2号航站楼到3号航站楼大约半小时。

旅客：好的，我知道了。非常感谢。

乘务员：不客气。

Dialogue 2: The connecting flight/Stopover

Situation: Between two scheduled flights, the aircraft needs cleaning and refuelling at the airport.

Principle: Flight attendants should remind passengers of taking all the personal belongings with them before disembarking.

音频扫一扫

Example

PAX: Excuse me, Miss. How long do we have to wait in the terminal and why?

FA: About 30 minutes, Sir. That's because the aircraft needs cleaning and refuelling.

PAX: Do I have to take all my belongings with me?

FA: Yes. You may not leave your carry-on baggage in the overhead locker. Please do take your boarding pass and valuables with you.

PAX: Got it.

FA: And the ground staff will give you another boarding pass later.

PAX: Alright.

FA: Please do pay attention to the re-boarding announcement.

PAX: OK.

情景会话2：中转（过站）航班

旅客：你好，乘务员，我们需要在候机楼等多久？为什么要下去等呢？

乘务员：大概需要等待30分钟。因为飞机需要清洁和加油。

旅客：所有的东西都要带下去吗？

乘务员：是的。您不可以把行李留在行李架内。请一定随身带好您的登机牌和贵重物品。

旅客：明白了。

乘务员：下机后，地面工作人员会再给您发一张登机牌的。

旅客：好的。

乘务员：请您一定留意再次登机广播。

旅客：好的。

Dialogue 3: The transfer service and city introduction

Situation: Flight attendants share the airline culture and traditional Chinese culture with passengers by introducing the airline lounge and Beijing.

Principle: Flight attendants should be well-prepared.

Example

FA: Excuse me, Sir. Your transfer flight is 9 p.m. and you may go to our airline lounge to have a rest.

PAX: Your airline lounge? I haven't heard of it before. Can you introduce it for me?

FA: Yes. I'm glad to introduce it for you. The lounge was launched at Terminal 3 of Beijing Capital International Airport in March, 2019. There are more than 10 function areas in the lounge, such as traditional lounge area, food and beverage area, relaxing area, viewing area, audio and video area, VIP room, bathroom and others. You may go and have a try in the lounge.

PAX: How about the meal service?

FA: Our lounge team will offer you custom-made meals at your request. And we also provide capsule coffee for coffee fans with advanced coffee machine.

PAX: Thank you for your introduction. How can I go there?

FA: After landing, you may ask the ground staff for help. They are glad to help you.

PAX: OK. By the way, could you please tell me something about Beijing?

FA: No problem. Beijing is the capital of China and a fascinating mixture of the old and new. It is the political, cultural and administrative center of the People's Republic of China. The Tian'an Men Square is the largest city square in the world with an area of 440,000 square meters. The Palace Museum, also called the Forbidden City, was once the palace for emperors in Ming and Qing Dynasty. It has a unique structural design. The Great Wall is regarded as a symbol of the ancient civilization of China.

PAX: Wow, amazing! The world's cultural and natural heritage is an important outcome of the development of human civilization and natural evolution, and an important vehicle for the exchanges and mutual learning between civilizations.

FA: Certainly. To well protect, inherit and make good use of these precious treasures is our shared responsibility, and is of vital importance to the continuity of human civilization and the sustainable development of the world.

PAX: Sure. Any delicious food there?

FA: If you would like to try the local food, I would suggest the famous Peking roast duck. It tastes distinctively Chinese! You can buy the roast duck in the terminal building. Wish you have a good time there!

情景会话 3：中转服务与城市介绍

乘务员：先生，您好，您的中转航班是晚上九点，您可以去我们航空公司的休息室休息下。

旅客：你们公司的休息室？我之前从没听说过。你能给我介绍一下吗？

乘务员：好的。很高兴向您介绍我们公司的休息室。休息室设于北京首都国际机场的 3 号航站楼，于 2019 年 3 月正式投入使用。休息室设置有传统休闲区、餐饮区、放松区、景观区、视听区、贵宾房、卫生间等十余个功能区。您可以去那儿感受下。

旅客：休息室的餐食如何呢？

乘务员：我们休息室团队将为宾客提供个性化的餐食服务，同时我们还使用高端的咖啡机为咖啡爱好者提供胶囊咖啡。

旅客：谢谢你的介绍，我怎么去那里呢？

乘务员：落地后您可以询问地面人员，他们会很乐意帮助您。

旅客：好的。你能顺便给我介绍下北京吗？

乘务员：没问题。北京作为中国的首都，是一个新旧交融、魅力无限的地方。北京是中华人民共和国的政治、文化和行政管理中心。天安门广场是世界上最大的城市广场，面积 44 万平方米。故宫，又名紫禁城，曾经是明清历代皇帝的宫殿，它的建筑风格非常独特。长城被认为是中国古代文明的象征。

旅客：哇，真不错！世界文化和自然遗产是人类文明发展和自然演进的重要成果，也是促进不同文明交流互鉴的重要载体。

乘务员：是呀。保护好、传承好、利用好这些宝贵财富，是我们的共同责任，是人类文明赓续和世界可持续发展的必然要求。

旅客：当然。那儿有什么美食吗？

乘务员：如果您想品尝当地美食，我给您推荐有名的北京烤鸭，这道菜很有中国特色。您在候机楼内就可以买到。希望您在那儿度过一段愉快的时光！

Dialogue 4: Spring Festival

音频扫一扫

Situation: The Spring Festival travel rush poses challenges to China's public transportation system. That people working far away rush back to the hometown creates the Spring Festival travel rush. And many foreign passengers would like to come back home or travel around China at this time. These foreign passengers are curious about Chinese festival culture.

Principle: Flight attendants should be professional and answer questions patiently.

Example

FA: Happy New Year!

PAX: Uh... I'm a bit confused. New Year's Day was over weeks ago.

FA: I am talking about the Chinese New Year, Spring Festival.

PAX: Oh, right, it slipped my mind. Why do you celebrate two New Years?

FA: Chinese New Year is set according to the lunar calendar. Chinese Spring Festival, also called Lunar New Year, comes on the first day of Chinese lunar calendar and lasts for almost half a month. Chinese have been celebrating the New Year in this fashion for thousands of years. It is the most important festival when the whole family get together. It is similar to Christmas in the western culture.

PAX: I noticed that your company was very empty in the past couple of days.

FA: That is because everyone goes home for Chinese New Year. Traditionally, Spring Festival is also called "guo nian", meaning "pass into the new year". It is a family holiday, not so much a party holiday.

PAX: OK. Will you set off firecrackers?

FA: Naturally, but the most important thing that we do during the New Year is to eat! So make sure to bring your appetite!

情景会话 4：春节

乘务员：新年快乐！

旅客：嗯……我有点儿迷糊了，新年不是几周前就过去了吗？

乘务员：我是说中国的新年，春节啦。

旅客：哦，对了，我都忘了。你们为什么要庆祝两个新年啊？

乘务员：春节是根据农历而定的。中国的春节，也称作农历新年，从农历正月初一开始持续大约半个月时间。中国人庆祝这个节日的习俗已经延续几千年了。它是中国人最重要的举家团圆的节日，就如同圣诞节之于西方人一般。

旅客：我发现这几天你们公司里空荡荡的。

乘务员：因为大家都回家过年啦。在民俗文化中，春节也被称作"过年"，意思是"进入新年"。这是个家庭团聚的日子，不太属于狂欢的节日。

旅客：这样啊。你们会放鞭炮吗？

乘务员：会的，不过过年期间最重要的事情就是吃，所以准备好大吃一顿哦！

音频扫一扫

Dialogue 5: Lantern Festival

Situation: Culture is defined as the social behavior and norms found in human societies. Culture is considered a central concept in anthropology, encompassing the range of phenomena that are transmitted through social learning in human societies. Yuan Xiao Jie, also called Lantern Festival, is the first significant feast after Chinese Lunar New Year, so called because the most important activity during the night of the event is watching various wonderful Chinese lanterns.

Principle: Flight attendants should be well-prepared before the festival flight.

Example

PAX: Hi, Miss, I've really had a great time in Beijing during the Spring Festival. I'm so sad that it's coming to the end.

FA: Don't get too sad. We still have a red letter day coming up.

PAX: Really? What day is that?

FA: The Lantern Festival! It is one of China's most important and interesting festivals. It's on the fifteenth day of the first lunar month.

PAX: But it's already the middle of February, didn't we miss it?

FA: No, Chinese people go by the lunar calendar to celebrate this holiday. The Lantern Festival marks the end of the Chinese New Year celebrations.

PAX: Okay, so fill me in, what do Chinese people do on this special day?

FA: Well, in Chinese we call it "Yuan Xiao Jie". The first month of the Chinese lunar calendar is called Yuan month, and in ancient times "*xiao*" means night.

PAX: I see, so why is it called the Lantern Festival in English then?

FA: Yuan Xiao Jie, also called Lantern Festival, is the first significant feast after Chinese Lunar New Year, so called because the most important activity during the night of the event is watching various wonderful Chinese lanterns. In early times, young people were chaperoned in the streets in hopes of finding love. Matchmakers tried to hook them up. The brightest lanterns were signs of good luck and hope.

PAX: What about nowadays?

FA: Nowadays people enjoy guessing lantern riddles and eating *tangyuan*.

PAX: Lantern riddles?

FA: Lantern riddles guessing is a unique game about Chinese characters.

PAX: I think I had better practice my Chinese so that I can crack the riddles. What about "*tangyuan*"?

FA: *Tangyuan* (rice dumplings) has long been a Chinese ethnic specialty food, adding more atmosphere to the festival. *Tangyuan/yuanxiao* is the indispensable food for the Yuan Xiao Jie (Lantern Festival). With the round shape and sweet taste, it represents a wish for reunion and happiness.

PAX: Wow... Amazing! Anything else?

FA: People like to fly Kongming Lanterns in the night of the festival, which dated back to Han Dynasty when an emperor lit a lantern for Buddhism worship.

PAX: You do that nowadays?

FA: That's right, good luck and have a happy Yuan Xiao Jie!

情景会话 5：元宵节

旅客：嗨，我今年在北京过了一个非常愉快的春节，我很难过它就要结束了。

乘务员：不要太难过，我们还有一个重要的节日马上就要到了。

旅客：真的吗？什么节？

乘务员：元宵节。它是中国最重要和最有趣的节日之一，在正月十五这一天。

旅客：但是现在已经二月中旬了，难道我们没错过吗？

乘务员：没有，中国人按农历过这个节。过完元宵节才意味着中国春节节庆的结束。

旅客：好吧，那快跟我说说中国人怎么过这个节？

乘务员：好，在中文中，我们叫它"元宵节"。因为按照中国的农历，第一个月叫作"元月"，而在古时候，"宵"是夜晚的意思。

旅客：哦，我知道了，那么为什么英文管它叫灯笼节呢？

乘务员：元宵节，也被称为灯（笼）节，是农历新年后首个最重要的节日，之所以这么命名是因为当天晚上最重要的活动就是看各式各样精美绝伦的中国花灯。在古时候，年轻人会在陪伴下到街上去寻找姻缘，媒人们会尽力牵线搭桥，最亮的灯笼就代表着好运和希望。

旅客：那么现在呢？

乘务员：现在人们会猜灯谜、吃汤圆。

旅客：灯谜？

乘务员：猜灯谜是元宵节独特的文字游戏。

旅客：我想我最好努力练习我的中文，这样我就能猜出灯谜了。那"汤圆"呢？

乘务员：汤圆作为节日特色食品，在中国由来已久，为这个节日增添了浓厚的节日氛围。汤圆/元宵是元宵节不可或缺的特色美食。它是圆形的，味道甜美，代表着团团圆圆，和和美美。

旅客：哇，真有趣！还有吗？

乘务员：人们喜欢在这天晚上放孔明灯，这一传统可以追溯到汉朝，当时有一位皇帝"燃灯表佛"。

旅客：那你们现在还会放孔明灯吗？

乘务员：没错，祝你好运，元宵节快乐！

Dialogue 6: Spraying against insect infestation

Situation: The crew members need to spray the cabin during certain flights.

Principle: Flight attendants should follow the standards.

Example

PAX: Excuse me, what's in your hand? And what are you going to do?

FA: I'm going to spray the cabin.

PAX: But what for?

FA: According to the quarantine regulations of the local government, we must spray the cabin against insect infestation prior to arrival.

PAX: Oh, I see. But is it harmful to health?

FA: This is non-toxic spray. But if you are sensitive to this spray, you can place a handkerchief or

音频扫一扫

napkin over your nose and mouth.

    PAX: OK. I'll accept your recommendation.

    FA: Thank you for your cooperation!

情景会话 6：喷洒杀虫剂

    旅客：打扰一下，你手上拿的是什么？你要干什么？

    乘务员：我要在客舱内喷药。

    旅客：为什么？

    乘务员：根据当地政府检疫规定，我们必须在飞机抵达机场前喷洒杀虫剂。

    旅客：哦，我明白了。但是杀虫剂对健康有害吗？

    乘务员：这是无毒喷液。但是如果您对此过敏的话，可以用手帕或纸巾捂住口鼻。

    旅客：好的，我接受你的建议。

    乘务员：谢谢您的合作！

Ⅲ. Popular Words and Phrases

domestic flight		国内航班
international flight		国际航班
departure	[dɪˈpɑːtʃə(r)]	*n.* 出发，启程
arrival	[əˈraɪvl]	*n.* 到达
round trip ticket		往返票
one way ticket		单程票
non-stop flight		直达航班
reconfirm	[riːkənˈfɜːm]	*v.* 再确认，再证实
available	[əˈveiləbl]	*adj.* 有空的，可获得的
alternative	[ɔːlˈtɜːnətɪv]	*n.* 供替代的选择
prohibited goods		违禁品
connecting time	[kəˈnektiŋtaɪm]	转机时间
connect	[kəˈnekt]	*v.* 连接
connecting passenger		转机旅客
transit passenger		过境旅客
transit visa		过境签证
transit information		中转信息
transit counter		中转柜台
transit lounge		中转候机室
transfer	[trænsˈfɜː]	*v.* 转移
catch	[kætʃ]	*v.* 追，赶
endorse	[ɪnˈdɔːs]	*v.* 改签
endorsement	[ɪnˈdɔrsmənt]	*n.* 改签
refuel	[riˈfjʊəl]	*v.* 给……再加燃料
terminal building	[ˈtɜːmin(ə)l ˈbɪldɪŋ]	候机楼
address	[əˈdres]	*n.* 地址
accommodation	[əkɔməˈdeɪʃ(ə)n]	*n.* 住宿
purchased	[ˈpɜːtʃəst]	*adj.* 购买的，买到的
sealed	[siːld]	*adj.* 密封的
receipt	[rɪˈsit]	*n.* 收据，发票
designated	[ˈdezɪgneɪtɪd]	*adj.* 指定的，选定的

assistance	[ə'sɪstəns]	*n.* 帮助
gate/ boarding gate		登机口
continent	['kɒntɪnənt]	*n.* 洲
aircraft type		机型
Asia	['eɪʒə]	*n.* 亚洲
North America	[nɔːθ ə'merɪkə]	北美洲
South America	[saʊθ ə'merɪkə]	南美洲
Europe	['jurəp]	*n.* 欧洲
Oceania	[ˌəʊsɪ'ɑːnɪə; −ʃɪ−]	*n.* 大洋洲
Africa	['æfrɪkə]	*n.* 非洲
ancient	['eɪnʃənt]	*adj.* 古代的
various	['veərɪəs]	*adj.* 多样的
activity	[æk'tɪvətɪ]	*n.* 活动
celebrate	['selɪbreɪt]	*v.* 庆祝
solar calender		阳历
lunar calendar		阴历，农历
be originated from		起源于……
lantern	['læntən]	*n.* 灯笼
invent	[ɪn'vent]	*v.* 发明
register	['redʒɪstə(r)]	*v.* 登记，注册
spray	[spreɪ]	*v.* 喷；喷射，喷洒
spray against insects		喷药杀虫
non-toxic	[nɒn'tɒksik]	*adj.* 无毒的
insecticide	[ɪn'sektɪˌsaɪd]	*n.* 杀虫剂
disinfectant	[ˌdɪsɪn'fektənt]	*n.* 消毒剂 *adj.* 消毒的

IV. Practical Expressions

1. What's the flight number and departure time of your transfer flight?

您的中转航班号和起飞时间是什么？

2. Excuse me, Sir. I will arrange you to sit in the front row before descending so that you can de-plane earlier. Is that OK?

您好，先生，飞机降落之前我会给您调到前排的座位，以便您能提前下飞机。这样可以吗？

3. Excuse me, Madam. Your next flight is the international flight of ×× Airline. Now you are at Terminal 3, so please go to Terminal 2 to check in.

女士，您好，您下一个航班是××航空公司的国际航班，您现在需要从T3航站楼到T2航站楼办理转机手续。

4. We'll land at T2. Please get your baggage at T2 and then go to T1 to check in for your next flight.

我们将停靠在2号航站楼。您需要在那里提取行李，然后去1号航站楼登记换乘接下来的航班。

5. You can go to T1 to check in. But if the transfer time is within 3 hours, the transfer procedure can be done in the transfer hall on the first floor of T2.

您可以去1号航站楼办理登机手续。但如果中转时间在3个小时以内的话，转机手续可以在2号航站楼的一楼办理。

6. Sorry, I'm not sure about the ground service, but after landing please ask our ground staff. They will help you with the transit. Don't worry!

抱歉，我对地面服务还真是不太清楚，但是落地后您可以询问我们的地服人员。他们会帮助您完成转机事宜。请不要担心！

7. You may go to the transit counter for your connecting flights.
如果您转乘其他航班，请到中转柜台办理转乘手续。

8. Your next flight will take off in 4 hours. You've got plenty of time to make the transit.
您的下一个航班在4小时后起飞，您的转机时间很充裕。

9. We are pleased to welcome you to our comfortable transfer lounge in Departure Hall of T3 for free.
欢迎您去我们舒适的中转休息室休息，那里免费提供中转候机服务，就在3号航站楼的出发厅。

10. It's because the airplane needs cleaning and refuelling.
因为飞机需要清洁和加油。

11. You may not leave your carry-on baggage in the overhead locker. Please do take your boarding pass and valuables with you.
您不可以把行李留在行李架内。请一定随身带好您的登机牌和贵重物品。

12. Please pay attention to the re-boarding broadcast.
请留意再次登机的广播。

13. Madam, your liquid makeup must be put into individual containers of 100-milliliter or less and placed inside a clear, one-liter plastic bag.
女士，您的液体状化妆品必须装在100毫升或以下的独立容器中，并将其放置在一个1升大小的透明塑料袋中。

14. Chinese Spring Festival, also called Lunar New Year, comes on the first day of Chinese lunar calendar and lasts for almost half a month.
中国的春节，也称作农历新年，从农历正月初一开始持续大约半个月时间。

15. It is the most important festival when the whole family get together. It is similar to Christmas in the western culture.
它是中国人最重要的举家团圆的节日，就如同圣诞节之于西方人一般。

16. Traditionally, Spring Festival is also called "guo nian", meaning "pass into the new year".
在民俗文化中，春节也被称作"过年"，意思是"进入新年"。

17. Yuan Xiao Jie, also called Lantern Festival, is the first significant feast after Chinese Lunar New Year, so called because the most important activity during the night of the event is watching various wonderful Chinese lanterns.
元宵节也被称为灯节，是农历新年后首个最重要的节日，之所以这么命名是因为当天晚上最重要的活动就是看各式各样精美绝伦的中国花灯。

18. This traditional festival falls on the 15th day of the first month of the lunar calendar.
这个传统佳节在农历（阴历）的正月十五。

19. The Lantern Festival marks the end of the Chinese New Year celebrations.
过完元宵节才意味着中国春节节庆的结束。

20. As the name suggests, people celebrate this festival by flying paper lanterns.
如同它的名字暗示，人们放纸灯笼庆祝这个节日。

21. Lantern riddles guessing is a unique game about Chinese characters.
猜灯谜是元宵节独特的文字游戏。

22. *Tangyuan* (rice dumplings) has long been a Chinese ethnic specialty food, adding more atmosphere to the festival.
汤圆作为节日特色食品，在中国由来已久，为这个节日增添了浓厚的节日氛围。

23. *Tangyuan* / *yuanxiao* is the indispensable food for the Yuan Xiao Jie (Lantern Festival).
汤圆/元宵是元宵节不可或缺的特色美食。

24. With the round shape and sweet taste, it represents a wish for reunion and happiness.

元宵是圆形的，味道甜美，代表着团团圆圆，和和美美。

25. Lion dance is a time-honoured custom in Lantern Festival. People performed lion dance praying for a good harvest year.

舞狮是元宵节一项历史悠久的习俗，人们舞狮祈求风调雨顺，五谷丰登。

26. Chinese traditional culture is broad and profound, to name a few, *Book of Changes*, *qigong* and martial arts, etc. Chinese martial arts, also called "*Wushu*", has a long history. It has gradually become an international event.

中国的传统文化博大精深，比如《易经》、气功、武术等。中国武术历史悠久，现在已成为一项国际竞技项目。

27. Harmony is a defining/ core value of China's cultural tradition. It is an ideal that the Chinese nation has never ceased to pursue.

"和"是中国文化传统的基本精神，也是中华民族不懈追求的理想境界。

28. Beijing is the capital of China and a fascinating mixture of the old and new.

北京作为中国的首都，是一个新旧交融、魅力无限的地方。

29. Where are you from?（Where do you come from?）

你是哪里人？（你来自何处？）

30. Is it your first time to come to Beijing? What's your impression of Beijing?

你是第一次来北京吗？你对北京有何印象？

31. I recommend you Peking roast duck as the dinner this evening. It tastes distinctively Chinese!

我推荐你晚饭吃北京烤鸭，这道菜很有中国特色。

32. I would be happy to recommend a restaurant in the central area. If you would like to try local food, I may suggest Quanjude Roast Duck Restaurant. It is popular and famous for its roast duck.

我非常乐意给您推荐一家市中心的餐厅。如果您想品尝当地美食，我可以给您推荐"全聚德"烤鸭店，那儿的烤鸭非常有名。

33. Wish you have a good time in Beijing! (I hope you enjoy yourself in Beijing.)

祝您在北京玩得愉快！（我希望您在北京玩得开心。）

34. The Tian'an Men Square is the largest city square in the world with an area of 440,000 square meters.

天安门广场是世界上最大的城市广场，面积44万平方米。

35. I recommend the Great Wall, which is a well-known tourist resort. The Great Wall is regarded as a symbol of the ancient civilization of China.

我建议您去参观长城，那是一处非常著名的景点。长城被认为是中国古代文明的象征。

36. The Palace Museum, also called the Forbidden City, was once the palace for emperors in Ming and Qing Dynasty. It has a unique structural design.

故宫，又名紫禁城，曾经是明清历代皇帝的宫殿，它的建筑风格非常独特。

37. Beihai Park is an imperial garden with a history of over 800 years.

北海公园是一座有八百多年历史的皇家园林。

38. Yong He Gong, once the palace for Emperor Yong Zheng, is the biggest and most well-preserved Lama Temple.

雍和宫原为雍正皇帝的府邸，是北京最大、保存最完好的喇嘛寺。

39. Beijing National Stadium, the main competition venue of the 29th Olympic Games, is located in the south of Beijing Olympic Park.

北京国家体育馆位于北京奥林匹克公园南部，是第29届奥林匹克运动会的主体育场。

40. The National Aquatics Centre is also known as "The Water Cube". The building's structural design is based on the natural formation of soap bubbles.

国家游泳中心也称作"水立方"，它的结构设计是基于自然形成的肥皂泡。

Ⅴ. Tips

1. Regular Transfer/ Transit Procedures 常规转机流程

(1) If passengers have an onward boarding pass, please: follow the directional sign to departures level for boarding gates; go through security screening; check your gate number and time and reach your boarding gate at least 30 minutes before the departure time.

(2) For passengers without an onward boarding pass, please: check your transfer desk's location; follow the directional sign to the designated transfer desk areas for check-in; follow the directional sign to departures level for boarding gates; go through security screening; check your gate number and time and reach your boarding gate at least 30 minutes before the departure time.

2. Infectious Disease Prevention and Control 传染性疾病防控

（1）disinfectant (*n.*) 消毒剂 (*adj.*) 消毒的

disinfectant 在用作名词时指代用于消毒的化学药物，即消毒剂。在与如 solution、wipes 等名词合用时，则变化成形容词，即消毒的。在机上卫生防疫包中有相关用品。同样的表达还有：

antiseptic solution 消毒液

antiseptic wipes 消毒湿巾

alcohol 酒精

sanitizer 消毒剂、洗手液

alcohol-based hand rub/sanitizer 含酒精洗手液

（2）mask (*n.*) 口罩

传染性疾病防控需戴口罩、勤洗手，给自己居住、生活的环境消毒。mask 可以表示面具、面膜，也可以表示口罩。

facemask 面罩

surgical mask 医用外科口罩

wear mask 戴口罩

（3）disposable gloves 一次性手套

disposable 表示用完即抛的，我们生活中常见的，比如 disposable slippers 一次性拖鞋，disposable chopsticks 一次性筷子

（4）goggles (*n.*) 护目镜

（5）protective suit 防护服

（6）negative pressure ambulance 负压救护车

negative 原表示负面、消极的，和 pressure 相连后代表的是有着可以最大限度地减少医务人员与病人间交叉感染概率的负压舱。负压救护车即防护型救护车，主要用于重大传染病人的安全隔离与转运。

Ⅵ. Supplementary Reading

1. Transfer / Transit Passenger 转机旅客

(1) International Transfer Passengers with a Domestic Connection Flight

Passengers arriving from abroad are subject to visa and passport controls to enter the country at the Arrivals Floor before they proceed for their domestic connection flight. The passenger then proceeds to the Domestic Terminal and finalizes his/ her transfer procedure in the relevant lounge by presenting his/ her boarding card issued in the country of origin. If a boarding card is not issued at the origin airport then the passenger needs to go through check-in at the Domestic Terminal. If your journey continues on a different airline, please ensure that you have the relevant information on whether or not you need to claim your luggage and check your ticket. According to their procedures, some airlines transfer the luggage automatically onto the connection flight. Therefore, the passenger does not have to claim their luggage in between flights. Please ensure that your luggage is labeled until your final destination to ensure that it is not left in the terminal.

(2) International Transfer Passengers with an International Connection Flight

A boarding card is issued for the passenger (if not issued in the country of origin) at the transit desk of the relevant handling company on the Arrivals Floor. The passenger does not go through passport control. Instead, he/ she directly proceeds through the transit area into the International Departures area. Baggage will be automatically transferred to the connecting flight.

(3) Domestic Transfer Passengers with an International Connection Flight

A passenger arriving on a domestic flight to continue flying abroad proceeds to the International Terminal and finalizes his/ her transit procedures by going through passport control with the boarding card issued in the origin country and going to the relevant lounge. If a boarding card is not issued then one should be obtained at the international check-in counters. Please ensure that your luggage is labeled until your final destination to ensure that it is not left in the terminal.

(4) Domestic Transfer Passengers with a Domestic Connection Flight

If a passenger arrives on a domestic flight and has a domestic connection flight, he/she proceeds to the Domestic Terminal Isolated Area and then into the relevant lounge provided that he/ she has a boarding card for the entire journey and that the baggage is checked in until the final destination. If the baggage is not checked in until the final destination and/ or he/ she has not got a boarding card then he/ she claims the baggage and goes through check-in again at the relevant counter within the Departures Lounge.

(5) Passengers Continuing Their Journey on the Same Flight

Should the grounding time of the relevant flight be excessively long, both international and domestic transit passengers are issued a transit card and taken to the transit lounge. They are taken back on board the same aircraft once refuelling and/ or maintenance procedures are completed. Should the grounding time not be sufficient, the passengers remain on board. Refuelling is done while passengers wait on board. Baggage remains in the aircraft during transit flights.

2. Transfer and culture diversity: Themed flight 转机与文化多样性：主题航班

On May 18, 2023, International Museum Day, China Eastern Airlines operated the "Explore the East, Journey with China" themed flight on its MU2805/6 round-trip service between Nanjing and Chengdu Tianfu.

At the boarding area, China Eastern Airlines set up a prominent promotional display board reading "Welcome Aboard the 'International Museum Day' Themed Flight," immediately sparking passengers' anticipation for this unique journey from the moment they arrived. Flight attendants handed out specially designed "International Museum Day Commemorative Boarding Passes" to passengers at the boarding gate. The back of these passes featured images of two renowned museum treasures: the Ming Dynasty Gold Cicada on a Jade Leaf and the Han Dynasty Ox-shaped Bronze Lamp Inlaid with Silver. A QR code was also included; scanning it allowed passengers to discover the stories behind these artifacts.

China Eastern Airlines and Nanjing Museum worked together to launch this "Air Museum" activity. Through distributing the co-branded commemorative boarding passes, broadcasting educational content about museums during the flight, gifting museum collection catalogues, and releasing the "Dongdong's Wonderful Museum Tour" series of short videos, the initiative aimed to enable more people to safeguard collective national memory and appreciate the charm of Chinese culture.

【背景阅读】2023年5月18日是国际博物馆日，当天中国东方航空公司在MU2805/6南京—成都天府往返航班上开展了"博览东方·同行华夏"国际博物馆日主题航班服务。东航在登机口旁摆放了印有"欢迎乘坐'国际博物馆日'主题航班"的宣传展板，十分醒目，让乘机旅客从登机的那一刻起就对这段不一样的航程有了期待。在登机口旁，东航空乘人员将精心制作的"国际博物馆日纪念登机牌"递给旅客，纪念登机牌背面展现了两件"镇院之宝"——明代金蝉玉叶与汉代错银铜牛灯的图案，并附有二维码，扫码即可了解这两件文物的故事。南京博物院与中国东方航空公司联手，共同开启"空中博物馆"之旅，通过发放博物馆联名纪念登机牌、机上广播科普博物馆知识、赠阅博物馆藏品图册、推出《东东博物馆奇妙游》系列短视频等方式，守护民族记忆，让更多人领略中华文化的魅力。

3. Hajj Charter Flight 朝觐包机

The Hajj is an annual Islamic pilgrimage to Mecca, Saudi Arabia, the holiest city for Muslims, and a mandatory religious duty for Muslims must be carried out at least once in their lifetime by all adult Muslims who are physically and financially capable of undertaking the journey and can support their family during their absence. Literally speaking, Hajj means heading to a place for the sake of visiting. The word "Hajj" means "to attend a journey", which connotes both the outward act of a journey and the inward act of intentions. Normally, the Hajj flight will be arranged specifically each year.

VII. Exercises

1. Can you list some Chinese festivals and describe the corresponding activities?

(1)

(2)

(3)

(4)

2. Translate the following words and phrases into Chinese or English.

round trip ticket	insecticide
transit passenger	住宿
transit visa	阳历
catch	庆祝
terminal building	登记，注册
ancient	无毒的
lunar calendar	中转信息
spray	中转柜台

3. Translate the following sentences into Chinese or English.

(1) 您的中转航班的航班号和起飞时间是什么？

(2) 您好，飞机降落之前我会给您调到前排的座位，以便您能提前下飞机。这样可以吗？

(3) 我们将停靠在2号航站楼。您需要在那儿提取行李，然后去1号航站楼换乘接下来的航班。

(4) You may go to the transit counter for your connecting flight.

(5) You may not leave your carry-on baggage in the overhead locker. Please do take your boarding pass and valuables with you.

(6) Yuan Xiao Jie, also called Lantern Festival, is the first significant feast after Chinese Lunar New Year, so called because the most important activity during the night of the event is watching various wonderful Chinese lanterns.

4. Group work: choose one topic to start a conversation. (TIME LIMIT: 5 minutes)

(1) Spring Festival

(2) Lantern Festival

(3) Spraying against insect infestation

Civil Aviation

Project 8

Special Situations
特殊情况

Task 18　Lost Items 丢失物品

Ⅰ. Warm-up Questions

1. What will you do if a passenger tells you that he/she lost his/ her wallet on board?

2. Why do passengers on board need to keep eyes on their own luggage?

3. As a flight attendant, if you find a pair of glasses in the lavatory and then a passenger comes to claim, what should you do?

4. How to assist a passenger in finding his / her in-flight lost item?

Ⅱ. Dialogues

Dialogue 1: "I can't find my cellphone."

音频扫一扫

Situation: Losing something can be annoying and inconvenient or totally nerve-wracking, depending on what's gone missing. Some passengers may not find out the situation of losing personal belongings until getting on board.

Principle: Flight attendants should comfort the passengers and help them find out the lost articles, such as by making an announcement.

Example

PAX: Excuse me, I can't find my cellphone.

FA: When did you find it lost? Did you switch it off during the security check?

PAX: Er... I'm not sure.

FA: Could you please offer us some details about your cellphone?

PAX: It's a white HUAWEI phone.

FA: Don't worry. Let me make an announcement for you.

FA: (Announcement) Ladies and Gentlemen, may I have your attention please! Any passenger who has found a white cellphone, please contact our cabin crew immediately. Meanwhile, other passengers who have seen the article please offer us relevant clues. Thank you!

(After a period of time...)

FA: Sorry, we haven't found your cellphone on board. Would you write down your name, address, phone number and details of your cellphone, please? If we get it, we will contact you as soon as possible.

PAX: OK. Maybe I forgot to take it after the security check. How can I find it?

FA: Miss, after arriving, you may contact the Lost and Found Office of the departure airport by dialing this number on this note.

情景会话 1："我的手机找不到了"

旅客：打扰一下，我的手机不见了。

乘务员：您是什么时候发现手机丢失的？安检时您关机了吗？

旅客：呃……我记不清楚了。

乘务员：您能具体描述一下您的手机吗？

旅客：是一部华为手机，白色的。

乘务员：别急。我来给您播报个寻物广播吧。

乘务员：（广播）各位女士，各位先生：请注意，现在广播寻物，如有旅客拾到一部白色手机，请立即与乘务员联系，其他旅客如有发现这部手机的，也请为我们提供相关线索。我们谨代表失主向您表示感谢！

（过了一段时间……）

乘务员：对不起，我们没能在客舱内找到您的手机。请写下您的姓名、地址、联系电话并具体描述一下您的手机。我们一找到，会马上联系您。

旅客：好吧。也可能是过安检的时候我忘记拿了。我怎么找呢？

乘务员：女士，落地以后您可以联系起飞机场的失物招领处，拨打便签上的这个电话就可以了。

音频扫一扫

Dialogue 2: Lost and Found

Situation: Some passengers may not find out the situation of losing personal belongings until getting on board.

Principle: Flight attendants should comfort the passengers and help them find out the lost articles.

Example

PAX: Please help! I left my jacket at the airport, can you help me find it?

FA: Calm down, Sir. I'm sorry to hear that. Do you remember where you left it?

PAX: Yes, at the café. Right at the entrance of the airport.

FA: Okay, can you leave your contact number and describe your jacket for me? I will report the matter to our ground crew. If they have any information about it, they will contact you.

PAX: Sure, it's black and there is a card in the pocket.

FA: And this is the number of the Lost and Found Department. If any passengers found your jacket, they might have handed it to them.

PAX: Thank you, you've been very helpful.

情景会话 2：失物招领

旅客：请帮帮我！我把夹克忘在机场了，能帮我找找吗？

乘务员：先生，您别急，很遗憾听到这个消息。您还记得放在什么位置了吗？

旅客：记得！就在机场门口的那家咖啡馆里。

乘务员：好的，那请您留下联系方式并描述一下您的夹克，我会请地面人员协助寻找，一有消息就马上告诉您。

旅客：没问题，是件黑色的夹克，口袋里还有一张卡片。

乘务员：另外，这是机场失物招领处的电话，如果有其他旅客拾到您的夹克，可能会交给他们保管。

旅客：谢谢你帮我做了这么多。

Dialogue 3: Found the lost item

Situation: A passenger may lose something on board. Another passenger finds out the lost item and tells the cabin crew.

Principle: Flight attendants should comfort the passenger and help him or her get the lost article back.

Example

PAX1: Excuse me, Miss?

FA: Yes, Madam. May I help you?

PAX1: I just found a wallet at the corner. Maybe someone lost it carelessly.

FA: Okay, thanks. I'll handle it.

PS: (Announcement) Good afternoon, ladies and gentlemen! Anyone who lost a wallet, please contact our flight attendants to get it back. Thank you for your attention!

PAX2: Hello? I just heard the announcement. I can't find my wallet.

FA: I see. Could you please describe your wallet, such as the color?

PAX2: It is black and made of leather. There are three tickets, a photo of my family, some money and credit cards.

FA: All right. Here you are. Take care!

PAX2: Thank you so much!

FA: Don't mention it.

情景会话3：旅客捡到遗失物品（物归原主）

旅客1：您好？

乘务员：您好，女士，有什么可以帮助您的？

旅客1：我刚刚在角落里发现了一个钱包，估计是有人不小心弄丢了。

乘务员：好的，谢谢您，请交给我来处理。

乘务长：（广播）女士们，先生们，下午好！如果有人丢失了钱包，请与我们的空乘人员联系取回，谢谢！

旅客2：您好，我刚听到广播，我的钱包不见了。

乘务员：我知道了。能描述下您的钱包吗？比如颜色之类的。

旅客2：它是黑色皮质的。里面有三张车票，一张我的全家福照片，一些现金和信用卡。

乘务员：好的，给您。请小心保管。

旅客2：非常感谢！

乘务员：不客气。

Dialogue 4: Contacting the police/ Report the in-flight theft

Situation: Losing something can be annoying and inconvenient or totally nerve-wracking. Some passengers may lose something on board. If necessary, call the police.

Principle: Flight attendants should comfort the passenger and help him or her get the lost item.

Example

PAX: Excuse me, Miss? I can't find my wallet! I've checked everywhere I could, but I just couldn't find it.

FA: Don't worry, Sir. When and where did you lose it?

PAX: I put it in my green backpack. And the backpack was put in the overhead bin. I went to the lavatory for about 10 minutes because of several passengers waiting in front of me. When I came back, I just couldn't find it.

FA: Have you checked your carry-on luggage, other than the backpack? Have you checked the seat pocket in front of you, or the area under your seat?

PAX: Yes! I even asked around and checked the aisle. My credit cards, cash... all my money... the memory card... If I couldn't find it, how would I attend the meeting?

FA: I do understand how you feel now. I'll help you find it.

(After one hour...)

PAX: We've been looking for my wallet over an hour... But we've got nothing... Please call the police.

PS: Okay.

(Before landing...)

PS: (Announcement) Ladies and gentlemen, at the request of a passenger, we have contacted the police. All passengers are required to remain seated after landing. Thank you for your cooperation!

情景会话4：机上偷盗报案

旅客：乘务员！我找不到我的钱包了！我能找的地方都找过了，就是找不到。

乘务员：先生，您别着急。您什么时候丢的？在哪里丢的？

旅客：我就把钱包放在行李架里的绿色背包里。我去了趟卫生间，大概十分钟，因为卫生间门口有不少旅客在排队。当我回来的时候，就怎么也找不着了。

乘务员：您检查过除了背包以外的随身行李吗？有没有检查过座椅前方口袋，或者您座椅下方的区域？

旅客：当然了！我周围的人都问过了，连过道都看过了。我的信用卡、现金……所有的钱……内存卡……如果我找不到它，我将怎么出席会议呢？

乘务员：我非常理解您此时的感受。我会帮您一起找的。

（一个小时后……）

旅客：我们找钱包都找了一个多小时了，但是什么也没找着……请帮我报警吧。

乘务长：好的。

（落地前……）

乘务长：（广播）女士们，先生们，由于一位旅客丢失物品并已向警方报案，请各位旅客在飞机落地后坐在原位等候。谢谢合作！

Ⅲ. Popular Words and Phrases

Lost and Found		失物招领
detail	['di:teɪl]	n. 细节，详细信息
contact information		联系信息
ground staff		地勤（地服）人员
recall	[rɪˈkɔːl]	v. 回忆
make an announcement		广播
consult	[kənˈsʌlt]	v. 咨询
describe	[dɪˈskraɪb]	v. 描述，形容
description	[dɪˈskrɪpʃn]	n. 描述，说明，形容

Ⅳ. Practical Expressions

1. When and where did you lose it?

您什么时候丢的？在哪里丢的？

2. Would you please offer us some details about your cellphone?

您能具体描述一下您的手机吗？

3. Let me make an announcement for you.

我给您播报个寻物广播吧。

4. Any passenger who has found a cellphone, please contact our cabin crew immediately.

如有旅客拾到一部手机，请立即与我们的乘务员联系。

5. Would you please write down your name, address, phone number and details of your cellphone?

请写下您的姓名、地址、联系电话并具体描述一下您的手机。

6. After landing, you may contact the Lost and Found Office of the departure airport. Here is the phone number.

落地以后您可以联系起飞机场的失物招领处。这是电话号码。

7. Any passenger who lost a laptop, please contact our flight attendants. Thank you!

哪位旅客丢失了一台笔记本电脑，请与我们的乘务员联系。谢谢！

8. At the request of a passenger, we have contacted the police. All passengers are required to remain seated after landing. Thank you for your cooperation!

由于一位旅客丢失物品并已向警方报案，请各位旅客在飞机落地后坐在原位等候。谢谢合作！

V. Tips

Cabin Announcement: Lost Items 客舱广播：丢失物品

(Lost and Found) Ladies and gentlemen, any passenger who lost a laptop, please contact our flight attendants. Thank you!

(Contacting the police) Ladies and gentlemen, at the request of a passenger, we have contacted the police. All passengers are required to remain seated after landing. Thank you for your cooperation!

VI. Supplementary Reading

1. Passenger Lost Items 旅客遗失物品

After the disembarkation or before the embarkation of passengers, any valuable article picked up by a flight attendant in charge of cabin safety should be reported to the chief purser for scrutiny by two persons at the spot of discovery. Lost articles should be recorded one by one.

Purser should deliver the lost articles to relevant departments and keep the receipts properly. In case the lost article is picked up in journey and it is proven that the article belongs to the passenger who lost it, the flight attendants in charge of cabin safety should return it to the owner after confirmation. In the event that a passenger declares that he/ she has lost a valuable thing after embarkation, flight attendant should ask the details of the lost article and provide any possible assistance in looking for it.

2. Theft on Board 机上失窃

In case a theft occurs on board, flight attendants should timely report to the purser, and the purser will report to the captain, who will notify the next arriving airport of it as follows: the name of the lost article and its value; the location of the lost article; whether the passenger wants to report to the security department. If the passenger wants to report to the security department, flight attendants should explain the following to him/ her: If the police are involved, inconvenience may arise and passengers may not deplane as scheduled.

Prior to landing, the purser should make an announcement that a passenger has lost a valuable thing, which the matter has been reported to the police and passengers are requested to remain seated after landing. Flight attendants should do their best to explain that it is not the crew who take the action.

VII. Exercises

1. Can you list the procedures of assisting passengers in finding their lost items?

(1)

(2)

(3)

2. Translate the following words and phrases into Chinese or English.

detail	consult
valuables	失物招领
recall	联系信息
make an announcement	地服人员

3. Translate the following sentences into Chinese or English.

(1) 您什么时候丢的？在哪里丢的？

(2) 您能具体描述一下您的手机吗？

(3) 请写下您的姓名、地址、联系电话并具体描述一下您的手机。

(4) After landing, you may contact the Lost and Found Office of the departure airport. Here is the phone number.

(5) Any passenger who lost a laptop, please contact our flight attendants. Thank you!

4. Group work: choose one topic to start a conversation. (TIME LIMIT: 10 minutes)

(1) "I can't find my cellphone."

(2) Found the lost items on board.

(3) The in-flight theft.

Task 19　Flight Delay 航班延误

I . Warm-up Questions

1. What are the common reasons for flight delay?

2. Why do passengers oftentimes blame airlines for flight delay, even if it is because the weather condition is terrible?

3. How to comfort passengers on board during the time of flight delay?

II . Dialogues

Dialogue 1: Air traffic control

Situation: Aircraft lines up for a long time for take-off because of air traffic control. During the waiting time, some passengers may have questions.

Principle: Flight attendants should listen to these passengers first, and then explain patiently.

Example

PAX1: Miss? The aircraft door has been closed. Why can't we take off now?

FA: It's true. The aircraft door has been closed. However, there is a lot of traffic right now, so we have to wait for the clearance from the Air Traffic Control Tower.

PAX1: Because of what?

FA: We have to wait for some more minutes due to the air traffic control.

PAX2: What's the reason of the delay?

FA: I'm so sorry. The flight has been delayed because of the air traffic control.

PAX2: What is air traffic control?

FA: Generally speaking, air traffic control can make sure aircrafts fly safely without getting close to each other.

PAX2: When shall we take off?/ Well, how long shall we wait for?

FA: There are 2 aircraft lining up ahead of us. Please remain seated. We'll take off soon. We will let you know as soon as we have any further information.

情景会话 1：航空管制

旅客1：乘务员，现在什么情况啊？关机门了，为什么还不起飞？

乘务员：您好，舱门虽然关闭了，但这时候起飞的飞机比较多，我们还需要等待航空管制塔台的指挥。

旅客1：是什么原因呢？

乘务员：由于航空管制，我们的飞机还要等待一段时间。

旅客2：飞机为什么延误啊？

乘务员：很抱歉，因为航空管制，我们的航班延误了。

旅客2：什么是航空管制呢？

乘务员：通常来说，航空管制可以控制起飞流量，让飞机间距不至于太近，以确保安全飞行。

旅客2：我们会什么时候起飞？/还要等多久？

乘务员：现在我们的飞机排在第三位，请您在座位上休息等候，很快将会起飞。一旦有进一步的消息，会立刻告知您。

Dialogue 2: Bad weather condition

Situation: As is often the case, flights delay because of bad weather condition. During the waiting time, some passengers may have questions.

Principle: Flight attendants should listen to these passengers first, comfort them, and then explain patiently. Make announcements according to the changing situation.

音频扫一扫

Example

FA1: Excuse me, Mr. Qi. I'm sorry to inform you that we will delay due to the bad weather condition.

PAX1: What's the weather leading to the delay?

FA1: There is a thunderstorm over the airport, so we can't take off now.

PAX1: When will we take off?/ How long are we going to wait for?

FA1: After the weather gets better, we will apply for departure from the Air Traffic Control Tower, and we will keep you informed. Thank you for your patience.

PS: (Announcement) Ladies and gentlemen, we are so sorry to inform you that our departure will be slightly delayed due to the weather condition. There is a heavy thunderstorm around this city. For the safety, we cannot take off now.

PAX2: What? How long shall we wait for?

FA2: To be honest, it is hard to say. It is the thunderstorm season in Shenzhen. Our captain is contacting with the ground staff. If we have further information, we will inform you as soon as possible.

PAX2: Oh, my God! What's the departure time?

FA2: Well, I am so sorry to tell you that we don't have the exact time for departure because of the air traffic control. Due to the bad (unfavorable) weather, many flights have been delayed. I do understand how you feel now. If there is anything I can help you, please let me know. I will try my best to help you. By the way, it is hot today, would you like a cup of ice water?

PAX2: Fine.

(After a while...)

FA2: We cannot take off now because of the bad weather. We'll keep you updated as soon as more information becomes available and apply for the take-off clearance as soon as the weather is getting better.

(After 50 minutes...)

PS: (Announcement) Ladies and gentlemen, the captain has just advised us that our aircraft cannot take off at this time because of the bad weather and we will have to return to the terminal. We will keep you updated as soon as more information becomes available. We sincerely apologize for the delay and any inconvenience!

情景会话2：天气不好

乘务员1：打扰了，戚先生，抱歉地通知您，由于天气状况不好，我们将会推迟起飞。

旅客1：请问具体什么天气导致航班延迟起飞呢？

乘务员1：由于机场上空的暴风雨，我们现在无法起飞。

旅客1：具体什么时间能起飞？／我们还要等多久呢？

乘务员1：等天气一有好转，我们马上就会向航空管制塔台申请起飞并广播通知。谢谢您的耐心等待。

乘务长：（广播）女士们，先生们，很抱歉地通知您，由于天气原因，我们的航班将有些延误。今天这座城市有强雷雨，为了安全，我们现在不能起飞。

旅客2：啊？要等多久啊？

乘务员2：老实说，这很难讲。深圳进入了雷雨季节，我们的机长正在和地服人员联系。如果有进一步消息，我们将尽快通知您。

旅客2：天哪！什么时候能起飞啊？

乘务员2：嗯，很抱歉，因为航空管制，现在还没有一个确切的时间。天气不好，很多航班都延误了。我特别理解您现在的心情，如果有能帮到您的地方，请告诉我，我将竭诚为您服务。另外，今天挺热的，您需要一杯冰水吗？

旅客2：好吧。

（过了一会儿……）

乘务员2：由于恶劣天气，我们的飞机现在不能起飞。如有最新消息，我们会及时向您更新，同时，当接到天气转好的信息时，我们会尽快申请排队，争取能够尽快起飞。

（等待50分钟后……）

乘务长：（广播）女士们，先生们，我们刚刚收到机长通知，由于天气原因，飞机暂时不能起飞，因为等待时间较长，我们决定安排大家到候机室休息等候。当我们收到进一步的消息时，会及时地通知您。对于航班的延误和给您带来的不便，我们深表歉意！

Dialogue 3: Aircraft deicing

Situation: In winter, flights delay a little bit because of aircraft deicing. During the waiting time, some passengers may have questions.

音频扫一扫

Principle: Flight attendants should keep information updated, comfort them and explain patiently. Make announcements according to the changing situation.

Example

PS: (Before deicing) Ladies and gentlemen, I am the purser of this flight. The deicing procedure is to start. During this period, the air-condition system of the cabin needs to be turned off for a short period. We hope you can understand, and we're sorry for the inconvenience. Thank you!

PAX: Excuse me, Miss.Why are we still waiting here?

FA: Yes. It's because of the deicing procedure.

PAX: How many minutes left?

FA: I just got the latest information. It takes about 20 minutes.

(After a while...)

PS: (After deicing) Ladies and gentlemen, the procedure of deicing has been done. The plane is going to take off. Today's flight time is 3 hours and 30 minutes. Thank you for your understanding and support during the waiting time and wish you a comfortable journey!

情景会话3：飞机除冰

乘务长：（除冰前）女士们、先生们，我是本次航班的乘务长，除冰工作即将开始，在此期间，客舱空调系统需要关闭一小段时间，由此给您带来的不便，希望能够得到您的谅解。谢谢！

旅客：乘务员，我们为什么还待在这里呢？

乘务员：嗯，这是因为我们的飞机还在除冰。

旅客：还有多长时间？

乘务员：我刚收到最新消息，还需要20分钟左右。

（过了一会儿……）

乘务长：（除冰后）女士们，先生们，飞机的除冰工作已经完成，感谢您在等待期间对我们工作的理解与支持，飞机即将起飞，今天的飞行时间是3小时30分钟，祝愿您有一段舒适的旅程。谢谢！

Dialogue 4: Poor visibility

Situation: Occasionally, flights are delayed or even cancelled because of poor visibility. During the waiting time, some passengers may have questions.

音频扫一扫

Principle: Flight attendants should keep information updated, comfort them and explain patiently. Make announcements according to the situation and apologize sincerely.

Example

PAX: Excuse me, Miss. What's the reason for the delay?

FA: I'm sorry, Sir. There is heavy fog over the airport. The visibility is so poor that the plane can't take off now. I'm afraid we have to wait till the fog lifts and the weather gets better/ improved.

PAX: How long do we have to wait?

FA: I am not sure, Sir. But I will let you know as soon as I receive the information.

PAX: I see, but my son and daughter are thirsty and hungry.

FA: I will bring you some water and bread. I'll be back soon.

PAX: Thank you.

FA: You're welcome.

FA: Sir, we will take off in 10 minutes and arrive on schedule.

/ Sir, I'm afraid we will have to stay here overnight.

PAX: Oh, no, that's too bad!

FA: Don't worry. We'll provide free food and accommodation for every passenger.

PS: (Announcement) Ladies and gentlemen, we regret to inform you that our flight is cancelled due to the poor visibility. Please take all your hand luggage with you, including your boarding pass, valuables and travel documents. Check that you have nothing left on board. If you need any assistance, please contact our ground staff after disembarkation. We apologize for the inconvenience and thank you for your understanding!

情景会话 4：能见度低

旅客：乘务员，请问一下，延误的原因是什么？

乘务员：对不起，先生。机场雾大。能见度太低了，飞机现在无法起飞。恐怕我们只能等到雾散去，天气转好以后了。

旅客：我们要等多久啊？

乘务员：现在还不能确定，先生。不过，我一得到消息会马上通知你们的。

旅客：我知道了。但是我的儿子和女儿口渴了，肚子也饿了。

乘务员：我马上为您取些水和面包吧。我很快就回来。

旅客：谢谢。

乘务员：您客气了。

乘务员：先生，我们10分钟之后起飞，并且会准时落地的。

/ 先生，恐怕我们得在这里过夜了。

旅客：噢，不！这太糟糕了！

乘务员：请不要担心。我们将为每位旅客提供免费的餐食和住宿。

乘务长：（广播）女士们，先生们，非常抱歉地通知您，由于机场能见度低于放行标准，本次航班被迫取消。所有旅客请携带全部手提行李下机，包括您的登机牌、贵重物品和旅行证件。请确认您没有在飞机上遗留任何您的个人物品。如果您需要任何帮助，请下机后联系我们的地勤人员。由此给您带来的不便，我们深表歉意，感谢您对我们工作的理解。

Dialogue 5: Mechanical problem(s)

Situation: Occasionally, flights are delayed or even cancelled because of technical problems. When flights are cancelled or delayed, passengers may be entitled to explanation or even compensation.

音频扫一扫

Principle: Flight attendants should keep information updated, comfort them and explain patiently. Make announcements according to the situation and apologize sincerely.

Example

FA: (Announcement) We are so sorry to inform you that we will delay for take-off due to the mechanical problem.

PAX: How long will the delay last?

FA: Don't worry about that. Please wait a moment. Our maintenance personnel are troubleshooting.

PAX: Er... What's the problem?

FA: A minor technical problem. By the way, would you care for something to drink?

PAX: Just water.

(After a while...)

PS: (Announcement) The mechanical problem has been resolved after troubleshooting and testing. / (Announcement) We are sorry to inform you that we have to change to another aircraft because of the technical problem. Please disembark with all your belongings. We sincerely apologize for the inconvenience!

情景会话5：机械故障

乘务员：（广播）我们抱歉地通知您，由于机械故障，我们的航班将推迟起飞。

旅客：还会延误多久？

乘务员：请不要着急，您稍等一会儿。我们的机务维修人员正在积极排除故障。

旅客：呃……是什么故障呢？

乘务员：是一个小的技术故障。请问您想喝些什么吗？

旅客：水就行了。

（过了一会儿……）

乘务长：（广播）本架飞机经过维修和测试，机械故障已排除。

/（广播）我们抱歉地通知您，由于机械故障无法排除，我们需要换乘另外一架飞机，请您下机时带好随身物品。对此带来的不便我们深表歉意！

Dialogue 6: Multiple reasons

Situation: Occasionally, flights are delayed or even cancelled because of multiple reasons. When flights are cancelled or delayed, passengers may be entitled to explanation or even compensation.

Principle: Flight attendants should keep information updated, comfort them and explain patiently. Make announcements according to the situation and apologize sincerely.

音频扫一扫

Example

PAX1: Excuse me, Miss? It's already 9:30 p.m. now. Why don't we take off?

FA: We are still waiting for the take-off clearance, Sir.

PAX1: But the time on my boarding pass is 9:30 p.m. Are we delayed?

FA: Sir, the time on the boarding pass is the time to close the cabin door. Don't worry. I believe we'll be taking off soon.

(After a while...)

PAX1: Hi! It's 10:30. I'm pretty sure we get delayed. May I know the reason?

FA: It's the bad weather on route, and Beijing area makes the air traffic control.

PAX1: Then what time can we take off?

FA: I'm sorry. We haven't received any information about the take-off time yet. Once we get the time for departure, we will make an announcement to let you know. Sorry for that.

PAX2: Now what? Why are we still here?

FA: Some passengers decide to cancel their flights, so we need to open the cabin door to let them disembark. And we also need to find out their check-in luggage from the cargo hold. Then... check the cabin and queue from the last one...

PAX2: Oh, my god!

FA: I understand your feeling and we do apologize!

PAX2: I'm very hungry, can I have my meal on ground?

FA: Sorry, Sir. We provide snacks for passengers, which are selected peanuts and biscuits, because this is a night flight.

PAX2: Anything else? I'm allergic to peanuts and I don't like biscuits.

FA: Well, we have baked bread from the business class. May I bring some to you?/ If you don't mind, I can get some for you.

PAX2: OK. Thanks.

FA: My pleasure.

(After half an hour...)

PS: (Announcement) As some passengers have cancelled their flights, for your safety, we will be conducting security check of the cabin. We appreciate your cooperation and apologize for any inconvenience!

情景会话6：多种原因延误

旅客1：请问一下，现在已经9:30了。我们为什么还不起飞？

乘务员：先生，我们正在等待起飞指令。

旅客1：但是登机牌上的起飞时间是9:30。我们延误了是吗？

乘务员：先生，登机牌上的时间表示的是飞机关闭舱门的时间。不要担心，我相信我们很快就会起飞的。

（过了一会儿……）

旅客1：你好！现在10:30了，我确定我们延误了。我想知道为什么？

乘务员：因为航路上天气不好，而且北京地区现在航空管制。

旅客1：那我们几点能起飞？

乘务员：我很抱歉，我们现在还没有收到任何有关起飞的消息。一旦知道起飞时间，我们会第一时间进行广播，让大家知道。

旅客2：现在又是什么情况？为什么我们还在这里？

乘务员：航班中有部分旅客决定终止行程，所以我们需要滑回打开舱门，让他们下飞机。同时，还需要把他们的托运行李找出来，从飞机上卸下并清舱。然后，检查客舱，再重新排队。

旅客2：噢，天哪！

乘务员：我理解您的感受，非常抱歉！

旅客2：我现在好饿，能在地面就餐吗？

乘务员：抱歉，先生。因为是夜航，本次航班准备的是小吃，精选花生和饼干。

旅客2：还有别的吗？我对花生过敏，也不喜欢吃饼干。

乘务员：这样啊，我们有商务舱的烤面包。我给您拿些吗？/如果您不介意，我可以给您拿些。

旅客2：好的，多谢了。

乘务员：不客气的。

（半小时后……）

乘务长：（广播）由于部分旅客临时取消航程，为了确保您的安全，我们的客舱将重新进行安全检查。谢谢您的合作，由此给您带来的不便，敬请谅解。

Dialogue 7: Circling

Situation: Occasionally, flights delay because of circling. During the waiting time, some passengers may have questions.

Principle: Flight attendants should keep information updated, comfort them and explain patiently. Make announcements according to the situation and apologize sincerely.

音频扫一扫

Example

PAX1: Excuse me, how long will it take to arrive at the connecting airport?

FA: Madam, we regret to inform you that due to the unfavorable weather at Nanjing Lukou Airport, we'll land at Shanghai Hongqiao Airport instead. We expect to land in about 2 hours and 20 minutes.

PAX1: Oh, my god!

FA: We shall keep you updated. We appreciate your understanding and apologize for any inconvenience.

(After two hours...)

PAX2: Excuse me, Miss? I've already seen the airport. Why not descend? We have been circling around for half an hour.

FA: Due to the unfavorable weather and poor visibility at the airport, we will circle over the airport until the weather clears up. We shall keep you updated as soon as further information becomes available.

PAX2: Well...

PS: (Announcement) Ladies and gentlemen, the captain has advised us that due to the congestion at the airport caused by the unfavorable weather and poor visibility, we are unable to land at the moment. Our plane is expected to arrive in about 40 minutes. Thank you for your understanding and cooperation!

情景会话7：空中盘旋

旅客1：请问我们还有多久到经停站？

乘务员：您好，女士。抱歉地通知您，由于南京禄口机场天气状况不好，我们决定降落在上海虹桥机场，预计在两小时二十分钟后着陆。

旅客1：哦，天哪！

乘务员：一有新的消息我们就会及时告知您。给您带来不便非常抱歉，感谢您的理解！

（两小时后……）

旅客2：乘务员，我已经看到地面了，为什么我们还不降落？都在空中盘旋半个小时了。

乘务员：由于目的地机场天气不好，能见度太低，不符合降落标准，飞机暂时无法降落，我们将在机场上空盘旋等待天气转晴。一有进一步的消息，我们将及时通知您。

旅客2：这样啊……

乘务长：（广播）女士们，先生们，我们刚刚收到机长通知，由于机场天气不好、能见度太低造成机场繁忙，飞机暂时无法降落，本次航班将推迟落地时间，我们预计在四十分钟后着陆。感谢您的理解与配合！

Ⅲ. Popular Words and Phrases

delay	[dɪˈleɪ]	*n.* 延误
weather	[ˈweðə]	*n.* 天气
unfavorable	[ʌnˈfeɪvərəbl]	*adj.* 不良的；不宜的，不顺利的
weather condition		天气情况
weather forecast/ report		天气预报
sunny	[ˈsʌnɪ]	*adj.* 阳光充足的
rainy	[ˈreɪnɪ]	*adj.* 下雨的

rainy period		雨季
plum rain season		梅雨季节
dog days of the summer		三伏天
heavy rain	[ˈhevɪ reɪn]	暴雨
rainstorm	[ˈreɪnstɔːm]	n. 暴雨
thunderstorm	[ˈθʌndəstɔːm]	n. 雷暴，雷雨
hurricane	[ˈhʌrɪk(ə)n]	n. 飓风，暴风
hail	[heɪl]	n. 冰雹
snowy	[ˈsnəʊɪ]	adj. 下雪的
overcast	[ˈəʊvəkɑːst]	adj. 阴天的
storm	[stɔːm]	n. 暴风雨
snow storm		暴风雪
heavy snow		大雪
foggy	[ˈfɒgɪ]	adj. 有雾的
cloudy	[ˈklaʊdɪ]	adj. 多云的
heavy fog		大雾
typhoon	[taɪˈfuːn]	n. 台风
frozen	[ˈfrəʊzn]	adj. 冻结的，冰冻的
icing	[ˈaɪsɪŋ]	n. & v. 结冰
ice-melter	[aɪs ˈmeltə]	n. 除冰车
circle over		盘旋于
temperature	[ˈtemprətʃə]	n. 温度
degree	[dɪˈgriː]	n. 度数
Celsius	[ˈselsɪəs]	adj. 摄氏的
Fahrenheit	[ˈfærənhaɪt]	adj. 华氏的
exact	[igˈzækt]	adj. 准确的
put off		推后
apologize	[əˈpɒlədʒaiz]	v. 道歉
apologize for		为……道歉
due to/ owning to		由于
make worse		使更糟糕
interval	[ˈɪntəv(ə)l]	n. 间隔
terminate	[ˈtɜːmɪneɪt]	v. 终止 adj. 结束的
queue	[kjuː]	n. & v. 排队
last sector	[laːst ˈsektə]	上一航段
catch up with		赶上
ground service		地面服务
approach	[əˈprəʊtʃ]	v. & n. 接近
Don't mention it.		不客气。
air traffic control		航空管制
cargo	[ˈkɑːgəʊ]	n. 货物

estimate	['estɪmeɪt]	v. 估计
late arrival	[leɪt ə'raɪvl]	晚点，迟到
load	[ləʊd]	v. 装载
on route		路线上，航线上
runway congestion		跑道堵塞
understanding	[ˌʌndə'stændɪŋ]	n. 理解

Ⅳ. Practical Expressions

1. I am sorry. Your flight has been delayed because of the air traffic control. We sincerely apologize for the inconvenience.

对不起，您乘坐的航班因为航空管制延误了。对此带来的不便我们表示真诚的歉意。

2. We have to wait for some more minutes due to the air traffic control.

由于航空管制，我们的飞机还要再等待一段时间。

3. The aircraft door has been closed. However, there is a lot of traffic right now, so we have to wait for the clearance from the Air Traffic Control Tower.

机门虽然关闭了，但这时候起飞的飞机比较多，所以我们还需要等待航空管制塔台的指挥。

4. We are waiting for the take-off clearance, and there are 2 aircraft lining up ahead of us. Please remain seated for the time being.

我们正在等待起飞的命令，现在我们的飞机排在第三位，请您暂时在座位上休息等候。

5. We are waiting for departure because of the air traffic control/ bad weather.

因为起飞流量控制/天气不好，我们正在等待起飞。

6. We cannot take off now because of the bad weather in Beijing. We'll update you as soon as more information becomes available.

由于北京的天气不好，我们的飞机现在不能起飞。如有最新消息，我们会及时向您更新。

7. We have to wait for 30 minutes due to the unfavorable weather condition on route. We'll provide you with further information.

由于航路天气不好，我们还须等待30分钟才能起飞，乘务组会随时将最新的信息告诉您。

8. We'll apply for the take-off clearance as soon as the weather is getting better.

天气一转好，我们就会请求起飞。

9. I'm afraid we have to wait until the weather gets better.

恐怕我们需要等到天气转好才能起飞。

10. Nanjing has a very long rainy period, called plum rain season, which is in June and July of the summer. It's the hottest period in Nanjing. We call it "dog days of the summer". Due to the bad weather, our plane is circling over the airfield.

在夏季的六七月份，南京会经历一段很长的雨季，被称为梅雨季节。现在正是南京最热的时期，被称为"三伏天"。由于天气不好，我们正在机场上空盘旋。

11. The airport has been closed due to the bad weather. For the safety reason, we are informed that the flight has been canceled.

由于天气不好机场已经关闭。出于安全考虑，我们被通知本次航班取消了。

12. We have to wait for a few minutes due to a minor technical problem.

我们的飞机有些小故障，正在维修排除，还需要等待一会儿。

13. We have to change to another aircraft because of the technical problem. Please disembark with all your belongings. We sincerely apologize for the inconvenience.

由于机械故障无法排除，我们需要换乘另外一架飞机，请您下机时带好随身物品。对此带来的不便我们深表歉意。

14. I'm sorry to tell you that our flight has been delayed due to mechanical problems.

很抱歉地通知您，由于机械故障，本次航班延误了。

15. Owing to the heavy air traffic, we'll wait until the take-off clearance is given.

由于空中航路拥挤，我们要等待通行许可（才能起飞）。

16. We have to wait until the ice on the runway has been cleared.

我们须等待跑道上的冰被清除。

17. Our plane can't take off until the cargo is loaded.

我们的飞机要装完货才能起飞。

18. We are waiting for a few passengers to complete boarding formalities.

我们正在等待几位旅客办理登机手续。

19. It's okay, our captain is now contacting with the ground staff/ air traffic controller.

不用担心，我们的机长正在和地面人员/塔台积极联络。

20. There are too many flights waiting for departure, and we are waiting in line.

很多飞机在等待起飞，我们正在排队等候。

21. We are currently No. X in line.

我们的飞机现在排在第X位。

22. We are waiting for clearing the obstacles on the runway.

我们正在等待清理跑道上的障碍物。

23. We are still waiting for the departure clearance.

我们还在等待起飞指令。

24. We will take off after 10 minutes.

我们将在10分钟之后起飞。

25. Don't worry. I will confirm the exact departure time now and let you know as soon as I receive the information.

别担心。我现在就去询问飞机确切的起飞时间，一有消息我就会马上通知您。

26. If we have any further information, we'll let you know immediately.

如果有进一步的消息，我们会立即通知你们的。

/ We will let you know as soon as we receive further information.

一有进一步的消息，我们会马上通知您。

27. I'm afraid we will have to stay here overnight.

恐怕我们将在这里过夜了。

28. We'll provide free food and accommodation for every passenger.

我们将为每位旅客提供免费食宿。

29. The time on the boarding pass is the time to close the cabin door. But don't worry. I believe we'll be taking off soon.

登机牌上的时间表示的是关闭舱门的时间。但是不要担心，我相信我们很快就会起飞的。

30. Could you please tell me the flight number and departure time of your next flight?

您能告诉我您接下来的航班号和起飞时间吗？

31. Don't worry, Sir/ Madam. We will try our best to solve the problem for you.

先生/女士，请不要担心。我们将尽力为您解决。

32. Excuse me, Sir/ Madam. If you need to transfer, I can help you contact the ground staff.

先生/女士，您好，如果您需要转机，我可以帮您联系地面工作人员。

33. Let me confirm it with our captain, and we will inform you as soon as we get the exact departure time. If you couldn't catch it, our ground staff would help you.

我来跟机长确认一下，一有准确的起飞时间我们会立刻告诉您的。如果您赶不上的话，我们的地面工作人员会帮您的。

34. We'll inform the ground staff if you'd like to cancel the flight. They will help you complete the relevant procedures.

如果您想取消这一段的行程，我们会通知地面工作人员。他们会帮助您办理相关手续。

35. If you need any assistance, please contact our ground staff after disembarkation. We apologize for the inconvenience and thank you for your understanding.

如果您需要任何帮助，请在下机后联系我们的地面工作人员。由此给您带来的不便，我们深表歉意，感谢您对我们工作的理解。

36. According to the regulation of CAAC, the departure time on your ticket refers to the time for closing cabin doors, but not for taking off. There are about 15 minutes between them.

根据民航局的规定，您机票上的时间是指飞机关闭舱门的时间，而非飞机起飞的时间。两者之间一般相差 15 分钟左右。

V. Tips

In-flight announcement in terms of flight delay 机上延误广播

Ladies and gentlemen, this is your purser speaking. The exact departure time can not be predicted for now. We can understand the limited space on board made you feel uncomfortable and the inconvenience we caused you. You will be updated as soon as possible if the latest information becomes available. Passengers request to change another flight: If you want to change or cancel your flight, please contact the cabin crew. Thank you for your understanding!

VI. Supplementary Reading

Deicing 除冰

Deicing is a process of removing snow, ice or frost from a surface. Anti-icing is understood to be the application of chemicals that not only de-ice but also remain on a surface and continue to delay the reformation of ice for a certain period of time, or prevent adhesion of ice to make mechanical removal easier.

On the ground, when there are freezing conditions and precipitation, deicing an aircraft is crucial. Frozen contaminants cause critical control surfaces to be rough and uneven, disrupting smooth air flow and greatly degrading the ability of the wing to generate lift and increasing drag. This situation can cause a crash. If large pieces of ice separate when the aircraft is in motion, they can be ingested in engines or hit propellers and cause catastrophic failure. Frozen contaminants can jam control surfaces, preventing them from moving properly. Because of this potentially severe consequence, deicing is performed at airports where temperatures are likely to be around 0℃ (32 °F). Deicing techniques are also employed to ensure that engine inlets and various sensors on the outside of the aircraft are clear of ice or snow.

VII. Exercises

1. Can you list different reasons for "flight delay"?

(1)

(2)

(3)

(4)

2. Translate the following words and phrases into Chinese or English.

delay	runway congestion
weather	天气预报
unfavorable	暴雨
typhoon	雷暴，雷雨
temperature	晚点
terminate	航路上

3. Translate the following sentences into Chinese or English.

(1) 由于航空管制，我们的飞机还要等待一段时间。

(2) 我们正在等待起飞的指令，现在我们的飞机排在第三位，请您在座位上休息等候。

(3) 由于天气不好机场已经关闭。出于安全考虑，我们被通知本次航班取消。

(4) 我们的飞机有些小故障，正在维修排除，还需要等待一会儿。

(5) We have to change to another aircraft because of the technical problem. Please disembark with all your belongings. We sincerely apologize for the inconvenience.

(6) Don't worry. I will confirm the exact departure time now and let you know as soon as I receive the information.

(7) We'll inform the ground staff if you'd like to cancel the flight. They will help you complete the relevant procedures.

4. Group work: choose one topic to start a conversation. (TIME LIMIT: 5 minutes)

(1) Flight delay due to air traffic control.

(2) Flight delay due to terrible weather.

(3) Flight delay due to mechanical problems.

Task 20　Complaints Handling 处理机上矛盾、投诉

I . Warm-up Questions

1. What are the common reasons for passengers' complaints?

2. Why listening comes first in terms of complaining?

3. How to deal with in-flight complaints?

II . Dialogues

Dialogue 1: "It is too crowded here."

Situation: The communication among flight attendants as well as between passengers and flight attendants is very significant. Whatever happens, to communicate with each other always brings a

音频扫一扫

better solution.

Principle: Listen first and then try to communicate. Flight attendants should be patient and consistent in terms of attitude, and handle the situation with flexibility.

Example

PAX1: Excuse me?

FA: Yes, Madam. May I help you?

PAX1: It is too crowded here. I can't even put my legs in.

FA: Don't worry. I'll help out.

PAX1: Thanks.

FA: That's all right.

(Turning around to the next row...)

FA: Excuse me, Madam. Would you please lean your seat back forward a little bit?

PAX2: Is there anything wrong? I think It's my personal right.

FA: Yes, it is. But you have squeezed another passenger's space. You might walk a mile in others' shoes.

PAX2: Fine.

FA: You are so considerate. Let me help you adjust your seat back.

情景会话1："（座位）这里太挤了。"

旅客1：打扰一下。

乘务员：您好，女士。有什么可以帮助您的？

旅客1：我的位子太挤了，我连脚都放不进去。

乘务员：别担心，我来帮您解决。

旅客1：谢谢。

乘务员：不客气。

（转身向前一排……）

乘务员：打扰一下，女士。您能把椅背往前倾一点儿吗？

旅客2：有什么问题吗？我觉得这是我的权利。

乘务员：是的，这是您的权利。但是您已经挤占了其他旅客的空间，您可以站在他人的立场上想一想。

旅客2：那好吧。

乘务员：您真善解人意，我来帮您调整座椅。

Dialogue 2: When someone speaks too loud

Situation: The communication among flight attendants as well as between passengers and flight attendants is very significant. Whatever happens, to communicate with each other always brings a better solution.

Principle: Listen first and then try to communicate. Flight attendants should be patient and consistent in terms of attitude, and handle the situation with flexibility.

Example

PAX1: Excuse me, Miss?

FA: Yes, Sir. May I help you?

PAX1: That lady in a red dress speaks too loud. I can't bear it any more.

FA: Don't worry. I'll help you.

音频扫一扫

PAX1: OK.

(Walking towards that lady in a red dress...)

FA: Excuse me, Madam. Could you please talk softly to avoid disturbing the others?

PAX2: What?

FA: I said "Could you please talk softly to avoid disturbing the others".

PAX2: Sorry for that. I just listened to music and could not notice that.

FA: Thanks for your cooperation.

PAX1: Anyway, it's quite lucky for us to have the chance traveling on the same flight.

PAX2: Yeah, I think you are right. Sorry for that.

(Walking along the aisle...)

PAX3: Excuse me? I can't sit here any longer. That group of people is making too much noise. They are disturbing everyone around, including me. If you can't do anything about it, you'll have to find another seat for me. I refuse to sit here any longer.

FA: Er... Yes, I do understand. I'm sorry that they are disturbing you. Have you spoken to them yourself?

PAX3: Of course not. I don't think they care about me or anyone else.

FA: Let me talk with them. If it doesn't work, I'll try to find another available seat for you. How about that?

PAX3: Well, OK.

情景会话2：有人说话声音太大

旅客1：打扰一下。

乘务员：您好，先生。有什么可以帮助您的？

旅客1：那位穿红裙子的女士说话声音太大了，我受不了了。

乘务员：别着急，我来帮您解决。

旅客1：好的。

（走向那位身着红色连衣裙的女士……）

乘务员：打扰一下，女士。您能轻声说话以免打扰到其他人吗？

旅客2：你说什么？

乘务员：我说，"麻烦您说话小声一些，以免打扰到其他人"。

旅客2：抱歉，我刚才听音乐，没注意到自己说话声音那么大。

乘务员：感谢您的配合。

旅客1：毕竟我们能够同乘一架飞机还是很幸运的。

旅客2：嗯，您说得对。刚才的事抱歉了。

（客舱巡舱中……）

旅客3：您好？我不想坐在这儿了，那群人太吵了。他们打扰到了周围的所有人，包括我在内。如果你们不解决的话，就得给我另找一个座位，我拒绝再坐在这个位子上。

乘务员：嗯，好的，我很理解您。我对他们影响到您表示抱歉。您跟他们说了吗？

旅客3：当然没有。我认为我说不管用，其他人说也没用。

乘务员：让我和他们谈谈吧。如果不管用，我会设法给您另外找个空座位，您看如何？

旅客3：好，可以。

Dialogue 3: Dissatisfied with the cleanliness

Situation: The cabin attendants should keep the cabin clean all the time, clear the cabin from time to time, keep the lavatory clean and provide adequate amount of tissues and toilet paper. Sometimes, passengers are not satisfied with the lavatory cleanliness or blanket cleanliness.

Principle: Flight attendants should apologize for the inconvenience and check the lavatory in time. If a passenger got a dirty and smelly blanket, flight attendants should bring him or her a clean one.

Example

PAX1: Excuse me? Why is this blanket so smelly?

FA1: Sir, we apologize for the unclean blanket and the dissatisfaction that you suffered. This airport terminal has not provided washing outsourcing service so far, and we are vigorously putting this service into operation. We will change a clean blanket for you immediately. We do apologize.

PAX1: It's okay. Just give me a clean one.

FA1: No problem. Just a minute.

FA2: Did you just press the call button, Madam?

PAX2: Yes. The toilets are dirty and the smell is disgusting.

FA2: Thank you for letting me know and I do apologize. I'll deal with the situation immediately. As soon as they have been cleaned, I'll let you know.

PAX2: Well, there are no snacks. The plane hasn't been cleaned and the service is awful. I'm going to complain about those.

FA2: I do apologize. I'll talk with the purser and try to make it up to you. Would you give us another chance?

PAX2: Fine, then.

情景会话 3：对清洁度不满

旅客1：乘务员？为什么这条毛毯有一股怪味？

乘务员1：先生，对于这条毛毯的清洁问题，我们深表歉意，非常抱歉没能为您提供满意的服务。此航站暂时还没有实现寝具的外站洗涤，我们也在积极协调努力推进此项工作尽快开展，我们马上为您更换一条干净的毛毯，真的非常抱歉！

旅客1：没事，给我换条干净的就行。

乘务员1：没问题。请稍等一下。

乘务员2：女士，请问刚才是您按的呼叫按钮吗？

旅客2：是的，卫生间太脏了，而且气味难闻。

乘务员2：谢谢您告诉我，很抱歉。我马上处理一下，只要打扫干净，就马上跟您说。

旅客2：航班中没有点心供应，飞机上不干净，服务也糟糕。我要投诉你们！

乘务员2：真的非常抱歉！我马上跟乘务长反映，看看有没有补偿措施。能请您再给我们一次机会吗？

旅客2：那，好吧。

Dialogue 4: Serve a passenger in bad mood

Situation: The communication among flight attendants as well as between passengers and flight attendants is very significant. Whatever happens, to communicate with each other always brings a better solution.

Principle: Listen first and then try to communicate. Flight attendants should be patient and consistent in terms of attitude, and handle the situation with flexibility.

Example

FA: May I help you, Sir?

PAX: I haven't got my meal while the others are having their meals. Why?

音频扫一扫

FA: Oh, sorry. Did you in your seat when we served meals?

PAX: I was just in the lavatory. I'm starving and please send my meal quickly.

FA: All right. What would you like to have, fish, chicken or vegetarian?

PAX: Chicken.

FA: And rice or noodles?

PAX: Noodles, of course.

FA: Wait a moment, please.

(A few minutes later...)

FA: Here's your chicken with rice. Enjoy your meal.

PAX: Why do you serve me rice? Do I order rice?

FA: Sorry, Sir. We have run out of noodles.

PAX: I don't like rice and I prefer noodles. I'd like to speak to the purser. Ask your purser to come here.

FA: I'm sorry. Just a moment.

(The flight attendant goes to the front cabin and tells the purser the situation.)

FA: Purser, a passenger seems in bad mood. He doesn't accept rice and insists on noodles. What should I do?

PS: Oh, I see. I'll be there immediately. Try to comfort him.

(A few minutes later...)

FA: This is our purser, Sir.

PS: What can I do for you?

PAX: I want noodles and I don't like rice. Understand?

PS: Could you listen to me?

PAX: Please.

PS: OK. We do have run out of noodles. I like noodles, too. I usually take instant noodles with me. If you want instant noodles, I'll get some to you. OK?

PAX: Sorry, Miss. How can I show you my appreciation? I've been through a lot recently. I haven't been respectful to this flight attendant. I have to say sorry to her.

PS: It's okay. We still have a lot to improve.

情景会话4：为一位心情不好的旅客服务

乘务员：先生，请问需要些什么？

旅客：别人都在用餐，而不给我，为什么？

乘务员：呀，抱歉。我们供餐的时候您在座位上吗？

旅客：我在卫生间。现在我饿了，请马上给我送餐。

乘务员：好的。您要吃点儿什么？鱼肉、鸡肉或素餐？

旅客：鸡肉。

乘务员：主食要米饭还是面条？

旅客：当然是面条。

乘务员：请稍等。

（几分钟后……）

乘务员：您的鸡肉和米饭，请慢用。

旅客：为什么是米饭？我要的是米饭吗？

乘务员：对不起，先生。面条已经没有了。

旅客：我不喜欢吃米饭，我要面条。我要找你们乘务长，你把她给我叫来。

乘务员：抱歉，稍等。

（乘务员走到前舱，跟乘务长报告了此事。）

乘务员：乘务长，有位旅客似乎心情不太好，他不要米饭，一定要面条，请问该如何处理？

乘务长：我知道了。我马上就过去。先稳定下他的情绪。

（几分钟以后……）

乘务员：先生，这是我们的乘务长。

乘务长：我能为您做点儿什么吗？

旅客：我要吃面条，不吃米饭，知道吗？

乘务长：您能听我解释下吗？

旅客：请便。

乘务长：是这样，我们的面条确实已经发完了。但是我和您一样喜欢吃面条，我经常随身携带方便面。如果您吃方便面的话，我去给您拿来，您看行吗？

旅客：对不起。我怎样感谢你呢？最近我经历了太多起起落落。刚才对这位乘务员有些不尊重，我得向她道歉。

乘务长：没关系。我们的服务也还有待提高。

Dialogue 5: "We've been waiting for drinks for a long time."

Situation: After making mistakes, flight attendants should listen first and then try to communicate with passengers.

音频扫一扫

Principle: Flight attendants should be patient and consistent in terms of attitude, and handle the situation with flexibility.

Example

FA: May I help you, Madam? I saw you pressed the call button.

PAX1: Yes, I certainly did. I told your colleague that it was too cold, and we asked for the cabin to be a little warmer, but now it's getting even colder.

FA: You're right. It is cold. I'm afraid it often takes about 20 minutes for the cabin to acclimatize after taking off. I'll get you a blanket in the meantime, if you'd like.

PAX1: Yes, please.

FA: I'll be back in a moment.

PAX2: Excuse me? We've been waiting for drinks for a long time. We finished eating twenty minutes ago.

FA: I do apologize. It's been so busy. What can I get you?

PAX2: Two Cokes.

FA: Oh dear, I am sorry, but we've run out of Coke. They've been very popular today. But I can offer you Seven-up or Pepsi, Sprite or something else.

PAX2: I don't believe it. It's the same old story. You always seem to run out.

FA: I'm so sorry, Sir. Would you like Seven-up, Pepsi or Sprite instead?

PAX2: No way, thank you.

FA: I do apologize for that.

情景会话5："我们等饮料已经很长时间了。"

乘务员：女士，我能帮您做点儿什么？我看到您按呼叫钮了。

旅客1：嗯，我确实按了。我告诉您的同事客舱内太冷了，我们要求提高客舱内的温度，但是现在反而变得更冷了。

乘务员：是冷了，恐怕要等到飞机起飞二十分钟后客舱温度才会上升。如果您愿意的话，我现在马上给您拿条毯子来。

旅客1：好啊。

乘务员：我马上去拿来。

旅客2：你好？我们等饮料已经很长时间了。吃完饭到现在已经有二十分钟了。

乘务员：很抱歉，一直太忙了，您要点什么？

旅客2：两杯可口可乐。

乘务员：天哪，对不起。我们可乐发完了，今天喝可乐的人特别多。但我可以给您七喜、百事可乐、雪碧或其他饮料。

旅客2：我不信，你们总是这一套说辞，总是说发完了。

乘务员：我只能说抱歉了，先生。您还要七喜、百事可乐或雪碧吗？

旅客2：不必了，谢谢。

乘务员：真的非常抱歉！

Dialogue 6: Making mistakes

Situation: In summer, passengers wear less clothes. The aisles in the cabin are relatively narrow. If flight attendants are not careful enough, they may bump into passengers when providing service.

Principle: Flight attendants should not be at a loss but pay attention to remedial measures. They need to ask about the passengers, apologize and explain the situation. When providing service with trolleys in the cabin, flight attendants should be careful. If necessary, passengers should be reminded of being careful, especially those with children. Effective communication is based on sincere care and polite behavior.

Example

PAX: Oh! What's wrong with you?

FA: Are you all right? Where does it hurt?

PAX: The trolley bumped into my leg, the right leg.

FA: I do apologize. Let me get you some ice!

PAX: Fine.

FA: As you could recognize, we encountered the turbulence just then. The trolley is heavy and the aisle is narrow. So I bumped into you accidentally.

PAX: I'm feeling better now. Never mind.

FA: Thank you for your understanding and kindness.

情景会话6：服务出错

旅客：啊！你怎么回事？

乘务员：您还好吗？您伤到哪儿了？

旅客：我的腿，右腿被餐车撞到了。

乘务员：非常抱歉！我给您拿些冰块敷一下。

旅客：好吧。

乘务员：您也感受到了，刚才我们遇到颠簸，由于餐车重并且过道狭窄。所以，我刚才不小心碰到了您。

旅客：算了，没事的，我现在感觉好多了。

乘务员：您人真好！非常感谢您的理解！

III. Popular Words and Phrases

compensation	[ˌkɒmpenˈseɪʃn]	n. 补偿，赔偿
recommended	[rekəˈmendɪd]	adj. 被推荐的，被建议的
interfere	[ˌɪntəˈfɪə(r)]	v. 干预，干涉
apologize	[əˈpɒlədʒaɪz]	v. 道歉，认错
inconvenience	[ˌɪnkənˈviːnɪəns]	n. 不便；麻烦
crowded	[ˈkraʊdɪd]	adj. 拥挤的
lean	[liːn]	v. 倾斜
squeeze	[skwiːz]	v. 挤，压
considerate	[kənˈsɪdərɪt]	adj. 体贴的
bear	[beə(r)]	v. 忍受
disturb	[dɪˈstɜːb]	v. 打扰，妨碍
refrain	[rɪˈfreɪn]	v. 忍住，克制
bear in mind		牢记，铭记

IV. Practical Expressions

1. I'm sorry you are not able to rest. Would you like me to change a seat in another part of the cabin? Alternatively, I can offer you a pair of earplugs or headphones to help lower the noise.

我很抱歉打扰了您的休息。您愿意换个座位吗？或者，我给您送一副耳塞或者耳机过来，以便降低吵闹声。

2. Excuse me, could you talk softly to avoid disturbing the others. Thank you for your understanding !

对不起，请您谈话声音小些，以免影响其他客人休息。谢谢您的理解！

3. Sir/ Madam, I am sorry to disturb you. Would you please kindly refrain from speaking so loudly?

先生/女士，我很抱歉打扰您。请您小点儿声说话好吗？

4. I'll ask him to turn down the volume.

我会让他把音量调低。

5. I may help you deal with that. There's nothing to get excited about.

我会帮您处理此事的。没必要激动。

6. Would you please lean your seat back forward a little bit, Sir?

先生，您能把椅背往前倾一点吗？

7. Would you mind changing to another seat?

您介意换到其他座位吗？

8. Would you please calm down and think about this for a while?

您能冷静下来想想吗？

9. I'll consult with him for you.

我会为您和他协商这件事的。

10. Some passengers have already complained about that.

有一些旅客已经在抱怨此事了。

11. It's quite lucky to have the chance traveling on the same flight.

能够同乘一架飞机还是很幸运的。

12. I apologize for the condition of the blanket. I will bring you another one straight away.

我非常抱歉毛毯的清洁问题。我马上给您更换一条毛毯。

13. I will get it for you right now. I'm sorry for keeping you waiting so long.

我马上给您拿来。抱歉让您久等了。

V. Tips

How to make up for mistakes? 犯错如何补救

Step 1: Figure out the situation.

Are you OK?/ Are you all right?

Where does it hurt?

Do you need any help? / Would you like ice compress?

I will try my best to help you.

Step 2: Apologize.

I'm so/ terribly sorry.（道歉意愿强烈）

I apologize for that.（道歉意愿强烈且正式）

I do apologize.（语气正式且更强烈）

Step 3: Explain and deal with the situation.

The trolley is heavy.

The aisle is narrow.

We encountered the turbulence just then. So I bumped into you accidentally.

VI. Supplementary Reading

Complaints 投诉

A complaint is any formal legal document that sets out the facts and legal reasons that the filing party or parties believe(s) are sufficient to support a claim against the party or parties against whom the claim is brought that entitles the plaintiff(s) to a remedy (either money damages or injunctive relief). In *Civil Law*, a "complaint" is the very first formal action taken to officially begin a lawsuit. This written document contains the allegations against the defense, the specific laws violated, the facts that led to the dispute, and any demands made by the plaintiff to restore justice. In some jurisdictions, specific types of criminal cases may also be commenced by the filing of a complaint, also sometimes called a criminal complaint or felony complaint. Most criminal cases are prosecuted in the name of the governmental authority that promulgates criminal statutes and enforces the police power of the state with the goal of seeking criminal sanctions, such as the State (also sometimes called the People) or Crown (in Commonwealth realms). In the United States, the complaint is often associated with misdemeanor criminal charges presented by the prosecutor without the grand jury process.

VII. Exercises

1. What are the common reasons for passengers' complaints?

(1)

(2)

(3)

2. Translate the following words into Chinese or English.

compensation	道歉，认错
recommended	拥挤的

inconvenience   倾斜

disturb   体贴的

refrain   忍受

干预，干涉

3. Translate the following sentences into Chinese or English.

(1) 对不起，请您谈话声音小些，以免影响其他客人休息。谢谢您的理解！

(2) 先生，您能把椅背往前倾一点儿吗？

(3) 您介意换到其他座位吗？

(4) Would you please calm down and think about this for a while?

(5) I apologize for the condition of the blanket. I will bring you another one straight away.

(6) I will get it for you right now. I'm sorry for keeping you waiting so long.

4. Group work: choose one topic to start a conversation. (TIME LIMIT: 5 minutes)

(1) Someone speaks too loud.

(2) Serve a passenger in bad mood.

(3) Making mistakes.

Project 9

Civil Aviation

Emergencies
紧急情况

Task 21 First Aid and Medical Assistance 应急医疗救护

I . Warm-up Questions

1. What is CPR and how to operate in-flight CPR?

2. Why is it important to make announcements to ask for help from medical personnel when a passenger feels dizzy, has a stomachache, sprains or gets other illnesses?

3. How to express your concern to a sick passenger on board?

4. How to deal with "Foreign Body Airway Obstruction"?

II . Dialogues

音频扫一扫

Dialogue 1: Airsickness (1)

Situation: Some passengers may suffer from airsickness on board and they would ask flight attendants for help.

Principle: If the sick passengers ask for in-flight airsick tablets, flight attendants should explain the situation and ask the passengers to sign their names before taking the tablets.

Example

PAX: Excuse me. I feel like vomiting./ I am overcoming with a feeling of nausea.

FA: Don't worry. Let me remove the armrests and adjust the seat back for you, so you can lie down and relax. A nice nap would be great for you. If you feel sick, you can use the airsickness bag in the seat pocket in front of you. Let me get you a blanket and a pillow. By the way, could I open the air-flow vent?

/ If you feel like vomiting, these are the airsickness bags and towel. Would you like me to switch on the air-flow knob for you?

PAX: Yes, thanks a lot.

FA: Let me get you a cup of warm water as well. I will be back soon.

(After a while...)

FA: Excuse me, Miss. Here is your blanket, pillow and a cup of warm water.

PAX: Thanks, but I am not feeling very well. Do you have airsickness tablets on board?

FA: Yes, we have. However, the tablets won't start to help so quickly. They work 30 minutes after usage. Besides, our body becomes more sensitive in the air. I'm afraid you may not feel good even if you take pills. So for your health, we don't suggest you take any pills on board. But if you insist, I will get for you, but you have to sign your name on the *Letter of Consent of Use of Drug*. Do you still need them?

PAX: Yes, I believe I really need one.

/ No, I don't.

FA: OK, I will bring one to you right now. Please sign your name here.

/ OK, have a good rest. If there is anything we can do for you, please let us know.

PAX: Thanks.

FA: It's my pleasure. By the way, there are some vacant seats close to the lavatory. Maybe it's more convenient for you. Would you like to sit there?

PAX: Sure.

FA: May I help you with your baggage? If there are valuables, please bring them with you all the time.

PAX: So considerate of you. Thanks a lot.

FA: With pleasure.

情景会话1：晕机（1）

旅客：打扰一下。我感觉不舒服，想吐。

乘务员：请不要担心，我来帮您放下扶手并调节座椅靠背，躺下来休息一会儿您可能会感觉好些。如果您感觉难受的话，请使用前排座椅口袋内的清洁袋。我给您拿条毛毯和枕头。对了，需要我打开通风口吗？

/ 如果您感觉想吐，这是为您准备的呕吐袋和毛巾，您看需要我为您打开通风口吗？

旅客：好的，十分感谢。

乘务员：我再给您倒杯温水吧。我很快就会回来。

（过了一会儿……）

乘务员：女士，打扰一下。这是您的毛毯、枕头和一杯热水。

旅客：谢谢，我还是感觉不舒服，请问机上有晕机药吗？

乘务员：是的，机上配有晕机药。但这种药片不会立即见效，在服用30分钟后才能起效。而且，我们的身体在空中变得更为敏感，恐怕您即使服了药也不一定会舒服。因此，为了您的健康着想，我们不建议您在飞行中用药。但是如果您坚持，我会为您提供，但请您务必在《药品使用知情同意书》上签名。那么，您现在还需要用药吗？

旅客：是的，我确实需要吃一片药。

/ 不了，我还是不用药了。

乘务员：好的，我现在就去给您拿一片，请您在这里签名。

/ 好的，您好好休息。如您有任何事情需要我们帮忙，可以随时联系我们。

旅客：谢谢了。

乘务员：不用谢。另外，靠近卫生间那边有几个空座位，那边对您来说可能会更方便，您想坐那儿去吗？

旅客：好的。

乘务员：我来帮您拿行李吧。如有贵重物品，请您随身携带。

旅客：非常感谢，你真体贴。

乘务员：很高兴帮到您。

Dialogue 2: Airsickness (2)

Situation: Some passengers may suffer from airsickness on board and they would ask flight attendants for help.

Principle: Flight attendants should pay attention to the passenger's symptom and ask about their feelings, then comfort them and offer assistance.

Example

FA: Are you alright, Sir? You look pale. / What's the matter?

PAX: I'm not feeling very well.

FA: What's your symptom?

音频扫一扫

PAX: I feel dizzy and I think I'm going to throw up.

FA: You might be airsick./ I think you're suffering from airsickness. You may find an airsickness bag in the seat pocket in front of you. I'll bring you some water.

PAX: Thank you.

FA: Is this your first time traveling by plane? It's quite normal if you don't often take the plane. Just relax. You may feel better if you don't think about it.

/ You may use the wet towel to wipe your face, which can make you feel better. You may also lie down and have a rest.

PAX: Alright.

FA: If you feel worse, please call us immediately.

PAX: OK.

情景会话2：晕机（2）

乘务员：先生，您还好吗？您看上去脸色苍白。/ 您怎么了？

旅客：我感觉不太好。

乘务员：您有什么症状？

旅客：感觉头晕，而且我觉得我快要吐了。

乘务员：您可能是晕机了。您可以在前排座椅口袋里找到清洁袋，我去给您拿杯水。

旅客：谢谢。

乘务员：这是您第一次乘坐飞机吗？如果您不经常坐飞机的话，这是很正常的。放松就好了。如果您不去想它，会感觉好些。

/ 您可以用湿毛巾擦擦脸，这样会感觉好些。您也可以躺下休息一会儿。

旅客：好的。

乘务员：如果您觉得症状加重，请马上叫我们。

旅客：好。

Dialogue 3: Feel pains in ears

音频扫一扫

Situation: As is often the case, passengers may feel pains in ears or suffer from tinnitus during the descending period. And they may ask flight attendants for help.

Principle: Flight attendants should pay attention to the passengers' symptom and ask about their feelings, then comfort them and offer assistance.

Example

PAX: Excuse me, Miss. I don't feel well.

FA: What's the matter？

PAX: I feel pains in my ears. It's quite uncomfortable. Could you please help me with that？

FA: Don't worry, Sir. You may not feel well in your ears because the aircraft is descending. Is this the first time that you travel by air?

PAX: Yes.

FA: That's alright. It's quite common for people who do not often take the plane. It's just because of the changes in pressure./ You feel pains in your ears because of a change in air pressure.

PAX: What should I do?

FA: You can relieve the earache by chewing a gum or a candy. Another method is to try to hold your nose with your fingers and blow your nose. Like this...

(The flight attendant showed the passenger how to do that.)

PAX: Let me have a try. Wow! It works.

FA: If you have any other requirement, please feel free to let me know.

PAX: Thank you very much!

情景会话 3：耳痛

旅客：打扰一下，我不太舒服。

乘务员：您怎么了？

旅客：我耳朵疼。真的很难受。您能帮帮我吗？

乘务员：别着急，先生。飞机下降过程中，您可能会感到耳部不适。这是您第一次坐飞机吗？

旅客：是的。

乘务员：没关系。这对于不经常坐飞机的人来说很常见。这是因为气压变化导致的。/ 您感到耳膜疼是由于气压的改变。

旅客：那我该怎么办？

乘务员：嚼块口香糖或糖果。还有另外一种方法，您只要用手捏住鼻子鼓气，就像这样……您的耳痛就会有所缓解。

（乘务员教旅客怎么做。）

旅客：我试试。哇，真的有效！

乘务员：如果您还有其他需要，请随时告诉我。

旅客：非常感谢。

Dialogue 4: Be in a coma

Situation: During intercontinental flights, passengers are easily affected by the limited space, which can induce diseases, such as a coma.

Principle: When a passenger is in an emergency, the crew need to seek professional assistance from medical staff by broadcasting. When a passenger is in a coma, flight attendants need to ask the passengers around him or her about his or her situation.

Example

PAX: Help! Help!

FA: What's going on? Hey, can you hear me, Sir? (Turning around to ask another passenger) Madam, what's going on?

PAX: We were just chatting and then suddenly he passed out. Please! You must save him!

FA: Calm down, Madam. Are you with him? Everyone, please go back to your seat. We need some space and fresh air!

PAX: No, we just met, and he told me he was travelling alone. I swear I didn't do anything!

FA: Okay, I'm going to search his pockets and bag for medicine. Please witness me.

音频扫一扫

情景会话 4：旅客昏迷

旅客：快来人！快来人！

乘务员：怎么了？嘿，先生，能听到我说话吗？（转身向另一位旅客询问）女士，他怎么了？

旅客：我们刚刚在聊天，突然他就晕倒了。请您救救他吧！

乘务员：女士，您先冷静一下，您与他同行吗？其他旅客，请回到座位就座，我们需要一些空间和新鲜空气。

旅客：不是，我们刚遇见。他说他是自己一个人旅行的。我发誓我什么也没有做！

乘务员：好的，现在我要检查他的口袋和包看看有没有药物。请做我的见证人。

Dialogue 5: Dizzy

Situation: During intercontinental flights, passengers are easily affected by the limited space, which can induce diseases, such as dizziness.

Principle: When a passenger is in an emergency, the crew need to seek professional assistance

音频扫一扫

from medical staff by broadcasting. When a passenger feels dizzy, flight attendants need to ask the passenger himself or herself as well as the passengers around him or her about details.

Example

FA: Excuse me, Miss. You look so pale. Do you feel uncomfortable?

PAX1: Yes, I've no idea what happened to me. I just feel dizzy and weak.

FA: Don't worry, Miss. Sometimes, hypoglycemia happens to the passengers who are traveling overnight by air. And I will report to the purser.

PAX1: Thank you.

FA: Miss, please have a cup of sweet water first. Don't worry. I will make an announcement to see if there are any medical personnel on board.

PAX1: You're so nice.

(Turning towards the passenger nearby...)

FA: Excuse me, this passenger feels dizzy. Could you help us look after her during the flight? If you notice anything wrong with her, you only need to press the call button to contact us at once. Thank you so much.

PAX2: No problem. I'd like to.

(After making the announcement...)

FA: I'm sorry to tell you that there is no medical personnel on board. But we have removed the armrests for you to lie down. And the passengers around you will help us look after you. I hope you will feel better soon.

PAX1: Thanks.

情景会话5：眩晕

乘务员：女士，打扰一下，您看起来脸色很苍白。您觉得不舒服吗？

旅客1：是的，我不知道我怎么了。就是感觉头晕，无力。

乘务员：别担心，女士。偶尔会有旅客夜航时发生低血糖症状的情况。我来报告给乘务长。

旅客1：谢谢您！

乘务员：女士，您先喝一杯糖水吧。别着急，我马上为您广播寻找医务人员。

旅客1：您真好心。

（转向邻座旅客……）

乘务员：打扰一下，这位旅客眩晕。能麻烦您在航班上帮我们照看一下她吗？如果您发现她有任何不正常的情况，只需要立即按呼唤铃叫我们即可。非常感谢您！

旅客2：没问题。我很乐意。

（客舱广播后……）

乘务员：很抱歉告诉您我们没能在飞机上找到医护人员。不过我们已经把座椅扶手放倒了便于您躺下休息。您周围的旅客会帮助我们照顾您的。希望您一会儿会舒服些。

旅客1：谢谢您！

Dialogue 6: Stomachache

Situation: During intercontinental flights, passengers are easily affected by the limited space, which can induce diseases, such as stomachache.

Principle: When a passenger is in an emergency, the crew need to seek professional assistance from medical staff by broadcasting. When a passenger suffers from stomachache, flight attendants need to ask him or her about details.

Example

PAX1: Excuse me, I have a stomachache.

FA: Don't worry, Sir. We'll help you. Let me put down the armrests and adjust the seat back.

音频扫一扫

Please lie down and relax. Here is the pillow and blanket.

PAX1: Thanks.

FA: When did the pain start？

PAX1: About 5 minutes ago.

FA: Where does it hurt? / In what way are you feeling sick？

PAX1: I'm getting the grabbing pain in my upper abdomen.

FA: What is your symptom?

PAX1: I have the burping and bloating.

FA: Sir, do you have any relevant pills with you?

PAX1: No, I have no pills.

FA: Prescription drugs can only be used when we get the indication from the doctor.

PAX1: But it hurts...

FA: Relax, we'll report this to our captain at once and make an announcement for looking for doctors. We'll try our best to help you.

(Turning towards the passenger nearby...)

FA: Madam, would you please take care of this passenger for a while? I'll be back soon. If there's any problem, please inform us by pressing the call button.

PAX2: It's okay.

PS: (Announcement) Ladies and gentlemen, may I have your attention please! There is a passenger feeling uncomfortable. If there is any medical qualified person on board, doctor or nurse, please identify yourself to the nearest cabin crew. Thank you!

(After a while... The sick passenger felt better...)

情景会话6：旅客胃痛

旅客1：打扰一下，我觉得胃疼。

乘务员：不要担心，先生。我们会帮助您的。我来放下扶手并调好座椅靠背，请躺下放松。这是为您准备的枕头和毛毯。

旅客1：谢了。

乘务员：您什么时候开始痛的？

旅客1：大概5分钟前。

乘务员：什么位置不舒服？

旅客1：我感到上腹部剧烈疼痛。

乘务员：您有什么症状吗？

旅客1：打嗝，胀气。

乘务员：先生，您有带相关的药吗？

旅客1：我没有药。

乘务员：只有得到医嘱我们才能使用处方药。

旅客1：但是好疼啊……

乘务员：放松。我会立即向机长报告并且广播寻找医生，我们会尽全力帮助您。

（转向邻座旅客……）

乘务员：女士，能请您暂时帮忙照看一下这位旅客吗？我马上回来，如果有什么问题请您立刻按呼唤铃通知我们。

旅客2：好的。

乘务长：（广播）女士们，先生们，请注意！现在有一位旅客身体不适，如果机上有医生或护士等具有行医资质人员，请与最近的机组人员联系。谢谢！

（过了一会儿……生病旅客情况好转……）

Ⅲ. Popular Words and Phrases

airsickness	[ˈɛrsɪknɪs]	n. 晕机
airsickness bag		呕吐袋
airsickness tablet		晕机药
disposal bag		清洁袋
vomit	[ˈvɒmɪt]	v. 吐出；呕吐 n. 呕吐；呕吐物
sick	[sɪk]	adj. 恶心的；不舒服的
uncomfortable	[ʌnˈkʌmftəbl]	adj. 不舒服的
choke	[tʃəuk]	v. 呛，噎，使室息
FBAO(Foreign Body Airway Obstruction)		气道异物梗阻（阻塞）
First Aid Kit		急救箱
Emergency Medical Kit		应急医疗箱
Universal Precaution Kit		卫生防疫包
consent	[kənˈsent]	n. & v. 同意
medicine	[ˈmeds(ə)n]	n. 药
pill	[pɪl]	n. 药丸
tablet	[ˈtæblɪt]	n. 药片
painkiller	[ˈpenˌkɪlə]	n. 止痛药
prescription drugs		处方药
indication	[ˌɪndɪˈkeʃən]	v. 指示；迹象
symptom	[ˈsɪmptəm]	n. 症状
ill	[ɪl]	adj. 生病的；不好的
dizzy	[ˈdɪzɪ]	adj. 头晕的
have difficulty in breathing		呼吸困难
faint	[feɪnt]	adj. & v. 无力（的）
chest congestion	[tʃest kənˈdʒestʃən]	胸闷
pain	[peɪn]	n. 痛苦，疼痛
ache	[eɪk]	n. 疼痛
headache	[ˈhedeɪk]	n. 头疼
backache	[ˈbækeɪk]	n. 背疼
toothache	[ˈtuːθeɪk]	n. 牙疼
stomachache	[ˈstʌməkeɪk]	n. 胃疼，腹痛
earache	[ˈɪəreɪk]	n. 耳朵疼
sore throat	[sɔː θrəut]	喉咙痛
abdomen	[ˈæbdəmən]	n. 腹部
grabbing	[ˈgræbɪŋ]	adj. 强烈的
burping	[bɜːpɪŋ]	n. 打嗝
bloating	[ˈbləutɪŋ]	n. 胀气
swallow	[ˈswɒləu]	v. 吞咽
fever	[ˈfiːvə]	n. 发烧
have a cold		感冒；伤风
headache	[ˈhedeɪk]	n. 头痛
get hurt		受伤
ice compress		冰敷
compress	[kəmˈpres]	n. 止血敷布；止血带

bandage	['bændɪdʒ]	n. 绷带
ulcer	['ʌlsə]	n. 溃疡
swelling	['swelɪŋ]	n. 肿胀
fracture	['fræktʃə]	n. 骨折
coma	['kəumə]	n. 昏迷
epilepsy	['epɪlepsɪ]	n. 癫痫
diabetes	[ˌdaɪə'biːtiːz]	n. 糖尿病
bleed	[bliːd]	v. 流血
nosebleed	['nəuzbliːd]	n. 鼻子出血
cough	[kɒf]	n. & v. 咳嗽
shock	[ʃɒk]	n. 休克
burn	[bɜːn]	n. & v. 烧伤
choke	[tʃəuk]	n. & v. 窒息，哽咽；阻塞
bruise	[bruːz]	v. & n. 碰伤；擦伤
nausea	['nɔːzɪə]	n. 恶心，反胃
diarrhea	[ˌdaɪə'rɪə]	n. 腹泻
angina	[æn'dʒaɪnə]	n. 心绞痛
asthma	['æsmə]	n. 哮喘，气喘
cardiac arrest	['kɑːdɪæk ə'rest]	心搏停止
heart attack	[hɑːt ə'tæk]	心脏病发作
childbirth/ give birth to.../ delivering		分娩
CPR (cardiac-pulmonary resuscitation)		心肺复苏术
fainting	['feɪntɪŋ]	n. 昏晕
food poisoning		食物中毒
heat stroke		中暑
lose consciousness		失去意识
allergic to...		对……过敏
ointment	['ɔɪntmənt]	n. 药膏，油膏，软膏
nitroglycerin	[ˌnaɪtrəu'glɪsərɪn]	n. 硝化甘油
allergy	['ælərdʒi]	n. 过敏症
urgent	['ɜːrdʒənt]	adj. 急迫的，紧急的
medical	['mɛdɪkəl]	adj. 医学的；医药的；医疗的
disinfectant	[ˌdɪsɪn'fɛktənt]	n. 消毒剂，杀菌剂
infectious	[ɪn'fɛkʃəs]	adj. 有传染性的；易传染的
influenza	[ˌɪnflu'enzə]	n. 流感
statement	['stetmənt]	n. 声明，（文字）陈述
communicable	[kə'mjunɪkəbl]	adj. 可以传达的，会传染的
qualification	[ˌkwɒlɪfɪ'keɪʃ(ə)n]	n. 资质

IV. Practical Expressions

1. What's the matter?
（遇有旅客需要医疗救护时）您怎么了？

2. Do you need medical assistance?
您需要医疗帮助吗？

3. Where do you feel the pain? / Do you have any pain? What is your symptom?
您感觉哪里不舒服？有什么症状吗？

4. Do you feel well enough to sit up?

您感觉自己能够坐起来吗?

5. Please explain your emergency to me slowly and clearly so that I can help you.

请您慢慢地清楚地描述一下您的症状以便我能帮助您。

6. Are you ill or injured?

您是生病还是受伤了?

7. Did you get hurt?

您受伤了吗?

8. When did the pain start？

什么时候开始痛的?

9. Where does it hurt?/ In what way are you feeling sick？

什么位置不舒服?

10. Is this your first time traveling by plane?

这是您第一次乘坐飞机吗?

11. I think you're suffering from airsickness.

我想您是晕机了。

12. Shall I bring you some water?

我给您拿些水来吧?

13. There is an airsick bag in the seat pocket in front of you.

前排座椅口袋里有清洁袋。

14. You may lie down and have a rest.

您可以躺下休息一会儿。

15. It's quite normal if you don't often take the plane. Just relax.

如果您不经常坐飞机的话,这是很正常的。放松就好了。

16. You may feel better if you don't think about it.

如果您不去想它,会感觉好些。

17. Do you feel headache, nausea or vomiting? Judging from your symptoms, I think you might be airsick.

您觉得头痛、恶心或想吐吗? 从您的症状来看,您可能是晕机了。

18. You don't need to worry about it. You are just a little bit tired.

您不用担心。您只不过是有点儿劳累过度。

19. You may remove the armrests and adjust the seat back to lie down and relax. A good sleep would be good for you.

您可以放下扶手并调整座椅靠背,躺下休息一会儿。好好睡一觉,您可能会感觉好些。

20. If you feel sick, you can use the airsickness bag in the seat pocket in front of you.

如果您晕机的话,请使用前排座椅口袋里的呕吐袋。

21. Don't worry. We'll help you. Let me put down the armrests and adjust the seat back. Please lie down and relax. Here is the pillow and blanket.

不要担心,我们会帮助您的。我来帮您放下扶手并调整座椅靠背,请躺下放松。这是为您准备的枕头和毛毯。

22. If you feel like vomiting, these are the airsickness bags and towel. Would you like me to switch on the air-flow knob for you?

如果您感觉想吐,这是为您准备的呕吐袋和毛巾,您看需要我为您打开通风口吗?

23. Do you have any pills with you?

您带药了吗?

24. Don't worry! I will try to look for a doctor on board for you.

您别担心! 我这就去试着找找看机上有没有医生。

25. Relax, we'll report this to our captain at once and make an announcement for looking for doctors. We'll try our best to help you.

请放轻松。我们会立即向机长报告并且广播寻找医生，我们会尽全力帮助您的。

26. The tablets won't work so quickly. They work half an hour after usage.

这种药片不会这么快见效的。服用后半小时才会起作用。

27. For your health, we don't suggest you take any pill on board.

为了您的健康着想，我们不建议您在飞行中用药。

28. If you insist, we will get it for you, but you have to sign your name on the form *Letter of Consent of Use of Drug*.

如果您坚持，我们会为您提供，但请您务必在《药品使用知情同意书》上签名。

29. Prescription drugs can only be used when we get the indication from the doctor.

只有得到医嘱，我们才能使用处方药。

30. Hope you'll be better soon.

希望您能快点儿好起来。

31. How are you feeling?

您感觉好点儿了吗？

32. There is a passenger who is seriously ill and we have to make an alternate. Thank you for your understanding!

由于一名旅客病情严重，飞机稍后备降，感谢您的理解！

33. Would you please take care of this passenger for a while? I'll be back soon. If there's any problem, please inform us by pressing the call button immediately.

能请您暂时帮忙照看一下这位旅客吗？我马上回来，如果有什么问题，请您立刻按呼唤铃通知我们。

34. You feel pains in your ears because of a change in air pressure.

您感到耳膜疼是由于气压的改变。

/ Please relax. Ear pressure is caused by the change of air pressure.

请放轻松。耳压是由于气压的变化引起的。

35. You may not feel well in your ears because the aircraft is descending.

飞机下降过程中，您可能会感到耳部不适。

36. You can relieve the earache by chewing a gum or a candy.

嚼块口香糖或糖果，您的耳痛会有所缓解。

37. Excuse me, Sir/ Madam. Do you know this passenger who gets ill?

您好，先生/女士，请问您认识这位生病的客人吗？

38. Excuse me, Sir / Madam. Have you ever suffered from emphysema?

您好，先生/女士，请问您得过肺气肿病吗？

39. I'll go and get the First Aid Kit. Let's stop bleeding first.

我去取一下急救药箱。我们先止住血。

40. Your blood pressure is relatively high. Do you have your prescribed medicine with you?

您的血压比较高，您有带自己的处方药吗？

41. He feels like everything around him is spinning.

他感到周围的东西在旋转。

42. He feels bloated and uncomfortable after meal. He has bouts of abdominal pain and the pain is mainly in the lower right part of the abdomen.

他餐后觉得肚子胀胀的，很不舒服。他感觉一阵阵地腹痛，痛点主要在肚子的右下方。

43. When he bends over or lies down, the chest pain gets worse.

他弯腰或躺下时，胸部更痛。

44. As the reason for the pain is not sure, we don't suggest you take any painkiller.

由于现在原因不明，我们不建议您使用止痛药。

45. I will make an announcement to see if there are any medical personnel on board.

我马上为您广播寻找机上的医务人员。

46. Do you need a wheelchair after landing? I can help you.

请问飞机落地之后需要帮您叫辆轮椅吗？

47. We can contact the airport ambulance service if it's needed.

如果情况需要，我们可以给您联系机场救护车。

48. First aid treatment has been given but he is still in unconsciousness.

他接受了机上急救，但还是没有恢复意识。

49. A passenger is unconscious after suffering from epileptic seizure.

一名旅客癫痫发作后失去知觉。

V. Tips

How to deal with stomachache? 旅客胃痛处理程序

Step 1：初步照顾。

Don't worry, Sir. We'll help you. Let me put down the armrests and adjust the seat back. Please lie down and relax. Here is the pillow and blanket. If you feel like vomiting, these are the airsickness bags and towel. Would you like me to switch on the air-flow knob for you?

Step 2：紧接着应该询问"是怎样的疼痛，哪里疼，什么时候开始的，等等"。

When did the pain start？

Where does it hurt？/ In what way are you feeling sick？

What is your symptom?

Do you have any pills with you?

Relax, we'll report this to our captain at once and make an announcement for looking for doctors. We'll try our best to help you.

Step 3：了解具体症状后，应立刻报告乘务长或机长旅客的座位号、症状、有无同行人员等，如需要获得允许使用氧气瓶，广播找医生并与医生沟通旅客的症状信息。

Step 4：听从机长指示。如果情节严重，准备返航或备降。向其他旅客做好解释工作。

There is a passenger who is seriously ill and we have to make an alternate. Thank you for your understanding!

Considerations：

As the reason for the pain is not sure, we don't suggest you take any painkiller.

Prescription drugs can only be used when we get the indication from the doctor.

Do you have any pills with you?

Would you please take care of this passenger for a while? I'll be back soon. If there's any problem, please inform us by pressing the call button immediately.

VI. Supplementary Reading

1. First Aid 急救

On-board first aid refers to immediate and temporary treatment given to someone who is accidentally injured or suddenly falls ill while waiting for the arrival of a doctor or sending the person in question to a medical unit for proper treatment. In an emergency case, a basic judgment is done as to the situation of the injured or the sick, and among other things, the following life-existence features are vital:

(1) Consciousness: Consciousness means the recognizing ability of the surrounding environment and the responding ability of the outside stimulation. An invalid is thought to be unconscious if he or she gives no response to the outside stimulation.

(2) Breathing: Breathing refers to the frequency of respiration. A single breath includes two processes, exhaling and inhaling. Normal breathing frequency for an adult is 15-20 times/minute, and breathing frequency for children is a bit faster than that of the adults. Breathing frequency may also vary due to various physiological and pathological reasons. Breathing is a way to obtain oxygen.

(3) Pulse: Pulse refers to the number of heartbeat per minute by feeling the artery of a person at the wrist or some other parts of the body. Regular pulse is 60-100 times/minute. Pulse may vary due to various physiological and pathological situations. It represents the status of blood circulation.

(4) Bodily Temperature: Normal body temperature is around 37℃. It matters little with age. Only under normal bodily temperature can human organism work properly.

2. CPR (Cardiac-pulmonary Resuscitation) 心肺复苏

Cardiac-pulmonary Resuscitation is a first-aid technology to treat the patient in sudden death, that is, a casualty stopping breathing, asphygmia and loss of consciousness. Cardiac-pulmonary Resuscitation is made in the following sequence: D, R, C, A, B, and D.

(1) D (danger) Confirm the safety of site conditions. The rescuer shall ensure he/ she and the rescue are in safe condition before taking treatment measures.

(2) R (response) Check the response of the patient. Judge consciousness, breathing and pulse. The method includes:

① Calling out: Calling out will express your concern; clap or shake the patient on his/ her shoulder.

② Check if there is any breathing: Immediately check if there is any breathing. Close the cheek to the patient's nose and mouth, and judge if the up-and-down movements of chest and abdomen are visible, if the breathing sound is audible, and if airflow can be felt at the mouth and nose.

③ Check if there is any pulse. Adult: use index finger and middle finger to press jugular vein near by the throat with the fingers to feel if there is any vascular pulsation. Infant: use index finger and middle finger to press brachial artery in the middle of inside of the upper arm to feel if there is any vascular pulsation.

④ Check if there is any trauma. Immediately stop bleeding in case of hemorrhea. If the patient has no response, then immediately take the following action.

(3) C (circulation) Chest compression.

The purpose of chest compression is: when the heart stops pumping, drive blood flowing in blood vessel by external force pressing the heart.

① The center part to be pressed: Press the lower half of the sternum for adults and one finger below the line of two nipples.

② For adults, overlap both palm bases, straight elbow joint and maintain arms down vertical to the ground by the weight of upper body and strength of the shoulders and arms; for children, it will be done with a single hand; for infants, it will be done with two fingers (middle finger and index finger) or embrace with both thumbs.

③ Rate of downward compression: For adults: 100 times/minute; for infants: 110 times/minute.

④ Strength of downward compression: For adults, the chest will sink 4-5 cm at each compression, for children and infants, it will reduce to 2-3 cm.

⑤ Conduct artificial respiration and chest compression alternatively: Mouth-to-mouth air blowing will be conducted two times followed by chest compression 30 times. The process will continue until: the invalid resumes spontaneous respiration and circulation, or the doctor diagnosed that the invalid has died.

(4) A (airway) Opening the airway.

Methods: Put the invalid lying face-up on a hard floor or on the ground, with head tilted backwards, jaw raised up, to such an extent that the imaginary line between the jaw angle and earlobe is perpendicular to the ground. The figure below is the three methods for opening the airway: chin lift, chin lift with head tilt, jaw lift with head tilt.

(5) B (breathing) Artificial respiration.

Mouth-to-mouth breathing method: Provided that the respiratory tract is free from obstruction, pinch the nostrils closed with the thumb and index finger, take a deep breath, open your mouth wide and place it over the patient's mouth, making a tight seal, and blow into the patient's mouth (effective air blowing is more than 2 seconds), and constantly blow twice. If the air cannot be blown in, it is necessary to re-identify if the respiratory tract has been opened or if there is any foreign object lodging in the nose, mouth, throat or chest. If a foreign object is found, it will be removed away and thereafter re-start the same procedure. If there is no Automated External Defibrillation (AED), after artificial respiration, immediately return to chest compression, repeat compression and artificial respiration.

(6) Defibrillate as early as possible

If there is an AED, it will immediately stop the above steps and defibrillate as instructed.

3. Rules and Storage of Passenger Oxygen 旅客用氧的规定与存储

Since oxygen is generally stored in high pressure gas cylinder and fluid oxygen device, it is under the management of dangerous goods. Therefore, CCAR-121 prohibits passengers from carrying any device for storing, generating or distributing oxygen on board. Currently, the company can't provide oxygen storage, generation and distribution equipment meeting the airworthiness standards. The company can't provide medical oxygen service for passengers in flight. To meet the regulation requirements of FAA, on the North America routes operated by the company, passengers may carry portable oxygen concentrator (POC) on board and use in cruise phase to improve physical comfort level. And all the aircraft are equipped with certain type of in-flight oxygen bottles.

By means of molecular sieve technology, POC separates oxygen from other gasses in the air, and provides the user with oxygen at a concentration of more than $90\% \pm 3\%$. The device does not have pressure storage part, its distribution structure has not pressure and does not generate oxygen, and the device is not dangerous goods certified by FAA, and has no special operation limits. US FAA has tested interference and authorized some electronic devices of specific manufacturer, and indicated on the surface of the product and approved to be used in flight.

4. First aid and medical assistance: Dozens of people work together to save the boy's badly damaged arm 应急医疗救护：多方协同救助断臂男孩

The airliner CZ6820 was being guided down the runway on April 30 at the Hetian (Kungang) airport in the Xinjiang Uygur autonomous region to prepare for its departure. It was then stopped by the request of a father who rushed to send his seven-year-old son with a badly damaged arm to a hospital in Urumqi, capital of Xinjiang. After the orthopedists in the hospital examined the arm, they suggested that as the injury was so severe that the arm would need to be severed and then reattached to properly align the bone fragments, otherwise the child would be disabled for life. They decided to transfer him to the affiliated TCM hospital of Xinjiang Medical University in Urumqi, which is more than 1,400 kilometers from Hetian prefecture. After the boy's wounds were bound up and the severed limb was preserved at a low temperature, he was sent to the Hetian airport to catch a flight to Urumqi. Soon, the plane stopped, returned to the parking bay and opened its cabin door. The child was lifted on a stretcher onto the plane.

The boy required surgery within eight hours to save his arm, and in a race against time, crew members and passengers, police, medical workers and many other people joined in to help. Zhao Yan, the flight's Chief Purser, said that as the doctors told her that the boy shouldn't fall asleep throughout the journey, she helped the boy to keep a clear mind by playing music. She also used ice cubes to cool down the severed limb. During the flight, some passengers also helped to take care of the boy.

It was at 2:10 am on May 1 when the seven-year-old finally arrived at the Affiliated TCM hospital of Xinjiang Medical University in Urumqi. The hospital prioritized his case and organized more than

20 doctors and nurses from departments including blood transfusion, orthopedics, emergency and anesthesiology. The surgery lasted for more than three hours and was successful. China Southern Airlines has opened the door of warmth, love, and life for the boy with a badly damaged arm, showcasing the responsibility of state-owned enterprises and the strength of China to the world, and forging a miracle of life rescue.

【背景阅读】2021年4月30日，新疆和田一名7岁男孩被拖拉机皮带轮绞断手臂，需紧急前往乌鲁木齐进行接臂手术。和田当地的医生告知孩子父亲，手术需要在6小时之内完成，否则细胞坏死后将无法治疗。当天和田（昆冈）机场飞往乌鲁木齐的最后一趟航班是中国南航的CZ6820航班，为救助该男孩，秉承"人民至上，生命至上"理念，经多方紧急协调，并征求101名旅客的同意，23时42分，刚从机场1号停机位滑行推出并准备起飞的班机接到指令，返回廊桥，二次开门。机场开启地面绿色通道，与时间赛跑，航班机组分工协作。乘务组协调旅客预留出了宽敞空间，准备好了冰块等物品。该航班的乘务长赵燕说，医生告诉她，男孩在旅途中不能睡着，她通过播放音乐帮助男孩保持清醒的头脑，用冰块冷却断肢。在飞行过程中，一些旅客还帮忙照顾男孩。地空联动，多方协同，机组成员、旅客、警察、医护人员和地勤人员等都加入了这场紧急救援之中。5月1日凌晨2点10分，小男孩到达乌鲁木齐的新疆医科大学附属中医医院。经过争分夺秒的抢救，手术持续了三个多小时，断臂终于接上了，南航为断臂男孩打开了温暖之门、爱心之门、生命之门，向世界彰显了央企担当、中国力量，铸造了生命救援奇迹。

VII. Exercises

1. How to express your concern to a sick passenger on board?

(1)

(2)

(3)

2. Translate the following words and phrases into Chinese or English.

airsickness bag	症状
disposal bag	晕机
consent	呛，噎，使窒息
medicine	急救箱
vomit	应急医疗箱
uncomfortable	药丸
headache	药片
stomachache	止痛药

3. Translate the following sentences into Chinese or English.

(1) 您感觉哪里不舒服？有什么症状吗？

(2) 请您慢慢地清楚地描述一下您的症状，以便我能帮助您。

(3) 这是您第一次乘坐飞机吗？

(4) 您觉得头痛、恶心或想吐吗？从症状来看，您可能是晕机了。

(5) You feel pains in your ears because of a change in air pressure.

(6) If you feel like vomiting, these are the airsickness bags and towel. Would you like me to switch on the air-flow knob for you?

(7) If you insist, we will get it for you, but you have to sign your name on the form *Letter of Consent of Use of Drug*.

(8) Do you need a wheelchair after landing? I can help you.

4. Group work: choose one topic to start a conversation. (TIME LIMIT: 15 minutes)

(1) Airsickness

(2) Feel pains in ears

(3) Stomachache on board

Task 22　Severe Turbulence 重度颠簸

Ⅰ. Warm-up Questions

1. What can be caused by encountering severe turbulence?

2. Why do both cabin crew and passengers need to fasten their seatbelts during turbulence?

3. How to deal with the situation when a passenger wants to use the lavatory during turbulence?

Ⅱ. Dialogues

音频扫一扫

Dialogue 1: Encountering turbulence

Situation: When encountering turbulence, passengers should remain seated and fasten their seatbelts.

Principle: Please make announcements in time when experiencing turbulence.

Example

PS: (Announcement) Ladies and gentlemen, as we expect turbulent weather, please return to your seats and fasten your seat belts. Kindly do not walk around in the cabin and do take care of your children.

FA: Excuse me, Sir. As we are encountering turbulence, please return to your seat at once and fasten your seatbelts.

PAX: I see... But I've been waiting here for such a long time!

FA: I can understand that it must be frustrating to wait for such a long time. However, it is a safety requirement that all passengers be seated with their seatbelts fastened during turbulence. Please feel free to use the lavatory when the "fasten seatbelts sign" is switched off. Thank you for your cooperation.

情景会话1：遇有颠簸

乘务长：（广播）女士们，先生们，由于飞机即将遇到不稳定气流，请您回到座位上并系好安全带。请不要在客舱内来回走动，有小孩的旅客请照顾好您的孩子。

乘务员：先生，您好，我们正遇有持续的气流颠簸，请您立即回到原位坐好，并系好安全带。

旅客：我知道……但是我已经站这儿等这么长时间了！

乘务员：（旅客不满颠簸时乘务员劝阻其暂缓使用卫生间时）我能理解您等了很长时间，一定心情不好。但是为了确保安全，所有旅客在颠簸期间都需要在座位上系好安全带。请您在安全带指示灯灭掉前不要使用卫生间。感谢您的配合。

Dialogue 2: Be affected by the signal of electronic devices

Situation: The navigation and communication system may be affected by the signal of electronic devices during the critical period, even worse with low visibility.

Principle: Flight attendants should monitor the cabin during the critical period.

Example

PS: (Announcement) Ladies and gentlemen, the captain has informed us that the aircraft will be operated in low visibility conditions. Now, please switch off all electronic devices and keep them off until the aircraft has reached the safety altitude. Thank you for your cooperation!

FA: Excuse me, Sir. The captain has informed us that our navigation and communication system is being interrupted.

PAX: Well, why are you talking to me?

FA: It could be your electronic devices. Now, please switch off your cellphone and laptop and keep them off until the aircraft has landed.

PAX: Oh! Of course. Sorry!

FA: Thank you for your cooperation.

情景会话 2：飞机受到电磁干扰

乘务长：（广播）女士们，先生们，根据机长指示，飞机正处于低能见度运行，请您立即关掉所有电子设备，保持电源关上直至飞机到达安全高度，感谢您的配合。

乘务员：先生，您好，根据机长指示，飞机的导航和通信系统正受到电磁干扰。

旅客：额，为什么只对我说呢？

乘务员：极可能是因为您的电子设备。现在请您立即关掉手机和笔记本电脑，并保持电源关上直至飞机落地。

旅客：哦，当然！马上关，真是抱歉！

乘务员：感谢您的配合。

III . Popular Words and Phrases

turbulence	['tɜ:bjʊl(ə)ns]	n. 颠簸
light/ moderate/ severe turbulence		轻度/中度/重度颠簸
available	[ə'veɪləbl]	adj. 可获得的
suspend	[sə'spɛnd]	v. 暂停
turn off		关闭
inconvenience	[ɪnkən'viːnɪəns]	n. 不便之处
moderate	['mɒd(ə)rət]	adj. 中度的
recommend	[ˌrekə'mend]	vt. 建议
rough air		扰动气流

IV . Practical Expressions

1. Please remain seated with your seat belts fastened. We are about to experience some turbulence.
请您坐好并且系好安全带。我们马上要遇到气流了。

2. According to the regulations of TSA, passengers are requested to return to their seats as staying at the door area/ emergency exits is not permitted.
根据美国运输安全管理局的规定，旅客必须回到座位上，禁止在门区和紧急出口处停留。

3. There will be turbulence at any time, so passengers are not allowed to stay in the service room for a long time. Would you please return to your seat till you feel better?

因为随时会有颠簸，所以旅客不可以长时间逗留在服务间内。等您感觉好些了就请回到座位上，好吗？

4. Our beverage service will start immediately after the seat belt sign is off. Now it's not safe to leave the seat.

我们的饮料服务在安全带信号灯关闭之后马上开始。现在离开座位不安全。

5. Because of turbulence, please return to your seats and fasten your seat belts.

由于受气流影响，飞机发生颠簸，请您回到座位上并系好安全带。

6. Kindly do not walk around in the cabin and do take care of your children.

请不要在客舱内来回走动，有小孩的旅客请照顾好您的孩子。

7. Please take care of your children and check their seat belts are securely fastened. Infants should be taken out of bassinets and be seated with infant seat belts fastened.

请带小孩的旅客照顾好您的孩子，确保他们系好安全带，将婴儿从摇篮中抱出让他们坐好，并帮他们系好婴儿安全带。

8. For your own safety, lavatories should not be used at this time. Passengers currently using lavatories should hold the handle firmly.

为了您的安全，在颠簸期间，卫生间暂停使用。正在使用卫生间的旅客请扶好把手。

9. As flight attendants are required to be seated, we shall be suspending cabin service until the aircraft is clear of turbulence.

由于乘务员需要留在座位上，我们将停止客舱服务直到飞机停止颠簸。

10. Some passengers were injured because their seat belts weren't fastened.

一些旅客受伤是因为他们没有系好安全带。

11. I can understand that it must be frustrating to wait for such a long time. However, it is a safety requirement that all passengers be seated with their seat belts fastened during turbulence.

我能理解您等了很长时间一定心情不好。但是为了确保安全，所有旅客在颠簸期间都需要在座位上系好安全带。

12. Please feel free to use the bathroom when the seat belt sign is switched off.

请您在安全带指示灯关闭前不要使用卫生间。

V. Tips

Cabin Announcements: Turbulence 客舱广播：颠簸

Ladies and gentlemen, because of turbulence, please return to your seats and fasten your seat belts. Kindly do not walk around in the cabin and do take care of your children. As flight attendants are required to be seated, we shall be suspending cabin service until the aircraft is clear of turbulence. Thank you for your cooperation!

VI. Supplementary Reading

1. Turbulence 飞机颠簸

During the flight, air turbulence may happen at any time. There are two categories of turbulence, predicted turbulence and unpredicted turbulence. The flight deck would notify the cabin crew before and during the flight of the information about predicted turbulence. The PIC will determine the level of turbulence and advise the purser. There are three levels of turbulence, mild, medium, and severe.

① Mild Turbulence

Cabin Situation: liquid swaying in containers; not difficult to operate food carts;

Service can be continued but hot drinks will not be provided to prevent accidental scald;

② Medium Turbulence

Cabin Situation: Liquid spilled out of a container with 70% glassful of drinks; difficult to operate food carts; difficult to walk in the cabin; difficult to stand upright without holding something tight;

Terminate service immediately, put away the pots containing hot drinks; push food carts and beverage carts back to the kitchen, then fasten and fix the carts; cabin crew retreat to their own seats and fasten seat belts;

③ Severe Turbulence

Cabin Situation: Objects flying or dropping; unfixed objects sliding back and forth; unable to stand upright or walk in the cabin;

Terminate service immediately, put on the breaks of carts; flight attendants should find nearby seats to sit in and fasten seat belts or hold fixed subjects to maintain stable.

2. Predicted Turbulence 可预知颠簸

During the flight, having received the information about impending turbulence, cabin crew should make appropriate preparation based on the precaution program as well as on the turbulence information provided by the flight deck; When the "Fasten seat belts" lamp illuminates and sends alarming sound, the cabin crew should use cabin broadcast to inform passengers to fasten their seat belts. In the case of mild turbulence, the crew could conduct seat belt checks while making broadcast; in the case of medium or severe turbulence, the "Fasten seat belts" announcement could be broadcast repeatedly while in the meantime flight attendants should retreat to their own seats and fasten seat belts. If necessary, the purser on duty should adjust the service plan based on the information provided by the flight deck.

3. Unpredicted Turbulence 突发性颠簸

When unpredicted turbulence occurs, cabin crew should first use broadcast to inform passengers to fasten their seat belts, meanwhile communicate with the flight deck and ask the pilots to switch on the "Fasten seat belts" lamp if it has not been switched on; Cabin crew should determine the level of turbulence and provide appropriate service in terms of the turbulence level; When the turbulence makes it impossible to continue service, cabin crew should terminate service and use broadcast to inform passengers to fasten their seat belts. The announcement can be broadcast repeatedly if necessary. Meanwhile, as required, cabin crew should protect themselves by implementing the following measures: If there is an empty seat nearby, take the seat and fasten the seat belt; Retreat to flight attendant seats immediately and fasten seat belts; Firmly hold on nearby fixed subjects to maintain stable.

4. Visibility 能见度

In meteorology, visibility is a measure of the distance at which an object or light can be clearly discerned. It is reported within surface weather observations and METAR code either in meters or statute miles, depending upon the country. Visibility affects all forms of traffic: roads, sailing and aviation. Meteorological visibility refers to transparency of air: in dark, meteorological visibility is still the same as in daylight for the same air.

A commercial aircraft flying into the clouds over somewhere. ICAO Annex 3 *Meteorological Service for International Air Navigation* contains the following definitions: the greatest distance at which a black object of suitable dimensions, situated near the ground, can be seen and recognized when observed against a bright background; the greatest distance at which lights of 1,000 candelas can be seen and identified against an unlit background; the range over which the pilot of an aircraft on the centre line of a runway can see the runway surface markings or the lights delineating the runway or identifying its centre line.

Ⅶ. Exercises

1. Could you please list several consequences after encountering severe turbulence?

(1)

(2)

(3)

2. Translate the following words and phrases into Chinese or English.

moderate turbulence	颠簸
severe turbulence	可获得的
turn off	暂停
inconvenience	中度的
recommend	

3. Translate the following sentences into Chinese or English.

(1) 请您坐好并且系好安全带。我们马上要遇到气流了。

(2) 由于受气流影响，飞机发生颠簸，请您回到座位上并系好安全带。

(3) 为了您的安全，在颠簸期间，卫生间暂停使用。正在使用卫生间的旅客请扶好把手。

(4) Kindly do not walk around in the cabin and do take care of your children.

(5) I can understand that it must be frustrating to wait for such a long time. However, it is a safety requirement that all passengers be seated with their seat belts fastened during turbulence.

4. Group work: choose one topic to start a conversation. (TIME LIMIT: 5 minutes)

(1) Encountering mild turbulence.

(2) Turbulence and suspending service.

(3) A passenger would like to use the lavatory when encountering medium turbulence.

Task 23　Dangerous Goods and Accidental Fire
危险品与意外失火

Ⅰ. Warm-up Questions

1. What are the reasons for in-flight fire?

2. Why is the use of lithium battery or power banks forbidden on board?

3. How will you calm passengers when you've extinguished a minor fire in the lavatory?

4. How to recognize in-flight fire as soon as possible?

Ⅱ. Dialogues

Dialogue 1: The in-flight oven is on fire!

音频扫一扫

Situation: During the cruising period, a flight attendant found that the oven is on fire.

Principle: The flight attendant should report the situation to the purser as soon as finding out the fire, and handle the situation professionally.

Example

FA2: Purser, oven No. 3 at the front galley is on fire.

PS: Got it. Please try to put it out and I'll report it to the captain.

(Flight attendant No.2 shuts off the No.3 oven and takes the nearest Halon Extinguisher to put out the fire...)

PS: (Calling the captain...) Captain, oven No. 3 at the front galley is on fire. We found white smoke as well as obvious fire. We are organizing fire fighting.The report is finished.

PS: (Calling flight attendants...) Attention! Attention! Oven No. 3 at the front galley is on fire. Please take all the available Halon extinguishers to the front galley.

FAs: Got it!

(After 2 minutes...)

FA3: I've already wore the Smoke Hood/ Protective Breathing Equipment. I'll take over the work of flight attendant No.2.

(Contacting the captain during the special situation...)

PS: Captain, we are trying our best to put out the fire. Four Halon Extinguishers have been used and the situation is under control.

FA4,5: (Comforting passengers...) Don't panic! Heads down! Bend over! Cover your nose and mouth with your clothes.

PS: Captain, the fire has been put out. Two Halon Extinguishers left. I've assigned a flight attendant to supervise the situation at the front galley. Anything else we need to do right now?

情景会话1：机上烤箱失火

乘务员2：乘务长，前厨房3号烤箱着火了。

乘务长：（确认火情后）知道了。我来向机长报告，你去尽力灭火。

（2号乘务员切断3号烤箱电源，拿起最近的海伦灭火瓶灭火。）

乘务长：（呼叫机长）报告机长，前厨房3号烤箱着火，烟雾白色，火焰红色，火势中等，我们正在组织灭火，报告完毕。

乘务长：（通知全体乘务员）全体乘务员请注意，前厨房3号烤箱着火，请带上所有能用的海伦灭火瓶速来支援灭火。

乘务员们：明白，收到。

（两分钟后……）

乘务员3：我已戴好防烟面罩，我来接替2号乘务员。

（灭火期间，与驾驶舱保持不间断地联系……）

乘务长：报告机长，我们正在积极灭火，已使用4个海伦灭火瓶，火势已得到控制，报告完毕。

乘务员4,5：（安抚旅客，在客舱过道中弯下腰大声提醒旅客）请不要惊慌！低下头！弯下腰！用衣服捂住口鼻。

乘务长：报告机长，火已被扑灭，海伦灭火瓶未全部用完，还剩两个。已派专人监控前厨房的情况，机长请指示。

Dialogue 2: The lithium battery fire

Situation: In case of lithium battery fire, use Water Extinguisher or other nonflammable fluid to cool battery core and device, cool the core of battery in fire, and prevent heat extending to adjacent battery core. If there is no Water Extinguisher, we may use other inflammable fluid to cool battery core and device. In case of open fire, Halon Extinguisher may control lithium battery fire to prevent the spread.

Principle: After Halon or Water Extinguisher is used, it will immediately and fully cover and soak the lithium battery with water or nonflammable fluid containing water, since only water or nonflammable fluid containing water can sufficiently cool lithium battery or battery core in lithium battery pack and prevent fire again.

Example

PAX: Fire! Fire!

FA1: The fire can be caused by the lithium power bank.

PAX: What can I do?!

FA2: Just leave your laptop on the tray table! Please stand up! Attention! Attention! All of the passengers, stay away from the fire at once! Don't panic! We are well trained to handle this situation!

FA1: Any incombustible liquid can be used to chill down the high temperature. We need it as much as possible.

(After putting out the fire...)

FA3: The lithium power bank is self-igniting, and it can be exploded easily once the after-combustion happens. Therefore, chilling it down by water instead of the powder extinguisher is the first action when emergency.

FA1: OK. I'll keep an eye on this. Please report the situation to our purser. Thank you!

情景会话2：锂电池失火

旅客：着火了！着火了！

乘务员1：火情极有可能是锂电池引起的。

旅客：我怎么办呢？！

乘务员2：将笔记本电脑留在小桌板上！站起来！其他旅客请注意！请尽快远离火源，不要惊慌，我们是受过专业训练的！

乘务员1：任何不可燃液体都可以降低温度，我们需要尽可能多的液体！

（明火熄灭后……）

乘务员3：锂电池自燃，一旦复燃，很有可能爆炸。因此，当情况紧急时首先使用水冷却，而不是用干粉灭火瓶。

乘务员1：好的，我会负责监控的。请你们把情况汇报给乘务长，谢谢！

Dialogue 3: Lavatory fire

Situation: A passenger smells something burning and immediately presses the call button.

Principle: A flight attendant should report the situation to the purser as soon as finding out something unusual on board, and handle the situation professionally.

Example

FA: Excuse me, Sir. May I help you?

PAX: I can smell a burning. Can you smell it?

FA: Yes, I can smell that as well. Maybe it's from the lavatory. Let me check!

(The smoke detector equipped in the lavatory alarms...)

PS: (Announcement) Ladies and gentlemen, we have a minor fire in the middle lavatory and we have handled the situation. Please remain seated and follow the cabin crew's instructions! Thank you!

FA: (Walking towards the passenger) For your safety, we'll relocate all the passengers near the fire. Would you please be seated to the rear of the cabin?

PAX: No problem. But I want to know what is the reason for the fire.

FA: Someone smoked in the lavatory and threw the cigarette butts into the garbage can. Now the fire is under our control. Thank you for your cooperation and assistance.

PAX: No worries.

情景会话 3：卫生间失火

乘务员：您好，先生。请问需要帮忙吗？

旅客：我闻到了一股焦味。你闻到了吗？

乘务员：是的，我也闻到了。可能是从卫生间冒出的，我去检查一下。

（卫生间的烟雾探测器警报响起……）

乘务长：（广播）女生们，先生们，客舱中部卫生间失火，火情已得到控制。请您在原位坐好，听从机组人员的指挥！谢谢！

乘务员：（走向旅客）为了您的安全，我们将重新调整火源附近所有旅客的座位，请您坐到后舱去好吗？

旅客：没问题。但是我想知道起火的原因是什么。

乘务员：有人在卫生间吸烟，并把烟头扔进了垃圾箱。现在我们已完全控制住火情。感谢您的理解和支持。

旅客：这没什么。

Ⅲ. Popular Words and Phrases

dry powder	[draɪ ˈpaʊdə]	干粉
lithium battery	[ˈlɪθiəm ˈbætəri]	锂电池
extinguisher	[ɪkˈstɪŋgwɪʃə]	n. 灭火器
self-ignite	[selfɪgˈnaɪt]	v. 自燃
external	[ɪkˈstɜːrnl]	adj. 外部的（internal 内部的）
combustion	[kəmˈbʌstʃən]	n. 燃烧
flame	[flem]	n. 火焰 v. 燃烧
chill down	[tʃɪl daʊn]	冷却
soak	[səʊk]	v. 浸泡
shower	[ˈʃaʊə]	v. 淋洒
incombustible	[ˌɪnkəmˈbʌstəb(ə)l]	adj. 不可燃的
prevent	[prɪˈvent]	v. 阻止
after-combustion		n. 复燃
occur	[əˈkɜː]	v. 发生

spark	[spɑːk]	v. 发出火星
blow up	[bləʊ ʌp]	爆炸
explode	[ɪkˈspləʊd]	v. 爆炸
rear cabin	[rɪə ˈkæbɪn]	后舱
restroom	[ˈrestruːm; −rʊm]	n. 卫生间
baggage hold		行李舱
fire warning (alarm)		火警
cargo compartment		货仓
evacuation	[ɪˌvækjʊˈeɪʃ(ə)n]	n. 撤离，疏散
open flame		明火
emergency slide/ escape		逃生滑梯
chute	[ʃut]	n. 降落伞
firefighting equipment	[ˈfaɪrˈfaɪtɪŋ ɪˈkwɪpm(ə)nt]	灭火设施
asphyxia/ suffocate	[əsˈfɪksɪə] / [ˈsʌfəkeɪt]	v. 室息
mobile	[ˈməʊbaɪl]	adj. 可移动的
portable	[ˈpɔːrtəbl]	adj. 于提的；轻便的
electronic device	[ɪˌlekˈtrɒnɪk dɪˈvaɪs]	电子设备
prohibit	[prəˈhɪbɪt]	v. 禁止
duration	[djuˈreɪʃn]	n. 持续，持续的时间，期间

Ⅳ. Practical Expressions

1. Attention! Attention! All of the passengers, stay away from the fire at once! Don't panic! We are well trained to handle this situation!

注意！注意！所有旅客，请尽快远离火源，不要惊慌，我们是受过专业训练的！

2. The fire can be caused by the lithium power bank.

火情极有可能是锂电池引起的。

3. Any incombustible liquid can be used to chill down the high temperature, we need it as much as possible.

任何不可燃液体都可以用于降低温度，我们需要尽可能多的液体！

4. The lithium power bank is self-igniting, and it can be exploded easily once the after-combustion happens. Therefore, chilling it down by water instead of the powder extinguisher is the first action when emergency.

锂电池自燃，一旦复燃，很有可能爆炸。 因此，当情况紧急时，首选水冷却而不是用干粉灭火。

5. For your safety, we'll relocate all the passengers near the fire. Would you please be seated to the rear of the cabin?

为了您的安全，我们将重新调整火源附近所有旅客的座位，请您坐到后舱去好吗？

6. Someone smoked in the lavatory and threw the cigarette butts into the garbage can. All of my colleagues are experienced and the fire is under our control.

有人在卫生间吸烟，并把烟头扔进了垃圾箱。我的同事们非常有经验，已完全控制住火情。

7. Excuse me, I am a crew member on this flight. This is non-smoking flight. Did you smoke in the lavatory just now?

您好，我是本次航班的一名机组成员，本次航班是禁烟航班，请问您刚才是否在洗手间吸烟？

8. Sir/ Madam, smoking in the lavatory may cause fire easily on board. And once the fire breaks out, the consequences will be devastating. Please cooperate with us and tell us where you left the cigarette stub so that we can eradicate the potential danger.

先生/女士，在洗手间吸烟极易引起火灾，一旦着火，后果不堪设想，希望您能及时告诉我们事情的真相，配合我们一起尽快消除火灾隐患，请问您将烟蒂扔在了哪里？

9. Sir/ Madam, your smoking in the lavatory just now was extremely dangerous, which has violated *Article 25 of Regulations on the Civil Aviation Security* as well as some other aviation rules. Please make sure it will not happen again.

先生/女士，你刚才在洗手间吸烟是非常危险的，你已经违反了《中华人民共和国民用航空安全保卫条例》第二十五条及其他民航法规规定。请保证不要再有类似情况发生。

10. As I informed you clearly that smoking on plane would jeopardize flight security, your behavior has seriously violated *Article 25 of Regulations on the Civil Aviation Security* and *Article 23 of Law of People's Republic of China on Security Administrative Penalties*. You have to put it out right away, or we will take whatever proper actions according to the law.

我已经明确地告知你，机上吸烟会影响飞行安全，你的行为已经严重违反了《中华人民共和国民用航空安全保卫条例》第二十五条的规定，以及《中华人民共和国治安管理处罚法》第二十三条的相关规定。请你立即将烟熄灭，否则我们将依法采取措施。

V. Tips

1. Procedures for Handling Lithium Battery Fire 锂电池失火处置程序

(1) Cut off or remove the external power from the equipment in fire (if applicable);

(2) Use Halon or water fire extinguisher;

(3) Immediately and constantly use water or other nonflammable fluid to soak the electronic devices in fire, reduce the temperature of the lithium battery cell, block heat dissipation, and prevent adjacent battery cell fire;

(4) If the device is connected to an aircraft power socket, remove other power from the socket until it has confirmed no failure in the aircraft system;

(5) Keep contact with the cockpit during fire fighting;

(6) In case of leakage or spillage, respond according to the corresponding manual.

Do not try to move the electronic device in fire or smoke to prevent any serious injury. Do not cover the electronic device by articles or try to reduce the temperature by ice.

2. Procedures for Handling Smoke/ Fire 灭烟/灭火程序

In performing smoke/ fire fighting procedures, it should establish a 3-person smoke/ fire fighting team, one for smoke/ fire fighting, one for communication, and the last one for assistance.

(1) Find out smoke/ fire source and determine the nature of smoke/ fire.

(2) Pull out circuit breakers of affected area and switch off the electrical power.

(3) Flight attendants protect themselves, with PBE, and take appropriate fire extinguishers.

(4) Report to the captain and keep communication with the cockpit crew. If necessary, ask the captain to cut off the electrical power of the smoke/ fire area.

(5) Take all available fire extinguishers to the region of the fire and keep them available for use.

(6) Monitor the situation and ensure the fire is extinguished.

Ⅵ. Supplementary Reading

1. Airplane Smoke/ Fire 机上烟雾/火灾

The interior of an airplane is made from man-made chemical materials all of which produce dense toxic smoke when a heat source is introduced or by burning. As heat is present, these smoke rise.

Classification of Smoke/ Fire on board:

Class A: Combustible substances, such as fabric, paper, wood, plastics, rubber, etc. Smoke: Grey/ brown, dense. Appropriate Fire Extinguisher: Water; Halon if it is close to the fire and easily to get, but it should wet the fire area by water after the fire has been put out.

Class B: Flammable liquids, grease, etc., such as aircraft fuel, hydraulic oil, lubricating oil, etc. Smoke: Black, very dense, with gasoline/ lubricant smell. Appropriate Fire Extinguisher: Halon.

Class C: Electrical equipment, such as oven and water heater. Smoke: Light grey/ light blue, very light, rapidly diffuse, with obvious acid smell. Appropriate Fire Extinguisher: Halon.

Class D: Flammable solid, such as magnesium, titanium, sodium and other flammable metals. Smoke: Light color, rapidly diffuse, usually with obvious sparks. Appropriate Fire Extinguisher: Halon.

2. Dangerous Goods 危险品

Dangerous goods are divided into nine classes in accordance with their different nature of danger, and some of them are further grouped into several types.

Class 1 – Explosives

Class 2 – Gases

Class 3 – Flammable liquids

Class 4 – Flammable solids, substances liable to spontaneous combustion and substances, which in contact with water and emit flammable gases

Class 5 – Oxidizing substances and organic peroxides

Class 6 – Toxic and infectious substances

Class 7 – Radioactive material

Class 8 – Corrosive material

Class 9 – Miscellaneous dangerous goods

Dangerous goods are differentiated in three hazard classes of package corresponding to its degree of danger. Hazard Class Ⅰ: More dangerous; Hazard Class Ⅱ: Medium level of danger; Hazard Class Ⅲ: Less dangerous.

Ⅶ. Exercises

1. What are the reasons for in-flight fire?

(1)

(2)

(3)

2. Translate the following words and phrases into Chinese or English.

external	duration
internal	锂电池
incombustible	灭火器
after-combustion	自燃
blow up	冷却
explode	后舱

3. Translate the following sentences into Chinese or English.

(1) 注意！注意！请尽快远离火源，不要惊慌，我们是受过专业训练的！

(2) 火情极有可能是锂电池引起的。

(3) 任何不可燃液体都可以帮助降低温度，我们需要尽可能多的液体！

(4) For your safety, we'll relocate all the passengers near the fire. Would you please be seated to the rear of the cabin?

(5) Excuse me, I am a crew member on this flight. This is non-smoking flight. Did you smoke in the lavatory just now?

4. Group work: choose one topic to start a conversation. (TIME LIMIT: 15 minutes)

(1) An in-flight oven is on fire.

(2) The lithium battery fire.

(3) The lavatory fire.

Task 24　Cabin Depressurization 客舱释压

Ⅰ. Warm-up Questions

1. What is depressurization?

2. How to identify different degrees of depressurization?

3. How would you say to the passengers when you teach them to use in-flight oxygen masks?

4. Why do flight attendants need to check the cabin and passengers after depressurization?

Ⅱ. Dialogues

Dialogue 1: Cabin Depressurization

Situation: Some passengers feel very uncomfortable. A passenger presses the call button.

Principle: The flight attendant should figure out the situation first and then report the situation.

Example

FA1: Excuse me, Madam. What can I do for you?

PAX1: I don't know why I feel stuffy in my chest.

FA1: Have you ever had this experience before?

PAX1: Never.

FA1: As far as I'm concerned, it's caused by cabin depressurization.

PAX1: What's the "cabin depressurization"?

FA1: In short, it's lack of oxygen. I shall report the situation to the purser and the captain immediately.

PS: (Announcement) Ladies and gentlemen, attention please! Our aircraft is now being depressurizing. Please fasten your seat belts and pull down the oxygen mask! Place it over your nose and mouth and slip the elastic band over your head to keep your breath normally. As our aircraft will make an emergency descent, please don't be panic and follow the instructions of our cabin crew.Thank you.

音频扫一扫

FA2: Are you clear? Please pull down the oxygen mask and cover your nose and mouth, just like this.

PAX2: OK, I see.

FA2: Don't be panic! Just breathe normally.

情景会话1：客舱释压

乘务员1：您好，女士，请问有什么可以帮您？

旅客1：我不知道为什么胸闷。

乘务员1：您以前有过这种感觉吗？

旅客1：从没有过。

乘务员1：据我判断，是由于客舱释压造成的。

旅客1：什么是"客舱释压"？

乘务员1：简单来说，就是缺氧。我将立即报告给乘务长和机长。

乘务长：（广播）女士们，先生们，请注意！我们的飞机现在正在释压，请您系好安全带，拉下氧气面罩，戴在口鼻上，正常呼吸。飞机将会紧急下降，请大家不要惊慌，听从乘务员的指挥，谢谢！

乘务员2：请问您听明白了吗？请您拉下氧气面罩，戴在口鼻上，就像这样。

旅客2：好的，我知道了。

乘务员2：不要惊慌，正常呼吸即可。

音频扫一扫

Dialogue 2: Reached the safety altitude after cabin depressurization

Situation: Flight attendants walk in the cabin and check the situation after cabin depressurization.

Principle: The flight attendant should figure out the situation first and then handle it professionally.

Example

PS: (Announcement) Ladies and gentlemen, our aircraft has reached the safety altitude. You can remove your oxygen mask now. If you need assistance, please contact our cabin crew. The flight attendants are doing cabin checks.

PAX1: Excuse me? Could you tell me what is the "safety altitude"?

FA1: The safety altitude refers to the altitude of 3000 meters or below. In this range of altitude, passengers aren't deprived of oxygen.

PAX1: What shall we do then?

FA1: We need to divert to a nearby airport for further inspection and maintenance. After all, safety is our priority.

PAX2: Excuse me, I think she may need oxygen.

FA2: Thank you for telling us.

(Turning around...)

FA2: Excuse me, do you have emphysema?

PAX3: No...

FA2: I see. Let me clean the makeup on your lip and put on the oxygen mask for you.

(At the same time...)

FA3: Did you get hurt, Sir?

PAX4: Yes. My right arm hurts, and it is bleeding.

FA3: Wait a second. Let me get a First Aid Kit. I will try to stop your arm from bleeding.

PAX4: All right.

情景会话 2：客舱释压后到达安全高度

乘务长：（广播）女士们，先生们，我们的飞机已经到达安全高度，现在，您可以取下氧气面罩了。如果您需要帮助，请与我们的客舱机组人员联系。现在，乘务员正在客舱进行检查。

旅客1：请问一下，什么是"安全高度"？

乘务员1：安全高度指的是海拔3000米或以下。在此范围内，旅客不会缺氧。

旅客1：那我们接下来怎么办？

乘务员1：我们需要调整航线，到附近机场进行检修。毕竟，安全是第一位的。

旅客2：打扰一下，我想她可能需要吸氧。

乘务员2：谢谢您通知我们。

（乘务员转身……）

乘务员2：请问您有肺气肿病吗？

旅客3：没有……

乘务员2：好的。让我来给您擦掉唇膏并戴上氧气面罩。

（与此同时……）

乘务员3：先生，请问您受伤了吗？

旅客4：是的，我的右臂受伤了，正在流血。

乘务员3：稍等一下，我去取一下急救药箱。我先给您止下血。

旅客4：好的。

III. Popular Words and Phrases

decompression	[ˌdiːkəmˈpreʃ(ə)n]	n. 减压；失压
depressurization	[diˌpreʃərɪˈzeʃn]	n. 释压
handle	[ˈhændl]	v. 处理
in the front		在前边
in the middle		在中间
in the rear		在后边
manage	[ˈmænɪdʒ]	v. 经营，管理
necessary	[ˈnesɪsərɪ]	adj. 必要的
pay attention to		注意
pull down		拉下
put out		熄灭
relocate	[ˌriːləʊˈkeɪt]	v. 重新安置
remain calm		保持冷静
collection	[kəˈlekʃ(ə)n]	n. 收取
decide	[dɪˈsaɪd]	v. 决定
explosive	[ikˈspləʊsiv]	adj. 爆炸的
breathe	[briθ]	v. 呼吸
normally	[ˈnɔː məlɪ]	adv. 正常地；通常地，一般地
instruct	[ɪnˈstrʌkt]	v. 通知；指示
extinguish	[ikˈstɪŋgwɪʃ]	v. 熄灭，扑灭
cruising	[ˈkruzɪŋ]	n. 巡航

Ⅳ. Practical Expressions

1. The oxygen mask is in the panel over your head.
氧气面罩储存在您头顶上方的嵌板内。

2. Oxygen masks will drop down from the compartment above your head if there is an emergency.
如遇有紧急情况，您头顶上方的氧气面罩会脱落。

3. Oxygen masks have dropped from the compartment above your seats.
您座椅上方的氧气面罩已脱落。

4. If you are traveling with a child, wear your oxygen mask first and then the child.
如果您与孩子一起乘机，请先佩戴好自己的氧气面罩，然后为孩子佩戴。

/ If you have an infant with you, please put on your mask first and then the infant.
如果您怀抱婴儿，请先佩戴好自己的氧气面罩，然后为婴儿佩戴。

5. One passenger is having difficulty in breathing. Request descent to a lower level to reduce cabin altitude.
一名旅客呼吸困难，请示下降到较低高度以减小客舱高度。

6. A passenger activated the overhead emergency oxygen generator.
一名旅客触发了顶部紧急氧气发生器。

7. The safety altitude refers to the altitude of 3000 meters or below. In this range of altitude, passengers aren't deprived of oxygen.
安全高度指的是海拔3000米或以下。在此范围内，旅客不会缺氧。

Ⅴ. Tips

Cabin Announcement: Cabin Depressurization 客舱广播：座舱释压

Ladies and gentlemen, Attention! Please sit down immediately. Pull an oxygen mask firmly towards yourself and place the mask over your nose and mouth and breathe normally. Put on your own mask first before assisting others. Please remain seated with your seatbelts fastened until further instructed.

Ⅵ. Supplementary Reading

1. Cabin Altitude 座舱高度

The pressure inside the cabin is technically referred to as the equivalent effective cabin altitude or more commonly as the cabin altitude. This is defined as the equivalent altitude above mean sea level having the same atmospheric pressure according to a standard atmospheric model such as the International Standard Atmosphere. Thus a cabin altitude of zero would have the pressure found at mean sea level, which is taken to be 101,325 pascals (14.696 psi).

2. Cabin Depressurization 座舱释压

Cabin pressurization is a process in which conditioned air is pumped into the cabin of an aircraft or spacecraft, in order to create a safe and comfortable environment for passengers and crew flying at high altitudes. For aircraft, this air is usually bled off from the gas turbine engines at the compressor stage, and for spacecraft, it is carried in high-pressure, often cryogenic tanks. The air is cooled, humidified, and mixed with recirculated air if necessary, before it is distributed to the cabin by one or more environmental control systems. The cabin pressure is regulated by the outflow valve.

(1) Type of Depressurization

Unplanned loss of cabin pressure at altitude is rare but has resulted in a number of fatal accidents.

Failures range from sudden, catastrophic loss of airframe integrity (explosive decompression) to slow leaks or equipment malfunctions that allow cabin pressure to drop undetected to levels that can lead to unconsciousness or severe performance degradation of the aircrew.

Uncontrolled decompression is an unplanned drop in the pressure of a sealed system, such as an aircraft cabin, and typically results from human error, material fatigue, engineering failure, or impact, causing a pressure vessel to vent into its lower-pressure surroundings or fail to pressurize at all. Such decompression may be classed as Explosive, Rapid, or Slow:

① Explosive decompression

② Rapid decompression

③ Slow/ Gradual decompression

(2) Reaction to cabin depressurization

① Reaction to lacking of oxygen

Altitudes	Symptoms
Sea level	Normal
10,000 feet	Headache, tiredness
14,000 feet	Sleepiness, headache, weakened sight, less concordance of muscle tissues, empurpling of nails, faint
18,000 feet	Reduction of memory capability, doing one action repeatedly except the above symptoms
22,000 feet	Convulsion, prostration, shock, unconsciousness
28,000 feet	Prompt occurrence of prostration and unconsciousness in 5 minutes

For people who are in poor health condition, reactions to the depressurization are stronger.

② Hours of effective consciousness

The hour of effective consciousness is the time during which human brain is sober enough to give sound judgments. In different altitudes, the hour of effective consciousness of a person in stationary status is very short. In the following table are altitudes versus hour of effective consciousness.

Altitudes	Hour of effective consciousness
22,000 feet	5-10 minutes
25,000 feet	3-5 minutes
30,000 feet	1-2 minutes
35,000 feet	30 seconds
40,000 feet	15 seconds

VII. Exercises

1. Can you list different degrees of cabin depressurization?

(1)

(2)

(3)

2. Translate the following words and phrases into Chinese or English.

decompression	释压
breathe	处理
normally	保持冷静
instruct	使熄灭，扑灭
cruising	

3. Translate the following sentences into Chinese or English.

(1) 氧气面罩储存在您头顶上方的嵌板内。

(2) 如遇有紧急情况，您座椅上方的氧气面罩会脱落。

(3) 如果您与孩子一起乘机，请先戴好自己的氧气面罩，然后再为孩子戴。

(4) If you have an infant with you, please put on your mask first and then the infant.

(5) Oxygen masks have dropped from the compartment above your seats.

4. Group work: choose one topic to start a conversation. (TIME LIMIT: 5 minutes)

(1) What is cabin depressurization?

(2) How to use in-flight oxygen masks?

(3) Reached the safety altitude after cabin depressurization.

Task 25　Hijacking and Explosive Objects Threat
劫机与爆炸物威胁

Ⅰ. Warm-up Questions

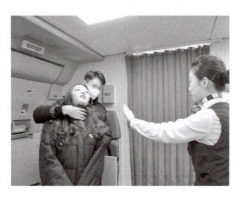

1. As a professional flight attendant, how to use words to comfort the hijacker on board?

2. How to deliver messages to colleagues when encountering in-flight hijacking?

3. What would you say to let the hijacker let go of a passenger hostage?

4. How to explain to passengers when you have just been informed that an explosive item might have been placed on board and have to examine all the in-flight baggage?

Ⅱ. Dialogues

音频扫一扫

Dialogue 1: Anti-hijacking

Situation: On the flight from Nanjing to Guangzhou, there seemed to be a fighting in the front cabin about 20 minutes ago. Some passengers are whispering. A flight attendant is walking through the aisle.

Principle: The principles of anti-hijacking is to ensure the safety of life and aircraft. Once the hijack happened, try to control the hijacker away from the cockpit, find out whether they have cahoots and weapons or not and report it immediately. Flight attendants should strictly implement the regulation of importing (entering into) and exporting (exiting) the cockpit. Be aware of safety when entering the cockpit in case of other people following in; when going out of the cockpit, flight attendants must first confirm no one outside the door through the observation mirror.

Example

PAX: Excuse me, Miss. What was happening in the front cabin just now?

FA: A hijacker attempted to rush into the cockpit and two security guards were fighting against him. The hijacking situation is now fully under control.

PAX: Wow. Amazing. The security guards are great! Shall we go to Guangzhou on time?

FA: However, our captain has decided to return to Nanjing for a thorough check. Further arrangements will be made after landing, and we will keep you informed.

PAX: OK, we understand.

FA: I don't think it'll be long before we continue our flight to Guangzhou.

PAX: I just hope we'll arrive at our destination safe and sound.

FA: Thank you for your understanding.

情景会话1：反劫机

旅客：乘务员？刚才前舱发生什么事了吗？

乘务员：一名劫机者试图冲进驾驶舱，两名安全员与之搏斗。现在劫机者已经被完全控制。

旅客：哇，太不可思议了。安保人员真是了不起！我们能准时抵达广州吗？

乘务员：即使这样，我们的机长还是决定返回南京做一次全面检查，下一步的安排将在落地后决定，到时我们会通知大家的。

旅客：好吧，我们理解。

乘务员：我想用不了多长时间我们就能继续飞往广州。

旅客：希望我们将平平安安抵达目的地。

乘务员：谢谢您的理解。

Dialogue 2: Explosive Objects Threat

音频扫一扫

Situation: On the flight from Chengdu to Beijing, all the passengers panic owing to the explosive objects threat. The flight attendants begin to examine all the baggage on board.

Principle: The principles of examining all the baggage is to ensure the safety of life and aircraft. Flight attendants should protect the cockpit and comfort on-board passengers.

Example

PS: (Announcement) Ladies and gentlemen, we have just been informed that an explosive item might have been placed on board. Our captain has instructed us to examine all the baggage on board. We apologize for the inconvenience and thank you for your cooperation.

FA1: Excuse me, Sir. Can you open your carry-on baggage for us to examine?

PAX1: Yes, here you are.

FA1: Please take off your shoes... Thank you.

FA2: Please show me your backpack.

PAX2: OK.

(20 minutes later...)

PS: (Announcement) Ladies and gentlemen, we have completed our baggage check, and no explosives could have been found on board.

PAX: Excuse me, Miss. Shall we arrive at Beijing Capital International Airport on time?

FA: Yes. The captain has decided to continue our flight. We'll arrive at the destination in about two hours and 40 minutes.

PAX: Thank you.

FA: Don't mention it.

情景会话2：爆炸物威胁

乘务长：（广播）女士们，先生们，我们刚接到通知，机上可能被放置了爆炸物。根据机长指示，我们必须检查机上所有旅客的行李物品。由此给您带来的不便，我们深表歉意，感谢大家配合！

乘务员1：打扰了，先生，能打开您的随身行李以便我们检查吗？

旅客1：好的，看吧。

乘务员1：请脱下您的鞋子……谢谢！

乘务员2：请给我看一下您的背包。

旅客2：好的。

（20分钟后……）

乘务长：（广播）女士们，先生们，我们已检查过所有行李，在机上未发现任何爆炸物品。

旅客：你好，乘务员。我们会准时抵达北京首都国际机场吗？

乘务员：是的，机长决定继续飞行。我们大约2小时40分钟后抵达目的地。

旅客：谢谢。

乘务员：别客气。

Ⅲ. Popular Words and Phrases

hijack	['haɪdʒæk]	v. 劫机 n. 劫持；威逼；敲诈
hijack victim		劫机受害者
trying to hijack aircraft		试图劫持客机
intimidate/ threaten	[ɪn'tɪmɪdeɪt] / [θret(ə)n]	v. 威胁
compel/ force	[kəm'pel] / [fɔːs]	v. 强迫
terrorist	['terərɪst]	n. 恐怖分子
terrorism	['terərɪzəm]	n. 恐怖主义
hostage	['hɒstɪdʒ]	n. 人质
compromise	['kɒmprəmaɪz]	v. 妥协
pilot-in-command	['paɪlət ɪn kə'mɑːnd]	n. 责任机长
spot commander, spot controller		现场指挥员
interference	[ˌɪntər'fɪrəns]	n. 干涉，干扰
anonymous call	[ə'nɒnɪməs kɔːl]	匿名电话
emergency evacuation		紧急撤离
the bomb disposal squad		拆弹人员
explosion	[ɪk'spləʊʒ(ə)n]	n. 爆炸
forced landing	[fɔːst 'lændɪŋ]	迫降
affect	[ə'fekt]	v. 影响
be devastating	[bi: 'devəsteɪtɪŋ]	不堪设想
behavior	[bɪ'heɪvjə]	n. 行为
be liable to	[bi: 'laɪəb(ə)l tu]	易于……
bomb	[bɒm]	n. 炸弹
carry out	['kærɪ aʊt]	施行

cease	[siːs]	v. 停止
certain procedure	[ˈsɜːt(ə)n prəˈsiːdʒə]	特定程序
claim	[kleɪm]	v. 反映，宣称
conduct	[ˈkɒndʌkt]	n. 行为
consequence	[ˈkɑnsəkwɛns]	后果
constraint measure	[kənˈstreɪnt ˈmeʒə(r)]	约束措施
crawl out	[krɔːl aut]	往外爬
criminal	[ˈkrɪmɪn(ə)l]	adj. 犯罪的 n. 罪犯
deal with		处理
deliberate damage	[dɪˈlɪb(ə)rət ˈdæmɪdʒ]	故意损坏
departure	[dɪˈpɑːtʃə]	n. 出发
detail	[ˈdiːteɪl]	n. 细节
detention	[dɪˈtenʃ(ə)n]	n. 拘留
Don't panic!		别惊慌！
drunk	[drʌŋk]	adj. 醉酒的
feature	[fiːtʃə]	n. 特征
fine	[faɪn]	v. 罚款
get down		下来；趴下
handcuff	[ˈhændkʌf]	n. 手铐
illegal	[ɪˈliːg(ə)l]	adj. 非法的
illicit behavior	[ɪˈlɪsɪt bɪˈheɪvjə]	违法行为
instruction	[ɪnˈstrʌkʃən]	n. 指示，命令
interrupt	[ɪntəˈrʌpt]	v. 打断，干扰
interview	[ˈɪntəvjuː]	v. 采访
immediately	[ɪˈmiːdɪətlɪ]	adv. 立即，马上
investigation	[ɪnˌvestɪˈgeɪʃ(ə)n]	n. 调查
jeopardize	[ˈdʒepədaɪz]	v. 危及
lead to		导致
legal responsibility		法律责任
make sure		确认，保证
mental condition		精神状况
parcel	[ˈpɑːs(ə)l]	n. 包裹
penalty	[pen(ə)ltɪ]	n. 处罚，罚款
performing duty		执行公务
propaganda	[prɒpəˈgændə]	n. 宣传品
permission	[pəˈmɪʃ(ə)n]	n. 允许
physical condition	[ˈfɪzɪk(ə)l kənˈdɪʃ(ə)n]	身体状况
potential danger	[pəˈtenʃl ˈdeɪndʒə(r)]	隐患
principle suspect		首要疑犯
printed material		印刷品
punishment	[ˈpʌnɪʃm(ə)nt]	n. 惩罚
radical action		过激行为
refuse	[rɪˈfjuːz]	v. 拒绝

restrain	[rɪ'streɪn]	v. 约束
restriction	[rɪ'strɪkʃ(ə)n]	n. 限制，管束
right away		立即，马上
severely	[sɪ'vɪəlɪ]	adv. 严重地
solve	[sɒlv]	v. 解决
spread	['spred]	v. 散发，传播
suspicious	[sə'spɪʃəs]	adj. 可疑的
take action		采取行动
take charge of		负责
threat	[θret]	n. 威胁
unauthorized	[ʌn'ɔːθəraɪzd]	adj. 擅自的
understanding	[ʌndə'stændɪŋ]	n. 理解
violate	['vaɪəleɪt]	v. 违反
witness	['wɪtnɪs]	v. 目击，看到

IV. Practical Expressions

1. A suspicious suitcase was found during the cabin inspection.
客舱检查中发现了一个可疑手提箱。

2. There is a suspicious parcel in the toilet. We think that it can be a bomb.
在洗手间里有一个可疑包裹。我们怀疑它是一枚炸弹。

3. Some explosives were discovered behind a panel near the back of the cabin.
客舱后部的一个面板后面发现了一些爆炸物。

4. A terrorist is trying to access the cockpit. He is about 30 years old. He is wearing a hat and backpack.
一名恐怖分子正试图接近驾驶舱，他大约30岁，头戴一顶帽子，背着双肩包。

5. Some of the hijackers are carrying sharp protruding weapons.
一些劫机者拿着锋利、尖锐的武器。

6. The situation is now under control.
现在局面得到了控制。

7. The cabin crew reports a passenger is behaving strangely.
客舱机组报告说一名旅客行为怪异。

8. Please stay away from here! Leave here immediately!
请大家不要围观！立即离开现场！

9. Don't panic. I'm a crew member. Follow my instructions！
别惊慌。我是机组成员，听从我的指挥！

10. Please leave here immediately. You are not allowed to take pictures or interview people here.
请马上离开。这里不允许照相和采访。

11. Please come here for security check.
请到这边来进行安全检查。

12. Sir/ Madam, I am the air marshal/ in-flight security officer of this flight. As your behavior has interrupted the attendant's normal work. Now I want you to stop your abnormal behavior immediately. Thank you for your cooperation.
先生/女士，我是本次航班的空中警察/安全员，鉴于你的行为已经影响了乘务员的正常工作，希望你立即对自己的行为有所克制，配合我们的工作，谢谢！

13. Hello, I am a crew member on this flight. May I help you ?

您好，我是本次航班的机组成员，请问有什么需要帮忙的吗？

14. I am a crew member on this flight. Please don't be nervous. Our airline will take every effort to help you.

我是本次航班的机组成员，请你不要紧张，我们航空公司会尽最大努力帮助你们的。

/ I am a crew member on this flight. I really understand your feelings at this moment. If there is anything we can do, we will try our best to help you.

我是本次航班的机组成员，我非常理解您现在的心情。如果有什么需要帮忙的，我们会尽力帮助您的。

15. As we are now counting the passenger number, please kindly be seated and refrain from using the lavatories until we complete the process. Thank you and we appreciate your cooperation!

现在我们正在重新核对旅客人数。请您协助我们在座位上坐好，暂停使用卫生间。谢谢！

Ⅴ. Tips

1. Handling of Hijacking 遭遇劫机时的处置方法

(1) When in flight, the first flight crew member who finds the aircraft being hijacked or who gets the information should immediately report to the captain, the purser and the air marshal or the security officer.

(2) After the hijacker is stable, get in touch with the hijacker for information or negotiation. Persuade him/ her or promise to accept his/ her requirements and find out further information, such as his/ her partners, seat number, purpose and demand.

(3) Walk in the cabin, keep an eye on the movements of passengers and pay attention to any suspicious signs or the hijacker's accomplices.

(4) Go on serving passengers, including serving meals. Stop serving alcoholic drinks. However, don't use meal and drinks carts.

(5) Don't inform passengers of the situation, lest they feel panic or confused.

(6) Protect the cockpit and don't let the hijacker break in and damage it.

(7) Listen to the captain's command, cooperate with the air marshal or the security officer and prepare for anti-hijack if the persons and the aircraft are sure to be safe.

2. Handling of Explosives 对爆炸物的处置

(1) Handling guidelines: Report immediately, react promptly, handle decisively and approach seriously.

(2) Handling requirements: Having high sense of responsibility, studying scientifically, avoiding reckless actions and handling correctly.

(3) Collecting information. While in the air, flight crew should detect the following information: the depositing location, shape, size, packing property of the explosive. See if there is any cord or tug attached to it, the initiate condition or the content of the warning and the disclosing time. Make sure if anybody has ever touched it.

(4) Procedures. Flight crew should make every possible effort to lower the flying altitude and try to land at a nearby airport first. After landing, taxi the plane into the safe parking lot as instructed by ground personnel. Evacuate passengers and crew members from the vicinity of the plane and danger zone.

Ⅵ. Supplementary Reading

1. Disruptive Acts On-board 机上扰乱行为

Disruptive acts refer to the behaviors on-board not complying with the code of conduct, not obeying crew members' instructions, and disturbing the cabin order. They mainly include: Race to occupy seats or overhead baggage compartment; Fight, pick quarrels and make troubles; Use mobile phones or other forbidden electronic devices in violation of rules; Steal, deliberately damage or move aircraft facility and equipment (e.g. survival items) without authorization or forcedly open emergency doors; Use fire or smoke (including electronic cigarettes); Molest persons in cabin or sexual harass; Propagate obscene articles and other illegal printed materials; Hinder crew members performing duties; Other behaviors disturbing the cabin order.

General Disruptive Acts On-board: Passengers violating the ban of smoking or the use of portable electronic devices on board; Theft on board; Drunk or poisoned passengers; Stowaways on board.

2. Acts of Unlawful Interference 非法干扰行为

Acts of unlawful interference refer to the acts or attempted acts such as to jeopardize the safety of civil aviation, i.e. Unlawful seizure of aircraft; Damage to aircraft in service; Hostage-taking on board aircraft or on aerodromes; Forcible intrusion on board an aircraft, or on the premises of an aeronautical facility; Introduction on board an aircraft or at an airport of a weapon or hazardous device or material intended for criminal purposes; Utilization of aircraft in service to cause death, injury or serious damage to property or environment; Communication of false information such as to jeopardize the safety of an aircraft in flight or on the ground, of passengers, crew, ground personnel or the general public, at an airport or on the premises of a civil aviation facility.

General Unlawful Interference Acts: Bomb threat; Hijacking.

Ⅶ. Exercises

1. How to comfort passengers in terms of explosive objects threat?
(1)

(2)

(3)

2. Translate the following words and phrases into Chinese or English.

hijack	紧急撤离
terrorist	行为
compromise	炸弹
interference	进行
devastating	强迫
be liable to	威胁
claim	人质
匿名电话	

3. Translate the following sentences into Chinese or English.
(1) 在洗手间里有一个包裹很可疑。我们怀疑它是炸弹。

(2) 客舱后部的一个面板后面发现一些爆炸物。

(3) 一名恐怖分子正试图接近驾驶舱，他大约30岁，头戴一顶帽子，背着双肩包。

(4) Some of the hijackers are carrying sharp protruding weapons.

(5) The situation is now under control.

(6) Don't panic. I'm a crew member. Follow my instructions！

4. Group work: choose one topic to start a conversation. (TIME LIMIT: 10 minutes)

(1) Use words to comfort a hijacker on board.

(2) A suspicious item on board.

(3) Explosive objects threat.

Task 26　Return, Diversion and Emergency Landing
返航、备降与迫降

Ⅰ. Warm-up Questions

1. What's the difference between diversion and forced landing?

2. Why do specific preparations need to be done before diversion?

3. How would you say to passengers when you have limited time to instruct them to put on and inflate life vests?

Ⅱ. Dialogues

Dialogue 1: Return to the original airport

音频扫一扫

Situation: First aid treatment has been given, but the passenger is still in unconsciousness.

Principle: If there's a sick passenger on board, the crew need to seek professional assistance from the medical staff by broadcasting. And flight attendants need to follow the captain's instructions of returning to the original airport or landing at an alternate airport.

Example

PS: (Announcement) Ladies and gentlemen, may I have your attention please? There is a passenger feeling uncomfortable. If there is any medical qualified person on board, doctor or nurse, please identify yourself to the nearest cabin crew. Thank you!

(After a while...)

PS: (Announcement) Ladies and gentlemen, we have been informed that we are returning to Nanjing due to a sick passenger on board. We are expected to arrive in 2 hours. We do apologize for any inconvenience.

PAX: What happened?

FA: There is a passenger who is seriously ill.

PAX: What shall we do then?

FA: We need to return to the original airport for medical assistance. Thank you for your understanding!

PAX: Thanks for telling me.

PS: (Announcement) Ladies and gentlemen, we have already returned to Nanjing Lukou International Airport. Our plane is still taxiing. Our captain is contacting with the relevant departments and we will keep you updated as soon as more information becomes available. We apologize for any inconvenience.

情景会话1：返航

乘务长：（广播）女士们，先生们，请注意！机上有位旅客生病，如果您是医生或护士等医护人员，请与离您最近的机组人员联系。谢谢！

（过了一会儿……）

乘务长：（返航前广播）女士们，先生们，我们刚刚收到通知，由于机上有重病旅客，需紧急医疗救助，我们即将返航回南京。预计在2小时后到达。对此带来的不便，我们深表歉意。

旅客：刚发生了什么？

乘务员：一名旅客病情严重。

旅客：那我们接下来怎么办？

乘务员：我们需要返航，回到起飞的机场获取医疗救护。谢谢您的理解！

旅客：谢谢你告诉我。

乘务长：（返航后广播）女士们，先生们，我们已经回到南京禄口国际机场，飞机还将滑行一段距离。飞机完全停稳后，机长将与相关部门联系后续事宜，请您在座位上耐心等候。进一步的消息，我们会随时广播通知您。对此带来的不便，我们深表歉意。

Dialogue 2: Diversion

音频扫一扫

Situation: Occasionally, there's an intermediate landing at another airport instead of the destination due to some mechanical problems.

Principle: Flight attendants need to follow the captain's instructions. The crew need to inform passengers of landing at an alternate airport by broadcasting.

Example

PS: (Announcement) Ladies and gentlemen, may I have your attention please? We are sorry to inform you that we will be making an intermediate landing at Shanghai instead of Beijing due to some mechanical problems. We'll land at Shanghai Hongqiao International Airport in 40 minutes. We apologize for the inconvenience! And thank you for your understanding!

PAX1: Oh, that's terrible! I've told my family my arrival time. I haven't seen them for 5 years.

PAX2: I have an important meeting to attend in Beijing this afternoon. If I can not get there on time, it will have to be put off and all the arrangements will be messed up.

PAX1: Excuse me, Miss? Mechanical problems? What kind of problems?

FA: I have no idea. If we have further information, we'll let you know as soon as possible.

PAX1: But who will arrange our accommodation in Shanghai?

FA: Our airline will do that. Please don't worry about it.

PAX2: But I'll miss the meeting this afternoon.

FA: I'm so sorry to hear that. But safety must be on the first place, right?

PAX2: Well, that's true.

FA: Thank you for your understanding!

情景会话2：备降

乘务长：（广播）女士们，先生们，请注意。我们抱歉地通知您，由于机械故障，我们不能继续前往北京，为了所有旅客的安全，现决定备降在上海虹桥国际机场。预计40分钟后到达。我们对此给您带来的不便深感歉意，并感谢您的理解。

旅客1：哦，太糟糕了。我已通知家人到达时间了，我已经5年没有见过我的家人了。

旅客2：我今天下午在北京还有个重要会议呢！我要是不能准时参加，会议就得延期，所有安排都将会被打乱。

旅客1：乘务员？机械故障？到底是什么故障？

乘务员：我不清楚。如果我们收到更多消息，会第一时间跟您说。

旅客1：但是谁来安排我们在上海的食宿呢？

乘务员：我们航空公司会做安排的。请别担心。

旅客2：但是我会错过今天下午的会议的。

乘务员：非常抱歉。但是安全永远是第一位的，您说呢？

旅客2：嗯，也对。

乘务员：感谢您的理解！

Dialogue 3: Prepared emergency evacuation—Emergency exits

音频扫一扫

Situation: It is very important that the passengers at the emergency exit areas can help the crew to open the exits in case of an emergency.

Principle: Flight attendants should follow the standard and ask the passengers in the exit area again whether they are willing to assist.

Example

PS: (Announcement) Ladies and gentlemen, our plane has eight emergency exits. Please locate the exit nearest to you. After landing, please leave by the exit nearest to you. Thank you!

(A flight attendant turns to a passenger sitting next to an over-wing exit...)

FA: Excuse me, Madam. You are sitting next to an emergency exit.

PAX1: Okay, I see.

FA: In the event of an emergency, do you think you can open the exit, Madam?

PAX1: Er... I'm not sure. Is the door very heavy?

FA: Not that heavy. But if you would like to sit somewhere else, I can arrange this for you.

PAX1: Thanks. I'd love that.

(The flight attendant turns to another passenger.)

FA: Excuse me, Sir. Would you mind changing your seat for one next to the emergency exit?

PAX2: Sure. I've sat there many times.

FA: Thank you, Sir.

情景会话3：有准备的应急撤离——应急出口

乘务长：（广播）女士们，先生们，本架飞机有八个应急出口。请找到离您最近的出口。落地后，请从离您最近的出口离开飞机。谢谢！

（一位乘务员向坐在机翼上出口附近座位的一位旅客走去……）

乘务员：女士，您好，您所坐的是应急出口座位。

旅客1：嗯，我知道。

乘务员：如果遇有紧急情况，您觉得自己可以打开应急出口的舱门吗？

旅客1：呃……我不确定。这个门很重吗？

乘务员：不是很重。但是如果您想要坐到别的座位上，我可以为您安排其他座位。

旅客1：谢了，我想换个座位。

（乘务员找到另一位旅客。）

乘务员：先生，您好，您介意换到应急出口处的座位吗？

旅客2：不介意呀，我之前坐过好多次应急出口处的座位。

乘务员：谢谢您，先生。

Dialogue 4: Ditching—Demonstration for the life vest

Situation: Before landing, flight attendants assist passengers in putting on life vests in terms of ditching.

Principle: Flight attendants should follow the standard procedure.

Example

PAX: Excuse me, could you tell me how to inflate my life vest?

FA: I suppose you didn't notice the life vest demonstration before take-off, Sir.

PAX: Sorry, I didn't.

FA: Never mind. You can slip the life vest over your head. Bring the waist strap around your waist. Fasten the buckle and tighten it by pulling outwards. To inflate your life vest, pull firmly on the red cord or just blow into the mouthpieces. Please do remember not to inflate it in the cabin. Do you understand?

PAX: Yes, I got what you just said. Could you tell me the reason why we are not suggested to inflate the life vest in the cabin? I think it may be too late to inflate it outside the cabin.

FA: Actually, if all passengers inflate their life vests except infants, there will be no room inside the cabin. And some broken metal from the aircraft may damage the life vests on the way out.

PAX: Oh, that's true.

情景会话4：水上撤离——救生衣演示

旅客：打扰一下，你能告诉我怎样给救生衣充气吗？

乘务员：先生，我猜您在起飞前没有注意看我们安全演示中救生衣的内容吧？

旅客：不好意思，确实没有。

乘务员：没关系的。您可以经头部穿好，将带子从后向前扣好、系紧，然后拉开充气阀门或向人工充气管内吹气来给救生衣充气。但请记住不要在客舱内充气。您清楚了吗？

旅客：好的，我明白你说的了。但你能告诉我为什么救生衣不能在客舱内充气吗？我觉得离开客舱再充气太晚了吧。

乘务员：事实上，如果所有的旅客都在客舱内充气，当然婴儿旅客除外，客舱里会特别拥挤。此外，在离开客舱的途中，从飞机上掉落的金属片会损坏救生衣。

旅客：噢，也对。

Dialogue 5: Brace for impact

Situation: Before an emergency landing, the purser is making an announcement about brace for impact.

Principle: Flight attendants should follow the standard procedure.

Example

PS: (Announcement) Ladies and gentlemen, attention, please. On the command of "brace for impact", please bend over and place your hands under your legs with your palms facing up; or cross your arms and hold the back of the seat in front of you. Place your head between your arms. When landing, the aircraft may bounce several times; hold your position until the aircraft has come to a complete stop. Then follow the instructions of cabin crew.

FA: Excuse me, Madam?

PAX1: Yes…

FA: You need to bend over more and place your hands under your legs with your palms facing up.

PAX1: I know. But I can't. It hurts my stomach. My head can't go that far...

FA: OK. Please cross your arms and hold the back of the seat in front of you. And place your head between your arms.

PAX1: That's better.

FA: Now please keep your head down. Brace for impact.

PAX2: OK. But am I doing right?

FA: That's right, Sir.

情景会话 5 ：防冲击姿势准备

乘务长：（广播）女士们，先生们，请注意，当听到 " 防冲击姿势准备 " 时，请低头弯腰，掌心朝上将双手放在腿下；或两臂交叉，抓住您前面的座椅靠背，将头置于两臂之间。落地时，飞机可能会有些颠簸，请保持这一姿势直到飞机完全停稳。落地后，请听从机组人员的指令。

乘务员：您好，女士。

旅客 1：嗯？

乘务员：请您再低些头弯点儿腰，掌心朝上将双手放在腿下。

旅客 1：我知道。但是我做不到，那样做的话我胃疼，我头够不着……

乘务员：好的。那请您两臂交叉，抓住您前面的座椅靠背，将头置于两臂之间。

旅客 1：好多了。

乘务员：现在请您低下头，做好防冲击姿势。

旅客 2：好的，我做得对吗？

乘务员：对的，先生。

Dialogue 6: Land Evacuation

音频扫一扫

Situation: For any airline, safety must be on the first place. Guaranteeing the safety of people on the aircraft is the most important responsibility of the crew.

Principle: Flight attendants should follow the standard evacuation procedure as well as handle the emergency situation with flexibility.

Example

FA: Release your seat belts and get out now! Release your seat belts and get out now...

PAX1: Help... help me, please. I cannot release my seat belt!

FA: Lift up the top of the buckle, Sir, quickly now.

PAX1: Thanks, I release it now.

PAX2: Excuse me, I have another question. Can you get my bag from the overhead compartment, please?

FA: Leave your bag there. Evacuate! Evacuate!

PAX2: I can't breathe... help me... I can't breathe (coughs)... the smoke!

FA: OK. Cover your nose and mouth with your clothes or blanket. Kneel down on the floor and follow the emergency floor lights. They will guide you to the exit.

PAX2: But I can't see anything.

FA: Hold onto the person in front of you, Sir. And follow him to the exit. OK... Jump! Jump!

PAX3: My glasses... I need my glasses.

FA: Remove your glasses and your high-heel shoes, Madam.

PAX3: Why?

FA: They're dangerous when using the emergency escape chute. The sharp objects could damage the escape slide and hurt passengers themselves at the same time.

PAX3: But they are Gucci.

FA: I'm afraid, Madam, for the safety, you have to.

PAX3: Fine, then.

情景会话6：陆地撤离

乘务员：解开安全带，现在撤离！解开安全带，现在撤离……

旅客1：帮……帮帮我。我解不开安全带了！

乘务员：先生，快点儿，向上抬起锁扣的最上面。

旅客1：谢谢，解开了。

旅客2：打扰下，我也有个问题。你能帮我把包从行李架上取下来吗？

乘务员：别带包了。撤离！撤离！

旅客2：帮帮我，我呼吸不了了……呼吸不了了（咳嗽）烟雾！

乘务员：好的，用你的衣服或毛毯捂住口鼻。顺着地板上的应急照明指示灯爬行。应急照明指示灯会引导你找到出口。

旅客2：但我什么也看不见。

乘务员：抓着你前方的人，先生。跟着他向出口走。好的……准备跳（滑梯）！跳！

旅客3：我的眼镜……我需要眼镜。

乘务员：女士，撤离时要摘下眼镜、脱下高跟鞋。

旅客3：为什么？

乘务员：因为在跳滑梯时它们会带来危险。这些尖锐物品既会损坏滑梯，同时也会给旅客自身造成伤害。

旅客3：但它们可是古驰（品牌）的。

乘务员：女士，出于安全考虑，您必须配合。

旅客3：那好吧。

Ⅲ. Popular Words and Phrases

diversion	[daɪˈvɜːʃ(ə)n]	n. 备降，改航
divert	[daɪˈvɜːt]	v. 改航
divert to		备降到……
alternate	[ˈɔltəneɪt]	v. 备降
alternate airport	[ˈɔltəneɪt ˈeəpɔːt]	备降机场
emergency landing		紧急迫降
ditching	[dɪtʃɪŋ]	n. 水上迫降
brace for impact		抱紧防撞（防冲击姿势）
completely	[kəmˈpliːtli]	adv. 完全地
evacuate	[ɪˈvækjueɪt]	v. 撤离，疏散
assigned emergency exit		指定的紧急出口
follow directions		听从指挥
high-heeled	[haɪ hiːld]	adj. （鞋）高跟的
head down		低下头
forward	[ˈfɔːwəd]	adv. 向前地
inflate	[ɪnˈflet]	v. 充气

identify	[aɪ'dentɪfaɪ]	v. 确认
remove sharp objects		除去尖锐物品
put apart		分开
stay calm		保持冷静
rescue	['reskjuː]	v. 援救
thorough check		彻底检查
blow into		向……里面吹气
examine	[ɪg'zæmɪn]	v. 检查
flat	[flæt]	adj. 平坦的
escape	[ɪ'skep]	v. 逃避，逃跑
soldier	['səʊldʒə(r)]	n. 士兵；军人
object	['ɒbdʒɪkt]	n. 物体，物品
denture	['dentʃə]	n. 假牙；托牙
hearing-aid	['hɪərɪŋ'eɪd]	n. 助听器
stretch	[stretʃ]	v. 伸展；延伸
impact	['ɪmpækt]	n. 碰撞，冲击，撞击
alternative	[ɔːl'tɜːnətɪv]	adj. 可选的；其他的
Survival Kit		救生包，救命包
sort out		解决（问题）

IV. Practical Expressions

1. Excuse me, Captain. What's the ditching type and preparing time?
机长，请问迫降的类型和准备时间？

2. All of the passengers must be evacuated.
必须撤离所有的旅客。

3. Attention, please! After the plane comes to a complete stop, evacuate from this exit! If this exit doesn't work, go to that one!
请注意！飞机完全停稳后，从这个出口撤离！如果这个出口不能使用，从那个出口撤离！

4. Please get all your tray sets and other service items ready for the cabin attendants to collect.
现在乘务员将收取您的餐盘和其他服务用具，请做好准备。

5. Place your seat back and table to the upright position and keep your seat belt fastened.
请调直座椅靠背，固定好小桌板，并系好安全带。

6. Ladies and gentlemen, if you are an airline staff, soldier, policeman or fire fighter, please notify us. We require your immediate assistance.
女士们，先生们，如果您是航空公司的雇员，军人、警察或消防人员，请与乘务员联系，我们需要您的协助。

7. For your safety during the evacuation, please remove all sharp objects such as pens, barrettes, knives, watches and jewelry items, untie the items like ties and scarves, take off high-heeled shoes and store them securely in your luggage.
为了疏散时保证您的安全，请取下随身携带的尖硬物品，如钢笔、发夹、小刀、手表和首饰，解下配饰，如领带和围巾，脱下高跟鞋，把这些物品放入行李内。

8. Please remove eye glasses, dentures and hearing-aids, and put them in your coat pockets.

请拿下眼镜、假牙和助听器，并将它们放在外衣口袋内。

9. The seat pocket in front of you should be kept empty. Please stow all your baggage in the overhead compartment or under your seat.

请不要把任何东西放在您前面的座椅口袋里。所有行李请放在座位底下或行李架上。

10. Now, the cabin attendant will show you two safety positions. First, keep the upper part of your body upright and strained, firmly grasp the arms of your seat with your hands and place your feet firmly on the floor. Second, cross your arms on the seat back in front of you; lower your head and place both your feet firmly on the floor.

现在乘务员将向您介绍两种防冲击姿势。第一种：上身挺直，收紧下颌，双手用力抓住座椅扶手，两脚用力蹬地。第二种：两臂交叉，紧抓前方座椅靠背，低头，两脚用力蹬地。

11. During emergency landing/ ditching, there may be some impacts. Therefore, please stay in your brace position until the aircraft comes to a complete stop.

飞机紧急着陆时，会有多次撞击，因此，请保持这种姿势直到飞机完全停稳。

12. Fasten seat belts, brace for impact!

系好安全带，防冲撞姿势准备！

13. The life vest is under your seat. Take it out and unwrap it, slip it on over your head. Fasten the buckles and pull tightly.

救生衣在您的座位底下。取出并撕开包装，将救生衣经头部穿好。将带子扣好，拉紧。

14. When you leave the aircraft, pull the red tab to inflate. If your vest needs further inflation, you can pull out the two mouthpieces in the upper part of the vest and blow into them.

当您离开飞机时，拉下救生衣两侧的红色充气把手。充气不足时，可将救生衣上部的两个人工充气管拉出，用嘴向里吹气。

15. The safety instructions are in your seat pocket, please read them carefully. If you have any questions, please ask a cabin attendant or a passenger near you.

在您前方座椅口袋里有安全说明书，请仔细阅读。如果您有疑问，请向乘务员或邻座旅客询问。

16. When evacuating, please leave the aircraft by the nearest exit and do not take any baggage. Inflate your life vest at the exit.

撤离时，请从最近的出口撤离，不要携带任何行李。（水上迫降）在到达出口时，打开救生衣的充气阀门。

17. Release seat belts! Don't take luggage!

解开安全带！不要带行李！

18. Stay down! Cover your mouth and nose! Come here!

低下身！捂住口鼻！到这边来！

19. Come here! One by one! Jump! Slide!

到这边来，一个接一个！跳，滑！

20. Come here! Inflate the life vest! Jump! Slide! Board the raft!

到这边来，救生衣充气！跳，滑！上船！

21. No exit, go that way!

此门不通，到那边去！

22. Anybody here? Answer me!

还有人吗？听到请回答！

V. Tips

Cabin Announcements: Diversion/ Rerouting 客舱广播：返航/备降

(Before Diversion/ Rerouting) Ladies and gentlemen, we have been informed that we are returning to XX airport/ we'll land at XX airport instead/ we will be making an intermediate landing at XX airport due to a sick passenger on board. We are expected to arrive in 2 hours and shall keep you updated as soon as more information becomes available. We apologize for any inconvenience.

(After Diversion/ Rerouting) Ladies and gentlemen, we have already returned to XX airport/ arrived at XX airport instead. Our plane is still taxiing, so please remain seated with your seat belt fastened and luggage stowed. Please also keep your mobile phone and other portable electronic devices off until the seat belt sign goes off. Our captain is contacting with the relevant departments and we will keep you updated as soon as more information becomes available. We apologize for any inconvenience.

VI. Supplementary Reading

1. Emergency Landing and Diversion 迫降与备降

An emergency landing is a prioritised landing made by an aircraft in response to an emergency containing an imminent or ongoing threat to the safety and operation of the aircraft or involving a sudden need for a passenger or crew on board to be on land, such as a medical emergency. It is usually a forced diversion to the nearest or most suitable airport, in which air traffic control must prioritise and give way immediately upon the declaration of the emergency.

Forced landing, the aircraft is forced to make a landing due to technical problems. Landing as soon as possible is a priority, no matter where, since a major system failure has occurred or is imminent. It is caused by the failure of or damage to vital systems such as engines, hydraulics, or landing gear, and so a landing must be attempted where a runway is needed but none is available. The pilot is essentially trying to get the aircraft on the ground in a way which minimizes the possibility of injury or death to the people aboard. This means that the forced landing may even occur when the aircraft is still flyable, in order to prevent a crash or ditching situation.

For example, on May 14, 2018, Sichuan Airlines Flight 3U8633, a domestic flight, had left the central Chinese city of Chongqing for the Tibetan capital, Lhasa. There were 128 people, nine of whom were crew, on board. During the flight, the heroic pilot Liu Chuanjian with other two pilots made an emergency landing after a cockpit windscreen was ripped out in mid-air. The jet's flight control unit was badly damaged by the resulting sudden decompression. Some parts of the system were reportedly sucked out of the gaping window, forcing the pilots to fly manually before landing the airliner safely at Chengdu.

Another example, on January 15, 2009, US Airways pilots board US Airways Flight 1549 from LaGuardia Airport to Charlotte Douglas International Airport. Few minutes into the flight, the aircraft strikes a flock of birds, disabling both engines. Without engine power and judging themselves unable to reach nearby airports, captain Chesley Sully Sullenberger decides to ditch the aircraft on the Hudson River and made a civil aviation miracle.

【背景阅读】

2018年5月14日四川航空3U8633航班机组成功处置特情，"中国民航英雄机组"成员与119名乘客遭遇极端险情，在万米高空直面强风、低温、座舱释压的多重考验，确保了机上全体人员的生命安全，创造了世界民航史上的奇迹。

2009年全美航空1549号航班迫降事件，机长切斯利•萨利•萨伦伯格在发动机失效的情况下，成功水上迫降在哈德逊河上，拯救了155名乘客和机组人员。

2. Ditching 水上迫降

(1) Introduce the use of the life vest. Distribute the infant life vest to the adult accompanying the infant and buckle the belt of infant life vest with the adult life vest. Inflate the life vest after holding infant from the seat after landing and inflate partial life vest after the child leaving the seat.

(2) Remind to inflate the adult life vest only after leaving the door, because the inflated life vest is difficult to pass the emergency exit and the passengers with inflated life vests are difficult to reach exits rapidly if the airplane quickly sinks into the water.

(3) The life vest must be put on the outside of all clothes to obviously distinguish with other objects on the water and to be found easily.

(4) Tell passengers that crew life vests are red.

(5) Release lifeboats. When the passengers and crew members board the lifeboat, the flight attendant responsible to release lifeboats should immediately cut off the connection ropes between boats and the airplane to make the boats departing from the airplane soon.

(6) Rescue the man fallen in water. After departing from the airplane, immediately look for survival fallen into the water, use the lifesaving equipment to rescue them into the boat and conduct emergency treatment for serious injured persons.

(7) Connect boats with each other and secure the location of boats. After leaving the fuel leaking area and fire area, connect all boats with each other, drop anchor to secure the location of boats, and take out Survival Kit. The lifeboat and persons may not be far away from the airplane, because most search and rescue work is carried out around the airplane and the airplane is much bigger than boat and person. At the same time, the distress site is the final point that external world may receive the information and each to be found.

(8) If possible, let the family members stay together. Carry blankets and cold protective clothing from the airplane and don't carry personal baggage.

3. Declaration and Implementation of Emergency Evacuation 应急撤离宣布和实施

After having received emergency evacuation instructions from flight crew, cabin crew should immediately conduct emergency evacuation; If cabin crew hasn't received instructions from flight crew in time, after the emergency lights illuminate, the purser should positively contact with the flight crew by all means, and implement according to the received instructions of flight crew; If evacuating from the aircraft is obvious in an emergency situation (e.g., smoke, fire, airframe serious damage, broken, explosion), the purser should positively contact with flight crew by all means, and implement according to the received instructions of flight crew; If can't get any instruction from flight crew, the purser should immediately organize to implement emergency evacuation, once confirmed the aircraft has emergency evacuation conditions.

A land evacuation time is 90 seconds, which means the period starting when the airplane comes to rest and ending when the last person evacuates from the airplane. The flotation time is no more than 60 minutes and normally is 20 minutes and however no less than 13 minutes. The occupants must evacuate within 13 minutes.

VII. Exercises

1. Could you list different types of emergency landing?

(1)

民航空乘英语实用口语教程 第三版

(2)

(3)

2. Translate the following words and phrases into Chinese or English.

diversion	denture
divert to	紧急迫降
alternate	水上迫降
brace for impact	撤离
stay calm	低下头
blow into	充气
soldier	取下尖锐物品
jewelry	援救
high-heeled	

3. Translate the following sentences into Chinese or English.

(1) 这排的旅客，请注意！飞机完全停稳后，从这个出口撤离！如果这个出口不能使用，从那个出口撤离！

(2) 如果您是航空公司的雇员，军人、警察或消防人员，请与乘务员联系，我们需要您立即协助。

(3) For your safety during the evacuation, please remove all sharp objects such as pens, barrettes, knives, watches and jewelry items, untie items like ties and scarves, take off high-heeled shoes and store them securely in your luggage.

(4) The seat pocket in front of you should be kept empty. Please stow all your baggage in the overhead compartment or under your seat.

4. Group work: choose one topic to start a conversation. (TIME LIMIT: 10 minutes)

(1) Return to the original airport.

(2) Ditching.

(3) Brace for impact.

Project 10

About Landing
着陆前后

Civil Aviation

Task 27　Preparations before Landing 着陆前的客舱准备

Ⅰ. Warm-up Questions

1. What is time difference and how would you explain it to the passenger who is interested in it?

2. How would you figure out the destination time and answer the question if a passenger asks about the local time?

3. Why is it necessary to ask some passengers about their in-flight feelings and suggestions?

Ⅱ. Dialogues

Dialogue 1: Adjust to the local time

音频扫一扫

Situation: Before landing, passengers would like to know the local time and time difference.

Principle: The flight attendant should look at the watch and think for a while before answering the questions.

Example

PAX: Excuse me, Miss. I've just been sleeping. What time is it now?

FA: Glad you've had a good rest. It's 5:11 in the morning Paris time.

PAX: What is the time difference between Beijing and Paris?

FA: Beijing is 7 hours ahead of Paris. The time in Beijing is 12:11.

PAX: Oh, thank you. I'll adjust my watch to the local time.

FA: Sure.

PAX: One more thing, could you tell me when we'll be landing at the airport?

FA: We'll arrive in about 50 minutes. The arrival time is around 6 a.m. local time.

情景会话1：调整到当地时间

旅客：打扰一下，女士。我刚才一直在睡觉。请问现在几点了？

乘务员：能好好休息一下真不错。现在是巴黎时间早上5:11。

旅客：北京和巴黎的时差是多少呢？

乘务员：北京比巴黎提前7小时。所以现在北京时间应该是中午12:11。

旅客：好的，谢谢你。我调一下我的手表，调到当地时间。

乘务员：好的。

旅客：还有个问题，能告诉我大概什么时候到达机场吗？

乘务员：我们在50分钟后就落地了。到达机场大约是当地时间早上6点。

Dialogue 2: The comment card

Situation: It is important for airlines to know more about passengers' needs and feelings in terms of cabin service.

Principle: Flights attendants should be polite and patient.

Example

FA: Sir, this is the comment card, would you please give us some advice? Your opinion is very important for us.

PAX: Sure!

FA: Thank you for your advice, Sir! And I would also like to say thank you for choosing flying with our airline and for supporting my work. Wish you have a good time in Paris!

PAX: Thank you for your efforts! I really enjoy it! By the way, can we expect a jet-bridge or remote stand?

FA: We're not sure. Thank you for your understanding!

音频扫一扫

情景会话 2：意见卡

乘务员：先生，这是我们的意见卡，希望您留下宝贵的建议。您的建议对我们非常重要。

旅客：好的。

乘务员：先生，非常感谢您提出的宝贵建议。非常感谢您选乘我们航空公司的班机旅行，同时也感谢您一路上对我工作的支持。祝您在巴黎旅途愉快！

旅客：感谢你们的努力。我真的很喜欢。顺便问一下，我们预计停靠在廊桥还是远机位？

乘务员：现在我们还不知道。感谢您的理解！

Dialogue 3: "How to get to the downtown?"

Situation: Before landing, a passenger wants to know the way to the downtown.

Principle: The flight attendant should answer questions patiently and professionally.

Example

PAX: Excuse me, when shall we arrive in Beijing?

FA: We shall arrive in about 40 minutes.

PAX: Then how far is the downtown from the airport?

FA: It's about 24 kilometers.

PAX: Where can I take a shuttle bus?

FA: Sorry, I'm not sure about it. You may consult the staff of the Information Counter. And they'll be able to help you.

PAX: Thanks. By the way, how much does it cost if I take a taxi?

FA: The taxi fare would be about 100RMB.

PAX: Can I bargain?/ Is bargaining possible?

FA: I'm afraid not, but you may have a try.

PAX: Thank you very much.

FA: My pleasure.

音频扫一扫

情景会话 3："如何去市区？"

旅客：请问，我们什么时候到达北京？

乘务员：大概40分钟后到。

旅客：机场离市区多远？

乘务员：大约24公里。

旅客：请问我在哪儿可以坐机场大巴？

乘务员：抱歉，我也不太清楚。您可以咨询机场问讯处的工作人员。他们一定会帮您的。

旅客：谢谢。顺便问问，打车大概多少钱？

乘务员：车费大概要100元。

旅客：能还价吗？

乘务员：恐怕不能，不过您可以试试。

旅客：非常感谢。

乘务员：不用客气。

Dialogue 4: The use of lavatories has been suspended

Situation: A passenger would like to use the on-board lavatory during descending.

Principle: The flight attendant should ask the passenger to go back to his or her seat and use the lavatory after landing.

Example

FA: Excuse me, Madam. I'm afraid that you have to go back to your seat and fasten your seat belt as the plane is landing soon.

PAX: I know the plane is landing, but I have to go to the lavatory first.

FA: I'm sorry to tell you that for the safety, the lavatories have to be closed before landing.

PAX: Then, when can I use it again?

FA: The aircraft is landing soon. It can be used once the aircraft comes to a complete stop.

PAX: Oh, I see.

FA: Thank you for your understanding.

情景会话4：卫生间暂停使用

乘务员：抱歉，女士。请您回到座位上并且系好安全带。我们的飞机很快就要落地了。

旅客：我知道飞机马上就要落地了，但我要先去一下卫生间。

乘务员：很抱歉，为了安全起见，卫生间在落地之前不可以使用。

旅客：那我什么时候能用卫生间呢？

乘务员：飞机很快就要着陆了。您可以在飞机落地停稳之后使用。

旅客：好的，我知道了。

乘务员：感谢您的理解。

Ⅲ. Popular Words and Phrases

arrival time		到达时间
be subject to		受到……的约束
final descent		最后的降落
latest weather report		最新天气预报
assistance	[ə'sɪst(ə)ns]	n. 援助
baggage claim area		行李提取处
be pleased to		很高兴，乐意于……

for the time being		暂时
inform	[ɪnˈfɔːm]	v. 通知；告诉；报告
proceed to		向某地进发
safety regulation		安全规则
watch out		当心
be careful	[bɪ ˈkeəfʊl; −f(ə)l]	当心
claim	[kleɪm]	v. 索取，认领
complete	[kəmˈpliːt]	adj. 完整的；完全的；彻底的
declare	[dɪˈkleə]	v. 宣布，声明；断言，宣称
equivalent	[ɪˈkwɪv(ə)l(ə)nt]	adj. 等价的，相等的
formality	[fɔːˈmælɪtɪ]	n. 礼节；拘谨；仪式；正式手续
free of charge		免费
outbound	[ˈaʊtbaʊnd]	adj. 出站的；驶向外国的，向外去的
park	[pɑːk]	v. 停放
remain seated		坐着不动，保持在原座位坐好
shift	[ʃɪft]	n. 转移
stopover	[ˈstɒpəʊvə]	n. 中途停留
concluding	[kənˈkluːdɪŋ]	adj. 结束的；最后的 (conclude 的现在分词)
appreciate	[əˈpriːʃieɪt]	v. 感激；欣赏

IV. Practical Expressions

1. This is the comment card, would you please give us some advice? Your opinion is very important for us. Thank you!

这是我们的意见卡，希望您留下宝贵的建议。您的建议对我们非常重要。谢谢！

2. Could you give us some advice to make your next flight more comfortable?

您能就机上服务给我们提些建议吗？以便我们下次能给您提供更舒适的服务。

3. Please close your table as soon as you finish filling in the form.

请您填好表格后把小桌板收好。

4. We will be landing in about one hour. It is sunny in Paris and the temperature is 20 degrees centigrade, 68 degrees Fahrenheit.

我们还有大约一个小时就到了。巴黎现在天气晴朗，温度是20摄氏度、68华氏度。

5. There is a six-hour time difference between Beijing and Munich. Now the local time is five fifteen.

慕尼黑与北京的时差是6小时，现在当地时间是5:15.

6. The weather in Munich is colder than that in Beijing. Please put on more clothes.

慕尼黑的天气比北京冷，请您注意添一些衣物。

7. The airport shuttle bus can take you downtown. The fare is 24 *yuan*.

您可以乘坐机场巴士到达市区。票价是每人24元。

8. Taxi charges 9 *yuan* per kilometer, and the taxi stand is on the ground floor.

出租车每公里计价为9元。出租车站在一楼。

9. It takes about two hours to reach downtown.

到达市中心大约需要两小时。

10. I will write down the hotel's name in Chinese, and then you can show it to the taxi driver.

我用中文把酒店的名字写下来，你把它交给出租车司机。他会带您去那儿。

11. I am not quite sure about that. May I suggest that you go to the Information Counter at the terminal building? They will provide assistance.

我不能确定。您最好去候机楼问讯处问一下，他们会帮助您的。

12. You may claim your checked baggage in the Arrival Hall with your luggage tag.

您可以凭行李牌在进港厅领取您的托运行李。

13. You need to go through entry formalities in the Arrival Hall.

您需要去进港大厅办理入境手续。

14. You may feel a little uncomfortable on your ears during descent. But don't worry, it can be relieved by swallowing.

下降期间您可能会感到些许耳痛。不过不要担心，您可以通过吞咽动作来缓解一下。

15. Please stay in your seat and we will accompany you to look for your family after landing.

请在座位上等一下，落地后我们会陪您一起去找您的家人。

16. When the plane has come to a complete stop, the ground staff will come and meet you with the wheelchair.

飞机完全停稳以后，地面工作人员会带着轮椅来接您的。

17. Would you please stay in your seat? When other passengers get off the plane, we'll be here to assist you.

请您在座位上稍等一下好吗？等其他旅客下飞机后，我们会来帮您的。

18. We will arrive at Beijing Capital International Airport T3.

我们将停在北京首都国际机场的3号航站楼。

19. For the safety, the lavatories have to be closed prior to landing. Please refrain from using it until the plane lands and comes to a complete stop.

为了安全，我们在着陆前关闭了卫生间。请等到飞机完全停稳后再使用。

20. I'm sorry to tell you that for the safety, the lavatories have to be closed before landing. It can be used once come to a complete stop.

抱歉，为了安全起见，卫生间在落地之前不可以使用。您可以在飞机停稳之后第一时间使用。

Ⅴ. Tips

Cabin Announcement: Descent 客舱广播：下降

Before or during the descent, the captain usually makes an announcement with the local time and the temperature at the destination airport and the time left until arrival. It is followed by an announcement from the flight attendant.

"Ladies and gentlemen, as we start our descent, please make sure your seat backs and tray tables are in their full upright position. Make sure your seat belt is securely fastened and all carry-on luggage is stowed underneath the seat in front of you or in the overhead bins. Thank you."

Ⅵ. Supplementary Reading

1. DOT (United States Department of Transportation) 美国交通运输部

The United States Department of Transportation (USDOT or DOT) is a federal cabinet department of the U.S. government concerned with transportation. It was established by an act of Congress on Oc-

 民航空乘英语实用口语教程 第三版

tober 15, 1966 and began operation on April 1, 1967. It is governed by the United States Secretary of Transportation.

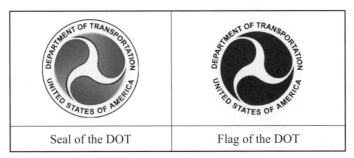

| Seal of the DOT | Flag of the DOT |

2. FAA (Federal Aviation Administration) 美国联邦航空局

The Federal Aviation Administration (FAA) of the United States is a national authority with powers to regulate all aspects of civil aviation. These include the construction and operation of airports, air traffic management, the certification of personnel and aircraft, and the protection of U.S. assets during the launch or re-entry of commercial space vehicles.

| Seal of the FAA | Flag of the FAA |

VII. Exercises

1. Answer the following questions according to the dialogues.

(1) What is time difference?

(2) How could you figure out the destination time?

(3) What are the ways of getting to know in-flight feelings of passengers?

2. Translate the following words and phrases into Chinese or English.

latest weather report   行李提取处

assistance   到达时间

claim   受到……的约束

formality   最后的降落

remain seated   安全规则

3. Translate the following sentences into Chinese or English.

(1) 这是我们的意见卡，希望您留下宝贵的建议。您的建议对我们非常重要。谢谢！

(2) 慕尼黑的天气比北京冷，请您注意添一些衣物。

(3) 您可以凭行李牌在进港厅领取您的托运行李。

(4) 飞机完全停稳以后，地面工作人员会带着轮椅来接您的。

(5) You need to go through entry formalities in the Arrival Hall.

(6) Could you please stay in your seat? When other passengers get off the plane, we'll be here to assist you.

(7) I'm sorry to tell you that for the safety, the lavatories have to be closed before landing.

4. Group work: choose one topic to start a conversation. (TIME LIMIT: 5 minutes)

(1) A jet-bridge or remote stand.

(2) How to claim the checked baggage?

(3) How to get to the downtown from the airport?

Task 28　After Landing 着陆后

Ⅰ. Warm-up Questions

1. What will you say to a passenger if he or she has difficulty in getting off the aircraft?

2. How to show your kindness during passengers' disembarkation?

3. How to say "goodbye" to passengers in diverse ways?

4. What's the content of connecting procedures?

5. How to do the connecting procedures effectively?

Ⅱ. Dialogues

音频扫一扫

Dialogue 1: After landing

Situation: A passenger stands up right after landing and he tries to open the overhead bin.

Principle: Flight attendants should monitor the cabin for landing. If we find passengers standing up and opening the overhead bins before the aircraft comes to a complete stop, make an announcement and stop them in time.

Example

PS: (Announcement) Ladies and gentlemen, we have just landed at Beijing Capital International Airport, Terminal 3. The ground temperature is 32 degrees centigrade/ degrees Celsius or 90 degrees Fahrenheit. Kindly remain seated with your seat belt fastened until the "fasten seat belts sign" goes off. We highly appreciate your patience and understanding. It's been our pleasure to serve you on this flight. Thank you for flying our airline. We look forward to seeing you again in the near future. Have a nice day! Goodbye!

FA: Sir, our aircraft is still taxiing. For your safety, please remain seated with your seat belt fastened and luggage stowed until the "fasten seat belts sign" is switched off.

PAX: I just saw the aircraft stopped.

FA: Due to airport congestion, we will be making a brief stop to wait for a parking bay. Please remain seated until the aircraft comes to a complete stop at the parking bay. Thank you!

PAX: Well, okay.

情景会话1：飞机着陆后

乘务长：女士们，先生们，欢迎您来到北京首都国际机场。我们将在3号候机楼进港。机舱外的温度是32摄氏度，90华氏度。飞机还将滑行一段距离，请您继续留在座位上并系好安全带，直到安全带指示灯关闭。非常感谢您的耐心等待与理解。机组成员再次感谢您选乘我们的航班。我们很荣幸与您共同度过了一段愉快的旅程，期待与您再次相会。祝您旅途愉快！再见！

乘务员：先生，我们的飞机还在滑行，为了您的安全，请关闭行李箱，在座位上坐好并系好安全带，直至安全带指示灯关闭。

旅客：我刚刚明明看到飞机停了呀。

乘务员：由于机场繁忙，我们的飞机需在此稍停等待停机位，稍后还将继续滑行。请您继续留在座位上，直到飞机完全停稳，谢谢！

旅客：嗯，好吧。

Dialogue 2: Disembarkation

Situation: The aircraft is parking at the apron and all passengers on board need to take the shuttle bus to the terminal building.

Principle: Flight attendants should assist special passengers in getting off the aircraft, such as the elderly.

Example

音频扫一扫

PS: (Announcement) Ladies and gentlemen, since our aircraft is parking at the apron, we will arrange shuttle buses to send all passengers to the Arrival Hall. As the outside temperature is comparatively low, kindly put on your jackets before disembarkation. Please mind your steps. Thank you!

FA: Excuse me, Miss. Would you please let this granny go first?

PAX1: Certainly.

FA: Thank you. (To the elderly) Madam, watch your steps, please. It's raining and very slippery outside. If you have an umbrella, you'd better get it ready in advance, please.

PAX2: It's so considerate of you.

FA: It's my pleasure. Hope you have a nice trip in China.

情景会话2：旅客下机

乘务长：（广播）女士们，先生们，由于我们的飞机停靠在远机位，您需要乘坐摆渡车前往候机楼。机舱内外温差较大，请您在下机前适当增加衣物。下机时，请小心台阶。谢谢！

乘务员：抱歉，女士。能让这位奶奶先走吗？

旅客1：当然可以。

乘务员：谢谢。（转向老奶奶）女士，请留意脚下。外面在下雨，脚底很滑。如果您带伞了，可以提前准备好。

旅客2：你可真体贴。

乘务员：很乐意为您服务。祝您在中国玩得开心。

Dialogue 3: Connecting procedures

Situation: After landing and before another flight, the flight attendants should communicate with the ground staff and conduct connecting procedures.

音频扫一扫

Principle: Flight attendants should conduct and confirm the connecting procedures patiently.

Example

(PS: Purser, AM: Airline Station Manager, CS1: Cleaning Staff, CS2: Catering Staff)

PS: Hello, Station Manager, I'm glad to see you again!

AM: Hello, Purser, nice to meet you too. Today we may have more than 285 passengers, and we haven't concluded the counter right now.

PS: OK. We will make full preparation.

AM: Here is the special order passengers' list. We have 2 wheelchair passengers, 3 infants and 2 of them order the baby bassinets on board, and 7 different kinds of special meal. There is also a special passengers' list. Here you are.

PS: Thank you.

CS1: Madam, the cabin is cleaned up, please check and sign your name.

PS: OK. Let me ask my colleagues to help me check the cleaning, please wait a minute.

CS2: Madam, here is the meal count, please check and sign your name.

PS: All right, 10 portions for the first class, 35 portions for the business class and 255 portions for the economy class, including 1 seafood meal, 1 Muslim meal, 2 gluten free meals and 3 baby meals. Great, everything is correct. Let me sign here.

情景会话3：航班交接

（PS: 乘务长，AM：站长，CS1：清洁人员，CS2：航食人员）

乘务长：您好，站长，很高兴又见到您！

站长：您好，乘务长，我也很高兴见到您。今天我们预计客人超过285人，现在还没有结柜台。

乘务长：好的，我们会做好充分的准备。

站长：这是特殊旅客单，我们有两名轮椅旅客，三名婴儿，其中两个婴儿申请了机上婴儿摇篮和七份特餐。这还有一份特殊旅客名单。给您。

乘务长：谢谢。

清洁人员：女士，客舱卫生打扫好了，请检查并签字。

乘务长：好的，我让我同事帮忙检查一下，请稍等。

航食人员：女士，这是餐食数量单，请检查后签字。

乘务长：好的，头等舱10份，商务舱35份，经济舱255份，包括一份海鲜餐、一份穆斯林餐、两份无麸质餐和三份婴儿餐。好的，数量都正确，我来签字。

Ⅲ. Popular Words and Phrases

arrival hall		到达大厅；进港大厅
disembarkation	[ˌdɪsˌembɑːˈkeɪʃn]	n. 下机
aerobridge	[ˈeərəʊbrɪdʒ]	n. 廊桥
apron	[ˈeɪprən]	n. 停机坪
shuttle bus		摆渡车
slippery	[ˈslɪpəri]	adj. 湿滑的，滑溜的
relevant	[ˈreləvənt]	adj. 有关的，相关联的
general aviation		通用航空
flight dispatcher		飞行签派员

procedure	[prə'siːdʒə]	n. 程序，手续，步骤
carousel	[ˌkærə'sel]	n. 旋转台
terminal	['tɜːrmɪnl]	n. 终端，终点站，航站楼

IV. Practical Expressions

1. The plane is still taxiing along the runway. For your safety, please remain seated.
飞机还在沿跑道滑行，为了您的安全，请在座位上坐好。

2. Please remain in your seat until the aircraft comes to a complete standstill.
飞机完全停稳以前，请不要离开座位。

3. Take your time, please. There will be enough time to collect your personal items.
别着急，您有足够的时间整理您的个人物品。

4. Please wait here for a while until the boarding bridge is in position.
请在这里稍候。您要等到廊桥接好后才能下机。

5. Thank you, Madam. It's so kind of you to make way for this senior gentleman.
女士，非常感谢您让这位老先生先走。

6. After landing, please take the transit bus. It will take you directly to the Arrival Hall.
落地后，请乘坐摆渡车，它将直接把您送到进港大厅。

7. I'm glad you like our blankets. However, we need to keep them in flight.
我非常高兴您喜欢我们的毛毯，但是很抱歉毛毯需要留在机上使用。

8. It is quite cold outside. Please dress warmly enough before you go out.
外面天气很冷，请下机前穿暖和，以免感冒。

9. Please make sure to take all your hand luggage and personal items when you disembark.
下机时请携带好您的手提行李和其他私人物品。

10. It's raining and very slippery outside. If you have an umbrella, get it ready in advance, please.
外面在下雨，脚底很滑。如果您带伞了，可以提前准备好。

11. Mind your steps, please.
请您小心台阶。

12. Thank you for flying with our airline. We are looking forward to seeing you again.
感谢您乘坐我们公司的班机，希望有幸再次为您服务。

13. Your stroller has been put at the boarding gate.
您的婴儿车已经放在登机口了。

14. The wheelchair is ready. Our ground staff will go with you to the baggage claim area. Then you can get back your own wheelchair.
轮椅已经准备好了。我们的地面工作人员会送您去行李提取处的。之后您就能取回自己的轮椅了。

15. Please get your passport ready. The immigration officer will check it when you disembark.
请将您的护照准备好，下机后有移民局官员进行检查。

16. Hope to see you again! Have a nice time!
下次见！祝您玩得开心！

17. Hope you will have a nice stay in Beijing.
希望您在北京过得愉快。

18. Clearly fill out the supply form for handing it over. Keep half of the supplies for the crew flying back. And please give me all the forms at least one hour before landing.

请清楚地填写交接单，要给回程留够至少一半的量。请最晚在着陆前一小时把所有表格都给我。

Ⅴ. Tips

Cabin Announcement: Landing 客舱广播：落地

Ladies and gentlemen, welcome to XX Airport. The local time is XX and the temperature is XX. For your safety, please remain seated with your seat belt fastened until the captain turns off the "fasten seat belts" sign. This will indicate that we have parked at the apron and it is safe for you to move about. Please check around your seat for any personal belongings you may have brought on board with you, and please be careful when opening the overhead bins. On behalf of our airline and the entire crew, I'd like to thank you for joining us on this trip and we are looking forward to seeing you on board again in the near future. Have a nice day!

Ⅵ. Supplementary Reading

Duty Period, Duty Time, Rest Period and Flight Time Limitations 值勤期、值勤时间、休息期和飞行时间限制

(1) Duty Period

It refers to the consecutive time period that begins when the crew member reports for duty after received the flight task assigned by the company, and ends when the task is removed.

(2) Duty Time

The period of time from one hour and a half prior to flight schedule to the public to terminated time after completion of flight task when crew arrive at crew rest places or sent back to base center assigned by the airlines, is the duty time of a flight attendant. Once delay occurs, during the time of performing duty for one time, rest time approved in designated places will not be considered as part of duty period.

(3) When a flight attendant is reassigned to duty, the air trip time for the flight attendant before flight mission will be counted in the duty time; the air trip time for the flight attendant after flight mission will not be counted in the duty time and rest period.

(4) Before a duty period, if the flight attendant has necessary work mission, including necessary training, learning, meeting and office work or other affairs assigned by the company, the mission time will be counted in the duty time. Otherwise, 8-hour rest period will be arranged for the flight attendant.

(5) Total flying time of flight attendants should be guaranteed to meet the following regulations:

① In any calendar week, a flight attendant may not exceed 40 hours of flight time.

② In any calendar month, a fight attendant may not exceed 110 hours of flight time.

③ In any calendar year, a flight attendant may not exceed 1,200 hours of flight time.

④ Period of time when a flight attendant performs safety and safeguard responsibilities shall be considered as part of flying time of the flight attendant.

(6) After a duty period, a flight attendant will have a rest period.

(7) Generally no person may arrange a flight attendant performing flight duty in his/ her rest period, and no flight attendant may accept a flight duty arranged by management department. In any consecutive 7 days, the flight attendant who is assigned one time or more than one time duty period, thus certificate hold should arrange them 36 consecutive hours rest period at least. When cabin attendants management department has assigned other tasks in his/ her rest period, task time can not

be counted in duty period. However, at least 8 hours of rest period should be arranged for the flight attendant before duty period.

VII. Exercises

1. How to say "goodbye" to passengers in diverse ways?

(1)

(2)

(3)

2. Translate the following words and phrases into Chinese or English.

disembarkation	停机坪
procedure	摆渡车
arrival hall	湿滑的
terminal	有关的，相关联的

3. Translate the following sentences into Chinese or English.

(1) 飞机还在滑行，为了您的安全，请在座位上坐好。

(2) 别着急，您有足够的时间整理您的物品。

(3) 请在这里稍候。您要等到廊桥接好后才能下机。

(4) 请乘坐摆渡车，它将直接把您送到进港大厅。

(5) 请留意脚下。外面在下雨，脚底很滑。如果您带伞了，可以提前准备好。

(6) The wheelchair is ready. Our ground staff will go with you to the baggage claim area. Then you can get back your own wheelchair.

4. Group work: choose one topic to start a conversation. (TIME LIMIT: 10 minutes)

(1) A passenger stands up right after landing and he tries to open the overhead bin.

(2) Show your kindness during passengers' disembarkation.

(3) Conduct the connecting procedures.

References 参考文献

[1] 李屹然. 民航空乘英语实用口语教程 [M]. 第2版. 北京：化学工业出版社，2022.

[2] 范晔，邹海鸥. 空中乘务情境英语 [M]. 第2版. 北京：清华大学出版社，2022.

[3] 余方敏. 实用空乘英语教程 [M]. 浙江：浙江大学出版社，2022.

[4] 孙庆芳，高锋. 空乘实用英语教程 [M]. 北京：清华大学出版社，2022.

[5] 林扬，余明洋. 民航乘务英语视听 [M]. 第4版. 北京：旅游教育出版社，2023.